asian

cooking companion

asian

cooking companion

vicky liley

APPLE

Contents

Introduction

Welcome to the Asian Cooking Companion! More than just a collection of recipes, this book takes you on a journey through the inspiring and exciting world of Asian cuisine, through thousands of years and across a myriad of cultures—without leaving your kitchen.

Today, Asian food is enjoyed all over the world, and it remains as exciting as it was when Marco Polo first laid eyes on the noodle in the thirteenth century or when people in Britain first sipped tea. Almost every mainstream cuisine style has been influenced by Asian cooking, from the early European trendsetters to the great chefs of today, and it has become a dominant flavor in the modern home where time and convenience reign.

Asian cuisine is united, but each country, and even region, is also unique, with its own specific customs. From the people of Southeast Asia and Sri Lanka to India, Korea, Japan and China, you'll find all walks of life. In some Asian countries, there's also the centuries-old influence of the West—both from the New World traders such as the Portuguese and Christopher Columbus, who brought the all-important chili, to the colonial Dutch, English and French.

Yet wherever you are in Asia, whether in the isolated mountain villages or the fast-paced cities, some customs will never change—the kitchen remains the heart of the home, and there's always rice, soy and tea.

Within these pages you'll find all the basics you need to prepare, cook and serve Asian-style meals at home. There are recipes with traditional ingredients and techniques, passed down through generations, as well as dishes born of today's fast-paced kitchens, using time-saving products off supermarket shelves. Also included are all the garnishes, sauces and accompaniments that make an Asian meal complete.

This book reflects the great diversity that is Asian cuisine, from recipes steeped in history to contemporary classics and ultramodern fusions of East and West. Apart from being full of wondrous flavors and textures, the recipes here are also healthy, using fresh ingredients, and easy to prepare—true to the Asian food philosophy.

We hope you enjoy your journey!

Equipment and utensils

While most of the recipes in this book can be prepared using standard good quality cooking equipment, there are a few items that an Asian cook couldn't live without—the wok, chopper and mortar and pestle, for example, can become lifelong friends in the kitchen. Sushi chefs have more specific requirements (see Chapter 6), but any good cookery store and many Asian markets will stock all the equipment you need.

Bamboo steamers

Bamboo steamers are indispensable in the Asian kitchen. The steamer's open-slat base allows steam to circulate easily and efficiently, while the lid is perfectly designed to allow excess steam to escape (through the tightly woven bamboo), with little condensation dripping back onto the food. They can also be stacked, allowing several dishes, or several batches of the same dish, to be cooked at once.

Bamboo steamers are available in many sizes at Asian markets; a 12-inch (30-cm) steamer will suit a standard 14-inch (35-cm) wok, and will hold a dinner plate for steaming whole fish. If there are large gaps between the slats, place food on a plate, parchment (baking) paper or leaves, and allowing space at the edges for steam to circulate.

Soak new bamboo steamers in cold water for at least 2 hours before use, to clean thoroughly. Steamers need only be rinsed in hot water after cooking. Allow them to dry thoroughly, then store in an airy place.

You can serve food in the steamer at the table, but place a plate under it to catch drips. If cooked food is to be left in the steamer for any length of time before serving, place a clean kitchen towel under the lid to absorb moisture.

Brazier or hibachi grill

Food grilled over small braziers imbuing them with charcoal smoke is much favored in Asian cuisine. Any Western outdoor grill or barbecue, or, more typically, a small Japanese-style hibachi, can also be used. The traditional charcoal brazier works like a chimney coal starter: it is stoked from the bottom, using paper and/or kindling, with coals resting above on a central rack. Once lit and covered with a white ash, the coals are ready for use.

Note: *Do not attempt to grill on top of a chimney coal starter.*

Both lava rock or ceramic briquette grills and indoor fan-forced grills can be used, but they will not imbue food with the same smoky flavors. Likewise, a broiler (grill) or a ridged grill pan is an alternative for indoor cooking.

It is better to use natural lump charcoal than charcoal briquettes, because it is pure and burns at a higher temperature. Avoid instant lighter liquids, fire sticks and other chemical agents, as these produce unpleasant fumes at the table. Never use gasoline or kerosene, as both are dangerously explosive.

Caution: When burning any form of charcoal indoors, always ensure the room is well ventilated to prevent carbon monoxide poisoning.

How to prepare a brazier

1. Charcoal is best lighted outdoors, directly in the brazier or hibachi (see Caution). To light coals, mound a small pile of charcoal atop a central rack. Tightly wrinkle newspapers and/or kindling in base, and set newspapers alight. If using a special chimney coal starter (as described above), do not use kindling. Alternatively, mound a small pile of charcoal around an electric fire starter and plug fire starter in. After 7 minutes, remove starter.

2. Once coals are covered with a layer of white ash, spread them evenly in the brazier or hibachi using tongs or a small shovel. If using a chimney coal starter, spill the lit coals onto the center grate of the brazier. Slide open the air vent at the bottom to stoke the coals; for lower heat, close the vent.

3. Place grill rack or basket on brazier and heat. To prevent sticking, hold a piece of fat with tongs and rub it along grids. Alternatively, brush lightly with oil.

4. When cooking soups and stews on the brazier, securely nestle terracotta pots or a wok atop coals. Fan the coals and open grill vents to increase heat while cooking.

Chopper

Also known as a Chinese chopper or cleaver, this Asian-style knife has a big rectangular blade and a wooden handle. It is used for chopping (through bone or shell), cutting (any food), crushing (garlic or herbs), fine slicing, shredding, mincing and grinding. A thick wooden board and sharpening stone go hand in hand with the chopper.

Chopping board

Traditional wooden chopping boards are popular in Asia, but resin boards are now widely available and are easier to keep free of odors. Before using a wooden board, wet the surface and wipe with a clean cloth. Disinfect once a week by boiling and drying in sunlight. If you use a plastic board, or don't have a pot big enough to boil the board in, scrub it with salt, using a scour pad, and rinse with boiling water.

Chopsticks for cooking

These are two to three times longer than chopsticks used for eating. Cooking chopsticks are extremely useful implements, as they enable you to easily manipulate food using only one hand.

Coconut grater

Coconut graters used to be a mainstay in Asian kitchens, but today grated coconut is often bought at the local market, where it is made fresh on the spot. While the hand-carved coconut graters, like those of Thailand, which were often shaped like miniature animals, are rapidly becoming museum pieces, tabletop and hand-held models are plentiful. Simply crack a coconut shell in half, drain the water and scrape out the meat with the grater.

Deghchi

This thick-based pan is used in Indian cooking. It is quite large, but shallower than a large saucepan, and traditionally has rounded sides and a tight-fitting lid. You can also use a large, shallow, thick-based pan with a lid.

Fish scaler

When cleaning and preparing fish at home, it is easiest to use a fish scaler, available from fish markets. Simply draw it up the body of the fish, working from tail to head. Do not use the back of a cleaver, as this may bruise the fish.

Gow gee press

This utensil, usually made of plastic, is used for making gow gee dumplings. Presses are sold in Asian markets.

Grater

There are several types of graters: brass, aluminum, stainless steel, ceramic and copper. Stainless steel graters are best for use at home; copper is popular with chefs for its sharp edges, but it needs to be well maintained. Choose a grater that is comfortable to hold and has closely packed, sharp teeth. When using the grater, particularly when grating ginger, use a circular motion. After each use, clean the grater then sprinkle with vinegar and brush it, to prevent rust.

Grilling racks and basket

Metal racks and baskets are used with braziers and hibachis for grilling food. Small, hand-held lattice wire baskets are convenient and allow foods to be securely caged for easier turning.

Hot pot

This circular clay pot with a cover is used for cooking soups and stews. It can be placed directly over a gas flame or on an electric hotplate, then transferred to the table, where it will keep the food hot during the meal. The Korean hot pot is called a ttukbaegi.

Japanese donabe

This earthenware cooking pot is used mainly for cooking stews or dishes that need simmering. Glazed on the inside, but left unglazed on the bottom, it sits directly on the heat source or is placed in the oven. A small hole in the lid allows steam to escape. The inner surface of the lid is usually patterned. Once food is cooked, the donabe doubles as a serving dish.

Kimchi jar (Hang-ari)

In a traditional Korean home, kimchi is stored to ferment in earthenware jars. These are put in a cool place where the temperature remains relatively even. These days, small quantities of kimchi are more likely to be stored in glass containers in the refrigerator.

Mortar and pestle

This is one of the essential utensils in the Asian kitchen. Mortar and pestle sets come in two forms: granite and pottery. While the pottery one is good for bruising ingredients such as long beans and pandan (screwpine) leaf, the granite one is faster at pulverizing fibrous mainstays such as lemongrass and galangal and for preparing traditional curry pastes.

When choosing a mortar and pestle, the larger the better, as the ingredients are otherwise likely to fly out during pounding. The small wooden mortar and pestles that are used for grinding spices are virtually useless for making pastes; the best alternative is a food processor.

Rice cooker

An automatic electric or gas rice cooker is highly recommended, as it controls the temperature and cooking time to always make perfect rice. Most rice cookers have a "Keep Warm" feature which maintains cooked rice temperature until the rice is required.

Skewers

Both bamboo and stainless steel skewers are available in many sizes. Stainless steel skewers require cleaning after each use. Bamboo skewers need soaking in water for 10 minutes before any food is threaded onto them to prevent them from burning. Or use fresh woody rosemary stems or bay leaf stems which have been soaked in water. Lemongrass, sugarcane and bamboo shoots can also be used as skewers for food.

Spice grinder

A good-quality spice grinder has both dry and wet mix attachments. You can also use any good-quality coffee grinder (kept only for spices). For wet spice mixes, you will need to use a spice grinder to first grind dry spices and then a small food processor to finish the spice mix with the fresh or wet ingredients.

Square omelette pan

A square-shaped omelette pan about 1 inch (2.5 cm) deep is traditionally used for making sushi omelettes. A thick pan that retains heat is ideal, but can be heavy to handle. You can substitute a conventional round skillet about 10 inches (25 cm) in diameter and trim the sides of the omelette once it has been cooked to make it square.

Steamboat or fire pot

Also called Mongolian hot pots, these are round, doughnut-shaped cooking vessels with a central heat source. The food is cooked in a hot broth at the table. The steaming broth is the source for the name "steamboat," while "fire pot" takes its name from the smoking center chimney filled with hot coals. This cooking technique is used in many Asian countries, from China and Vietnam to Korea and Japan.

Preparing a steamboat or fire pot

1. Prepare charcoal (see page 12).

2. Pour hot stock into the fire pot or steamboat. Always add liquid to a fire pot or steamboat prior to heating with hot coals, lest the solder joints of some models overheat and cause leakage. Stock should fill about two-thirds of pot. At this point, use tongs to add hot coals to center of chimney pot, filling no more than halfway up. Allow stock to boil gently. (See Cautions, below.)

3. Prepare ingredients according to recipe. Diners add ingredients to pot and use small wire ladles and chopsticks to retrieve cooked foods from stock. After guests have eaten meat and vegetables, add steamed rice or noodles. Ladle soup and rice or noodles into soup bowls.

Notes: If the steamboat has a lid attached to the chimney stack, it should be removed during cooking; cover to douse flame. Many models have a ring lid for the pot; this raises the temperature of the stock prior to cooking.

Cautions: Never place a coal-heated pot directly onto a table. It will char wood, melt plastic and may shatter materials such as glass. Place atop a fireproof base such as bricks or a stone slab. If there is a likelihood that the heat will conduct through the bricks onto the table, reinforce with a fireproof mat. Some electric pots require similar precautions.

Steamers

Stovetop steamers, with one or two handles, come in many sizes, shapes and materials. Steamer sets include a base saucepan, usually two baskets and one lid for the set. The steamer baskets can be bought separately, and are available in sizes that fit snugly into standard saucepans. Most woks double as steamers, as do "multifunctional" pasta pots with deep, perforated baskets with handles. (See also Bamboo steamers, page 10.)

Sticky rice steamer

Steamed rice is commonly cooked today in an electric rice cooker, but sticky (glutinous) rice stipulates tradition: a conical bamboo basket for the rice, and a deep, narrow rimmed pot on which the basket sits above the boiling water. These conical bamboo baskets are cheap, available through Asian groceries, and ensure that the sticky rice never touches the water, concentrating all the steam onto the rice. An ideal substitute for the water pot is a tall, narrow stockpot. Alternatively, use a steamer basket lined with cheesecloth (muslin) placed in a tightly fitting pot and a covered steamer.

Sushi bamboo rolling mat (Makisu)

Essential for making sushi rolls, this simple rolling mat is made of thin strips of bamboo woven with cotton string. After using the mat, scrub it with a brush and dry it thoroughly, otherwise it may become moldy. It is best to buy an all-purpose mat measuring 12 inches x 12 inches (30 cm x 30 cm), but larger and smaller ones are also available.

Sushi knives

Japanese chefs use knives that are traditionally made from the same steel that was used to make samurai swords; they are renowned for their strength and sharpness. Sharp, strong, good-quality steel knives are needed for sushi. Look after your knives and sharpen them regularly. Sushi chefs keep a damp cloth nearby, to wipe the knives clean from time to time while they work.

Knives used for filleting fish and for slicing fish for sashimi and sushi should be long and slender with a pointed end. Never use a serrated knife when cutting fish, as it will tear the flesh, spoiling its appearance.

The Japanese knife, houchou, has a single-edged blade, usually on the right side for right-handed use (though left-edged blades can be ordered). The deba-bouchou, used for filleting fish, is much heavier; its 16-inch (40-cm) length includes both blade and grip while its weight helps to make a sharp cut. Substitute a standard filleting or paring knife with a stainless steel blade about 5 inches (13 cm) long.

The yanagiba-bouchou, commonly called a "sashimi knife," has a carbon steel blade about 16 inches (40 cm) long, and is used for filleting small and medium-sized fish.

A stainless steel filleting knife, about 8 inches (20 cm) long, or a chef's knife, can be substituted.

A wide, heavy knife is useful for cutting through bone, as when removing a fish's head. For general chopping and slicing, a cleaver or chopper is most suitable.

Sushi rice-cooling tub (Hangiri)

The broad wooden hangiri, generally made of cypress, and with low sides, is designed specifically for cooling sushi rice, giving it the ideal texture and gloss. A nonmetallic flat-bottomed bowl can be used instead. The bigger the bowl the better, as you will then be able to stir and separate the rice grains properly. If using a hangiri, wash and dry it carefully after use then wrap it in a cloth and store it face down in a cool, dry place.

Sushi rice fan (Uchiwa)

An uchiwa is a flat fan made of paper or silk stretched over light bamboo ribs, and is traditionally used in Japan for cooling and separating the sushi rice. While it is delightful to own an uchiwa, a piece of heavy paper or cardboard will do the job just as well.

Tweezers

Japanese honehuki, or deboning tweezers, are heavy, with flat ends that grip bones and allow them to be pulled easily from fish. These are obtainable from a fish market. Sewing tweezers can be substituted, but the ends must be broad and flat not pointed.

Vegetable cutters

Many styles of stainless steel cutters—flowers, leaves and various decorative shapes—are available in kitchenware and Asian stores for cutting vegetables into attractive shapes and garnishes.

Wok

The word "wok" simply means "cooking vessel" in Cantonese—an indication of how versatile and indispensable this piece of equipment is. Its shape has remained unchanged for centuries. It accommodates small or large quantities of ingredients and allows control over how they are cooked. The large cooking surface evenly and efficiently conducts and holds heat, making a wok especially well suited for stir-frying. However, woks are also used for deep-frying, steaming, boiling and braising.

All woks are basically bowl-shaped, with gently sloping sides. Some have looped handles on opposite sides; others have a long wooden handle on one side. Woks are available in a range of sizes—a diameter of about 14 inches (35 cm) is versatile, and appropriate for recipes that yield four to six servings.

Woks were originally made from cast iron, but are now available in many different materials and finishes—nonstick woks are easy to clean but may not promote browning of foods as well as those made of rolled or carbon steel, while stainless steel or electric woks may not reach high temperatures. Round-bottomed woks work best on gas stoves, though a stand may be necessary to provide stability. Flat-bottomed woks are suited for electric stovetops as they sit directly and securely on the element.

Seasoning and cleaning a wok

Woks of carbon steel or rolled steel are coated with a thin film of lacquer to prevent rusting and this needs to be removed before the wok can be used. Place the wok on the stovetop, fill with cold water and add 2 tablespoons baking soda (bicarbonate of soda). Bring to a boil and boil rapidly for 15 minutes. Drain and scrub off coating with a nylon pad. Repeat process if any coating remains. Then rinse and dry the wok. It is now ready to be seasoned.

Carbon steel, rolled steel and cast iron woks require seasoning before use. This creates a smooth surface that keeps food from sticking and prevents the wok from discoloring. To season a wok, place over low heat. Have paper towels and vegetable oil handy. When the wok is hot, carefully wipe it with an oiled paper towel. Repeat the process with fresh towels until they come away clean, without any trace of color.

A seasoned wok should not be scrubbed clean with detergent after cooking. Instead, use hot water and a sponge or nylon pad. Dry the wok well after washing and store in a dry, well-ventilated place. Long periods without use can cause the oil coating on the wok to become rancid—using your wok is the best way to prevent this.

Wok shovels and utensils

Wooden and metal wok shovels have a rounded end, facilitating scraping along the contours of the wok. You can use a wooden or metal spatula or pancake turner. A slotted spoon, or a Chinese wire-mesh skimmer with a bamboo handle, is essential for correct lifting and draining of deep-fried food. Don't use metal tongs to lift food from the hot oil; a slotted spoon or wire-mesh skimmer are much safer options. Cooking chopsticks and wooden tongs are also handy utensils for cooking Asian dishes.

Wooden rice paddle (Shamoji)

A wooden rice paddle, called a shamoji, is traditionally used for turning and spreading sushi rice when cooling it, but any kind of broad, flat utensil will do the job. You can use a large wooden spoon or a wooden spatula. Because wood tends to absorb flavors, it is best to use your chosen spoon exclusively for sushi rice. Before using a wooden spoon for sushi rice, wet it thoroughly, or the rice will stick to it.

Serving Asian meals

Most Asian cultures have strong rituals and beliefs surrounding food, especially when it is served on formal occasions. And while the presentation of food remains as important as how it tastes, these days dining in the Asian home is a much more relaxed affair.

Plates and cutlery

It is perfectly acceptable to use standard plates, bowls and serving dishes, as well as forks, spoons and chopsticks, when serving an Asian-style meal. In fact, in many Asian homes, food stalls and restaurants, these are no different from anywhere else. However, the range of Asian homeware is infinitely varied and beautiful, and you will probably collect several sets, to suit various occasions. Whatever you use, it is important to choose serving dishes and utensils that suit the food style—deep, wide bowls for soups and curries, flat plates for sushi.

When eating with a spoon and fork (knives are not usually required at the table), many Asians, such as Thais and Malaysians, hold the spoon in the right hand, using it to place food in the mouth, with the fork in the left doing little more than positioning the food. It is considered bad etiquette to place a fork in the mouth—a bit like licking a knife blade.

How to serve Asian meals

Most Asian meals follow the Chinese tradition, where all the dishes are placed on the table at once so that they can be enjoyed together—the more dishes, the more ostentatious the occasion. Each diner has a small bowl of steamed rice, and places a spoonful of any one of the dishes onto their rice. Or their host may offer to serve them a portion of a dish. This is eaten, with some rice, before choosing another dish.

Vietnamese: When eating a Vietnamese dinner, do not accumulate different dishes on your plate at once. The Vietnamese eat with chopsticks, and also use Chinese-style soup spoons. Soup is regularly spooned over the rice to moisten it and, at the end, any remaining soup is poured into bowls and all rice is finished, for it is considered a bad omen if even one grain of rice is left. Some dishes are eaten with the hands, such as fresh spring rolls or when diners wrap food at the table.

Thai: A Thai meal follows the same style as the Chinese and Vietnamese, except diners are given plates of steamed rice, not bowls. It is considered bad manners for serving dishes to be passed around; rather, the host (or the person closest to a particular dish) offers to spoon a serving directly onto your plate. During a home meal, particularly, it is considered rude to begin eating before all the food is placed on the table; this rule of etiquette is less practiced when eating out. Unlike other Asian countries, most Thais eat with forks and spoons, not chopsticks, a custom going back to the royal court of Rama IV in the nineteenth century. Conversely, chopsticks are used when eating noodle dishes, or in some Chinese eateries. Before spoons, forks and even chopsticks, the traditional Thai way to eat was with fingers; this is still practiced today, particularly in areas where sticky rice is the preferred staple.

Indian: The customs surrounding food are very important in India, with many religious rituals associated with dining. Cleanliness is an essential part of the ritual, and diners wash their hands well both before and after the meal, whether in a restaurant or at home. Indians do not eat with cutlery; instead, they use a little bread or rice to soak up the sauce integral to many dishes or the fingertips of the right hand (which is considered the "holy" hand) to scoop up morsels and consume them, without actually inserting their fingers in their mouths. Of course cutlery may be used, both in Indian restaurants and at home.

Japanese: It is a given in Japan that food should appeal as much to the eye as to the palate, and it is presentation that changes the humblest meal into a dining experience. Japanese-style tableware is readily available in Asian markets and specialty stores— especially square and rectangular plates (these should be as flat as possible for presentation and to prevent the sushi from falling over), and any number of small soup and garnish bowls. If serving sake, heat it in a pitcher (tokkuri) and serve it in tiny china cups (sakazuki). Japanese chopsticks have more pointed ends than the Chinese variety, making it easy to handle sushi, sashimi and condiments. Those used at home and in restaurants are usually made of lacquered wood or bamboo; disposable chopsticks are also convenient; and steel is preferred for sashimi.

Korean: Table settings are very important in a Korean meal, from casual, everyday settings to formal ceremonial ones. Serving dishes are generally low flat bowls; porcelain bowls are used to serve sides. Rice is served in individual bowls; never place food over the rice before serving. Rice and soup are eaten with a spoon, and side dishes with chopsticks. Korean chopsticks are traditionally stainless steel or silver, and take an extra bit of skill to wield successfully. Spoons and chopsticks are never used at the same time; nor should you hold dishes in your hands while eating. After the meal, chopsticks and spoon are placed as they were laid out originally.

Preparing ingredients

Some ingredient preparation and cooking techniques are common across all Asian cuisines. Although many ingredients can now be easily purchased already prepared—such as commercial curry pastes and coconut cream—and these are perfectly acceptable and time-saving substitutes, there's nothing as authentic as making your own. This section includes step-by-step instructions for basic techniques and recipes; see also the introduction to each chapter and the Glossary for descriptions of specific ingredients.

Chili preparation

Chilies are freely added to many Asian dishes—especially those of Thailand, India, Korea and Vietnam. You can easily tame the piquancy of chilies in recipes. Generally, small chilies are hotter than larger varieties, so use larger chilies if a milder effect is preferred. In all chilies, the seeds and internal "ribs" are the hottest part, so you can scrape some or all of the seeds away before using. Surprisingly, adding whole chilies to a dish will make it less hot than if the chilies are chopped up. Likewise, coarsely chopped chilies will make dishes less hot than finely chopped chilies. If using whole or large pieces of chilies, simply avoid eating them.

When working with chilies, avoid touching your skin, eyes and nose, as fresh chilies contain volatile oils that can burn skin and tender membranes. Apply a barrier cream to hands prior to handling, or wear gloves. The soaking water from both dried and fresh chilies can also burn and cause a rash. Always wash your hands well in cool, soapy water after use, and thoroughly scrub the chopping board and knife. When the taste of chili overwhelms, immediately eat a spoonful of plain rice or a piece of banana, or drink milk. Do not down a glass of water, as it tends to spread the heat throughout the mouth.

Preparing dried chilies

1. Pull or cut stems off long chilies.

2. Roll the chili pod gently in the palm of your hand.

3. Turn the chili pod upside down and shake out the loosened seeds.

4. Soak pods in warm water for 10 minutes, then drain. Caution: Do not let the soaking liquid touch your hands, as it could burn your skin.

Roasting dried chilies

Slightly cooking dried chilies improves their flavor. Put the pods in a dry wok or a large, heavy frying pan over medium–high heat and toast, stirring constantly, until the chilies are fragrant and begin to brown, without burning. (Note: Ensure that the room is well ventilated.)

Roasting and peeling fresh chilies

In some recipes, such as Chili Dipping Sauce (see page 568), chilies are roasted and peeled to remove the slightly bitter skin and to improve the taste.

1. Skewer chilies on bamboo skewers or metal fondue forks and pass over a gas flame until blackened on all sides.

2. Alternatively, arrange chilies in a single layer on a baking sheet and place under a preheated broiler (grill), as close to heat source as possible, until blackened on all sides, turning as required.

3. Remove from heat and cover with a damp towel. Let stand until chilies are cool to the touch.

4. Peel skin and pull off stems, but do not remove seeds.

Carving a chili flower

Medium chili: These are ideal for the simplest of chili flowers. Make sure that the chilies are very crisp and fresh, either green or red.

1. Hold chili flat on a board and use a thin sharp knife to cut lengthwise from stem to tip. Make about 5 parallel cuts just through skin to seeds, but not across to the other side.

2. Plunge into ice water. Chili "petals" will curl back, while the seed cluster becomes the stamen. If parts of the flower remain closed, prod them gently with the knife and return the flower to the water. These keep for up to 36 hours if refrigerated in cold water.

Long chili: While these do not "blossom" as exquisitely as the shorter ones, they do resemble the beautiful kiriboon flower of Southeast Asia. Use a scalpel or a thin V-shaped garnishing knife (available at cookware shops and from some cake-decorating suppliers).

Make small V-shaped incisions along length of chili, in parallel rows. They should be about $\frac{1}{8}$ inch (3 mm) wide and no more than $\frac{1}{4}$ inch (6 mm) long. Plunge into ice water, as for medium chili, until the incisions curl back like a flower.

Coconut cream and milk

1. Shake a whole dried coconut to check for water inside. If there is none present, discard the coconut. Drill or nail holes in the eyes to drain the water. Hold the coconut in your hand, rested in a heavy tea towel. Use a large chef's knife to crack the coconut by scoring lightly across its circumference, then striking it sharply with the back of the knife to crack the shell. Take extra care, lest you cut your hand. Alternatively, drop the coconut onto a hard concrete surface, or hit it with a hammer.

2. Use a small hand grater to scrape out the coconut meat in shreds. Alternatively, pry the meat from the shell, peel off the brown inner skin, and grate the meat in a food processor.

3. Put grated coconut in a tea towel and wring it, or put it in a sieve and press it firmly with your knuckles or the back of a large spoon, to extract the cream; reserve liquid.

4. Add just enough warm or hot water to cover the shredded coconut and press it again to extract thick coconut milk; reserve. Repeat again, to extract thin coconut milk.

Cooking shrimp

To cook raw shrimp (prawns), bring an uncovered saucepan of salted water to boil, add shrimp and cook until they become firm and change color, 3–5 minutes. Remove and place in iced water until cool. Drain well. Refrigerate if not using immediately.

Crispy fried shallots (French shallots)

Packed with flavor and color, these are sprinkled over vegetables, noodles, rice and salads, and many soups are considered incomplete without them. The following recipe makes about 1 cup (8 oz/250 g); any unused fried shallots can be stored in an airtight container in the refrigerator.

2 cups (16 fl oz/500 ml) peanut oil
5 or 6 medium shallots (French shallots), about 5 oz (150 g), peeled
  and very thinly sliced

Heat oil in a medium saucepan over high heat until it reaches 375°F (190°C) on a deep-frying thermometer. Add shallots all at once and fry until golden, about 1 1/2 minutes. Remove with a slotted spoon and drain on a plate lined with paper towels.

Finely shredded herbs

Also known as chiffonnade, paper-thin shreds of herbs are achieved by rolling several leaves together into a tight cylinder, then slicing crosswise. This technique suits larger herb leaves such as kaffir lime and the many basils and mints which feature in Asian cuisine. When cutting kaffir lime leaves, first remove the tough center stem. Tender leaves such as basil and mint merely need to be pinched from their stems.

How to make curry pastes

In a mortar and pestle:

1. Begin by toasting then grinding the dry spices, while the inside of the mortar is still clean. Remove the powder. Then grind the other ingredients, starting with the hardest, most fibrous items and working down to the softer items. To facilitate pounding, coarsely cut the hardest ingredients, such as galangal and lemongrass, into pieces. Softer ingredients, such as garlic, can be added whole, as they mash easily.

2. Add wet ingredients to the mortar. Pound all wet ingredients to a paste using a pestle. If necessary, make the paste in 2 batches so that you can grind it effectively—the crushed ingredients will create a "cushioned" barrier.

3. Add all the ground ingredients and pound to combine. The texture should be pastelike and relatively smooth.

4. Cover tightly and store in the refrigerator—curry pastes keep for 3–4 days. For longer preservation, fry the curry paste prior to storage: In a wok, heat about $1/3$ cup (3 fl oz/90 ml) oil then add paste. Or fry the paste over low heat, stirring occasionally, until aromatic and color changes slightly, 3–5 minutes. Store the paste in the cooking oil, and cover tightly; keep for up to 2 months in the refrigerator or freeze indefinitely.

In a food processor: Coarsely chop all fresh ingredients. Place chopped ingredients and spices in a food processor. Pulse on and off until even in texture, then process continuously to make a relatively smooth paste. If necessary, add a small amount of water, 1 teaspoon at a time, to facilitate processing.

Noodles

For descriptions of types of noodles, see Glossary. For instructions on how to prepare noodles, see page 442 in the Rice and Noodles chapter.

Nori

Nori, the sheets of dark green seaweed used to wrap sushi, is usually purchased pre-toasted. Toasting is only required if nori is not purchased toasted or if it loses its crispness and needs to be freshened up. To toast nori: Place nori under the broiler (grill) or over a gas burner until crisp, 30 seconds to 1 minute. Only one side needs to be toasted. To store nori: Light will affect the flavor and color of nori, so keep nori in a cool dark place. Once opened, packages should be wrapped in plastic wrap, foil or freezer bags, or kept in an airtight container, without any contact with moisture. Open packets can be refrigerated for 1 month or frozen for 3–4 months.

Omelettes

Omelettes are used in a variety of Asian dishes, to wrap food as in the Vietnamese Pork Omelette Roll (see page 64) or thinly sliced as a garnish for fried rice, noodles or vegetables. (See also Thin Seasoned Omelette for Sushi on page 320.) The following recipe makes 1 omelette.

1–2 eggs
1 tablespoon water
pinch sugar
pinch salt (optional)
vegetable oil for cooking

Using a fork, beat egg(s) until blended. Add 1 tablespoon water and sugar, and salt if using. Heat an 8-inch (20-cm) frying pan over medium heat. Add enough oil to coat bottom. It should sizzle if a drop of water is added. Pour beaten egg into pan, lifting pan to tilt it quickly to allow egg to spread out evenly. Reduce heat to low and cook just until set, about 30 seconds. Carefully flip over omelette and cook a few seconds on second side. It should be firm and not runny. Transfer to a plate to cool.

Cooked omelettes, either stacked flat or rolled, can be wrapped tightly in plastic wrap and refrigerated for up to 2 days. For omelette strips, loosely roll 2–3 cooked omelettes into a cylinder, then cut crosswise into strips.

Egg gidan

Egg gidan is used in many Korean recipes for garnish. To make egg gidan: Fry egg white and yolk separately, tilting pan evenly to create a pancake. Remove and slice thinly.

Onions, Indian-style

Cooking onions correctly is an important step in making many Indian dishes, and the process must not be rushed or the onions will burn. The quantities below are similar to those found in many recipes in this book. Using a ratio of half oil to half melted unsalted butter gives both a good heating temperature and good flavor. Salt also adds flavor and helps onions to brown evenly.

1. Halve and thinly slice or chop 3 yellow (brown) onions. In a large, heavy saucepan, heat $1/2$ cup (4 fl oz/125 ml) combined vegetable oil and melted unsalted butter over medium–low heat. Do not overheat or butter will burn and taint onions.

2. Add onions and 1 teaspoon salt to pan. Cook, uncovered, stirring occasionally, until onions are dark golden brown, 15–20 minutes. Onions will begin to color around edge of pan—stirring helps to distribute heat and ensures even browning.

Peeling rhizomes

Fresh galangal, ginger and turmeric should be peeled before using. Removing the peel concentrates the flavors of the inner root and eliminates tasteless fiber. However, this step is considered optional by many. To peel rhizomes, pare thinly with a small paring knife. Wear gloves when cutting turmeric, as it stains skin.

Preparing rice paper sheets

As well as being used for spring rolls, softened, round rice paper sheets can also be served at the table, Vietnamese-style, for wrapping foods to eat.

1. Place dry stacked rice paper sheets on a plate.

2. Cover with a damp cloth that has been wrung dry, and wrap tightly with plastic wrap for 1–2 hours to soften sheets slightly. Shuffle sheets occasionally for even moisture distribution. Alternatively, place 2–3 cabbage leaves alongside rice paper sheets on a flat plate, cover tightly with plastic wrap and leave overnight.

3. The sheets should peel away individually; take care not to tear them. If still brittle, lightly moisten by either brushing with water or wiping with a damp cloth. Do not over-moisten.

4. Large, 9-inch (23-cm) rice paper sheets for enfolding foods at the table are cut into thirds or halves, then stacked; use scissors or shears to cut after softening. This makes them ideal for rolling bite-sized morsels. Precut sheets may be available from Asian markets.

Quick treatment for spring rolls

This treatment is especially suited for sheets used for spring rolls, but less suited for serving at the table.

1. Quickly dip each sheet, one at a time, into a pan of water (a shallow roasting pan works well).

2. Do not leave in water to soak, but pass sheet through water for a couple seconds, pat dry, then drain flat on a damp cloth. Do not over-moisten, as this leads to tearing, and sheets will not adhere easily when rolling. Be patient, as they will subsequently soften—taking from 15 seconds to a few minutes. Use immediately after they have softened, rolling into a spring roll.

3. If stacking, place sheets of waxed paper between rice paper sheets, as the greater volume of water used in this method can oversoak sheets and make them unusable.

Steamed rice

Though commonly referred to as "steamed," rice is actually boiled. This method can be used for 3–6 cups uncooked long-grain rice such as jasmine or basmati; it makes 6–12 cups of cooked rice. Alternatively, use an automatic rice cooker (see Equipment).

1. Rinse rice in several changes of water, until water runs clear, but do not overwork rice, lest grains break. Drain.

2. Place rice in a deep, medium to large, heavy-based saucepan or pot with a tight-fitting lid. Fill with just enough water to cover rice by 1 inch (2.5 cm). (Traditionally, cooks measured by placing their index finger on top of rice and adding enough water to reach the first joint.) Bring to a boil, uncovered, over high heat and cook until craters form in rice. Immediately cover tightly and reduce heat; simmer until tender, about 20 minutes. Do not lift lid whilst cooking.

3. Use a rice paddle to fluff up rice and loosen grains.

Sushi rice

Sushi rice is called shari, which means "a tiny piece of Buddha's bone," because of its shape and precious nature. Making it requires practice. Good sushi rice has a delicate balance of sweet and sour, is firm yet sticky, and shines like a pearl.

The measurements of sugar and vinegar are seasonal and regional. In Japan, in the summer, a little more vinegar is used, and in western Japan, sushi is sweeter than in the eastern part. All quantities can be adjusted to suit personal taste. Do not refrigerate cooked sushi rice: this causes the gluten to congeal, reducing the stickiness and lessening the flavor. Cooked sushi rice will not keep for more than 1 day.

White sushi rice

Makes about 8 cups (2$^1/_2$ lb/1.25 kg).

5 cups (2$^1/_4$ lb/1.1 kg) short-grain rice
5 cups (40 fl oz/1.25 L) water
$^1/_2$ cup (4 fl oz/125 ml) sake (optional)

1. Put rice in a large bowl and add cold water to cover. Stir rice briskly with your hands to remove any dirt. Cover rice with your hands as you carefully drain away cloudy water. Repeat process two more times. By the third rinsing, water should be clear. (Avoid washing rice too many times, as it removes starch and nourishment and also breaks grains.)

2. Place rice in a strainer to drain. In summer, it will need about 30 minutes, in winter about 1 hour.

3. If using an automatic rice cooker, place rice and water in rice cooker and turn on. Machine will cook rice and tell you when it is ready.

   If cooking rice on a stovetop, place drained rice and water in a heavy-bottomed saucepan and cover with a tight-fitting lid. Bring to a boil over medium heat. Do not remove lid while cooking. When water boils, raise heat to high and boil for about 3 minutes. If pot boils over, adjust heat. Reduce heat to medium and boil for 5 minutes. Reduce heat to low and cook for 5–10 minutes. Remove from heat and remove lid. The rice should have absorbed the water. You may wish to follow the practice of some sushi bars and add sake to the rice before removing from heat. This makes the rice puff up and adds flavor.

4. Place cheesecloth (muslin) or a clean kitchen towel over saucepan, re-cover and let stand for 10–15 minutes to finish cooking.

Sushi vinegar

1/2 cup (4 fl oz/125 ml) rice vinegar
1 teaspoon salt
1 tablespoon sugar
1 teaspoon mirin

1. Place vinegar and salt in a small saucepan over low heat and stir until salt is dissolved. Add sugar and mirin and continue to stir briskly until sugar is dissolved. Do not let mixture boil. Remove from heat when saucepan is too hot to touch.

2. Place hot rice in a wooden rice tub or a large, flat-bottomed nonmetallic bowl. Spread rice evenly over bottom of tub or bowl.

3. Add sushi vinegar slowly to rice and, using rice paddle or large flat wooden spoon, distribute evenly through rice. Do not stir rice; instead, slice paddle through rice, then lift rice and turn.

4. Use a handheld fan to cool rice. Continue mixing and fanning until rice cools to room temperature. Rice is then ready to use; if not using immediately, cover with a damp, clean kitchen towel to prevent rice from drying out until required.

Brown sushi rice

2 cups (13 oz/400 g) uncooked short-grain brown rice
3 cups (24 fl oz/750 ml) water

Sushi vinegar

1/4 cup (2 fl oz/60 ml) rice vinegar
2 tablespoons sugar
1/4 teaspoon salt

Rinse brown rice once and cook as for white sushi rice until most liquid is absorbed, 30–35 minutes. Remove from heat and let stand, covered, for 10–15 minutes. Combine ingredients of sushi vinegar, stir into rice as for sushi rice and fan to cool.

Thai crudités

A selection of raw vegetables and herbs is a standard inclusion at the Thai table. Usually this accompanies a dipping sauce, though these crudités are not plunged into the dip; instead, a small spoonful of the sauce is combined with rice, and the crudités are eaten as an accompaniment. A wide range of vegetables are offered, from baby corn to slices of eggplant and cucumber, lightly bruised long beans cut into 2-inch (5-cm) lengths or tied into small knots, okra and strips of cabbage. Fresh herbs are also eaten with dishes as accompaniments. A selection can include sweet Thai basil, mint and lead tree (kra thin). Lettuce and other greens, such as water spinach (morning glory), are also served.

Toasting nuts and seeds

1. Place nuts or seeds, such as peanuts, cashews and sesame seeds in a dry wok or frying pan over medium heat, and toast, stirring constantly, until lightly golden and fragrant. Take care not to burn them, especially once the nuts or seeds start to color.

2. Alternatively, preheat the oven to 400°F (200°C/Gas 6). Spread the nuts or seeds on a rimmed baking pan and toast for 8–12 minutes, shaking the pan once to ensure even browning. Nuts and seeds should not be overcooked, lest they become bitter.

Toasting spices

1. For fresher flavor, use whole spices, then toast and grind them yourself. Because spices all toast at different times, toast them separately in a dry wok or frying pan over medium–high heat, stirring constantly, until fragrant. This will take anywhere from a few seconds to no more than 90 seconds. The general rule is to use your nose: once fragrant, remove the spice from the heat immediately, lest it burns and becomes acrid.

2. Transfer toasted spices to a mortar, let cool and then grind.

Tofu preparation

Tofu is widely available from Asian markets, natural foods stores and most supermarkets. Label descriptions and textures can vary among manufacturers, so experiment to see which types and brands best suit your needs. (See Glossary for descriptions of different types of tofu and tempeh.)

In general, firm and extra-firm Chinese-style tofu is best for stir-fries, kabobs or dishes that require tofu to hold its shape. Japanese-style silken tofu, whether soft or firm, can hold its shape in soups and even some stir-fries if handled very carefully, and can also be used in other recipes such as dips and sauces.

Tofu is available in refrigerated plastic containers, refrigerated vacuum-sealed packs or shelf-stable sealed cartons that require no refrigeration until opened. Once opened, all tofu must be kept refrigerated in sealed containers covered with water that is changed daily. It should be used within 5–7 days if not frozen (see below). Tofu should smell slightly sweet. Discard it if it smells sour, feels slippery or is tinged with pink or green. Deep-fried tofu will keep for about 10 days; seasoned tofu should be used within 3–4 days.

Once opened, tempeh should be used within 5 days, or frozen for up to 3 months. If gray or black spots appear, caused by the active mold, just cut them off, but discard any tempeh that feels slippery or smells of ammonia.

Freezing and defrosting tofu

Tofu can be frozen for up to 3 months, and even used in cooking while still frozen, but the texture becomes firmer and more crumbly and the color darkens slightly. As the water in the tofu freezes, it expands to form small pockets. When the tofu thaws and the water drains away, the pockets remain, giving the tofu a crumbly texture and the ability to absorb flavors like a sponge. Especially when the tofu is cut into pieces, these small pores allow the tofu to absorb more flavor from marinades and sauces. If crumbled, defrosted tofu resembles ground meat. A similar texture can be achieved by breaking up a firm or extra-firm block of tofu and stir-frying it in a splash of oil until it is dry. Freezing silken tofu is not recommended, as freezing ruins its delicate texture.

Defrost tofu quickly by puncturing holes in the top of the plastic container and microwaving it for 5–7 minutes. It can also be defrosted in warm water, and the excess moisture gently squeezed out. Tofu can be defrosted at room temperature, which should take about 3 hours, but ideally it should be thawed overnight in the refrigerator. Drain and press thawed tofu before use to expel any excess liquid.

Tempeh can be defrosted by microwaving it on HIGH for 45–60 seconds or leaving it in the refrigerator overnight.

How to cut tofu

Tofu can be sliced, diced, crumbled or cut into decorative shapes with a melon baller or biscuit cutter.

1. Cut a block of tofu in half horizontally into 1–2 slices.

2. Cut vertically into strips of required thickness.

3. Give block a quarter turn and, holding tofu gently, slice to make cubes.

Removing excess moisture from tofu

Removing excess moisture from tofu makes room for other liquids, such as marinades and sauces, to be absorbed and prevents excess liquid from diluting sauces and dressings. It also prevents tofu from spattering when frying.

Draining: The first step is simply pouring off the water that surrounds the tofu in the packet. Further draining can be done in a colander.

Pressing: Although not necessary for firm and extra-firm tofu, pressing tofu before use removes even more moisture and makes the tofu firmer and less watery. The simplest method for pressing tofu is to wrap it in paper towels, place 2 dinner plates on top and leave it to drain for 20–30 minutes, or longer for a drier, firmer texture. Put a weight, such as a can of vegetables, on top and leave to drain into the sink for 20–30 minutes. Pat tofu dry before cooking.

Patting dry: Place sliced or diced tofu on a paper towel, cover with another paper towel and gently pat to absorb any excess surface moisture before cooking.

Pan drying: Slice or dice drained tofu and heat it in a nonstick or lightly greased frying pan over medium–high heat. Any excess moisture will evaporate and the tofu will brown lightly, giving it a slightly nutty flavor and a firmer texture.

Oven drying: Place sliced or diced tofu in a lightly greased baking dish and bake in a preheated 375°F (190°C/Gas 5) oven until excess moisture is released, 5–10 minutes. Drain, then return the tofu to the turned-off oven to evaporate any remaining moisture and firm the texture.

Grill drying: Place sliced or diced tofu under a preheated broiler (grill) and heat until lightly browned, about 5 minutes on each side. Besides evaporating any excess liquid, the texture will be firmer and the browning will bring out a nutty flavor. Grilled tofu is also available in cans and refrigerated packs.

Vegetable garnishes

Asian cuisine is often elaborately decorated with exquisite garnishes, from finely shredded kaffir lime leaves, or fresh ginger julienne, to ornately carved pumpkins or watermelons. Thai cooks are especially renowned for carving fruits and vegetables, and, indeed, in Thailand, the craft is taught at an early age. Commonly, fruits and vegetables take on the simple forms of flowers, such as roses (see page 23 for chili flower).

Rolling a tomato rose

1. Take a firm, medium to large red tomato. Beginning at its base, pare the skin thinly around the tomato in a continuous spiral about ¾-inch (2-cm) wide. Do not let the skin break.

2. Lay the skin on a working surface, skin-side up, then pinch and roll into a tight spiral nest.

3. Stand it upright, and gently prod outside layers to open like a rose. The center should remain tight like a bud. If desired, decorate with a couple of basil leaves to the side. Store under a damp paper towel in the refrigerator no longer than 2–3 days, until the edges wrinkle.

Scallion brushes and curls

1. Using a sharp knife, remove the root section from each scallion (shallot/spring onion). Cut the paler green section of each scallion into 2-inch (5-cm) sections. Discard the darker green section, or save for another use.

2. To make scallion brushes: Make ¼ inch (6 mm) cuts in each piece, forming a fringe.

3. To make scallion curls: Slice scallion pieces lengthwise into fine strips.

4. Place scallion brushes or strips in a bowl of ice water. Refrigerate until scallions curl, about 15 minutes. Drain and use to garnish or flavor your favorite recipes.

Lemon and lime zest curls

1. Using a citrus zester, firmly scrape the zest from lemons, limes, oranges or grapefruits. Use the zest to garnish and flavor your favorite recipes. If a zester is unavailable, remove zest with a vegetable peeler.

2. Remove any white pith from zest pieces.

3. Using a very sharp knife, finely slice zest. Place zest in a bowl of ice water. Refrigerate until zest curls, about 15 minutes. (If you are using a zester, it is generally not necessary to place zest in ice water.)

Appetizers & entrees

exquisitely presented morsels of food and bite-sized bundles are trademarks of Asian cuisine, yet many of the spring rolls, fish cakes and wontons which make ideal appetizers and entrees in the West were never designed to start a meal. Traditionally, in many Asian cultures, such as Thai, Vietnamese and Indian, there are no distinct courses. Main meals consist of an array of dishes, sometimes up to ten, with accompaniments and sides—the glory lies in a table laden with many plates and bowls offering a range of foods to balance a meal and tempt the palate. Conversely, in Japan, sashimi was always eaten before the main meal.

Likewise, dim sum is an ideal way to start an Asian meal at home, although the tradition began in the Guangzhou (Canton) region of China when teahouses started offering a few small snacks to attract locals and travelers. In the West the terms dim sum (meaning "dot hearts,'" "heart warmers" or "heart's delight"), or yum cha (meaning "to drink tea"), are used interchangeably, referring to a cacophony of small, mostly hot dishes, accompanied by a pot or two of tea. Perhaps one of the earliest forms of "fast food," dim sum has evolved to a high level, with some top restaurants offering hundreds of varieties.

In Asia, especially Hong Kong, dim sum is served from early morning to late afternoon. In other countries it's strictly a morning and lunchtime ritual—with Sunday mornings becoming the new tradition in most Western cities with a sizeable Chinese population.

At home, dim sum is a different story. Because you can't make the huge selection available in a restaurant, dim sum becomes perfect as a starter or appetizer to a main meal, and it is also exceptional with pre-dinner drinks or cocktails—simply serve one or two different dishes. Dim sum can also be served as brunch: allow 8–10 bite-sized pieces per person.

The great beauty of Asian food is its flexibility. You can adapt almost any recipe for a main meal into an appetizer, or turn an entree into a main by increasing the quantities. If you're serving in authentic styles, plan lots of complementary dishes, a mixture of large and small sizes, some of which can be conveniently made well in advance, and serve them at once, inviting guests to help themselves, in no particular order. Or, if preferred, you can simply serve an appetizer before a main course that consists of a few dishes.

As well as being adaptable, many of the recipes in this chapter can be prepared ahead of time, leaving the cooking to be done at the last minute. Others are so quick and easy that they can simply be thrown together just before serving. You can also serve the ingredients of some appetizers, such as fresh spring rolls, in separate plates and bowls at the table, allowing guests to create their own dishes—an excellent way to start an Asian meal.

Basic techniques for appetizers

Once you've mastered a few basic techniques, you'll find that the range of Asian appetizers and entrees you can make is infinite. In this section you will find instructions for the main techniques, such as rolling and cooking spring rolls and making wontons. (See also individual recipes and Preparing ingredients, pages 22–33.)

Making fresh spring rolls

1. Soften a rice paper sheet following directions on page 27, then lay, smooth side down, on a damp cloth. Lay a lettuce leaf slightly off center along bottom of sheet. Add herb leaves of your choice, first removing any stems that might pierce rice paper. Top with bean sprouts and softened dried or fresh thin rice noodles. The pile of fillings should be long and narrow, in the shape of a horizontal rectangle.

2. Fold over the two sides of rice paper sheet to enclose two narrow ends of filling. Crease rice paper gently, then lay a few shoots of Chinese chives along top side of filling so that the ends stick out beyond edges of rice paper by about $\frac{1}{2}$ inch (1.2 cm). Arrange 3 thin slices meat or halved shrimp on rice paper, about $\frac{3}{4}$ inch (2 cm) above chives, again horizontally along lines of filling. Meat should be cut very thin, into slices about 1 inch x 1$\frac{1}{2}$ inches (2.5 cm x 4 cm) each, and medium shrimp should be sliced lengthwise and placed skin-side down.

3. Bring bottom of rice paper sheet up and over filling and press gently to compact. (At this point, you may need to lightly brush rice paper sheet with water along the two sides to facilitate rolling and sealing.) Continue rolling the filling into a fat cigar shape about 4 inches (10 cm) long and 1$\frac{1}{4}$ inches (3 cm) wide, ensuring that filling is compact. Take care not to tear sheet. Gently press rice paper sheet to seal it to itself.

Note: If sheets are too wet, they will not adhere. Keep covered with plastic wrap while making remaining rolls.

Making fried spring rolls

1. Soften a rice paper sheet following directions on page 27. Wipe each rice paper sheet lightly with a damp cloth before using. If you like, add 1 teaspoon sugar to soaking water, as this will give it a crispier texture when fried. Cut off bottom and top thirds of a sheet to make 2 quarter moons. Lay one of these pieces at bottom edge of a full rice sheet to reinforce it. Reserve center section for individually wrapping foods at the table, or trim corners with scissors to make more quarter-moon pieces.

2. Spoon a heaping tablespoon of filling across bottom middle of sheet, slightly off center. Press filling lightly into a cylindrical shape.

3. Fold bottom edge of rice paper sheet over filling, pressing gently to remove any air bubbles that might burst during cooking. Fold the two sides inward, creasing to reinforce fold, then proceed as in Step 3 on page 38. Lightly smear final fold at top with a paste of flour and water. The roll should be about $\frac{2}{3}$ inches x 2 inches (1.75 cm x 5 cm) in size. Cover lightly with plastic wrap to prevent drying, then fill remaining rice paper sheets in the same way.

4. In a wok or deep-fryer, heat 4 inches (10 cm) oil to 325–350°F (170–180°C) and fry spring rolls until crisp and golden brown, about 5 minutes (see Caution). Using a skimmer, transfer to paper towels to drain. Keep warm in a low oven.

Caution: When deep-frying, make sure the wok or deep fryer is never filled more than one-third full, as the oil can froth up to double its volume when food is added, and any spilled oil can catch on fire.

Making basic dumplings

1. Place round wonton wrappers onto a work surface and cover with a damp kitchen towel. Place one wrapper on a work surface, spoon in filling, brush edges with water and fold in half to form a semicircle.

2. If you have a gow gee press, working with one wrapper at a time, lay it flat in the press and spoon filling into the center. Brush edges of wrapper with water. Close gow gee press firmly to seal edges together.

3. Square or round wonton wrappers can also be formed into little pouches around filling. Gather edges around filling to form a basket. Gently squeeze the center of dumpling to expose the filling at the top. Tap the base of dumpling on work surface to flatten it. Set aside, covered with plastic wrap, while you make the remaining dumplings.

Making steamed buns

1. Divide dough into walnut-sized rounds. Roll or press each piece out to a circle. Cover dough with a damp kitchen towel.

2. Working with one dough round at a time, spoon filling into the center.

3. Gather edges together and twist to seal dough. Cut out squares of parchment (baking paper) and place buns, sealed side down, onto paper.

Agedashi tofu

Serves 4 as an entree

20 oz (600 g) silken firm tofu, drained and pressed (see pages 31–32)
2 tablespoons cornstarch (cornflour)
vegetable or sunflower oil, for deep-frying
3/4 cup (6 fl oz/180 ml) Dashi 1 (see page 572)
2¹/2 tablespoons soy sauce
2¹/2 tablespoons mirin
1/4 cup (2 oz/60 g) shredded daikon
1 tablespoon grated fresh ginger
1 scallion (shallot/spring onion), green part only
1 tablespoon fine bonito flakes (katsuobushi)

Cut tofu into 12 equal cubes. Toss in cornstarch, shaking off any excess. Fill a frying pan or wok one-third full with oil and heat to 365°F (185°C). Deep-fry tofu in batches until lightly browned all over, 5–6 minutes. Drain on paper towels.

In a small saucepan, combine stock, soy sauce and mirin and bring to a simmer. Place 3 pieces of tofu in each serving bowl. Arrange daikon, ginger and onion on top and pour sauce around tofu. Sprinkle with bonito flakes and serve immediately.

Note: *Agedashi tofu is a classic Japanese tofu dish.*

Variation: *Season cornstarch with chili flakes, fresh herbs, or black and white sesame seeds.*

Baked chicken purses

Makes 20 purses

1 tablespoon vegetable oil

4 cloves garlic, finely chopped

1 bird's eye chili, seeded and finely chopped

6$^1/_2$ oz (200 g) ground (minced) chicken

3 tablespoons Thai sweet chili sauce

2 teaspoons fish sauce

1 tablespoon chopped fresh Thai basil

2 tablespoons chopped fresh cilantro (fresh coriander)

sea salt and freshly ground pepper to taste

5 scallions (shallots/spring onions)

5 sheets frozen ready-made puff pastry sheets, thawed

1 egg, beaten

Chili Dipping Sauce (see page 568) or soy sauce, for serving

Heat oil in a wok over medium heat and stir-fry garlic and chili for 1 minute, or until fragrant. Add chicken and stir-fry until opaque, about 3 minutes. Remove from heat. Stir in sweet chili sauce, fish sauce, basil, cilantro, salt and pepper. Mix well. Let cool completely.

Meanwhile, cut each scallion into 4 pieces lengthwise. Put in a bowl and add boiling water to cover. Let stand for 1 minute. Drain and rinse under cold running water. Drain again.

Preheat oven to 425°F (220°C/Gas 7). Line 2 baking trays with parchment (baking) paper. Using a $^1/_4$-inch (6-mm) cutter, cut puff pastry into 20 rounds. Spoon 2–3 teaspoonfuls of chicken filling into center of each round. Brush edges of each round with egg. Fold pastry over filling to form a semicircle, and press edges firmly together. Tie a scallion length around each. Place on prepared parchment. Brush with beaten egg.

Bake until golden and crisp, 12–15 minutes. Serve warm, with dipping sauce or soy sauce.

Baked crab and noodle cakes

Makes 8 cakes

4 oz (125 g) cellophane (bean thread) noodles
vegetable oil, as needed
8 large fresh basil leaves
6 oz (180 g) fresh or canned crabmeat
1/3 cup (3 fl oz/90 ml) coconut milk (see page 24)
1 tablespoon red curry paste
2 eggs, beaten
1 tablespoon fish sauce
2 tablespoons chopped fresh cilantro (fresh coriander)
2 teaspoons lime juice
Sweet Chili Relish (see page 592), for serving
1 small red chili, seeded if desired, and sliced, for serving (optional)

Soak noodles in boiling water for 10 minutes. Drain and pat dry with paper towels.

Preheat oven to 350°F (180°C/Gas 4).

Brush 8 cups of standard muffin pan with oil. Place 1 basil leaf in each muffin cup. Line cups with noodles, dividing evenly.

In a bowl, combine crabmeat, coconut milk, curry paste, eggs, fish sauce, cilantro and lime juice. Mix well. Pour over noodles.

Bake cakes until firm to touch, 15–20 minutes. Remove from oven and allow to cool in pan.

Remove from pan and serve warm with sweet chili relish. Garnish with chili slices, if desired.

Broiled beef wrapped in piper leaves

Makes about 60 wraps

4 oz (125 g) fresh pork fatback,
  ground or finely diced

1 lb (500 g) ground (minced) beef,
  preferably sirloin (rump)

1/4 cup (3/4 oz/20 g) finely chopped
  brown or pink shallots (French shallots)

3 large cloves garlic, finely chopped

1 fresh small red chili, seeded and
  finely chopped

2 tablespoons fish sauce

1 tablespoon sugar

1 teaspoon salt

1 teaspoon ground pepper

juice of 1 lemon

about 60 piper (betel) leaves or grape
  leaves

60 wooden toothpicks

FOR ACCOMPANIMENTS

Table Greens (see page 437)

rice paper sheets, prepared
  (see page 27)

Nuoc Cham Nem Sauce
  (see page 582)

In a bowl, combine all ingredients except piper leaves. Use your hands to knead well, for about 3 minutes. Meanwhile, soak 60 wooden toothpicks in water for a few minutes to prevent charring.

Place a piper leaf, dark side down, on a work surface. Place about 1 tablespoon filling in center of leaf and roll into a tiny cylinder about 2 inches (5 cm) long and 3/4 inch (2 cm) thick. Make sure that meat is fully covered by the leaf; covering the two ends is optional. Skewer with a toothpick. Continue with remaining meat and leaves.

Prepare a charcoal grill (barbecue) or brazier following directions on page 20, or preheat an oven broiler (grill) with the grilling rack set about 5 inches (12 cm) from heat source. Cook parcels, turning twice, until cooked through, 8–10 minutes. Watch carefully, as they tend to char quickly.

Serve with table greens, tearing lettuce to enfold the cooked parcel and adding other fresh herbs to taste, and rice paper sheets for wrapping. Dip into nuoc cham nem sauce, spooning some of the vegetables onto the roll.

Chicken cockscomb dumplings

8 oz (250 g) ground (minced) chicken

4 scallions (shallots/spring onions),
   finely chopped

1 teaspoon grated fresh ginger

3 canned water chestnuts, drained and
   finely chopped

2 tablespoons finely chopped, drained
   canned bamboo shoots

2 teaspoons rice wine

2 teaspoons salt

1 teaspoon sugar

1 teaspoon soy sauce

1 teaspoon Asian sesame oil

1 tablespoon oyster sauce

1$^1/_2$ tablespoons cornstarch (cornflour)

16 round wonton wrappers

6 cups (48 fl oz/1.5 L) water

1 tablespoon vegetable oil

Lime Cilantro Dipping Sauce
   (page 579), for serving

In a bowl, combine ground chicken, scallions, ginger, water chestnuts, bamboo shoots, rice wine, 1 teaspoon salt, sugar, soy sauce, sesame oil, oyster sauce and cornstarch. Using wet hands, mix until well combined.

Place wonton wrappers on work surface and cover with a damp kitchen towel. Working with one wrapper at a time, place in a gow gee press and put 2 teaspoons filling in the center. Brush edges of wrapper with water. Close gow gee press firmly to seal edges together. Alternatively, place wrapper on work surface, spoon in filling, brush with water and fold in half to form a semicircle. Pinch edges together to make a frill. Cover with a damp kitchen towel and repeat with remaining wrappers.

Pour water into a medium wok or saucepan, add remaining 1 teaspoon salt and vegetable oil, and bring to a boil. Working in batches, cook dumplings in boiling water for 5 minutes. Remove from pan with a slotted spoon. Run cold water over cooked dumplings.

Serve immediately with lime cilantro dipping sauce.

Note: *These dim sum are so named because they resemble the crest of a rooster.*

Chili-herb shrimp skewers

Makes 20 skewers

1/3 cup (3 fl oz/90 ml) olive oil

2 tablespoons grated fresh ginger

2 garlic cloves, finely chopped

2 small pieces lemongrass, finely chopped

1 small red chili, seeded and finely chopped

2 limes or lemons, juiced

1/4 cup (1/3 oz/10 g) chopped mixed fresh herbs of choice

4 lb (2 kg) jumbo shrimp (green king prawns), peeled and deveined

2 tablespoons olive oil, for cooking

20 short bamboo or metal skewers

lime or lemon wedges, for garnish

In a large bowl, combine 1/3 cup olive oil, ginger, garlic, lemongrass, chili, lime juice and herbs. Mix well. Add shrimp and toss until well coated in marinade. Cover with plastic wrap and refrigerate for 1 hour.

Warm 2 tablespoons oil in a frying pan over medium heat. Drain shrimp. Working in batches, fry shrimp until they just change color, 2–3 minutes. Thread shrimp onto skewers and serve immediately with lime or lemon wedges.

Chili stir-fried squid

Makes 4 small servings

4 cleaned squid tubes, about 12 oz (375 g) total

2 tablespoons vegetable oil

1 teaspoon Asian sesame oil

3 cloves garlic, finely chopped

1–2 small red chilies, seeded and finely chopped

Cut squid in half lengthwise, then cut into strips 3/4 inch (2 cm) wide. Heat oils in a wok or frying pan over medium heat. Fry garlic and chili until aromatic, about 1 minute. Add squid and stir-fry for 1 minute. Do not overcook. Remove from heat and serve hot.

Chinese pork sausage buns

Makes 12 buns

1 cup (4 oz/125 g) self-rising flour

2 teaspoons baking powder

2 teaspoons superfine (caster) sugar

2 teaspoons lard

$1/_4$–$1/_3$ cup (2–3 fl oz/60–90 ml) warm milk

6 Chinese pork sausages

1 tablespoon hoisin sauce, plus extra for serving

2 teaspoons soy sauce

Sift flour and baking powder into a bowl and add sugar. Rub lard into dry ingredients using your fingertips. Gradually add enough milk to make a soft dough. Turn out dough onto a floured work surface and knead for 1–2 minutes, until smooth. Wrap in plastic wrap and let stand for 30 minutes. Meanwhile, cut sausages in half crosswise. Place in a bowl with 1 tablespoon hoisin sauce and soy sauce, mix until well coated, cover, and let stand for 25 minutes.

Turn out dough onto a floured work surface and knead for 1 minute. Roll into a thick snake shape 12 inches (30 cm) long, and cut into 12 pieces. Cover dough with a damp kitchen towel to prevent drying out. Working with one piece of dough at a time, rub it between floured hands to form a thin snake about 4 inches (10 cm) long. Wrap dough around sausage in a spiral pattern, leaving ends of sausage exposed, and place on an oiled tray. Repeat with remaining dough and sausages.

Line a bamboo steamer with banana leaves or parchment (baking) paper. Half-fill a medium wok with water (steamer should not touch water) and bring to a boil. Working in batches, arrange buns in prepared steamer, allowing room for buns to spread. Cover, and place steamer over boiling water. Steam for 15 minutes, adding more boiling water to wok when necessary. Lift steamer off wok and carefully remove buns. Serve warm with hoisin sauce.

Cilantro and lime mini fish cakes

Makes 36 cakes

1 lb (500 g) redfish fillets or skinless, boneless white-fleshed fish fillets

1 tablespoon Thai red curry paste

1 tablespoon fish sauce

1 egg, beaten

2 teaspoons brown sugar

1 clove garlic, finely chopped

4 kaffir lime leaves, finely shredded, or 2 teaspoons grated lime zest

2 tablespoons chopped fresh cilantro (fresh coriander)

2 scallions (shallots/spring onions), finely sliced

1/2 cup (2 1/2 oz/75 g) finely sliced green beans

3 tablespoons vegetable oil, for frying

12 bamboo skewers

1/2 cup (4 fl oz/125 ml) light soy sauce, for serving

lime wedges and extra skewers, for serving

Place fish fillets, curry paste, fish sauce, egg, sugar and garlic in a food processor. Process until mixture forms a thick paste, about 20 seconds. Transfer to a bowl. Add lime leaves, cilantro, scallions and beans. Using wet hands, mix until well combined. Form mixture into 36 balls. Flatten each to form a patty shape.

Warm oil in a frying pan over medium heat. Working in batches, fry fish cakes until golden, about 1 minute on each side. Remove fish cakes from pan and drain on paper towels, then place 3 fish cakes on each skewer.

Serve with soy sauce for dipping and fresh lime wedges on skewers for garnish. (Pictured on page 6.)

Hint: Fish cake mixture can be prepared 2 hours ahead. Keep covered and refrigerated.

Clams with black bean sauce

Serves 6–8

1 lb (500 g) fresh clams in shells, shells cleaned

FOR BLACK BEAN SAUCE
2 teaspoons vegetable oil
2 cloves garlic, finely chopped
2 teaspoons grated fresh ginger
2 teaspoons fermented black beans, rinsed and chopped
2 tablespoons soy sauce
$1/3$ cup (3 fl oz/90 ml) water
2 tablespoons oyster sauce

Place clams in a bamboo steamer and cover with lid. Half-fill a medium wok with water (steamer should not touch water) and bring to a boil. Place steamer over boiling water and steam until clam shells open, 3–4 minutes (discard any clams that do not open). Lift steamer off wok and carefully remove clams.

To make black bean sauce: Heat oil in a small saucepan over medium heat. Fry garlic and ginger until aromatic, about 1 minute. Add black beans, soy sauce, water and oyster sauce. Bring to a boil, then reduce heat and simmer for 1 minute. Serve drizzled over clams.

Hint: *Black beans should be rinsed and drained before use as they can be very salty. Store unused black beans in a covered container in the refrigerator.*

Curried mango dip

Serves 4–6

1 tablespoon vegetable oil
1 onion, finely chopped
1 teaspoon mild curry powder
10 oz (300 g) plain (natural) yogurt

2 tablespoons mango chutney
mixed fresh vegetables and baby
  pappadams, for serving

Heat oil in a small frying pan over medium heat. Add onion and cook until softened, about 1 minute. Stir in curry powder and cook until aromatic, about 1 minute. Remove pan from heat and allow to cool. Gently stir in yogurt and mango chutney. Spoon into a serving bowl, place in center of a platter and surround with vegetables such as Belgian endive (chicory) leaves, slices of carrot, celery, red and green bell peppers (capsicums), English (hothouse) cucumber, blanched cauliflower florets and blanched asparagus spears. If desired, fry the pappadams in hot vegetable oil or microwave on high according to directions on package.

Curried mixed nuts

Makes 3 cups (15 oz/470 g)

3 tablespoons vegetable oil
1 cup (5 oz/150 g) cashew nuts
1 cup (5 oz/150 g) blanched whole
  almonds
1 cup (5 oz/150 g) raw peanuts

1 tablespoon sea salt
1 teaspoon Garam Masala
  (see page 575)
1/2 teaspoon chili powder

In a wok or skillet, heat oil over medium heat. Add cashews and cook, stirring constantly, until lightly browned, 1–2 minutes. Using a slotted spoon, transfer to paper towels to drain. Repeat to fry almonds, then peanuts. Combine nuts in a medium bowl. Add remaining ingredients and stir until well combined. Serve at room temperature.

Curried tofu puffs with herbed coconut sauce

Makes 24 puffs

FOR HERBED COCONUT SAUCE
1/2 cup (4 fl oz/125 ml) thick coconut
  cream (see page 24)
2 tablespoons chopped fresh mint
2 tablespoons chopped cilantro (fresh
  coriander) leaves

3 1/2 oz (105 g) firm or extra-firm tofu,
  drained and shredded
1/3 cup (1 oz/30 g) fresh soy and
  linseed bread crumbs
1 scallion (shallot/spring onion), green
  part only, finely chopped
1 garlic clove, finely chopped
2 tablespoons Red Curry Paste (see
  page 586)
12 large deep-fried tofu puffs
1/4 cup (2 fl oz/60 ml) ketjap manis

To make herbed coconut sauce: Mix coconut cream, mint and cilantro, stirring until well combined. Set aside.

Preheat oven to 400°F (200°C/Gas 6). Lightly grease a baking sheet or line it with parchment (baking) paper.

In a large bowl, combine tofu, bread crumbs, scallion, garlic and curry paste. Cut each tofu puff in half diagonally and make a pocket inside with fingers. Fill each puff with about 1 teaspoon of tofu mixture. Brush each puff, including filling, with ketjap manis. Place puffs on baking sheet and bake until crisp and lightly browned, 8–10 minutes. Serve with herbed coconut sauce for dipping.

Hint: Soy and linseed bread is available from health food stores and some supermarkets.

Fresh spring rolls with shrimp

Makes 12 rolls

12 medium shrimp (prawns), cooked, peeled and deveined
3¹/₃-oz (100-g) packet dried rice vermicelli noodles
12 butter (Boston) lettuce leaves
12 fresh mint leaves, preferably peppermint
12 garlic chives, cut crosswise into thirds
12 sheets rice paper, about 9 inches (23 cm) in diameter

FOR ACCOMPANIMENTS
Vietnamese Bean Sauce (see page 594)
Nuoc Cham Nem Sauce (see page 582)

Remove tails from shrimp and cut shrimp in half lengthwise. Set aside.

Prepare dried noodles as described on page 442. Using scissors, cut noodles into manageable lengths.

Remove core from lettuce leaves. If using larger leaves, cut them so they are about 2 inches (5 cm) wide. Remove stems from mint.

To make spring rolls, soften a rice paper sheet following directions on page 27, then assemble the rolls as described on page 36. Make sure to place shrimp halves, skin-side down, toward top of sheet, so they clearly show through final layer. Likewise, before final roll, arrange 2 or 3 chives lengthwise to poke out about ¹/₂ inch (1.2 cm) from each end.

Cover with plastic wrap to prevent rice paper from drying out. Rolls can be made up to 1–2 hours in advance. Serve with bean sauce or nuoc cham nem sauce.

Variation: Substitute 12 very thin slices roasted pork loin for the shrimp, and proceed as above.

For vegetarian: Omit shrimp. Add 8 oz (250 g) bean sprouts to filling, plus thinly sliced dried tofu skin, as desired.

Gyoza (Japanese pork and vegetable dumplings)

Serves 10 as an entree

1/3 **large cabbage, finely shredded**

2 **teaspoons salt**

1 **lb (500 g) ground (minced) pork shoulder**

1/2 **bunch (1 oz/30 g) garlic chives, finely chopped**

1 1/2 **tablespoons sugar**

1 **tablespoon soy sauce**

2 **teaspoons garlic powder**

1 **tablespoon Asian sesame oil**

2 1/2 **tablespoons grated fresh ginger**

1 **tablespoon sake**

1 **tablespoon potato flour**

60 **gyoza wrappers or round wonton wrappers**

vegetable oil, for frying

few drops of sesame oil, for frying

FOR DIPPING SAUCE

Nihaizu (see page 581)

chili oil, to taste

2 **scallions (shallots/spring onions), thinly sliced**

Place cabbage in a large bowl. Add salt and mix into cabbage, squeezing it well with your hands. Salt draws excess moisture from cabbage. Drain as much as you can. Add remaining ingredients and mix until well combined.

Holding a wrapper in one hand, place 1 teaspoon of filling in center of wrapper. Bring one side of wrapper to meet other side, then make 4 or 5 pleats along edges to enclose filling into a neat bundle. It may be necessary to use a little water to help edges adhere. (Note: freeze any unwanted dumplings before cooking.)

In a nonstick frying pan over medium–high heat, heat 2 tablespoons vegetable oil. Add a few drops of sesame oil. Place dumplings closely together and cook for 1 minute. Add water to pan until it comes halfway up the sides of dumplings. Cover and cook on medium heat until all water has evaporated. Remove lid and add 2 tablespoons oil to pan and cook until bottoms are well browned.

To make dipping sauce: Combine nihaizu, chili oil and scallions. Remove dumplings from pan and serve with dipping sauce. (Pictured on page 34.)

Lotus leaf wraps

5 dried lotus leaves, cut in half

1^1/$_3$ cups (9 oz/280 g) short-grain rice, washed and drained

4 Chinese dried mushrooms

1 tablespoon vegetable oil

2 teaspoons grated fresh ginger

6^1/$_2$ oz (200 g) ground (minced) chicken

4 oz (125 g) jumbo shrimp (green king prawns), peeled, deveined and finely chopped

2 Chinese pork sausages, finely chopped

1 tablespoon soy sauce

1 tablespoon rice wine

1 tablespoon oyster sauce

2 teaspoons cornstarch (cornflour) mixed with 1 tablespoon water

Soak lotus leaves in hot water until softened, about 15 minutes. Drain. Line a bamboo steamer with parchment (baking) paper, spread drained rice over it and cover steamer. Half-fill a medium wok with water (steamer should not touch water) and bring to a boil. Place steamer over boiling water and steam until rice is tender, 25–30 minutes, adding more boiling water to wok when necessary. Remove steamer from wok, allow rice to cool, then divide it into 10 equal portions.

Place mushrooms in a small bowl, add boiling water to cover and let stand until softened, 10–15 minutes. Drain, squeeze excess liquid from mushrooms and finely chop, discarding thick stems.

Heat oil in a wok over medium heat. Fry ginger until aromatic, about 30 seconds. Add chicken and shrimp, and stir-fry until mixture changes color, about 3 minutes. Add sausages, mushrooms, soy sauce, rice wine and oyster sauce, and cook for 1 minute. Stir in cornstarch mixture, bring to a boil and stir until sauce thickens, about 2 minutes. Remove from heat and allow to cool.

Place lotus leaves on work surface. Spoon a portion of rice into the center of each leaf. Place 3 teaspoons of chicken mixture over rice, molding rice around it. Fold leaf over rice to form a parcel and secure with raffia or twine.

Half-fill a large wok with water (steamer should not touch water) and bring to a boil. Working in batches, arrange leaf parcels in steamer, cover and place steamer over boiling water. Steam for 15 minutes, adding more boiling water to wok when necessary. Lift steamer off wok and carefully remove parcels. Cut open to serve.

Mini spring rolls

Makes 20 rolls

2 tablespoons vegetable oil

2 cloves garlic, finely chopped

2 teaspoons grated fresh ginger

$3^1/_2$ oz (100 g) ground (minced) pork

$3^1/_2$ oz (100 g) ground (minced) chicken

2 oz (60 g) ground (minced) shrimp (prawns)

2 stalks celery, finely chopped

1 small carrot, finely chopped

6 canned water chestnuts, drained and finely chopped

4 scallions (shallots/spring onions), finely chopped

1 cup (3 oz/90 g) shredded Chinese cabbage

2 teaspoons cornstarch (cornflour)

2 tablespoons oyster sauce

1 tablespoon soy sauce, plus extra for serving

2 tablespoons chicken stock

1 teaspoon Asian sesame oil

20 mini spring roll wrappers, about $4^1/_2$ inches (11.5 cm) square

2 teaspoons cornstarch (cornflour) mixed with 2 tablespoons water

4 cups (32 fl oz/1 L) vegetable oil, for deep frying

Heat 1 tablespoon oil in a wok over medium heat. Add garlic and ginger, and cook until aromatic, about 1 minute. Stir in ground pork, chicken and shrimp, and cook, stirring, until mixture changes color, about 3 minutes. Remove from heat and transfer to a bowl.

Using same wok, heat remaining 1 tablespoon oil over medium heat. Add celery, carrot, water chestnuts, scallions and cabbage. Raise heat to high and stir-fry until softened, about 2 minutes. In a small bowl, combine cornstarch, oyster sauce, soy sauce and stock. Add to wok, bring to a boil, reduce heat to medium and cook until sauce thickens, 1–2 minutes. Remove from heat and allow to cool completely. Stir in cooled pork mixture and sesame oil, and mix well.

Separate spring roll wrappers, place on a work surface and cover with a damp kitchen towel. Place 1 wrapper on work surface and, using your fingertips, wet edges with cornstarch and water mixture. Place 1 tablespoon of filling in center of wrapper and roll up diagonally, tucking in edges. Seal edges with cornstarch mixture. Repeat with remaining wrappers.

Heat vegetable oil in a large wok until it reaches 375°F (190°C) on a deep-frying thermometer, or until a small bread cube dropped in oil sizzles and turns golden. Working in batches, add rolls and fry until golden, about 1 minute. Using a slotted spoon, remove from oil and drain on paper towels. Serve immediately, with soy sauce for dipping.

Paper-wrapped shrimp rolls

Makes 20 rolls

1 1/2 lb (750 g) jumbo shrimp (green king prawns), peeled, deveined and finely
    chopped
3 teaspoons grated fresh ginger
2 cloves garlic, finely chopped
4 scallions (shallots/spring onions), finely chopped
1 tablespoon cornstarch (cornflour)
20 rice paper wrappers, about 8 inches (20 cm) square
2 tablespoons cornstarch (cornflour) mixed with 1 1/2 tablespoons water
1/4 cup (2 fl oz/60 ml) vegetable oil, for deep-frying
hoisin sauce, for serving

In a bowl, combine shrimp, ginger, garlic, scallions and cornstarch. Using wet hands, mix
until well combined. Working with one wrapper at a time, plunge it into a shallow bowl
of warm water until softened, 1–2 minutes. Lay it on work surface and place
1 1/2 tablespoons of shrimp filling in center. Brush edges of wrapper with cornstarch
mixture. Fold wrapper over filling, tucking in edges, and roll up to form a neat parcel.
Cover with a damp kitchen towel and set aside. Repeat with remaining ingredients.

Heat oil in a wok or frying pan until it reaches 375°F (190°C) on a deep-frying
thermometer, or until a small bread cube dropped in oil sizzles and turns golden. Working
in batches, add parcels and fry until golden on both sides, about 2 minutes. Shake pan
from time to time to prevent parcels from sticking. Remove from oil and drain on paper
towels. Serve hot with hoisin sauce.

Hint: Substitute spring roll wrappers or pancakes for rice paper wrappers.

Peanut and chili bundles

Serves 8–10 as appetizer, 6 as entree

1 cup (5^1/$_2$ oz/165 g) unsalted roasted peanuts
1 small red chili, seeded and finely chopped
8 scallions (shallots/green onions), finely chopped
^{1}/$_4$ cup (^{1}/$_3$ oz/10 g) chopped fresh cilantro (fresh coriander)
^{1}/$_2$ cup (4 fl oz/125 ml) lemon juice
^{1}/$_2$ cup (1 oz/30 g) fresh white bread crumbs
1 teaspoon superfine (caster) sugar
24 wonton wrappers
4 cups (32 fl oz/1 L) vegetable oil, for deep-frying
lime wedges, for serving
Sweet Chili Relish (see page 592) or soy sauce, for serving

Place peanuts in food processor and process until fine. Transfer to a bowl. Add chili, scallions, cilantro, lemon juice, bread crumbs and sugar. Mix well.

Place wonton wrappers on work surface and cover with damp towel to prevent them from drying out. Working with one wrapper at a time, place 1 teaspoon of peanut filling in center. Brush edges with water, gather edges together and twist to seal. Set aside, and cover with plastic wrap. Repeat with remaining wonton wrappers.

Heat oil in a wok until it reaches 375°F (190°C) on deep-frying thermometer or until a small bread cube cropped in oil sizzles and turns golden. Working in batches, add wontons and fry until golden, 1–2 minutes.

Using a slotted spoon, remove from wok and drain on paper towels. Serve bundles hot, with lime wedges and with sweet chili relish or soy sauce for dipping.

Peking duck pancakes

PANCAKES

$3/4$ cup (3 oz/90 g) all-purpose (plain)
   flour

$1/3$ cup ($1 1/2$ oz/45 g) cornstarch
   (cornflour)

2 eggs, beaten

$3/4$ cup (6 fl oz/180 ml) water

$1/4$ cup (2 fl oz/60 ml) milk

2 teaspoons superfine (caster) sugar

1 tablespoon vegetable oil

FILLING

15 scallions (shallots/spring onions)

2 carrots, peeled and cut into thin
   sticks

1 Chinese roast duck

$1/4$ cup (2 fl oz/60 ml) hoisin sauce

1 tablespoon rice wine

12 chives

$1/3$ cup (3 fl oz/90 ml) hoisin sauce, for
   serving

To make pancakes, sift flour and cornstarch into a bowl. In a separate bowl, whisk together eggs, water, milk and sugar. Make a well in center of dry ingredients, gradually add egg mixture, and beat until smooth.

Heat oil in a frying pan over medium heat, pour in 2 tablespoons of pancake batter and swirl pan gently to form a round pancake. Cook until golden, about 2 minutes. Turn and cook other side for 10 seconds. Remove from pan and repeat with remaining batter and oil.

To make filling. Cut into each end of scallions with a sharp knife or scissors to form a fringe. Place scallions and carrots in a bowl of iced water and refrigerate for 15 minutes, or until scallions curl. Remove meat and skin from duck and roughly chop. Combine hoisin sauce and rice wine.

Lay pancakes on work surface and place 1 tablespoon of duck meat and skin in center of each one. Top with 1 teaspoon of hoisin and rice wine mixture. Add a scallion curl and 3–4 carrot sticks. Roll and secure with a chive, trimming off any excess chive. Serve with hoisin sauce as a dipping sauce.

Pork omelette roll Vietnamese-style

Makes 6 rolls

6 dried black mushrooms

1 bunch garlic chives, trimmed

6 eggs

vegetable oil, for cooking

1¼ lb (625 g) finely ground (minced) lean pork

1 teaspoon ground pepper

3 tablespoons fish sauce

butter (Boston) lettuce leaves, for serving (optional)

softened rice vermicelli (see page 442), for serving (optional)

Nuoc Cham Sauce (see page 582), for serving (optional)

Soak mushrooms in hot water for about 20 minutes, then drain, squeezing to remove all liquid. Use scissors or a small knife to cut away and discard tough stems. Cut mushroom caps into thin julienne and set aside. Cut chives into 8-inch (20-cm) lengths.

Prepare 6 thin, flat omelettes, as described on page 26.

In a food processor, combine ground pork, pepper and fish sauce and process until well blended, about 1 minute. Alternatively, use your hands to knead well, about 3 minutes. The smoother the paste, the better. Divide meat into 6 portions.

Lay out an omelette and spread 1 meat portion evenly on it. Lay strips of mushroom and chive shoots evenly across the entire top, arranging them horizontally to facilitate rolling. Tightly roll omelette into a cylinder. Wrap tightly with plastic wrap, twisting the ends to secure. Repeat with remaining omelettes. Place wrapped rolls in a steamer over—but not touching—rapidly boiling water. Cover tightly with a lid and steam for about 20 minutes, or until the meat is thoroughly cooked.

Use tongs to remove the rolls from the steamer. Let the rolls cool, then remove plastic wrap and cut the rolls into rounds about ¼ inch (6 mm) thick. Arrange these on a platter, such as in the fan shape of a peacock's tail. These rolls are traditionally served plain. If desired, accompany with lettuce leaves, softened rice vermicelli and nuoc cham sauce. Tear a piece of lettuce to enfold the roll with some noodles and fresh herbs of choice, and dip into sauce.

Pork sui mai dumplings with chili oil

Makes 16 dumplings

5 oz (150 g) ground (minced) pork

5 oz (150 g) jumbo shrimp (king
   prawns), shelled and deveined

2 cloves garlic, finely chopped

1 tablespoon grated fresh ginger

1/4 teaspoon salt

2 tablespoons chopped fresh cilantro
   (fresh coriander)

1 tablespoon chopped fresh
   Vietnamese mint

16 wonton wrappers

FOR CHILI OIL

1 tablespoon chili oil

2 teaspoons ketjap manis

1 tablespoon finely chopped garlic

1 teaspoon Chinese red vinegar

In a food processor, combine pork, shrimp, garlic, ginger and salt. Process for
20 seconds, or until well blended. Transfer to a bowl and add cilantro and mint. Using
wet hands, mix until well combined.

Place 1 wonton wrapper on a work surface. Cover remaining skins with a clean damp
kitchen towel. Place 1 tablespoon of pork filling in center of wonton skin and brush edges
of skin with water. Gather edges around filling, forming a basket. Gently squeeze center
of dumpling so that filling is exposed at top. Tap base of dumpling on work surface to
flatten. Set aside on a tray and cover with plastic wrap. Repeat with remaining wonton
wrappers and filling.

Line a medium-sized bamboo steamer with parchment (baking) paper. Fill a medium-sized
wok about one-third full with water (steamer should not touch water). Bring water to a boil.
Arrange dumplings in steamer. Cover with lid. Place steamer over boiling water. Steam for
12 minutes, adding more water to wok as necessary.

Meanwhile, stir all chili oil ingredients together in a small bowl. Lift steamer off wok and
carefully remove dumplings from steamer. Serve hot, with chili oil for dipping.

Pot stickers

Serves 4

8 oz (250 g) ground (minced) lean pork
1 onion, finely chopped
1 cup (3 oz/90 g) finely shredded green cabbage
2 teaspoons grated fresh ginger
1 tablespoon Asian sesame oil
1 tablespoon soy sauce
1 teaspoon white pepper
24 round wheat wonton wrappers
4 tablespoons vegetable oil
2 cups (16 fl oz/500 ml) chicken stock (see page 588), or as needed
light soy sauce for serving

In a bowl, combine pork, onion, cabbage, ginger, sesame oil, soy sauce and pepper. Mix well.

Place wonton wrappers on work surface and cover with damp kitchen towel. Working with one wrapper at a time, lay it on work surface and place 1 teaspoon of filling in the center. Brush edges with water, fold wonton in half and press edges together to seal. Using your fingertips, pinch frill around each folded wonton if desired. Set aside, covered with plastic wrap. Repeat with remaining wrappers.

Heat 1 tablespoon vegetable oil in a heavy-bottomed pan over medium–high heat. Swirl to cover entire bottom of pan. Working in batches, fry filled wontons until golden brown on both sides, about 1 minute each side. Coat pan as needed with remaining 3 tablespoons vegetable oil.

Return pot stickers to pan and add enough stock to come halfway up sides of pot stickers. Cover and simmer until stock is almost absorbed, about 10 minutes. Uncover and cook until stock is completely absorbed and bottoms of pot stickers are crisp. Repeat with remaining pot stickers. Serve pot stickers warm with soy sauce.

Note: These dumplings are so named for the way they tend to stick to the pot during cooking. Though messy, they have an authentic flavor and appearance.

Salmon money bags

Makes 12 bags

9 oz (280 g) Atlantic salmon, bones and skin removed, finely chopped
3 tablespoons cream cheese
3 scallions (shallots/spring onions), finely chopped
2 teaspoons grated fresh ginger
¹/₄ teaspoon salt
pinch five-spice powder
1 teaspoon grated lime zest
1 egg yolk
12 wonton wrappers
12 chives
Sweet Chili Relish (see page 592) or soy sauce, for serving

In a bowl, combine salmon, cream cheese, scallions, ginger, salt, five-spice powder, lime zest and egg yolk. Using wet hands, mix until well combined.

Place wonton wrappers on work surface and cover with a damp kitchen towel. Working with one wrapper at a time, lay it on work surface and place 2 teaspoons of filling in the center. Brush edges of wrapper with water. Gather edges together and twist to seal. Cover with a damp kitchen towel and set aside. Repeat with remaining wonton wrappers.

Line a medium bamboo steamer with parchment (baking) paper. Half-fill a medium wok with water (steamer should not touch water) and bring to a boil. Arrange filled wontons in steamer, cover and place steamer over boiling water. Steam for 8 minutes, adding more boiling water to wok when necessary. Lift steamer off wok and carefully remove dumplings. Dip chives into bowl of hot water and tie one loosely around the top of each money bag. Serve warm with sweet chili relish or soy sauce, for dipping.

Note: This steamed dim sum recipe is a Western adaptation of a traditional favorite.

Scallops steamed in shells

Makes 4 small servings

24 scallops in their shells
2 tablespoons vegetable oil
4 cloves garlic, finely chopped
6 scallions (shallots/spring onions),
  chopped

GINGER AND SCALLION SAUCE

6 scallions (shallots/spring onions), cut
  into shreds
3 tablespoons vegetable oil
2-inch (5-cm) piece fresh ginger, cut
  into fine shreds
1 green chili, seeded and sliced
4 tablespoons soy sauce
2 tablespoons water

Clean scallops and return to shells. Heat oil in a small saucepan over medium heat and fry garlic until aromatic, about 1 minute. Add scallions and cook for 1 minute. Remove from heat. Spoon garlic and scallions over scallops.

Half-fill a medium wok with water (steamer should not touch water) and bring to a boil. Working in batches, arrange scallops in a bamboo steamer, cover, and place steamer over boiling water. Steam until scallops are tender, 7–10 minutes, adding more boiling water to wok when necessary. Lift steamer off wok and carefully remove scallops.

To make ginger and scallion sauce: Place scallions in a small bowl and set aside. Heat oil in a small saucepan over medium heat and fry ginger and chili until aromatic, about 1 minute. Remove from heat and stir in soy sauce and water. Bring to a boil and pour over scallions. Let stand for 2 minutes before serving with scallops.

Shiitake and garlic chive dumplings

Makes 20 dumplings

DUMPLING DOUGH

$^1/_2$ cup (2 oz/60 g) Chinese wheat flour, sifted

$^1/_4$ cup (1 oz/30 g) potato or corn starch flour, sifted

pinch salt

$^1/_2$ cup (4 fl oz/125 ml) water

1 tablespoon solid vegetable shortening

sesame oil, for brushing

banana leaves, for serving

Lime and Soy Dipping Sauce (see page 579), for serving

FILLING

12 dried shiitake mushrooms, soaked in hot water for 30 minutes, drained and finely chopped

4 tablespoons garlic chives, finely chopped

4 scallions (shallots/spring onions), finely chopped

2 teaspoons freshly grated ginger

1 clove garlic, finely chopped

1 small red chili, seeded and finely chopped

$^2/_3$ cup (4 oz/125 g) finely chopped water chestnuts

$^1/_2$ cup (3 oz/90 g) finely chopped carrots

2 teaspoons potato or corn starch

$^1/_2$ teaspoon salt

1 teaspoon dark sesame oil

1 tablespoon soy sauce

In a bowl, combine the flours and salt. Mix the water and shortening in a saucepan and bring to a boil. Immediately pour the water mixture into the flour mixture and mix quickly using a wooden spoon. Press to form a smooth white dough. Roll into a thick cylinder and wrap in plastic. Set aside.

In a bowl, mix all filling ingredients until combined. Unwrap and cut the dough into 20 pieces. Working 5 at a time so the dough does not dry out, flatten each piece into a 4-inch (10-cm) round using the blade of a Chinese chopper or a palette knife, lightly brushed with sesame oil to prevent the dough from sticking. Divide the filling evenly among the dough pieces. Brush half the edge of each piece with sesame oil and fold each to form semi-circles. Crinkle and press the edges firmly together so they stick. Brush each dumpling with sesame oil.

Steam dumplings on a piece of banana leaf or waxed paper for 15 minutes. Serve hot, on a fresh banana leaf and with dipping sauce.

Shrimp and snowpea shoot dumplings

Makes 15 dumplings

4 oz (125 g) fresh snowpea (mange-tout) shoots, roughly chopped

4 oz (125 g) jumbo shrimp (green king prawns), peeled, deveined and coarsely chopped

2 teaspoons grated fresh ginger

3 teaspoons oyster sauce

1 teaspoon soy sauce

1 teaspoon rice wine

1/4 teaspoon salt

1/2 teaspoon sugar

1 teaspoon Asian sesame oil

1 tablespoon cornstarch (cornflour)

15 round wonton wrappers

soy sauce, for serving

Blanch snowpea shoots in a pan of boiling water for 1 minute. Drain and refresh immediately in cold water. In a bowl, combine snowpea shoots, shrimp, ginger, oyster sauce, soy sauce, rice wine, salt, sugar, sesame oil and cornstarch. Using wet hands, mix until well combined.

Place wonton wrappers on work surface and cover with a damp kitchen towel. Working with one wrapper at a time, place 3 teaspoons of filling in the center and brush edges of wrapper with water. Fold three sides of wrapper into the center, forming a triangular shape. Using your fingertips, press edges of wrapper together. Cover with a damp kitchen towel and set aside. Repeat with remaining wonton wrappers.

Line a medium bamboo steamer with parchment (baking) paper. Half fill a medium wok with water (steamer should not touch water) and bring to a boil. Arrange dumplings in steamer, cover, and place steamer over boiling water. Steam for 10 minutes, adding more boiling water to wok when necessary. Lift steamer off wok and carefully remove dumplings. Serve warm, with soy sauce.

Shrimp balls

1 lb (500 g) jumbo shrimp (green king prawns), peeled and deveined

2 cloves garlic

3 teaspoons grated fresh ginger

2 teaspoons fish sauce

1/4 teaspoon salt

1/4 cup (1 oz/30 g) cornstarch (cornflour), plus extra for coating

4 scallions (shallots/spring onions), roughly chopped

2 tablespoons finely chopped canned water chestnuts

1/4 cup (2 oz/60 g) finely chopped canned bamboo shoots

3 cups (24 fl oz/750 ml) vegetable oil, for deep-frying

lime wedges, for serving

Chili Dipping Sauce (see page 568), for serving

Place shrimp, garlic, ginger, fish sauce, salt and cornstarch in a food processor and process until smooth. Transfer to a bowl. Stir in scallions, water chestnuts and bamboo shoots. Using wet hands, mix until well combined.

Coat hands in cornstarch and form 1 tablespoon of shrimp mixture into a ball. Toss shrimp ball in cornstarch, shaking off any excess. Repeat with remaining mixture.

Heat oil in a large wok until it reaches 375°F (190°C) on a deep-frying thermometer, or until a small bread cube dropped in oil sizzles and turns golden. Working in batches, add shrimp balls and fry until golden, about 2 minutes. Using a slotted spoon, remove from oil and drain on paper towels. Serve hot with lime wedges and dipping sauce.

Note: These shrimp balls can be steamed or deep-fried; you can also thread them onto skewers after cooking, for serving.

Shrimp dumplings

Serves 6 as appetizer, 3–4 as entree

8 oz (250 g) jumbo shrimp (king prawns), peeled and deveined

2 tablespoons finely chopped drained canned water chestnuts

2 scallions (shallots/spring onions), chopped, plus shredded scallions, for serving

1 tablespoon light soy sauce

1/2 teaspoon Asian sesame oil

12 wonton wrappers

soy sauce, for serving

Place shrimp in food processor and process until smooth. Transfer to bowl. Add water chestnuts, chopped scallions, 1 tablespoon soy sauce and sesame oil. Mix until well combined.

Place wonton wrappers on work surface and cover with damp kitchen towel to prevent them from drying out. Working with one wrapper at a time, lay it on work surface and place 1 teaspoon of shrimp filling in the center. Brush edges with water, then gather edges together and twist to seal. Set aside, and cover with plastic wrap. Repeat with remaining wonton wrappers.

Line a bamboo steamer with parchment (baking) paper. Half fill a wok with water (steamer should not touch water) and bring water to a boil. Arrange filled wontons in steamer, cover, and place steamer over boiling water. Steam for 20 minutes, adding more water to wok when necessary. Lift steamer off wok and carefully remove dumplings from steamer.

Arrange dumplings on individual plates and garnish with shredded scallions. Serve warm, with soy sauce for dipping.

Shrimp toasts

Makes 14 toasts

4 slices stale white bread

1 lb (500 g) jumbo shrimp (green king prawns), peeled and deveined

2 cloves garlic

2 teaspoons grated fresh ginger

1 teaspoon sugar

1/2 teaspoon salt

1 tablespoon cornstarch (cornflour)

1 egg white

1 teaspoon Asian sesame oil

4 scallions (shallots/spring onions), finely chopped

1 egg, beaten

1 cup (4 oz/125 g) dry bread crumbs

3 cups (24 fl oz/750ml) vegetable oil, for deep-frying

Quick Sweet-and-Sour Sauce (page 585), for serving

Remove crusts from bread and cut each slice into 4 triangles. Allow bread to dry out at room temperature.

Place shrimp, garlic, ginger, sugar, salt, cornstarch, egg white and sesame oil in a food processor and process until smooth. Transfer to a bowl, then stir in scallions.

Place 1 tablespoon of shrimp filling in the center of each bread triangle. Brush shrimp filling and bread edges with beaten egg and sprinkle with bread crumbs. Pat shrimp mixture into a pyramid shape and shake off any excess crumbs.

Heat oil in a large wok until it reaches 375°F (190°C) on a deep-frying thermometer, or until a small bread cube dropped in oil sizzles and turns golden. Working in batches, fry toasts until golden on both sides, 1–2 minutes. Using a slotted spoon, remove from oil and drain on paper towels. Serve hot, with sweet-and-sour sauce.

Note: *This Western-adapted recipe is a favorite in many dim sum tea houses.*

Spicy pork puffs

Makes about 12 rolls

3 scallions (shallots/spring onions), halved lengthwise

6 oz (180 g) ground (minced) pork

2 teaspoons sambal oelek

3 cloves garlic, finely chopped

1/4 cup (1/3 oz/10 g) finely chopped fresh cilantro (fresh coriander)

1/4 teaspoon sea salt

1/4 teaspoon ground white pepper

1 sheet frozen puff pastry, thawed

1 egg, beaten

1/4 cup (2 fl oz/60 ml) light soy sauce, for serving

Put scallions in a bowl and add boiling water to cover. Let stand for 1 minute. Drain and rinse under cold running water.

Preheat oven to 450°F (230°C/Gas 8). Line a baking tray with parchment (baking) paper.

In a bowl, combine pork, sambal oelek, garlic, cilantro, salt and pepper. Put puff pastry on a work surface, and cut into 4 rectangles. Place a line of pork mixture along the center of each pastry piece. Brush edges of pastries with beaten egg. Fold long sides of each pastry over pork filling, overlapping slightly, then seal to form a neat sausage roll. Trim away any excess pastry. Cut each roll into crosswise pieces 1 inch (2.5 cm) wide.

Place on prepared pan, sealed side down. Brush tops with beaten egg. Tie a scallion around each piece. Brush each again with beaten egg. Bake until golden and crisp, about 15 minutes. Remove from oven and serve hot, with soy sauce for dipping.

Split-chickpea patties

Makes about 22 patties

1¹⁄₂ cups (10 oz/300 g) split chickpeas (garbanzo beans)

1 yellow (brown) onion, chopped

¹⁄₄ bunch fresh cilantro (fresh coriander), leaves and stems chopped

2 teaspoons grated fresh ginger

2 teaspoons finely chopped garlic

2 fresh green chilies, finely chopped

4 teaspoons fennel seeds

1¹⁄₂ teaspoons cumin seeds

18 fresh curry leaves, finely chopped

salt to taste

vegetable oil, for deep-frying

Mint Raita (see page 580) or Cucumber Raita (see page 571), for serving

Place chickpeas in a bowl, add hot water to cover and soak for 2 hours. Drain and reserve 1 cup (8 fl oz/250 ml) soaking water.

Place chickpeas in a food processor and process until finely crushed, adding 1–2 tablespoons soaking water if necessary to make a smooth, thick paste. Add onion, cilantro, ginger, garlic, chilies, fennel, cumin, curry leaves and salt, and process until well chopped and combined.

Shape 2 tablespoons of chickpea mixture into a small patty and place on a baking sheet. Repeat with remaining mixture.

Fill a karhai or wok with vegetable oil to a depth of 3 inches (7.5 cm). Heat oil over medium–high heat to 375°F (190°C) on a deep-frying thermometer. Cook patties in hot oil in batches of six, turning occasionally, until light golden brown, 1–2 minutes. Use a slotted spoon to remove patties to paper towels to drain.

Just before serving patties, refry in batches in hot oil until golden brown, 1–2 minutes. Drain on paper towels. Serve immediately, with raita.

Note: You can do the initial frying of patties up to 6 hours ahead.

Steamed pork buns

Chili Dipping Sauce (see page 568), or
  soy sauce, for serving

DOUGH

1 1/2 teaspoons active dry yeast
1/2 cup (4 fl oz/125 ml) warm water
1/4 cup (1 3/4 oz/50 g) superfine
  (caster) sugar
1 cup (4 oz/125 g) all-purpose (plain)
  flour
1/2 cup (2 oz/60 g) self-rising flour
3 teaspoons butter, melted

FILLING

2 tablespoons vegetable oil
3 teaspoons grated fresh ginger
2 cloves garlic, chopped
1 tablespoon hoisin sauce
1 tablespoon oyster sauce
1 tablespoon soy sauce
1 teaspoon Asian sesame oil
3 teaspoons cornstarch (cornflour)
  mixed with 1 tablespoon water
8 oz (250 g) Chinese barbecue pork,
  finely chopped
6 scallions (shallots/spring onions),
  finely chopped

To make dough: in a small bowl, combine yeast with 2 tablespoons warm water,
1 teaspoon sugar and 1 teaspoon all-purpose flour. Mix until well combined. Cover with
a kitchen towel and let stand in a warm place until frothy, about 15 minutes.

Sift remaining all-purpose flour and self-rising flour into a large bowl. Add remaining sugar,
yeast mixture, remaining warm water and melted butter. Using a wooden spoon, mix to
form a soft dough. Turn out onto a floured work surface and knead until smooth and
elastic, 3–5 minutes. Place dough in a large oiled bowl, cover and let stand in a warm
place until doubled in bulk, about 1 hour.

To make filling: Heat oil in a wok or frying pan over medium heat and fry ginger and
garlic until aromatic, about 1 minute. Add hoisin, oyster and soy sauces and sesame oil.
Cook, stirring, for 2 minutes. Add cornstarch and water mixture, bring to a boil and stir
until sauce thickens, about 2 minutes. Remove from heat and stir in pork and scallions.
Transfer to a bowl and let cool completely.

Punch down dough. Turn out onto a floured work surface and knead until smooth, about
5 minutes. Divide dough into 16 pieces. Roll or press out each piece to form a 2 1/4-inch
(6-cm) circle. Cover dough with a damp kitchen towel. Working with one round of dough

at a time, spoon 2 teaspoons of filling into center. Gather edges together, twist to seal and cover with a kitchen towel. Repeat with remaining dough.

Cut out 16 squares of parchment (baking) paper and place buns, sealed side down, on paper. Half fill a medium wok with water (steamer should not touch water) and bring to a boil. Working in batches, arrange buns in steamer, cover, and place steamer over boiling water. Steam for 15 minutes, adding more boiling water to wok when necessary. Lift steamer off wok and carefully remove buns. Using scissors, snip top of each bun twice, to resemble a star. Serve warm, with dipping sauce.

Steamed vegetable buns

Makes 16 buns

Chili Dipping Sauce (see page 568) or
  soy sauce, for serving

DOUGH
1¹/₂ teaspoons active dry yeast
¹/₂ cup (4 fl oz/125 ml) warm water
¹/₄ cup (1³/₄ oz/50 g) superfine
  (caster) sugar
1 cup (4 oz/125 g) all-purpose (plain)
  flour
¹/₂ cup (2 oz/60 g) self-rising flour
3 teaspoons butter, melted

FILLING
2 tablespoons vegetable oil
1 teaspoon grated fresh ginger
2 cloves garlic, chopped
4 bunches bok choy, finely chopped
3 bunches choy sum, finely chopped
1 carrot, finely chopped
6 scallions (shallots/spring onions),
  finely chopped
1 teaspoon Asian sesame oil
2 tablespoons Thai sweet chili sauce

To make dough, follow directions as for Steamed Pork Buns (see opposite).

To make filling: Heat oil in a wok or frying pan over medium heat and fry ginger and garlic until aromatic, about 1 minute. Add bok choy, choy sum, carrot and scallions. Stir-fry for 2 minutes. Remove from heat and stir in sesame oil and chili sauce. Transfer to a bowl and allow to cool completely.

Continue preparing dough as directed opposite, to make 16 dough rounds, and fill each with 2 teaspoons of vegetable filling. Steam vegetable buns for 15 minutes, adding more boiling water to wok when necessary. Carefully remove buns and serve warm, with dipping sauce.

Stuffed crab claws

12 cooked crab claws

1 lb (500 g) jumbo shrimp (green king prawns), peeled and deveined

2 cloves garlic

3 teaspoons grated fresh ginger

1 egg white

2 teaspoons fish sauce

1/4 teaspoon salt

4 scallions (shallots/spring onions), roughly chopped

1/4 cup (1 1/2 oz/45 g) finely chopped celery

1/4 cup (1 oz/30 g) cornstarch (cornflour)

3 cups (24 fl oz/750 ml) vegetable oil, for deep-frying

Lime Cilantro Dipping Sauce (see page 579), for serving

BATTER

1/2 cup (2 oz/60 g) cornstarch (cornflour)

1/2 cup (2 oz/60 g) all-purpose (plain) flour

1/2 teaspoon baking powder

1/2 teaspoon salt

1 cup (8 fl oz/250 ml) water

The shell around the larger end of the crab claw is generally lightly cracked when purchased. Remove the shell, leaving shell on nipper end as a handle for holding the crab claws.

Place shrimp, garlic, ginger, egg white, fish sauce and salt in a food processor and process until smooth. Transfer to a bowl. Stir in scallions and celery. Divide shrimp mixture into 12 portions. With wet hands, flatten each portion in palm of hand. Place flesh end of crab claw into center of shrimp mixture. Wet hands again and mold shrimp evenly all over crab flesh.

To make batter: Sift cornstarch, flour, baking powder and salt into a mixing bowl. Gradually add water, mixing to a smooth batter (this can also be done in a food processor).

Heat oil in a large wok or saucepan until it reaches 375°F (190°C) on a deep-frying thermometer, or until a small bread cube dropped in oil sizzles and turns golden. Dip crab claws in cornstarch, shaking off any excess. Working in batches, and holding nipper end of crab claw, dip into batter. Fry until golden, 2–3 minutes. Using a slotted spoon, remove from oil and drain on paper towels. Serve hot, with lime cilantro dipping sauce.

Sugarcane shrimp

Makes 12 canes

12-inch (30-cm) piece of fresh
  sugarcane or one 12-oz (375-g) can
  sugarcane packed in light syrup,
  drained

1 lb (500 g) shelled raw shrimp (green
  prawns), deveined

1 teaspoon fish sauce

2 tablespoons finely ground (minced)
  fresh pork fatback (optional)

6 cloves garlic, finely chopped

2 tablespoons finely chopped brown or
  pink shallots (French shallots)

1/2 teaspoon ground pepper

2 teaspoons sugar

1 egg white

1 tablespoon fish sauce

1–2 tablespoons ground rice (see Hint)

FOR ACCOMPANIMENTS
Vietnamese Bean Sauce (see page 594)
Nuoc Cham Nem Sauce (see page 582)

Use a cleaver to peel sugarcane, then hack it crosswise into 4-inch (10-cm) pieces. Split each piece lengthwise into quarters. Canned sugarcane is usually thinner; simply cut it in half lengthwise. You should have 12 pieces.

In a bowl, toss shrimp with 1 teaspoon fish sauce. Let stand for 15 minutes. Wipe well with paper towels, then squeeze any excess moisture from shrimp. Transfer to a food processor and chop finely. Add pork fatback if using, garlic, shallots, pepper and sugar and process to a sticky paste, scraping sides of container as necessary. Add egg white, 1 tablespoon fish sauce and ground rice, and process again. Chill slightly to facilitate molding into small balls, if desired. Lightly moisten your hands with oil and shape about 2 tablespoons of paste into a mound around each piece of sugarcane. Leave about 1 inch (2.5 cm) sugarcane exposed at each end.

Prepare a charcoal grill (barbecue) or brazier (see page 12), or preheat a broiler (grill) with the grilling rack set about 5 inches (12 cm) from heat source. Cook, turning occasionally, until dark golden on all sides, 3–5 minutes. Watch carefully; they tend to char quickly. Alternatively, preheat oven to 350°F (180°C/Gas 4) and bake, turning occasionally, for about 30 minutes. Serve with bean sauce or nuoc cham nem sauce.

Hint: To make ground rice, in a wok or small frying pan over low–medium heat, stir 2–3 tablespoons sticky (glutinous) rice until golden brown, 3–5 minutes. Transfer to a mortar and pound to a coarse powder with a pestle.

Vegetable pakoras

Makes about 28 pakoras

BATTER

2²/₃ cups (14 oz/440 g) chickpea (garbanzo bean) flour

1 teaspoon whole ajwain seeds

¹/₂ teaspoon chili powder

salt to taste

4 teaspoons vegetable oil

about 1¹/₄ cups (10 fl oz/300 ml) water

vegetable oil, for deep-frying

1 red bell pepper (capsicum), seeded and cut into ¹/₂-inch (12-mm) dice

1 medium desiree potato, peeled and cut into ¹/₂-inch (12-mm) dice

1 large red (Spanish) or yellow (brown) onion, cut into ¹/₂-inch (12-mm) dice

1 medium globe eggplant (aubergine), unpeeled, cut into ¹/₂-inch (12-mm) dice

Mint Raita (see page 580), for serving

To make batter: In a bowl, combine flour, ajwain, chili powder and salt. In a small saucepan, heat oil until it begins to smoke, then quickly stir into flour mixture. Add enough water to form a thick, smooth batter.

Fill a karhai or wok with vegetable oil to a depth of 3 inches (7.5 cm). Heat oil over medium–high heat to 375°F (190°C) on a deep-frying thermometer. Meanwhile, add all diced vegetables to batter and mix well.

Working in batches, carefully drop 1 heaping tablespoon of mixture for each pakora into hot oil. Cook, turning as necessary, until light golden brown, 1–2 minutes per side. Use a slotted spoon to remove pakoras to paper towels to drain. Repeat with remaining batter.

Just before serving pakoras, refry them in batches of seven, turning once, until crisp and golden brown, 1–2 minutes. Drain on paper towels. Serve immediately, with raita.

Hint: *You can do the initial frying of pakoras up to 6 hours ahead.*

Variation: *Instead of dicing vegetables, you can cut them into thin slices, dip them in batter, then deep-fry slices until golden brown.*

Vegetable samosas

PASTRY

3 cups (12 oz/375 g) all-purpose
  (plain) flour

salt to taste

3 tablespoons melted butter

about 3/4 cup (6 fl oz/180 ml) warm
  water

vegetable oil, for deep-frying

FILLING

1 lb (500 g) desiree or pontiac
  potatoes, boiled whole and cooled

4 teaspoons vegetable oil

1 1/2 teaspoons cumin seeds

1 teaspoon finely chopped fresh ginger

1/2 teaspoon chili powder

1 small fresh green chili, finely
  chopped

1/4 bunch fresh cilantro (fresh
  coriander), leaves and stems chopped

1 teaspoon chat masala

juice of 1 lemon

salt to taste

To make pastry: Sift flour and salt into a bowl. Stir in melted butter. Add enough warm water, cutting into flour mixture with a round-bladed knife, to form a firm dough. Knead dough lightly in bowl until smooth. Wrap in plastic wrap and set aside for 20 minutes.

To make filling: Peel potatoes and mash coarsely in a bowl. In a saucepan over medium heat, heat oil and briefly toast cumin seeds until fragrant. Stir in ginger, then add potatoes, chili powder and chili. Cook, stirring gently, for 3 minutes. Add cilantro, chat masala, lemon juice and salt, and mix well. Remove from heat and let cool.

Divide dough evenly into 6 portions. Shape each into an oval and roll out on a lightly floured work surface until about 9 inches (23 cm) long and 5 1/2 inches (14 cm) wide. Cut each oval in half crosswise. Hold one half-oval on your hand with the straight edge in line with your forefinger. Wet a finger and moisten straight edge. Place fingers of your other hand in centre of half-oval, folding sides in so edges overlap to form a cone. Press overlapped edges to seal. Hold cone with open end uppermost. Spoon one-twelfth of potato mixture into cone and use a wet finger to moisten edge of opening. Pinch edges of opening together to seal and enclose filling. Place samosa on a lightly floured baking sheet. Repeat with remaining dough and potato filling.

Fill a karhai or wok with vegetable oil to a depth of 5 inches (12.5 cm). Heat oil to 375°F (190°C) on a deep-frying thermometer. Carefully place four samosas in hot oil and cook, turning often, until crisp and dark golden brown, 3–4 minutes. Use a slotted spoon to remove samosas to paper towels to drain. Serve immediately.

Vegetable spring rolls

Makes 18 rolls

4 Chinese dried mushrooms

1 oz (30 g) cellophane noodles

2 tablespoons vegetable or canola oil

3 cloves garlic, chopped

2 tablespoons grated fresh ginger

6 scallions (shallots/spring onions), including some green parts, finely chopped

2 cups (6 oz/180 g) shredded Chinese (napa) cabbage

2 medium carrots, peeled and grated

$1/3$ cup chopped fresh cilantro (fresh coriander)

1 cup ($3^{1}/_{2}$ oz/105 g) fresh bean sprouts

2 tablespoons Thai sweet chili sauce plus extra, for serving

2 teaspoons fish sauce

18 frozen square spring roll wrappers, about $8^{1}/_{2}$ inches (21.5 cm), thawed

1 egg white, lightly beaten

3 cups (24 fl oz/750 ml) vegetable or canola oil, for deep-frying

Put mushrooms in a small bowl and add boiling water to cover. Let stand for 10 minutes. Drain, squeezing out excess liquid. Thinly slice mushrooms, discarding tough stems.

Put noodles in a bowl and add boiling water to cover. Let soak for 10 minutes. Drain. Using scissors, coarsely cut noodles into shorter lengths.

Heat oil in a wok or large skillet and stir-fry garlic and ginger for 1 minute, or until fragrant. Add scallions and cabbage. Stir-fry for 2 minutes, or until cabbage softens. Remove from heat. Stir in carrots, cilantro, bean sprouts, noodles, mushrooms, 2 tablespoons chili sauce, and fish sauce. Mix well. Let cool completely.

Place 1 spring roll wrapper on a work surface. Brush edges of wrapper with egg white. Place 1 heaping tablespoon of filling in center of wrapper. Roll the bottom of the wrapper diagonally over filling. Fold in sides and roll up diagonally. Seal edges with egg white. Repeat with remaining wrappers and filling.

In a large wok, heat oil to 375°F (190°C), or until a small bread cube dropped in oil sizzles and turns golden. Fry spring rolls in batches until golden, about 2 minutes. Using a wire-mesh skimmer, transfer to paper towels to drain. Serve hot, with Thai sweet chili sauce for dipping.

Vietnamese fried crab nems

$^1/_2$ oz (15 g) dried, or 1 oz (30 g) fresh,
tree ear or cloud mushrooms (black
or white fungus)

1 carrot, peeled and shredded

1 small onion, shredded

1 cup (2 oz/60 g) bean sprouts, rinsed
and drained

3 scallions (shallots/spring onions),
including green parts

1$^1/_2$-oz (45-g) packet dried rice
vermicelli noodles

8 oz (250 g) cooked or lump crabmeat,
picked over for shell

1 egg, beaten

ground pepper to taste

1 teaspoon sugar dissolved in
1 cup (8 fl oz/250 ml) water

1 tablespoon flour dissolved in
2–3 teaspoons water

about 30 sheets rice paper, about
9 inches (23 cm) in diameter

about 4–6 cups vegetable oil, for
deep-frying

FOR ACCOMPANIMENTS

Nuoc Cham Nem Sauce (see page 582)

Table Greens (see page 437)

If using dried tree ear or cloud mushrooms, soak them separately in several changes of water to remove grit, then drain, squeezing to remove all water. Fresh tree ear mushrooms should be quickly rinsed, and patted dry; then remove tough whitish core and discard, and cut mushroom into thin strips.

Pat shredded carrot and onion with a cloth to remove excess moisture. Cut bean sprouts into $^1/_2$-inch (12 mm) lengths. Cut scallions into thin rounds. Cook noodles according to packet directions or following instructions on page 442. Using scissors, cut noodles into manageable lengths.

Squeeze crabmeat firmly in your hand to extract any moisture. In a bowl, combine crabmeat, vegetables and noodles. Add egg and toss to coat; season with pepper.

To make rolls, soften a rice paper sheet in the sugar water following directions on page 27. Add 2–3 heaping tablespoons of filling, and roll up diagonally, tucking in edges. Seal edges with flour mixture. Cover lightly with plastic wrap to prevent drying, and fill remaining wrappers in the same way. In a wok or deep-fryer, heat 4 inches (10 cm) oil to 325–350°F (170–180°C) and fry rolls in batches, until crisp and golden brown, about 5 minutes. Transfer to paper towels to drain. Keep warm in a low oven while cooking successive batches.

Soups

from the subtle nature of miso and congee to hot and spicy laksa and the intensely flavored pho, Asian soups are now famous, and enjoyed all over the world. However, soups that originate in Japan, Korea, India, Malaysia, Vietnam, China and Thailand are more than just delicious—they promote a well-being that demonstrates the power of good food.

For the most part, soups are seen in Asian countries as health tonics or medicines vital for energy, and for restoring the body to its optimum state. In China, for example, chicken soup is thought to have essential healing properties, and is given for recuperation and to promote a stronger immune system. Pho, the famous Vietnamese soup, is also health-conscious and is believed to be a "mind-clearing tonic," while the spice and citrus of Thai soups stimulate the appetite during hot seasons and help to cool the body.

Every Asian country has at least one national soup, based on local ingredients and tradition. For the Vietnamese, it is pho, usually served for breakfast in order to fortify the mind and body for the day ahead. Typically, the rich pho broth is poured over thin slices of raw lean beef—these cook as the broth comes to the table, for a minute or two, so that they are perfectly pink on the inside—or thin slices of steamed chicken.

The Malaysians have laksa, which means "ten thousand," referring to the enormous variety of vegetables that can be added to the soup as condiments. Laksa is from the cuisine called Nonya, a fusion of Chinese and Malay food. In Malaysia, laksa is sold only at markets or at hawkers' stands, and traditionally consists of rice noodles in a sour-flavored fish soup made from a paste that is an exciting blend of dried shrimp, nuts and spices, including turmeric, which gives it its glorious sunshine color. While a seafood laksa is the most authentic style, chicken and vegetable are very popular in the West.

Hot and sour flavors and coconut milk bases typify Thai soups, like the classic tom yam, with kaffir lime leaves and lime juice imperative for that distinctive sour but fragrant tang. Another delicious flavor in Thai cooking comes from galangal, a root that is not dissimilar to ginger but is slightly tangier. Substitute galangal for ginger or vice versa, depending on which you come across. Relative to other Asian soups, though, Thai soups are lighter and do not have noodles.

In Japan, soups are based on clear stocks or are made with fermented beans and rice or barley (miso). Typical of Japanese cuisine, they are very simple in appearance and flavor and are virtually fat free. However, like pho and laksa, many have noodles and a seafood or meat topping, commonly beef or pork. Japanese clear soups are delicate, the perfect partner to sushi.

Many of the soups in this chapter are based on traditional recipes— some are centuries old, steeped in history and culture. However, there are also modern variations of the favorites, quick and easy soups with a fusion of flavors which are right at home in the contemporary kitchen.

Preparing and serving Asian soups

Whichever the country of origin, all soups start with one vital ingredient—a good-quality stock. Likewise, a good pot for cooking soup is indispensable. In Asia, eating soup is a communal activity that takes place at any time of the day or night—whether in a market, at a street stall or at home—so for serving you'll need individual bowls, chopsticks and little spoons, with an array of condiments alongside.

Making stock

Undoubtedly, making your own stock at home will be superior to any store-bought product, as most purchased varieties have some kind of coloring and/or preservatives, and definitely do not have the authentic flavors that you can add to your own. (See Stocks, pages 588–591.) Asian stocks, in particular, are enhanced by a variety of herbs and spices, such as ginger, galangal and lemongrass, many of which are seasonal.

If you do use a commercial stock, choose a good-quality one and simmer it with your own selection of flavorings, such as ginger, garlic, lemongrass or kaffir lime leaves. While it's still not the "real thing," it's a lot closer than what comes out of the packet. Remember the philosophy that underlies all Asian cooking—food should be good for body and soul—so use homemade stock wherever possible.

Equipment for soup

To make soup, you can use a large saucepan with a lid or a stock pot, preferably one with a heavy base. Some soups can be cooked in a wok. Or use an authentic cooking vessel such as a donabe, deghchi or hot pot (see Equipment, pages 10–19).

For serving main meal-type soups, a big soup bowl is essential. White porcelain or "chinaware" is economical and durable, the reason for its popularity throughout the centuries. Likewise, the typical blue-patterned bowls from Thailand are timelessly stylish and widely available too. Some of the traditional soup bowls have lids, which adds an authentic touch and keeps the soup warm.

For lighter soups, such as Japanese miso and clear soup, small cup-like bowls are used, to facilitate sipping (for example, between sushi bites). These are available in an amazing range of beautiful styles, from finest porcelain and classic Japanese lacquered bowls to modern ceramics glazed in contemporary colors.

Asian soups are usually served with porcelain spoons (for slurping the liquid) and chopsticks (for picking up meat, noodles and vegetables), but of course you can use a spoon and a fork. Like bowls, the Asian soup spoons are usually made of white porcelain, sometimes with red stamps or blue patterns, but they are increasingly available in more modern forms and colors.

Condiments, if served, are placed in separate little bowls, often matching the soup bowls and spoons, and set on the table so diners can add them to their soup bowls.

Preparing ingredients

As well as the soup itself, there are a host of ingredients which can enhance the meal and turn it into a stylish affair. Some Asian soups, such as laksa and pho, are always served with a colorful choice of condiments, such as sliced chili peppers, mint leaves, crispy fried shallots (the crowning glory of many an Asian soup) and lemon or lime wedges, in little bowls and dishes.

You can prepare condiments and garnishes such as thinly sliced omelette in advance of serving the meal, and place them on the table for guests to help themselves, which also makes this style of meal very convenient for the cook.

Soup herbs and greens

In Vietnamese tradition, a platter of herbs and greens is served at the table with soup, each diner picking from the central platter. This accompaniment also suits a range of other soup styles, such as laksa and hot pots. The selection of fresh herbs can include scallions (shallots/spring onions), eryngo (sawtooth coriander) leaves, cilantro (fresh coriander) sprigs, Vietnamese mint (rau ram), dill and bean sprouts, as well as other condiments.

To prepare herbs, simply trim stems and rinse leaves, but keep sprigs whole. Rinse bean sprouts, and remove "tails" if desired. To serve, arrange leaves and herbs in a large bowl or platter and place in center of table.

Storing and freezing soups

Don't forget that many soups can be made in advance and stored, tightly sealed in containers, in the refrigerator or the freezer. Of course stocks and soup bases can also be stored. In general, any soup that does not contain dairy products (such as cream) or coconut milk (whether fresh or canned) can be frozen. Some soups, however, such as clear soup or combination soup, must be made immediately before serving, though the ingredients can often be prepared beforehand.

Beef and coconut milk soup with Thai herbs

Serves 4

2 cloves garlic

2 tablespoons finely chopped fresh ginger

3 shallots (French shallots), peeled

1 teaspoon galangal powder

$1/2$ teaspoons sea salt

$1/2$ teaspoon white peppercorns

4 fresh cilantro (fresh coriander) roots

1 small red chili

3 tablespoons light olive oil

12 oz (375 g) round or rump steak, cut into 1-inch (2.5-cm) cubes

5 cups (40 fl oz/1.25 L) coconut milk (see page 24)

3 cups (24 fl oz/750 ml) pho beef stock (see page 591)

2–3 tablespoons lemon juice

2 stalks lemongrass, bottom 4 inches (10 cm) only, cut into 2-inch (5-cm) pieces

3 fresh or 6 dried kaffir lime leaves

2 teaspoons palm sugar or dark brown sugar

1 tablespoon fish sauce

$6 1/2$ oz (200 g) baby English spinach leaves

Combine garlic, ginger, shallots, galangal, salt, peppercorns, cilantro, chili and
2 tablespoons oil in a food processor and process to a smooth paste, 1–2 minutes.

Heat remaining oil in a large saucepan over medium heat. Add paste and cook, stirring,
until fragrant, 3–4 minutes. Add meat and cook for 3–4 minutes, turning to coat meat
and brown it slightly. Add coconut milk, stock and lemon juice and bring mixture to a
steady simmer. Add lemongrass, lime leaves, palm sugar and fish sauce and simmer until
meat is tender, about 30 minutes. Remove lemongrass and lime leaves. Season to taste
with fish sauce if soup is not salty enough and lemon juice if it is not tangy enough.

Stir in spinach leaves and let soup stand until leaves are wilted, about 1 minute. Serve
immediately.

Beef laksa

Serves 4

10 oz (300 g) lean beef tenderloin
  (fillet)

3 tablespoons lime juice

3 tablespoons light olive oil

1 teaspoon chili oil

1 small red chili, chopped

2 scallions (shallots/spring onions),
  white part only, finely chopped

1 clove garlic, finely chopped

2 tablespoons finely chopped fresh
  cilantro (fresh coriander)

$1/4$ cup (2 oz/60 g) laksa paste
  (see page 578)

4 cups (32 fl oz/1 L) beef, pho beef or
  vegetable stock (see Stocks, pages
  588–591)

4 cups (32 fl oz/1 L) coconut milk (see
  page 24)

2 teaspoons fish sauce

2 cups (4 oz/125 g) baby spinach
  leaves

4 oz (125 g) mixed fresh mushrooms
  (enoki, cremini, shiitake, button),
  sliced if large, for garnish

4 oz (125 g) deep-fried tofu (about
  4 pillows), sliced, for garnish

4 large sprigs cilantro (coriander),
  for garnish

$1/4$ cup (2 oz/60 g) crispy fried onions
  or shallots (French shallots), for
  garnish (see page 24)

Wrap beef tenderloin in plastic wrap and freeze until partially frozen, about 1 hour. Remove from freezer and slice into very thin strips. Place in a ceramic or glass bowl and add 1 tablespoon lime juice, 1 tablespoon olive oil, chili oil, chili, scallions, garlic and cilantro. Mix gently to combine marinade ingredients. Cover and refrigerate for 1 hour.

Heat remaining oil in a large saucepan over medium–high heat until hot, about 1 minute. Add laksa paste and cook, stirring, until very fragrant, about 5 minutes. Add remaining lime juice, stock, coconut milk and fish sauce, reduce heat to medium and bring mixture to a steady simmer. Simmer for 15 minutes. Stir in spinach and simmer until leaves have wilted, about 1 minute.

Remove beef from refrigerator. Ladle soup into individual bowls and add beef and marinade. Top with garnishes, finishing with crispy fried onions. The beef and mushrooms will cook in the stock. Serve immediately.

Beef pho

Serves 4

1-inch (2.5-cm) knob fresh ginger, peeled

¼ cup (1 oz/30 g) brown or pink shallots (French shallots), peeled

6 cups (48 fl oz/1.5 L) beef pho stock (see page 591)

1 star anise

1 brown or black cardamom pod, lightly crushed

1-lb (500-g) packet rice noodles or rice sticks

2 tablespoons coarsely chopped Chinese (flat/garlic) chives

2 scallions (shallots/spring onions), including green parts, coarsely chopped

1 small onion, thinly sliced

6 oz (180 g) beef tenderloin (fillet), sliced paper thin

FOR ACCOMPANIMENTS

Soup Herbs (see page 437), including eryngo (sawtooth coriander) leaves, peppermint and bean sprouts

2 fresh medium or long red chilies, cut into small rings

fish sauce or Nuoc Cham Sauce (see page 582)

1–2 lemons, cut into wedges

Preheat oven to 400°F (200°C/Gas 6). Enclose ginger and shallots in a square of aluminum foil. Roast for about 20 minutes. Remove from foil, chop ginger and shallots, and add to stock in a large pot. Add star anise and cardamom. Bring stock to a boil, then reduce heat to low and simmer for at least 30 minutes. Set aside. Prepare dried noodles as described on page 442. Fresh noodles, direct from the packet, can also be used.

Immediately before serving, remove star anise and cardamom from stock. Bring stock to a boil. Plunge noodles into boiling water for a moment to reheat. Drain immediately and place in warmed individual bowls. Divide chives, scallions and onion among bowls. Toss meat into boiling stock, then ladle meat and boiling stock into each bowl. Accompany with soup herbs, chilies, fish sauce and lemon wedges. Squeeze wedges of lemon into individual bowls.

Note: Banh pho or rice noodles generally come in three widths, but noodles that are ⅛ inch (3 mm) wide are normally used for pho.

Beef with cabbage soup

Serves 4

1 red chili

4 shallots (French shallots), peeled

2 cloves garlic, peeled

1 teaspoon galangal powder or
  1 tablespoon chopped fresh galangal
  or fresh ginger

1/2 cup (1/2 oz/15 g) fresh cilantro
  (fresh coriander) leaves

2 tablespoons finely grated lime zest

1 teaspoon coriander seeds

1 teaspoon cumin seeds

5 black peppercorns

1 teaspoon paprika

1/4 teaspoon turmeric

1/4 cup (2 fl oz/60 ml) light olive oil

1 medium yellow (brown) onion,
  chopped

1 lb (500 g) blade, round or chuck
  steak, cut into 1-inch (2.5-cm) cubes

6 cups (48 fl oz/1.5 L) pho beef stock
  (see page 591)

2 cups (16 fl oz/500 ml) coconut milk
  (see page 24)

4 medium, ripe tomatoes, chopped

2 teaspoons fish sauce

3 cups (9 oz/280 g) shredded white or
  Chinese cabbage

Combine chili, shallots, garlic, galangal, cilantro, lime zest, coriander seeds, cumin seeds, peppercorns, paprika, turmeric and oil in a food processor and process to a smooth paste, about 2 minutes.

Place paste in a large saucepan over medium–low heat and cook, stirring, for 5 minutes. Add a little more oil if mixture starts to stick to bottom of pan. Add onion and meat and cook, stirring, until onion is soft and meat is slightly browned, about 5 minutes. Add stock, coconut milk, tomatoes and fish sauce, increase heat to medium and bring mixture to a steady simmer. Simmer until meat is tender, about 1 1/2 hours.

Stir in cabbage and cook until cabbage is soft, about 10 minutes.

Ladle into individual bowls and serve.

Chicken and mushroom soup

Serves 4

4 Chinese dried mushrooms

4 cups (32 fl oz/1 L) chicken stock
(see page 588)

2 cloves garlic, finely chopped

1 teaspoon grated fresh ginger

1 tablespoon rice vinegar

2 teaspoons palm sugar

1 chicken fillet, about 5 oz (150 g),
thinly sliced

6 scallions (shallots/spring onions),
chopped

2 lemongrass stalks, bruised and sliced

1 small red chili, seeded and chopped

Place mushrooms in small bowl, add boiling water to cover and allow to stand until softened, 10–15 minutes. Drain, and squeeze excess liquid from mushrooms. Thinly slice, discarding thick stems. Place broth, garlic, ginger, vinegar and sugar in wok. Bring to a boil, reduce heat to low and simmer, uncovered, for 5 minutes. Stir in sliced mushrooms, chicken, scallions, lemongrass and chili. Simmer until chicken is opaque, about 15 minutes. Serve hot, ladled into bowls.

Chicken and noodle soup

Serves 4

4 Chinese dried mushrooms

8 oz (250 g) egg noodles

1/2 cup (2 oz/60 g) shredded snow
peas (mange-tout)

1 tablespoon vegetable oil

1 tablespoon light soy sauce

1 tablespoon rice wine

4 cups (32 fl oz/ 1 L) chicken stock (see
page 588)

11/2 cups (8 oz/250 g) shredded
cooked skinless chicken meat

1/2 cup (2 oz/60 g) fresh bean sprouts,
rinsed

Prepare mushrooms as directed above and cook egg noodles as directed on package. Drain and set aside. Place snow peas in a bowl and add boiling water to cover. Let stand for 1 minute, then drain and refresh immediately in cold water. In a wok or saucepan over medium–high heat, warm oil. Add sliced mushrooms and stir-fry for 1 minute. Add noodles, snow peas, soy sauce, rice wine, stock and chicken. Bring to boil, stirring occasionally. Serve hot, ladled into bowls and garnished with bean sprouts.

Chicken coconut milk soup

Serves 4–6

2 cups (16 fl oz/500 ml) coconut cream (see page 24)

1 cup (8 fl oz/125 ml) coconut milk (see page 24)

2 stalks lemongrass, white part only, peeled and cut into 1-inch (2.5-cm) pieces

1/2-inch (12-mm) piece galangal, thinly sliced

2 tablespoons coarsely chopped shallots (French shallots), preferably pink

10–15 small fresh chilies, halved lengthwise

1 cup (4 oz/125 g) canned or 2 cups (8 oz/250 g) fresh straw mushrooms, rinsed, drained and halved

12 oz (375 g) boneless, skinless chicken breasts, thinly sliced

2–3 tablespoons fish sauce, to taste

3 kaffir lime leaves, stems removed

1/2 cup (1/2 oz/15 g) coarsely chopped fresh cilantro (fresh coriander)

2 tablespoons fresh lime juice

2 scallions (shallots/spring onions), chopped

In a wok or large saucepan over high heat, combine coconut cream, coconut milk, lemongrass, galangal, shallots, chilies, and mushrooms. Bring to a boil, reduce heat, and simmer for 3–5 minutes. Add chicken, stirring well. Add fish sauce and lime leaves. Return to a boil. Add half the cilantro and turn off heat.

Stir in lime juice. Transfer to bowls for serving, garnish with scallions and remaining cilantro, and serve.

Hint: *For a less rich soup, replace the coconut cream with an equal quantity of coconut milk. For a less spicy broth, keep the chilies whole.*

Note: *"Tom kha gai" is one of Thailand's best-known soups, with a creamy consistency and a lovely lemony flavor. The fibrous ingredients in this dish—kaffir lime leaf, galangal and lemongrass—are not eaten. Just push them aside.*

Chicken ginseng soup

Serves 4

1/3 cup (1³/₄ oz/50 g) sticky (glutinous) rice, soaked in water for about
   30 minutes
1 fresh young chicken (about 1 lb/500 g), washed
1 whole bulb garlic
5 dates
2 whole finger-thick, fresh ginseng roots, washed
1 scallion (shallot/spring onion), roughly chopped
salt and freshly ground black pepper to taste

Spoon rice into cavity of chicken. Make a slit in flap of flesh on each side of cavity
entrance. Push end of right drumstick through slit on left side and end of left drumstick
through slit on right. Alternatively, tie or skewer cavity closed.

Place chicken in a large saucepan and cover with water. Add garlic, dates and ginseng.
Bring to a boil, then reduce heat to low and simmer until liquid turns yellowish, about
1 hour.

Transfer whole chicken and liquid to a large bowl. Accompany with separate bowls of
chopped scallion, salt and pepper for diners to add to taste.

Notes: It is believed that this Korean hot soup is energy food. It is eaten in
summer to energize the body by replacing lost body heat. The traditional wisdom
is that hot food keeps the mind and body strong throughout the summer.

Ginseng is widely cultivated in Korea. Tasting similar to parsnip, it is used in soups,
stews and teas, and is believed to have properties that strengthen and rejuvenate
the body.

Chicken laksa

Serves 4

2 large skinless, boneless chicken
   breast halves, 1 lb (500 g) total

2 tablespoons light olive oil

sea salt and freshly ground black
   pepper

$^1/_2$ cup (4 oz/125 g) laksa paste (see
   page 578)

3 tablespoons lemon or lime juice

3 cups (24 fl oz/750 ml) coconut milk
   (see page 24)

3 cups (24 fl oz/750 ml) chicken stock
   (see page 588)

2 cups (10 oz/300 g) cherry tomatoes

6 oz (180 g) thick dried rice noodles

1 cup (5 oz/150 g) pineapple pieces,
   about $^1/_2$ inch (12 mm)

1 small cucumber, peeled and sliced

2 tablespoons chopped fresh mint
   leaves

$^1/_4$ cup fresh cilantro (fresh coriander)
   leaves

$^1/_4$ cup (2 oz/60 g) crisp fried shallots
   (French shallots) (see page 24)

Brush chicken breasts with 2 teaspoons oil. Heat a cast iron frying pan or stovetop grill pan over high heat until very hot, about 5 minutes. Cook chicken breasts until tender and cooked through, 4–5 minutes on each side. Season with salt and black pepper. Remove and set aside.

Heat remaining oil in a large saucepan over medium–high heat. Stir in laksa paste and cook until fragrant, 4–5 minutes, stirring frequently. Add lime juice, coconut milk and chicken stock and stir until mixture is thoroughly combined. Reduce heat to medium and simmer for 10 minutes. Add tomatoes and simmer for 5 minutes.

Place noodles in a large bowl and add boiling water to cover. Allow to stand until noodles are soft, about 3 minutes. Drain noodles, rinse under warm water and set aside.

Slice chicken breasts into thin slices. Spoon noodles into individual bowls and ladle soup over them. Top with chicken slices and remaining ingredients, finishing with a sprinkling of shallots. Serve immediately.

Chili-corn soup

Serves 4

3 tablespoons light olive oil

2 red chilies

1 medium yellow (brown) onion

2 cloves garlic, peeled

1 teaspoon dried shrimp paste
  (optional)

2 teaspoons finely grated lime zest

1 tablespoon chopped fresh ginger or
  fresh galangal or 2 teaspoons
  galangal powder

1 tablespoon coriander seeds

1 teaspoon cumin seeds

$1/2$ teaspoon fennel seeds

$1/2$ teaspoon ground cardamom

8 cups (64 fl oz/2 L) chicken or
  vegetable stock (see Stocks, pages
  588-591)

4 cups (24 oz/750 g) fresh or frozen
  corn kernels

2 teaspoons fish sauce

1 tablespoon lime juice

1 roasted red bell pepper (capsicum),
  peeled and seeded

1 teaspoon chili paste or sambal oelek

Combine 2 tablespoons oil, chilies, onion, garlic, shrimp paste, lime zest, ginger and spices in a food processor and process to a smooth paste, 2–3 minutes.

Heat remaining oil in a large saucepan over medium heat and add paste. Cook, stirring, until fragrant, 3–4 minutes. Add stock, increase heat to medium–high and bring liquid to a steady simmer. Add corn, fish sauce and lime juice and simmer until corn is tender, about 5 minutes.

Let soup cool slightly. Working in batches if necessary, ladle into a food processor and process until smooth, 2–3 minutes. Return to saucepan and reheat before serving.

In a food processor, process bell pepper and chili paste until smooth, about 2 minutes.

Ladle soup into individual bowls and garnish with a little chili paste.

Coconut and pumpkin Thai-style soup

Serves 4

12 oz (375 g) pumpkin, peeled and cut into 1-inch (2.5-cm) pieces

2 tablespoons lime juice

1 large yellow (brown) onion, chopped

2 cloves garlic, chopped

2-inch (5-cm) piece fresh ginger, chopped

3 red chilies

1 stalk lemongrass, bottom 3 inches (7.5 cm) only, finely chopped

1 teaspoon dried shrimp paste

3 cups (24 fl oz/750 ml) coconut milk (see page 24)

1 cup (8 fl oz/250 ml) chicken or vegetable stock (see Stocks, pages 588-591)

1 tablespoon fish sauce

$1/2$ cup ($1/2$ oz/15 g) baby basil leaves, for garnish

Place pumpkin pieces in a large bowl and add lime juice. Stir to combine and set aside.

Place onion, garlic, ginger, chilies, lemongrass and shrimp paste in a food processor and process until smooth, 2–3 minutes. In a large saucepan, combine onion mixture with $1/4$ cup (2 fl oz/60 ml) coconut milk. Cook over medium–high heat until mixture is fragrant and reduced, about 5 minutes. Add remaining coconut milk, stock and fish sauce and cook over medium–high heat, stirring, until liquid begins to bubble. Simmer for 5 minutes. Add pumpkin pieces and lime juice and simmer until pumpkin is tender, 10–15 minutes.

Ladle soup into individual bowls and serve sprinkled with basil leaves.

Combination short and long soup

3¹/₂ oz (105 g) egg noodles

2 tablespoons vegetable oil

1 chicken breast fillet, skin removed

4 oz (125 g) ground (minced) chicken

1 cup (3 oz/90 g) shredded Chinese (napa) cabbage

¹/₄ cup (2 oz/60 g) chopped canned water chestnuts

2 teaspoons soy sauce, plus extra for serving

1 teaspoons Asian sesame oil

1 teaspoon grated fresh ginger

12 wonton wrappers

1 egg, beaten

6 cups (42 fl oz/1.5 L) chicken stock (see page 588)

1 tablespoon dry sherry

12 jumbo shrimp (king prawns), peeled and deveined, tails intact

6¹/₂ oz (200 g) baby spinach or bok choy, trimmed

4 oz (125 g) Chinese barbecue pork, sliced

Cook noodles as directed on package or on page 442. Drain and set aside. Heat 1 tablespoon vegetable oil in a wok or frying pan over medium heat. Add chicken breast and cook, turning once, until juices run clear when pierced with skewer, about 5 minutes on each side. Remove from pan and allow to cool. Slice chicken and set aside.

Heat remaining 1 tablespoon vegetable oil in the same pan over medium–high heat. Add ground chicken and stir-fry until it changes color, about 5 minutes. Add cabbage and stir-fry for 2 minutes. Stir in water chestnuts, soy sauce, sesame oil and ginger. Remove from heat and let cool.

Place wonton wrappers on work surface and cover with a damp kitchen towel. Working with one wrapper at a time, lay it on work surface and place 1 teaspoon ground chicken in the middle. Brush edges with beaten egg, fold wrapper diagonally and curl around finger to form a tortellini-like shape. Set aside, covered with plastic wrap. Repeat with remaining wonton wrappers.

Combine chicken stock and sherry in a saucepan. Bring to a boil, reduce heat to low and simmer, uncovered, for 5 minutes. Add shrimp and wontons and simmer until shrimp change color, about 3 minutes. Stir in noodles, spinach, pork and sliced chicken and simmer until noodles, pork and chicken are heated through, 4–5 minutes. Ladle into individual bowls. Offer soy sauce at the table, to be added to taste.

Curry yogurt soup

Serves 2

2 tablespoons vegetable oil

1 green Thai or Anaheim chili, seeded and chopped

4 cloves garlic, finely chopped

1 tablespoon grated fresh ginger

4 dried red chilies

1 teaspoon cumin seeds

1/2 teaspoon chili powder

1/2 teaspoon ground turmeric

8 fresh curry leaves

2 cups (16 oz/500 g) plain (natural) yogurt

sea salt to taste

1/2 cup (4 fl oz/125 ml) coconut milk (see page 24)

1/4 fresh red Thai or Anaheim chili, seeded and cut into very fine 2-inch
  (5-cm) lengths

In a medium saucepan, heat 1 tablespoon of oil over medium heat and fry chili, garlic, ginger, dried chilies, cumin seeds, chili powder, turmeric, and 4 of the curry leaves for 2–3 minutes, or until fragrant.

Reduce heat to low and stir in yogurt and salt. Cook for 5 minutes, stirring (do not boil). Stir in coconut milk and cook for 1 minute, stirring constantly. Remove and discard dried chilies. Spoon into serving bowls.

In a small skillet, heat remaining 1 tablespoon of oil and fry remaining 4 curry leaves and shredded fresh red chili until the chili curls, about 30 seconds. Using a slotted spoon, transfer to paper towels to drain. Garnish each soup bowl with curry and chili leaf mixture.

Ginger and spice soup

Serves 4

1 tablespoon vegetable oil

1 medium yellow (brown) onion, chopped

3 stalks lemongrass, bruised

4 cloves garlic, chopped

2 small red chilies, seeded and chopped

2 curry leaves

2 kaffir lime leaves, finely sliced

1-inch (2.5-cm) piece fresh galangal, chopped

2-inch (5-cm) piece fresh ginger, chopped

1 tablespoon grated palm sugar

pinch salt

7 cups (56 fl oz/1.75 L) clear vegetable stock (see page 590)

2 tablespoons lemon juice

2 tablespoons fresh cilantro (fresh coriander) leaves, chopped

1/2 lb (250 g) enoki or oyster (abalone) mushrooms

4 sprigs watercress

Warm oil in a large pot over medium–high heat. Add onion, lemongrass, garlic, chili, curry and kaffir lime leaves, galangal, ginger and sugar. Stir-fry until the aromas start to release, about 2 minutes. Add salt, stock and lemon juice and bring to a boil. Simmer, uncovered, for 10 minutes. Strain, then return liquid to a clean pot. Discard solids. Return to a boil.

Divide the cilantro, mushrooms and watercress equally among 4 bowls. Pour soup over the vegetables. Serve immediately.

Variation: Use steamed choy sum or bok choy leaves instead of watercress.

Hanoi chicken pho

Serves 4

2 cloves garlic, finely chopped

2 tablespoons soy sauce

2 boneless, skinless chicken breasts, about 6 oz (180 g) each

6 oz (180 g) dried rice noodles

8 cups (64 fl oz/2 L) pho chicken stock (see page 591)

4 scallions (shallots/spring onions), green and white parts, cut into strips

1 cup (1 oz/30 g) basil leaves, preferably holy basil

1/2 cup (1/2 oz/15 g) small mint leaves

7 oz (220 g) bean sprouts, watercress or snow pea (mange-tout) shoots, trimmed

2 tablespoons prepared chili paste or sambal oelek

Combine garlic, soy sauce and 1/2 cup (4 fl oz/125 ml) water in a large saucepan, with a lid, that can accommodate a bamboo steamer and its lid. Place over high heat and bring to a boil. Reduce heat to medium so liquid is at a steady simmer.

Line the bottom of a bamboo steamer with two pieces of wax paper, each cut to approximate size of a chicken breast. Place chicken breasts on wax paper in steamer, then set steamer inside saucepan. Cover steamer and saucepan and steam chicken until cooked through, 12–15 minutes (test by cutting through thickest part with a small, sharp knife). Check steaming liquid occasionally and add more water if necessary. Remove cooked chicken and set aside.

Place noodles in a large bowl and add boiling water to cover. Allow noodles to stand until soft, 3–4 minutes. Drain and set aside in colander.

In a large saucepan, heat pho stock over high heat until boiling. Slice cooked chicken into thin strips.

Quickly rinse noodles under very hot water, using a fork to separate them. Place noodles in individual bowls and top with chicken. Pour stock into bowls. Serve remaining ingredients in small bowls for diners to add to soup.

Indian spinach soup (Caldo verde)

Serves 4–6

2 tablespoons vegetable oil

2 yellow (brown) onions, thinly sliced

4 cloves garlic, finely chopped

1/2 teaspoon ground turmeric

1 bunch spinach, trimmed, rinsed well and chopped

1 1/2 cups (12 fl oz/375 ml) milk

1 1/2 cups (12 fl oz/375 ml) chicken or vegetable stock (see Stocks, pages 588-591)
  or water

4 teaspoons butter, frozen

1/2 teaspoon freshly grated nutmeg

salt and freshly ground pepper to taste

heavy (double) cream, for garnish

In a large, heavy saucepan, heat oil over medium heat. Add onions and cook, stirring occasionally, until softened, about 5 minutes. Add garlic and turmeric, and cook, stirring, for 30 seconds. Add spinach leaves to pan and cook, tossing, just until spinach wilts. Remove from heat and let cool.

Place spinach mixture in a blender and process to a smooth puree, adding a small amount of milk if necessary. Return mixture to pan. Stir in remaining milk and stock, and bring to a simmer over medium heat. Simmer, uncovered, for 3 minutes. Add butter and nutmeg and season with salt and pepper. Simmer for 2 minutes.

Ladle into bowls and add a swirl of cream to each bowl before serving.

Japanese clear soup with shrimp and fish

Serves 4

4 cups (36 fl oz/1 L) water
1 small dried shiitake mushroom
$1/2$ teaspoon salt
$1/2$ teaspoon mirin
$1/2$ teaspoon instant dashi, or to taste
4 medium-sized cooked shrimp
 (prawns), deveined, shells removed
 and tails intact

4 thinly sliced pieces of white-fleshed
 fish, approximately $1 1/2$ inches
 x $3/4$ inch (4 cm x 2 cm), and $1/4$ inch
 (6 mm) thick, boiled
2 oz (60 g) tofu, cut into $3/4$-inch
 (1-cm) cubes
1 oz (30 g) enoki mushrooms
1 scallion (shallot/spring onion), thinly
 sliced
12 mitsuba leaves, for garnish

In a saucepan, bring water, shiitake mushroom, salt and mirin to a boil. Add dashi, stir until well dissolved and remove from heat; add more dashi for a stronger flavor, less dashi for a milder flavor. Remove shiitake mushroom from soup and thinly slice, then return to soup. Place a shrimp in each bowl. Divide fish pieces, tofu, enoki mushrooms, scallions and mitsuba leaves among bowls. Pour soup into each bowl and serve.

Japanese watercress soup

Serves 4

6 cups (48 fl oz/1.5 L) chicken or
 vegetable stock (see Stocks, pages
 588-591)
2 tablespoons soy sauce

2 eggs
4 cups (4 oz/125 g) watercress sprigs
white pepper to taste
soy sauce to taste (optional)

Heat stock and soy sauce in a large saucepan over medium–high heat. Bring liquid to a steady simmer. Simmer for 3–4 minutes. Increase heat to high and bring liquid to a boil. In a small bowl, using a fork, lightly whisk eggs then stir into soup. Keep stirring until eggs are set. Soup must be boiling for eggs to set.

Reduce heat to medium–low and add watercress. Simmer until watercress is wilted, about 2 minutes. Season with white pepper, and soy sauce if desired. Ladle into individual bowls and serve immediately.

Korean beef ball soup

Serves 4–5

4 oz (125 g) stewing (gravy) beef

8 cups (64 fl oz/2 L) water

light soy sauce to taste

4 oz (125 g) ground (minced) beef

2 tablespoons all-purpose (plain) flour

2 eggs, beaten

vegetable or sunflower oil, for frying

1 egg, separated

crown daisy leaves (see Note), for
   garnish (optional)

FOR STEWING BEEF SEASONING

1 teaspoon table salt

1 teaspoon sesame oil

1 clove garlic, finely chopped

freshly ground black pepper to taste

FOR GROUND BEEF SEASONING

1 teaspoon salt

2 teaspoons finely chopped scallions
   (shallots/spring onions)

1 oz (30 g) firm tofu, crumbled

1 clove garlic, finely chopped

1 teaspoon sesame oil

freshly ground black pepper to taste

To prepare and use stewing beef seasoning: Combine ingredients in a small bowl. Thinly slice beef and coat in seasoning. Transfer to a medium saucepan, add water and boil for 20 minutes. Add soy sauce to taste.

Meanwhile, mix ground beef in small bowl with ground beef seasoning ingredients. Using wet hands, form beef into bite-sized balls. Coat beef balls in flour and dip in the beaten egg.

Heat $1\frac{1}{2}$ teaspoons oil in a frying pan and stir-fry balls until evenly browned, about 2 minutes. Remove and drain on paper towels. Fry egg white and yolk to make egg gidan (see page 26). Remove from pan and slice into thin strips. Add beef balls to boiling beef stock. Reduce heat to low and simmer for 5 minutes. Serve beef balls and stock in individual bowls, garnished with egg gidan and crown daisy leaves.

Note: Crown daisy leaves, or "ssukgat," come from a variety of chrysanthemum. They are used in Korean recipes as a kind of spinach and, with stems intact, in Asian stir-fries.

Malay chicken rice soup

2 teaspoons light olive oil

1 yellow (brown) onion, sliced

3 stalks celery, cut into thin strips

2 medium carrots, peeled and sliced

1 whole chicken, about 4 lb (2 kg)

8 cups (64 fl oz/2 L) water

2 stalks lemongrass, bottom 3 inches (7.5 cm) only, chopped into 2-inch (5-cm) pieces

2-inch (5-cm) piece fresh galangal or fresh ginger, sliced

2 large sprigs fresh cilantro (fresh coriander), including roots

2 teaspoons sea salt

$1/2$ teaspoon white pepper

$1^1/_2$ cups (11 oz/330 g) jasmine rice, rinsed until water runs clear

2 tablespoons finely chopped fresh chives

2 tablespoons crispy fried shallots (French shallots) (see page 24)

soy sauce, for serving

chili sauce, for serving

Heat olive oil in a large saucepan (large enough to hold whole chicken) over medium–high heat. Add onion, celery and carrots and cook, stirring, until onions are soft, about 5 minutes. Place chicken on top of vegetables and add 8 cups (64 fl oz/2 L) water to completely cover chicken. Add lemongrass, galangal, cilantro, salt and pepper and bring liquid to a steady simmer. Reduce heat to medium–low and simmer for $1^1/_2$ hours, occasionally skimming any oil and scum from surface.

Drain mixture, reserving chicken and stock and discarding other solids. Allow chicken to cool slightly, then chop, with a large, heavy knife or cleaver, into medium-sized sections (wings, quartered breasts, drumsticks and thighs). Return stock to a large saucepan and add rinsed rice. Bring stock to a boil over high heat. Boil until rice is cooked, about 15 minutes. Stir in chives.

Ladle soup and rice into individual bowls and place chicken on top. Sprinkle with crispy fried shallots and serve immediately, accompanied by small bowls of soy sauce and chili sauce for each diner to add if desired.

Note: This traditional Malaysian dish is a meal in itself; in Malaysia, it is sold at local markets and street stalls and enjoyed at any time of day.

Miso soup

4 cups (32 fl oz/1 L) water
$1/4$ cup (2 fl oz/60 ml) white (shiro)
  miso paste
$1/2$ teaspoon instant dashi, or to taste
cubed silken tofu, as desired

2 scallions (shallots/spring onions),
  thinly sliced
1 tablespoon wakame seaweed,
  soaked for 2 minutes in warm water

Place water in a saucepan and bring to a boil. Place miso paste in a small strainer, holding it over saucepan, and press miso through strainer with back of a wooden spoon. Discard any grainy miso left in strainer. Return soup to boil and add dashi.

Divide tofu, scallions and seaweed among individual serving bowls. Pour soup into each bowl, and serve immediately.

Miso soup with scallops and caviar

12 white sea scallops without roe
1 tablespoon mirin
1 tablespoon olive oil
2 cups (16 fl oz/500 ml) water

$1^1/2$ tablespoons white miso paste
4 teaspoons salmon caviar
4 scallions (shallots/spring onions),
  green parts only, halved lengthwise

Place scallops on a plate and drizzle mirin over them. Heat olive oil in a grill pan or frying pan over medium–high heat. Add scallops to pan, reduce heat to low, and cook on each side until opaque. Transfer scallops to a plate and set aside.

In a medium saucepan, bring water to a boil. Reduce heat to a simmer. In a cup, mix miso paste with 1 tablespoon boiling water, then pour into saucepan. Add scallops and cook until heated through (do not overcook).

Place 3 scallops in each of 4 bowls and gently ladle soup over them. Tie each scallion leaf in a knot and place alongside scallops.

Miso soup with tuna and ginger

Serves 4

1/4 cup (2 oz/60 g) miso paste

6 cups (48 fl oz/1.5 L) light fish stock (see page 589) or water

2-inch (5-cm) piece fresh ginger, thinly sliced

4 scallions (shallots/spring onions), white part only, cut into thin strips

6 oz (180 g) soft tofu, cut into 1/2-inch (12-mm) cubes

2 tablespoons shredded seaweed

8 oz (250 g) sashimi-quality tuna

1 tablespoon wasabi powder

1/4 cup (1 1/2 fl oz/45 g) Japanese pickled ginger

Place miso paste in a large saucepan with fish stock and ginger and stir over medium heat until liquid reaches a steady simmer and miso paste is completely dissolved, about 10 minutes. Reduce heat to low and add scallions, tofu and seaweed. Simmer for 3 minutes.

Meanwhile, slice tuna into very thin strips. Prepare wasabi paste by mixing wasabi powder with 2 teaspoons water (or enough to form a thick paste) and stirring until smooth.

Pour miso soup into individual bowls and accompany with sliced tuna, wasabi paste and pickled ginger. Dip tuna in hot soup to cook it slightly, then eat soup and tuna with wasabi and pickled ginger. Serve with spoons or sip soup directly from bowls.

Note: Miso is a traditional soup that can be served as an accompaniment to any Japanese meal. It is usually enjoyed as a part of a traditional Japanese breakfast.

Hints: Other ingredients can be added to basic miso soup. Cooked meat, seafood or vegetables such as clams, lobster, pork, daikon, onion, eggplant (aubergine) and enoki mushrooms can be added to individual bowls just before filling with soup and serving. The amounts added depend on individual preference.

Mushroom wonton and spinach noodle soup

Serves 4

9 oz (280 g) mixed oyster, shiitake and
button mushrooms

1/2 teaspoon white pepper

1/2 teaspoon sea salt

3 tablespoons chopped fresh cilantro
(fresh coriander)

1 tablespoon grated fresh ginger

2 cloves garlic, roughly chopped

1 fresh or 2 dried kaffir lime leaves,
finely chopped, or 2 teaspoons finely
grated lime zest

4 water chestnuts, finely chopped

1 small egg, lightly beaten

20 wonton wrappers

8 cups (64 fl oz/2 L) chicken or
vegetable stock (see Stocks, pages
588-591)

1/2 lb (250 g) fresh egg noodles

8 oz (250 g) baby English spinach
leaves or shredded English spinach
leaves

Combine mushrooms, pepper, salt, cilantro, ginger, garlic and kaffir lime leaf in a food
processor and process until smooth, about 2 minutes. Transfer mixture to a bowl and stir in
water chestnuts and egg.

Lay wonton wrappers on a dry surface. Working with one wrapper at a time, place
1 heaping teaspoon of mushroom mixture in the center of the wrapper. Wet edges with
a little water, using a pastry brush or your finger, and fold edges in to form a bundle. Press
edges together to secure filling. Repeat with remaining wrappers.

Place stock in a large saucepan over medium heat and bring to a steady simmer.

Bring a large pot of water to a boil. Add noodles and cook until tender, 5–7 minutes.
Drain and rinse noodles and add to stock.

Add wontons to stock and simmer until cooked through, 5–6 minutes. Stir in spinach and
cook until wilted, 2–3 minutes.

Ladle soup into individual bowls and serve immediately.

Mussels in spiced coconut milk broth

Serves 4

1 large yellow (brown) onion, sliced

3 cloves garlic

1 teaspoon ground coriander

1/4 teaspoon turmeric

2 small red chilies

1 stalk lemongrass, bottom 3 inches (7.5 cm) only, chopped

2 tablespoons lemon juice

1 tablespoon light olive oil

2 cups (16 fl oz/500 ml) fish stock (see page 589)

2 cups (16 fl oz/500 ml) coconut milk (see page 24)

2 teaspoons fish sauce

4 lb (2 kg) mussels in their shells, scrubbed

2-inch (5-cm) piece fresh ginger, very finely sliced lengthwise and julienned

1/2 cup (1/2 oz/15 g) fresh cilantro (fresh coriander) leaves

Combine onion, garlic, coriander, turmeric, chilies, lemongrass and lemon juice in a food processor and process to a fine paste, 2–3 minutes.

Heat oil in a very large saucepan, with a lid, over medium heat. Add paste and cook, stirring, until fragrant, about 5 minutes.

Add fish stock, coconut milk and fish sauce, increase heat to high and bring liquid to a boil. Add mussels, then cover saucepan tightly and cook, shaking saucepan occasionally, until all mussels have opened, 7–8 minutes. Discard any mussels that do not open. Add ginger and cilantro and stir to combine thoroughly.

Serve immediately in large bowls.

Octopus and squid laksa

Serves 4

1 tablespoon Asian sesame oil

3 tablespoons fish sauce

5 tablespoons (3 fl oz/80 ml) lime juice

1 tablespoon honey

2 small red chilies, finely chopped

1/4 cup (1/4 oz/7 g) finely chopped fresh cilantro (fresh coriander)

2 tablespoons finely chopped fresh mint

8 oz (250 g) baby octopus, trimmed of head and beak

8 oz (250 g) small whole squid, cleaned, trimmed and cut into rings 1/2 inch (12 mm) thick

1 tablespoon peanut oil

1 medium yellow (brown) onion, chopped

2 tablespoons grated fresh ginger

2 cloves garlic, finely chopped

1 tablespoon chili paste or sambal oelek

1 teaspoon ground coriander

1/4 teaspoon turmeric

2 cups (16 fl oz/500 ml) coconut milk (see page 24)

4 cups (32 fl oz/1 L) fish stock (see page 589)

8 oz (250 g) deep-fried tofu

4 sprigs mint

4 sprigs basil

1 small red onion, very thinly sliced

1 small cucumber, sliced and julienned

1 red chili (optional), sliced

1/4 cup (2 oz/60 g) crispy fried shallots (French shallots) (see page 24)

Combine sesame oil, 2 tablespoons fish sauce, 2 tablespoons lime juice, honey, chilies, cilantro and mint in a glass or ceramic bowl. Add squid and octopus, then cover and refrigerate. Allow to marinate for 3 hours.

Heat peanut oil in a large saucepan over medium–high heat. Add onion, ginger, garlic, chili paste, ground coriander and turmeric and cook, stirring, until onion is soft and mixture is fragrant, about 5 minutes. Add remaining lime juice, coconut milk, fish stock and remaining fish sauce. Bring liquid to a boil, then reduce heat to medium–low and simmer for 15–20 minutes.

Preheat broiler (grill). Remove squid and octopus from marinade and discard marinade. Grill squid and octopus until cooked through and tender, 3–4 minutes for squid, 4–5 minutes for octopus. Add squid and octopus to simmering soup and stir. Ladle into individual bowls and pile high with remaining ingredients, finishing with crispy fried shallots.

Penang-style seafood laksa

Serves 4

2 tablespoons peanut oil

1 medium yellow (brown) onion, sliced

2 tablespoons laksa paste (see page 578)

8 cups (64 fl oz/2 L) fish stock (see page 589)

$1/4$ cup (2 fl oz/60 ml) lime or lemon juice

7 oz (220 g) dried rice noodles

1 lb (500 g) firm white-fleshed fish fillets, skin and bones removed, cut into 8 pieces

8 oz (250 g) scallops or shrimp (prawns)

4 deep-fried tofu pillows, halved

5 oz (150 g) bean sprouts, trimmed

4 quail eggs, hard boiled, peeled and halved (or 2 hard boiled chicken eggs, peeled and quartered)

4 small sprigs mint

4 small sprigs basil

$1/4$ cup (2 oz/60 g) crispy fried shallots (French shallots) (see page 24)

Heat oil in a large saucepan over medium heat. Add onion and cook until it begins to soften, 3–4 minutes. Add laksa paste and continue to cook, stirring, until onion is soft and paste is fragrant, about 4 minutes. Add fish stock and lime juice, increase heat to medium–high and bring liquid to a steady simmer. Simmer for 10 minutes.

Meanwhile, place noodles in a large bowl and add boiling water to cover. Allow to stand until noodles are soft, 3–5 minutes. Drain, then rinse noodles in very hot water and set aside.

Add fish to laksa broth and simmer until cooked through, 4–5 minutes. Add scallops and tofu and cook for 1 minute.

Rinse noodles under very hot water, using a fork to separate. Spoon noodles into individual bowls and ladle soup over, piling fish and scallops in the center. Top with remaining ingredients, finishing with crispy fried shallots. Serve immediately.

Pork and noodles in broth

1-inch (2.5-cm) knob fresh turmeric, or
   3 teaspoons ground turmeric
1 1/4 lb (625 g) boned pork leg,
   preferably hock, shank or knuckle
1/4 cup (2 fl oz/60 ml) fish sauce
2 tomatoes, quartered or cut into wedges
4 cups (32 fl oz/1 L) beef stock (see
   page 588)
2 carambolas (star fruits), preferably
   slightly unripe, cut into 1/4-inch
   (6-mm) stars (optional)
1 tablespoon tamarind puree, or to taste
1 taro stem (Vietnamese rhubarb),
   about 4 oz (125 g)

salt to taste
12-oz (375-g) packet dried rice
   vermicelli
3 scallions (shallots/spring onions),
   including green parts, coarsely
   chopped

FOR ACCOMPANIMENTS
Soup Herbs (see page 437) including
   fresh cilantro (fresh coriander) sprigs,
   Vietnamese mint (rau ram) and bean
   sprouts
fresh long red chilies, sliced
2 lemons, cut into wedges

Using a pestle, pound turmeric in a mortar (alternatively, use a grater). Soak extracted juice and pulp in 1 tablespoon water, from 3–4 minutes up to a few hours; then strain. Cut pork into 1-inch (2.5-cm) cubes. Retain any rind, as this enriches the broth. In a bowl, combine fish sauce, turmeric and pork. Toss to coat (use a spoon, as turmeric will stain your hands) and let stand for 1–2 hours.

Pour meat and marinade into a large pot. Add tomatoes and stock. Bring to a low boil, then reduce heat to low and cover. Simmer until meat is tender, about 2 1/2 hours. Add more water if it cooks dry. Add carambola if using, and tamarind puree to taste. (The carambola will slightly sour the broth, so add more tamarind judiciously.) If using taro, peel stem by pulling upward at base. It should come away easily in ribbonlike strips; do not use a potato peeler. Cut taro into julienne, about 2 inches (5 cm) long. Lightly sprinkle with salt and leave for 5 minutes. Then press gently to remove any bitter juice. Rinse and press again, wipe with a damp cloth, then add to pot. Cook until barely tender, 2–3 minutes.

Prepare dried noodles as described on page 442, and set aside. Just before serving, plunge noodles momentarily into a pot of boiling water to reheat. Drain immediately, and divide among 6 large soup bowls. Ladle soup over noodles. Sprinkle with chopped scallions and serve, accompanied by soup herbs, chilies and lemon wedges.

Pork and spinach noodle soup

Serves 4

1 tablespoon light olive oil

1¹/₂ lb (750 g) pork tenderloin (fillet),
  trimmed of fat and sinew

2 tablespoons soy sauce

¹/₂ teaspoon ground white pepper

¹/₄ cup (2 oz/60 g) miso paste

8 cups (64 fl oz/2 L) water

1 lb (500 g) fresh thick egg noodles

6 oz (180 g) baby English spinach
  leaves

2-inch (5-cm) piece fresh ginger, peeled
  and julienned

1 small red onion, cut into very thin
  slices

Heat oil in a large cast iron frying pan over medium–high heat. Add pork and cook,
turning, until well browned, 8–10 minutes. Add soy sauce and white pepper. Remove
from pan and set aside. Place miso paste and water in a large saucepan over
medium–high heat and cook, stirring, until miso paste is dissolved, 4–5 minutes. Reduce
heat to low.

Bring a large saucepan filled with water to a boil, add noodles and cook until tender,
5–7 minutes. Drain, then add noodles to miso soup. Add spinach and cook until wilted,
about 1 minute. Cut pork into thin slices. Ladle noodles and soup into large bowls and top
with sliced pork, ginger and onion. Serve immediately.

Pork, somen noodle and scallion soup

Serves 4

8 oz (250 g) somen noodles

4 cups (32 fl oz/1 L) chicken stock (see
  page 588)

1 tablespoon dry sherry

1 tablespoon light soy sauce

6 scallions (shallots/spring onions),
  sliced

4 oz (125 g) Chinese barbecue pork,
  sliced

chili oil, for serving

Cook noodles in boiling water until tender, about 3 minutes. Drain and divide among
4 individual bowls. Place stock, sherry and soy sauce in a saucepan. Bring to a boil.
Reduce heat to low and simmer for 5 minutes. Add scallions and pork. Cook for
1 minute. Ladle soup over noodles. Serve chili oil at the table, to be added to taste.

Ramen noodle miso soup

Serves 4

1/4 cup (2 oz/60 g) miso paste

2 tablespoons rice wine vinegar

6 cups (48 fl oz/1.5 L) vegetable stock
(see page 590) or water

1 lb (500 g) fresh ramen noodles

2 tablespoons light olive oil

2 Asian eggplants (aubergines), about
4 oz (125 g) each, cut crosswise into
1/2-inch (12-mm) slices

1/2 lb (250 g) mixed green leaf
vegetables, such as baby English
spinach, baby bok choy, Chinese
spinach and snow pea (mange-tout)
sprouts, chopped if large

4 oz (125 g) mushrooms, such as
shiitake, button or oyster varieties,
chopped

5 scallions (shallots/spring onions),
sliced, for garnish

Combine miso paste, rice wine vinegar and stock in a large saucepan over medium–high heat. Cook, stirring, until miso paste is dissolved. Reduce heat to low and simmer gently while preparing the rest of the soup.

Bring a large pot of water to a boil, add noodles and cook until tender, 4–5 minutes. Drain noodles and set aside.

Heat oil in a frying pan over medium heat and cook eggplant slices on both sides until soft and golden, about 2 minutes per side. Set aside.

Add green leaf vegetables and mushrooms to simmering soup and cook until wilted and soft, 2–3 minutes.

Spoon noodles into individual bowls and ladle soup over noodles. Top with eggplant and scallions and serve immediately.

Roast duck and sweet potato soup

Serves 4

2 medium sweet potatoes

1 tablespoon plus 2 teaspoons light
 olive oil

2 large red onions, very thinly sliced

3 cloves garlic, finely chopped

2-inch (5-cm) piece fresh ginger, grated

8 cups (64 fl oz/2 L) chicken stock (see
 page 588)

2 small red chilies, thinly sliced

grated zest of 1 lime

1 Chinese roast duck, meat removed
 from bones

1 teaspoon fish sauce

2 tablespoons lime juice

freshly ground black pepper

1/2 cup (1/2 oz/15 g) fresh cilantro
 (fresh coriander) leaves plus 4 sprigs

1/2 cup (1/2 oz/15 g) small basil leaves

1/2 cup (1/2 oz/15 g) small mint leaves

Preheat oven to 400°F (200°C/Gas 6). Place sweet potatoes on an oven rack and bake until a skewer inserted through thickest part meets with no resistance, 30–40 minutes. Remove sweet potatoes from oven and set aside to cool. When cool enough to handle, remove skins and chop flesh into pieces.

Heat 1 tablespoon oil in a large saucepan over medium heat. Add half the onion slices, half the garlic and half the ginger and cook, stirring, for 3–4 minutes. Add chicken stock and bring liquid to a steady simmer. Simmer for 15 minutes. Reduce heat to medium–low and add chopped sweet potato. Cook for 2–3 minutes, then remove from heat and allow to cool slightly. Place mixture, working in batches, in a food processor and puree until smooth, about 3 minutes. Return pureed mixture to large saucepan and keep hot enough to serve.

Heat remaining oil in a large frying pan or wok. Add remaining onion, chilies, remaining garlic and ginger, lime zest and duck and cook, tossing and stirring, for 1 minute. Remove from heat and add fish sauce, lime juice, black pepper, cilantro, basil and mint. Stir until combined.

Ladle soup into individual bowls, top with the duck mixture and serve immediately.

Roast duck laksa with papaya and Chinese spinach

Serves 4

2 teaspoons light olive oil

$1/4$ cup (2 oz/60 g) laksa paste (see page 578)

2 cups (16 fl oz/500 ml) coconut milk (see page 24)

4 cups (64 fl oz/1 L) chicken stock (see page 588)

3 tablespoons lime juice

1 tablespoon fish sauce

1 Chinese roast duck (meat from breast and thigh bones removed and chopped, legs intact)

1 bunch small Chinese spinach, bok choy or choy sum, trimmed, or $3^1/2$ oz (100 g) baby English spinach leaves

1 small papaya, peeled, seeded and cut into $1/2$-inch (12-mm) pieces

1 small cucumber, peeled and sliced

1 medium red onion, finely sliced

4 tablespoons crispy fried shallots (French shallots) (see page 24)

8 small sprigs fresh cilantro (fresh coriander) or basil

Heat oil in a large saucepan over medium heat and add laksa paste. Cook, stirring, until paste is fragrant, 4–5 minutes. Add coconut milk, chicken stock, lime juice and fish sauce and cook for 15 minutes. Add more fish sauce for a saltier flavor.

Stir in duck and Chinese spinach and cook until duck is heated through and spinach is wilted, 2–3 minutes.

Ladle soup into individual bowls and top with papaya, cucumber, red onion, crispy fried shallots and cilantro sprigs. Serve immediately.

Salmon ball and Chinese spinach soup

Serves 4

1 lb (500 g) salmon fillet, skin and any
  bones removed, cut into 1-inch
  (2.5-cm) pieces

4 scallions (shallots/spring onions),
  green and white parts, finely chopped

1 tablespoon finely chopped fresh ginger

2 cloves garlic, finely chopped

1 small red chili, finely chopped

1/2 teaspoon white pepper

1/2 teaspoon sea salt

2 teaspoons finely grated lime zest

2 tablespoons finely chopped fresh
  cilantro (fresh coriander)

1 large egg white, lightly beaten

9 cups (72 fl oz/1.25 L) fish stock
  (see page 589)

1 tablespoon light olive oil

1 large red onion, sliced

2-inch (5-cm) piece fresh ginger, peeled
  and thinly sliced

1 large carrot, peeled and julienned

2 tablespoons lime juice

sea salt and ground white pepper

1/2 lb (250 g) Chinese spinach, bok
  choy, choy sum or baby English
  spinach, trimmed

Place salmon pieces in a food processor and process until fish is minced and forms a mass when a small amount is shaped, about 2 minutes. Place salmon in a bowl with scallions, ginger, garlic, chili, white pepper, salt, lime zest, cilantro and egg white. Mix until thoroughly combined. Line a sheet of parchment (baking) paper with waxed paper. Take a large teaspoonful of mixture and form it into a ball. Place on waxed paper. Repeat with remaining mixture.

Heat 1 cup (8 fl oz/250 ml) fish stock with 1 cup (8 fl oz/250 ml) water in a saucepan over medium–low heat. Bring mixture to a slow simmer. Add fish balls, 5 at a time, and simmer until just cooked through, about 4 minutes. Remove with a slotted spoon and set aside. Cover cooked fish balls loosely with plastic wrap so they do not dry out. Repeat with remaining fish balls.

Heat oil in a large saucepan over medium heat and add onion and ginger slices. Cook until onion begins to soften, 3–4 minutes. Add carrot pieces and cook for 2 minutes. Add remaining stock and lime juice and bring mixture to a steady simmer. Simmer for 15 minutes. Season to taste with salt and white pepper. Add spinach and fish balls and simmer until fish balls have heated through and spinach is wilted, about 3 minutes. Serve immediately, ladled into large bowls.

Seafood laksa

1¹/₂ tablespoons light olive oil

¹/₂ cup (4 oz/125 g) laksa paste (see page 578)

2 tablespoons lime or lemon juice

3 cups (24 fl oz/750 ml) coconut milk (see page 24)

3 cups (24 fl oz/750 ml) fish stock (see page 589)

6 oz (180 g) dried rice vermicelli noodles

12 oz (375 g) medium shrimp (prawns), peeled and deveined, tails left intact

16 oz (500 g) salmon fillet, cut into 8 pieces 1 inch (5 cm) thick

1 medium red onion, thinly sliced

1 medium cucumber, peeled and sliced

7 oz (220 g) bean sprouts, trimmed

5 oz (150 g) mustard cress shoots or snow pea (mange-tout) shoots

1 medium mango, 12 oz (375 g), peeled, seeded and diced

2 tablespoons small mint leaves

¹/₄ cup (2 oz/60 g) crispy fried shallots (French shallots) (see page 24)

Heat oil in a large saucepan over medium–high heat. Stir in laksa paste and cook, stirring, until fragrant, 4–5 minutes. Add lime juice, coconut milk and stock and stir until thoroughly combined.

Reduce heat to medium and simmer for 10 minutes. Place noodles in a large bowl and add boiling water to cover. Let stand until noodles are soft, 3–4 minutes. Drain noodles, rinse under warm water and set aside.

Add shrimp and salmon to soup and simmer until shrimp are cooked through and salmon is just cooked through, 3–4 minutes.

Rinse noodles under very hot water, using a fork to separate them. Spoon noodles into individual bowls and top with soup and seafood. Top with remaining ingredients, finishing with crispy fried shallots. Serve immediately.

Shrimp and coconut soup with hokkien noodles

Serves 4

1 lb (500 g) jumbo shrimp (king prawns)

1 stalk lemongrass, chopped, or 2 teaspoons grated lemon zest

1 carrot, peeled and sliced

1 stalk celery, sliced

1 onion, sliced

2 plum (Roma) tomatoes, chopped

1 bunch fresh cilantro (fresh coriander)

6 cups (48 fl oz/1.5 L) water

2 cups (16 fl oz/500 ml) coconut milk (see page 24)

$1^1/_2$ tablespoons red curry paste

1 teaspoon palm sugar or brown sugar

2 teaspoons fish sauce

8 oz (250 g) hokkien noodles

juice of 2 limes

Peel and devein shrimp; reserve heads and shells. Cover shrimp and set aside.

Place shrimp heads and shells in a large saucepan. Add lemongrass, carrot, celery, onion and tomatoes. Remove cilantro leaves from stems. Chop stems and add to saucepan; chop and reserve leaves. Pour in water. Bring to a boil, reduce heat to low, cover, and simmer gently, stirring occasionally, for 20 minutes. Strain through fine-mesh sieve. Measure 5 cups (40 fl oz/1.25 L) of stock.

Return measured stock to the saucepan. Stir in coconut milk, curry paste, sugar, fish sauce, noodles, lime juice, cilantro leaves and shrimp. Bring to a boil, reduce heat to low, cover, and simmer, stirring occasionally, until shrimp change color, 6–7 minutes.

Ladle into individual bowls and serve.

Shrimp, noodle and herb soup

Serves 4

2 lb (1 kg) shrimp (prawns), peeled, heads and shells reserved

2 tablespoons soy sauce

2 tablespoons lemon juice

1 large yellow (brown) onion, chopped

2-inch (5-cm) piece fresh ginger, sliced

4 fresh or 8 dried kaffir lime leaves

2 stalks lemongrass, cut lengthwise into 3 inch (7.5 cm) lengths each, or 4 strips
   lemon zest

sea salt to taste

8 oz (250 g) fresh egg noodles

$1/2$ cup ($1/2$ oz/15 g) fresh cilantro (fresh coriander) leaves

$1/2$ cup ($1/2$ oz/15 g) small basil leaves

4 cups (8 oz/250 g) chopped Chinese greens, such as bok choy, choy sum or
   English spinach

4 scallions (shallots/spring onions), thinly sliced, for garnish

Place shrimp in a glass or ceramic bowl and stir in soy sauce and lemon juice. Cover and refrigerate for at least 30 minutes. Place shrimp heads and shells in a large saucepan with onion, ginger, kaffir lime leaves and lemongrass. Add 8 cups (64 fl oz/2 L) water, place over medium–high heat and bring to a steady simmer. Simmer for 25 minutes. Add salt to taste. Strain and reserve broth. Discard solids.

Bring a large pot of water to a boil. Add noodles and cook until soft and cooked through, 5–7 minutes. Drain, rinse under very hot water and set aside.

Skim shrimp stock of any residue on surface and place in a large saucepan over medium–high heat. Bring to a steady simmer, then add noodles and shrimp and marinade. Reduce heat to low and simmer until heated through, about 1 minute. Add herbs and chopped greens and simmer until greens have wilted, about 1 minute.

Ladle into individual bowls and serve topped with sliced scallions.

Sour crabmeat soup

1 tablespoon light olive oil

2 medium red onions, sliced

2-inch (5-cm) piece fresh ginger, sliced

4 cloves garlic, finely chopped

2 stalks lemongrass, bottom 3 inches (7.5 cm) only, cut lengthwise into strips

1 small red chili, finely chopped

3 tablespoons lime juice

3 fresh or 6 dried kaffir lime leaves

8 cups (64 fl oz/2 L) fish stock (see page 589)

2 teaspoons fish sauce

1 lb (500 g) prepared crabmeat (picked from shells)

1 small red onion, very thinly sliced, for garnish

1 red chili, sliced crosswise, for garnish

Heat oil in a large saucepan over medium–high heat. Add onions and cook until onions begin to soften, about 3 minutes. Add ginger, garlic, lemongrass and chili and cook, stirring, until mixture is fragrant, about 3 minutes. Add lime juice, kaffir lime leaves, stock and fish sauce and bring mixture to a steady simmer. Simmer for 20 minutes.

Strain mixture through a fine sieve, discarding solids, and return liquid to saucepan. Heat over medium heat until it simmers, 2–3 minutes. Add crabmeat and simmer until heated through, 2–3 minutes.

Pour into individual bowls and serve immediately, garnished with slices of onion and chili.

Spicy crab and rice noodle soup

Serves 6

3 lb (1.5 kg) raw or cooked crab in its
shell, or 1¹/₂ lb (24 oz/750 g) lump
crabmeat, picked over for shell
6 cups (48 fl oz/1.5 L) water, or if using
precooked crab, Fish Stock or Quick
Seafood Stock (see page 589)
3 tablespoons vegetable oil
1 cup (4 oz/125 g) thinly sliced pink or
brown shallots (French shallots)

¹/₄ cup (2 fl oz/60 ml) Asian chili sauce
12-oz (375-g) packet dried rice noodles
1 bunch English spinach, stemmed and
rinsed well
2 tablespoons fish sauce, plus more for
serving
1–2 teaspoons salt, or to taste
freshly ground pepper to taste
1–2 lemons, quartered

If using raw crabs, scrub them with a scouring brush under cold running water, then
plunge them into a deep pot of lightly salted boiling water—about 6 cups
(48 fl oz/1.5 L). Cook for 10–15 minutes, depending on size. Remove crabs with
a slotted spoon, reserving cooking liquid. Clean crabs by pulling off apron flap from
under shell. Pry off top shell and rinse away breathing ducts or lungs. Break or cut body in
half, or cut large crabs into smaller pieces. Twist off claws, reserving pincers for garnish.
Refrigerate until ready to use.

In a small saucepan, heat oil over medium heat and sauté shallots with the chili sauce until
shallots are soft, 3–5 minutes; set aside.

Prepare dried noodles as described on page 442.

Bring 6 cups reserved cooking liquid from crab (or stock if using precooked crab) to a
rapid boil. Add remaining ¾ cup (3 oz/90g) shallots, spinach, crab and 2 tablespoons
fish sauce. Stir to combine, and taste; add salt if necessary. Remove from heat to avoid
overcooking the crab.

Immediately before serving, reheat noodles by plunging them into boiling water for
a moment, then draining them. Divide among warmed large, deep soup bowls. Ladle hot
soup over noodles, sprinkle with pepper, and add a dollop of reserved cooked chili sauce
to each. (This dish is traditionally served very spicy.) Serve piping hot, with additional fish
sauce to taste and lemon quarters on the side.

Note: *This dish is a morning-market specialty of Hue, Vietnam.*

Tom yam soup with vegetables

Serves 4–6

1 tablespoon vegetable oil

1 medium yellow (brown) onion, chopped

3 lemongrass stalks, bruised

2 cloves garlic, chopped

3 small red chilies, 2 whole, 1 seeded and finely sliced

2 kaffir lime leaves, finely sliced

7 cups (56 fl oz/1.75 L) clear vegetable stock (see page 589), simmering

1 teaspoon superfine (caster) sugar

pinch salt

2 tablespoons lemon juice

1 tablespoon tamarind paste, soaked in $1/4$ cup (2 fl oz/60 ml) water and strained

1 lb (500 g) canned straw mushrooms, drained and halved

4 scallions (shallots/spring onions), trimmed and finely chopped

2 tablespoons fresh cilantro (fresh coriander) leaves or holy basil, chopped

Warm oil in a large pot over medium–high heat. Add onion and stir-fry until onion begins to color, about 2 minutes. Add lemongrass, garlic, 2 whole chilies, and kaffir lime leaves and fry for 1 minute. Add vegetable stock, sugar and salt and simmer, uncovered, for 15 minutes.

Strain soup and transfer to a clean pot. Return soup to a boil and add lemon juice, tamarind water and mushrooms.

Divide among individual soup bowls for serving. Sprinkle with a combination of scallions, seeded and sliced chili and cilantro.

Udon noodle soup with sesame pork and fried enoki mushrooms

Serves 4

7 oz (220 g) dried udon noodles

1 tablespoon peanut oil

2-inch (5-cm) piece fresh ginger, peeled and grated

2 small leeks, white part only, thinly sliced

1 clove garlic, finely chopped

3 oz (90 g) fresh shiitake mushrooms, sliced

5 oz (150 g) button mushrooms, sliced

1 tablespoon soy sauce

1 tablespoon rice wine

6 cups (48 fl oz/1.5 L) chicken or beef stock (see Stocks, pages 588-591)

2 teaspoons Asian sesame oil

12 oz (375 g) pork tenderloin (fillet)

sea salt and white pepper

2 tablespoons finely chopped chives, for garnish

FRIED ENOKI MUSHROOMS

1/4 cup (2 oz/60 g) all-purpose (plain) flour

sea salt and freshly ground black pepper

1 1/2 cups (12 fl oz/375 ml) peanut oil, for frying

4 bundles (2 oz/60 g) enoki mushrooms, divided into smaller bundles of 2 or 3 mushrooms

Bring a large pot of water to a boil, add noodles and cook until tender, 7–9 minutes. Drain, rinse with warm water and set aside. Heat oil in a saucepan over medium–high heat. Add ginger, leeks, garlic and mushrooms and cook, stirring, for 4–5 minutes. Add soy sauce, rice wine and stock. Increase heat and bring to a boil, then reduce heat to medium–low and simmer until ready to serve.

Heat sesame oil in a frying pan over high heat. Add pork and cook, turning, for 4–7 minutes. Reduce heat to medium and continue to cook for a further 4–5 minutes. Remove pork, season and set aside for 5 minutes.

To make fried enoki mushrooms: In a bowl, combine flour with salt and black pepper to taste. Mix well. Heat oil in a large saucepan over high heat until a drop of flour sizzles rapidly when dropped in oil. Coat mushrooms in flour, shaking off excess. Fry mushrooms in hot oil until crisp and golden, about 40 seconds. Remove and drain on paper towels.

Cut pork into thin slices. Rinse noodles under very hot water, using a fork to separate them, and place in individual bowls. Pour soup over noodles and top with pork slices and fried mushrooms. Sprinkle with chives and serve immediately.

Vegetable and noodle soup (Buddha's delight)

Serves 4

4 oz (125 g) dried rice noodles

8 cups (64 fl oz/2 L) vegetable stock
(see page 590)

2 cloves garlic, chopped

1 piece of fresh ginger, about 1 inch
(2.5 cm), sliced

1 stalk lemongrass or zest of
1 lime, cut into 1-inch (3-cm) pieces

ground white pepper to taste

1 tablespoon soy sauce, or to taste

1 tablespoon lime juice, or to taste

8 oz (250 g) butternut squash
(pumpkin), cut into 1-inch (2.5-cm)
cubes

4 oz (125 g) green beans

8 baby sweet corn cobs

1 carrot, peeled and julienned

1 bunch (13 oz/400 g) baby bok choy,
leaves separated

1 green bell pepper (capsicum), seeded
and sliced

4 oz (125 g) snow peas (mange-tout)

1 tomato, cut into 1-inch (2.5-cm) cubes

2 sprigs fresh herbs, such as basil,
fresh cilantro (fresh coriander) or
chives

4 sprigs fresh mint, for garnish

chili paste or sambal oelek, for serving

Bring a large saucepan of water to a boil and add noodles. Remove from heat and allow to stand until soft, 4–5 minutes. Drain and divide among individual bowls.

Place stock in a large saucepan over medium–high heat, cover, and bring to a boil. Add garlic, ginger, lemongrass, white pepper, soy sauce and lime juice, reduce heat and simmer for about 1 minute. Add squash, beans, corn and carrot and cook until tender–crisp, about 2 minutes. Add bok choy, bell pepper, snow peas, tomato and herbs and cook until vegetables are tender, about 3 minutes.

Ladle soup over noodles and garnish with mint. Serve immediately with chili paste.

Vegetable laksa

Serves 4

4 tablespoons light olive oil

2 small red chilies, finely chopped

3 cloves garlic, finely chopped

2-inch (5-cm) piece fresh ginger, peeled and grated

1 stalk lemongrass, bottom 3 inches (7.5 cm) only, finely chopped

1 teaspoon ground coriander

1/2 teaspoon turmeric

1 teaspoon dark brown sugar

1/4 cup (2 fl oz/60 ml) lime juice

3 cups (24 fl oz/750 ml) coconut milk (see page 24)

3 cups (24 fl oz/750 ml) vegetable or chicken stock (see Stocks, pages 588-591)

4 medium yellow tomatoes, cut into quarters

8 oz (250 g) fresh thick rice noodles

2 medium Asian eggplants (aubergines), cut diagonally into 1-inch (2.5-cm) pieces

1 small green bell pepper (capsicum), seeded and cut into thin strips

1 small yellow bell pepper (capsicum), seeded and cut into thin strips

5 oz (150 g) bean sprouts

1/4 cup (2 fl oz/60 g) crispy fried shallots (French shallots) (see page 24)

Heat 2 tablespoons oil in a large saucepan over medium–high heat. Add chilies, garlic, ginger, lemongrass, coriander, turmeric and brown sugar and cook, stirring, until mixture is fragrant, 3–4 minutes. Add lime juice, coconut milk and stock. Increase heat to high and bring liquid to a steady simmer. Reduce heat to medium and simmer for 15 minutes. Add tomatoes and cook for 5 minutes.

Bring a large saucepan of water to a boil. Add noodles and cook until tender, about 3 minutes. Drain noodles and set aside.

Heat remaining oil in a heavy-bottomed frying pan over medium–high heat. Add eggplant slices in a single layer and cook until golden and cooked through, 3–4 minutes on each side.

Rinse noodles under very hot water, using a fork to separate them, and place in individual bowls. Ladle soup over noodles and top with eggplant, bell peppers, bean sprouts and crispy fried shallots.

Vegetable pho

Serves 4

6 cups (48 fl oz/1.5 L) vegetable stock
(see page 590)

6 cloves

4 black peppercorns

2-inch (5-cm) piece fresh ginger, peeled
and sliced

1 cinnamon stick

2 star anise

4 cardamom pods

1 tablespoon fish sauce

8 oz (250 g) green beans, sliced

8 oz (250 g) thick asparagus spears,
cut into 2-inch (5-cm) pieces

8 oz (250 g) dried rice noodles

6 oz (180 g) chopped Chinese greens,
such as bok choy or choy sum, or
English spinach

4 sprigs mint

4 sprigs fresh cilantro (fresh coriander)

chili sauce, for serving

fish sauce, for serving

lime wedges, for serving

Combine stock, spices and fish sauce in a large saucepan over medium–high heat and
bring to a steady simmer. Simmer until stock is infused with flavor, about 20 minutes.

Strain through a fine sieve. Discard solids, return stock to saucepan over medium heat
and simmer gently.

Bring a small saucepan of water to a boil. Add beans and asparagus and cook for
2 minutes. Drain, then set aside.

Place noodles in a bowl and cover with boiling water. Let stand until soft, about
5 minutes. Drain noodles and place in individual bowls.

Top noodles with Chinese greens, cooked beans and asparagus, and mint and cilantro
sprigs. Ladle stock into bowls.

Serve immediately, accompanied by chili sauce, fish sauce and lime wedges for each
diner to add according to taste. (Pictured on page 90.)

Vietnamese sour fish soup with turmeric

Serves 4–6

$^3/_4$-inch (2-cm) knob fresh turmeric, or
  2 teaspoons ground turmeric

4 tablespoons (2 fl oz/60 ml) fish sauce

1 teaspoon ground pepper

2 lb (1 kg) catfish, cut through the bone
  into $^3/_4$-inch (2-cm) steaks (cutlets), or
  about 20 oz (600 g) fish fillets

3 tablespoons vegetable oil

1 large leek or 3 baby leeks, white
  part only, well rinsed and thinly
  sliced, or 3 scallions (shallots/spring
  onions), including green parts, thinly
  sliced

2 small tomatoes, cut into wedges

1 tablespoon water

4 cups (32 fl oz/1 L) chicken or fish
  stock (see Stocks, pages 588–591)

1–2 carambolas (star fruits), preferably
  slightly unripe, coarsely cut

1 fresh long red chili, seeded and thinly
  sliced lengthwise

2 cups (4 oz/125 g) bean sprouts,
  rinsed and drained

$^1/_2$ bunch Chinese (flat/garlic) chives

$^1/_3$ cup ($^1/_2$ oz/15 g) very coarsely
  chopped eryngo (sawtooth coriander)
  leaves or 1 cup (1$^1/_3$ oz/40 g)
  coarsely chopped fresh cilantro (fresh
  coriander) sprigs

$^1/_3$ cup ($^1/_2$ oz/15 g) very coarsely
  chopped fresh dill

Steamed Rice (see page 28)

Soup Herbs (see page 437)

fish sauce or Nuoc Cham Sauce (see
  page 582)

Using a pestle, pound turmeric in a mortar; alternatively, use a grater. Soak extracted juice and pulp in 1 tablespoon water, from 3–4 minutes up to a few hours, then strain. Wear gloves to prevent turmeric staining your skin. In a small bowl, combine strained turmeric or turmeric powder, 3 tablespoons fish sauce and pepper. Coat fish pieces with sauce mixture and let stand at room temperature for 20 minutes.

In a medium pot, heat oil over medium heat. Add leek and stir, then cover, and cook for 2 minutes. Add tomatoes, remaining 1 tablespoon fish sauce and water, and stir. Cover and reduce heat to low. Cook until tomatoes are just soft, about 5 minutes. Add stock and bring to a boil. Add carambola, fish and its marinade, and half the chilies. Cook, increasing heat to high, until fish is opaque throughout, about 3 minutes for fillets and 5 minutes for steaks. Add bean sprouts, chives and herbs. Just before serving, garnish with remaining chili. Serve hot with steamed rice and an accompanying plate of soup herbs. Season to taste with fish sauce or nuoc cham sauce.

Chicken & duck

In Asia, as in many parts of the world, poultry is a favored meat source. There are infinite ways of preparing chicken, duck and other poultry, even in Asian cuisine alone.

Asia has, in fact, given contemporary world cuisine some of its favorite poutry dishes. For example, Chinese-style roast duck and soy chicken are now widely available from specialist Asian markets in most capital cities. These are cooked to perfection and ready to be enjoyed at home. And where would we be without tandoori chicken or chicken satay, both now appearing in sushi and sandwiches and on pizzas?

Many rural families in Asian countries still raise fowl at home, but in cities poultry is readily available from the local markets, where it can be bought live or butchered on the spot. In India and Thailand, where much of the population is vegetarian, poultry is less frequently consumed, but it is more popular than red meat. Conversely, in Muslim parts of Asia, where pork is not eaten, poultry is a mainstay.

Chicken is, of course, the predominant form of poultry in Asia. It is featured in spicy stir-fries and curries and fresh tangy salads, its portions delicately steamed, marinated and roasted, broiled or grilled. Duck, too, is immensely popular, and is also cooked in a huge variety of ways. Also found on the Asian menu are duckling, spatchcock and quail.

Chicken is one of the most economical and reliably available meats we can buy. It is also high in protein and other valuable minerals, low in calories (especially if the skin is removed), easily digested and versatile. All common forms of poultry, from duckling to partridge, can now be obtained from good butchers and even large supermarkets; a varied and convenient range of poultry cuts, including boneless breast and thigh fillets with or without skin, legs, wings and quarters, is also available. Poultry is also widely available fresh or frozen, free-range, corn-fed or organic, depending on your preference.

The recipes in this chapter are a combination of old and new, from authentic Thai roast duck and Indian braised chicken to quick cooking spicy skewers or stir-fries and salads. (See also chapters on Rice and noodles, Soups and Appetizers for more recipes with poultry.) Many of them use poultry in ways that are healthy and easy to prepare—typical of Asian cuisine. Recipes for poultry are very adaptable, and in many cases you can safely substitute both cuts and the types of poultry used. As always in this regard, Asian cuisine is very flexible.

Buying and preparing poultry

These days, most of us enjoy the luxury of buying our poultry already prepared and ready to cook, if not already cooked. However, with poultry, as with all ingredients, a good supplier is essential. Not only will you be assured of the best and freshest quality, but you'll be able to choose from a wide range of poultry types and cuts.

Cooking with poultry

Poultry is a very perishable food, and though easy to cook, it must be prepared with care. Frozen sections should be thawed before cooking, either at room temperature or in the refrigerator, and they should then be used immediately. Fresh poultry will keep in the refrigerator for 2–3 days. Care should also be taken to recook rather than just simply reheat frozen dishes that include poultry.

Preparing whole poultry

1. Rinse the inside and outside of the bird, for example a whole chicken, with cold running water. Drain and dry the bird thoroughly, but gently, with paper towels.

2. If using stuffing, spoon it into the body cavity, being careful not to pack it too tightly.

3. To truss, cut a length of kitchen string about twice the length of the bird. Tuck each wing tip under the back of the bird, and place the bird on its back. Slip the string under the wings, securing the wing tips to the body. Cross the string over the center of the back of the bird, then bring the ends under the drumsticks, returning the ends to the side. Tie the drumsticks together, wrap the string around the tail, pull tightly and tie to secure. Trim any excess string.

Cooking guide

You can use a thermometer to test the temperature of whole poultry and check if it is cooked. As a guide:

- 155°F (70°C) for chicken breast, 175°F (80°C) for chicken thigh
- 165°F (75°C) for turkey breast, 175°F (80°C) for turkey thigh
- 150°F (65°C) for duck breast, 175°F (80°C) for duck thigh

Alternatively, insert a thin skewer into the thigh joint of whole poultry; the juices should run clear if cooked.

If steaming poultry, the following cooking times can be used as a guide:

- Whole chicken, 3 lb (1.5 kg): 50–55 minutes
- Poussin or spatchcock, 12–14 oz (375–440 g): 30–35 minutes
- Boneless chicken breasts: 12–15 minutes
- Chicken legs: 15–20 minutes
- Chicken drumsticks: 12–15 minutes.

Allow 10–15 minutes extra cooking time for whole chickens with stuffing, or 5 minutes extra for stuffed chicken pieces.

Marinade for poultry

One of the simplest ways to prepare poultry is by marinating it before cooking.

- To make an Asian-style marinade for 1 lb (500 g) chicken or duck: Combine 2 tablespoons vegetable oil, 2 tablespoons Thai sweet chili sauce, 2 tablespoons lemon or lime juice, 3 chopped garlic cloves, 3 teaspoons grated ginger, 1 tablespoon chopped fresh cilantro (fresh coriander) leaves and salt and pepper to taste in a small bowl or screw-top jar. Coat poultry in marinade, cover and refrigerate for 10 minutes or more, then drain before cooking.

- To make a dry marinade: Combine the grated rind of 1 lemon or lime, 2 tablespoons chopped fresh cilantro (fresh coriander) leaves, 1 tablespoon chopped chervil and sea salt and freshly ground black pepper to taste. Brush poultry with oil, coat in marinade mixture then cover and refrigerate for several hours before cooking.

Buying Chinese-style duck and chicken

The convenience of being able to buy authentic Asian-style cooked chicken and duck cannot be overstated. Seek out a good quality Chinese deli, or "barbecue" store as they are often known, where these freshly cooked delicacies are often seen hanging in the window.

Chinese roast duck: May be purchased whole or by the half, chopped or not. Store in the refrigerator for up to 2 days. Use standard roasted duck or chicken in recipes if unavailable.

Chinese soy chicken: A glossy, golden chicken glazed in soy. Generally sold with a ginger dipping sauce. Store in the refrigerator for up to 2 days.

Andhra-style chicken pulao

Serves 10–12

5 cups (2 lb/1 kg) basmati rice

3 large yellow (brown) onions, halved
and thinly sliced

1/2 teaspoon salt, plus extra salt to
taste

7 fl oz (220 ml) vegetable oil and
melted unsalted butter combined

1 1/2-inch (4-cm) cinnamon stick

2 green cardamom pods

3 whole cloves

2 star anise

36 fresh curry leaves

2 1/2 lb (1.5 kg) chicken pieces or
1 whole 2 1/2-lb (1.5-kg) chicken cut
into 16 pieces

1 tablespoon finely grated fresh ginger

1 tablespoon finely chopped garlic

5 fresh green chilies, sliced lengthwise

1 2/3 cups (13 fl oz/400 ml) buttermilk

4 tomatoes, finely chopped

7 fl oz (220 ml) canned coconut milk

5 cups (40 fl oz/1.2 L) chicken stock
(see page 588) or water

1 cup (1 1/2 oz/45 g) chopped fresh
cilantro (fresh coriander)

1 lemon, cut into wedges, for serving

Preheat oven to 425°F (220°C/Gas 7). Place rice in a bowl and add cold water to cover. Swirl rice with your hand, let rice settle, then drain off water. Repeat six or seven times. Cover rice with water and set aside to soak for 20 minutes. In another bowl, combine onions with 1/2 teaspoon salt and set aside.

In a heavy deghchi or saucepan about 12 inches (30 cm) in diameter, heat oil and butter mixture over medium–low heat. Add cinnamon, cardamom and cloves, and cook until fragrant, about 30 seconds. Add star anise and half of curry leaves, and stir well. Add onions to pan and cook, uncovered, stirring often, until onions are dark golden brown, 10–15 minutes.

Add chicken pieces and cook, turning occasionally, until chicken is lightly browned, about 10 minutes. Add ginger, garlic, chili, remaining curry leaves, and buttermilk, and season with salt (not too much if using seasoned stock). Cook, uncovered, turning chicken occasionally, until chicken is cooked through and liquid reduces by half (liquid may look curdled), 10–15 minutes. Add tomatoes and coconut milk and cook, stirring often, until tomatoes are slightly soft, about 5 minutes. Add stock or water and mix well. Bring to a boil over medium–high heat.

Drain rice, add to pan and mix well. Cook, partially covered, until most of liquid is absorbed and steam holes appear in mixture, about 10 minutes.

Remove from heat and cover pan with a wet, clean kitchen towel. Cover tightly with lid, compressing towel around edge of pan. Bake in oven for 20 minutes. Remove from oven and set aside for 10 minutes. Sprinkle with cilantro and serve hot, accompanied by lemon wedges.

Baked chicken wings with noodle stuffing

Serves 4

3 1/2 oz (105 g) cellophane (bean thread) noodles

8 oz (250 g) ground (minced) chicken

1 teaspoon grated fresh ginger

1 clove garlic, finely chopped

2 teaspoons rice wine or dry sherry

1 tablespoon finely chopped fresh cilantro (fresh coriander)

12 large chicken wings

2 tablespoons soy sauce

1 tablespoon honey

cucumber slices, for serving

Sweet Chili Relish (see page 592), for serving

Soak noodles in boiling water for 10 minutes; drain. In a bowl, combine noodles, ground chicken, ginger, garlic, rice wine and cilantro an mix well. Preheat oven to 350°F (180°C/Gas 4). Oil a baking dish large enough to accommodate wings in one layer.

Using a small sharp knife, remove small drumstick from each chicken wing (and reserve for another use), leaving wing tip and middle section intact. Starting at top of middle joint (opposite end from wing tip), start gently separating skin from bone until you reach joint. Remove and discard bone.

You should now have wing tip with cavity of skin attached. Fill each cavity with about 1 tablespoon of chicken stuffing and close. Place into prepared baking dish. Repeat with remaining wings.

In a small bowl, combine soy sauce and honey and brush on wings. Bake until golden and tender, about 20 minutes. Serve hot or cold, garnished with cucumber slices and with chili relish for dipping.

Braised duck with pineapple

Serves 4

1 duck (about 3 lb/1.5 kg) or duck pieces
1/2 cup (2 oz/60 g) finely chopped brown or pink shallots (French shallots)
6 cloves garlic, finely chopped
about 1/2 teaspoon ground pepper
2 tablespoons fish sauce
2–3 tablespoons vegetable oil
3 cups (24 fl oz/750 ml) chicken or beef stock (see page 588)
2 tablespoons distilled rice alcohol or vodka
1 fresh pineapple, peeled, or 28-oz (850-g) can pineapple rings, drained
1 tablespoon sugar
1 teaspoon salt or to taste
1 tablespoon arrowroot or cornstarch (cornflour) mixed with 1 tablespoon water
fresh cilantro (fresh coriander) sprigs, for garnish
coarsely ground pepper, for serving

If using whole duck, begin by placing duck on a cutting board. Pull each leg away from body and use a cleaver or large chef's knife to cut through the joint attaching it to the body. Likewise, pull each wing away from body and cut through its joint. Cut duck carcass in half lengthwise by cutting through bones connecting breast and back. Remove and discard any large bones as necessary. Now cut down along backbone, turn over duck, and cut lengthwise through breastbone. You should have 8 pieces. Cut each section crosswise through the bones into bite-sized pieces.

In a large bowl, toss duck pieces with shallots, garlic, pepper and fish sauce. Let stand at room temperature for 1 hour or refrigerate overnight. Using a slotted spoon, transfer duck to a plate, reserving marinade. Pat duck dry with paper towels.

In a large frying pan or heavy pot, heat oil over medium heat. Add duck pieces, skin-side down, and cook until golden brown and all fat has been extracted, about 15–20 minutes. Drain off and discard fat.

Transfer duck to a heavy pot. Add stock, liquor and reserved marinade. Bring to a very gentle boil, then immediately reduce heat to low, cover, and cook at a bare simmer until tender, 20 minutes.

Meanwhile, cut fresh pineapple in half lengthwise, then into half-moons $\frac{1}{2}$-inch (1.2-cm) thick. Use a small paring knife to remove core. If using canned pineapple rings, cut in half crosswise. In a large, nonstick frying pan over medium heat, lightly brown pineapple pieces, sprinkling with sugar to create a light caramel glaze. Alternatively, use a large frying pan oiled with 1 tablespoon vegetable oil or butter, or vegetable oil cooking spray. Remove from heat and set aside.

When duck is almost done, add pineapple and taste for seasoning, adding salt if necessary. Cook for a few minutes for flavors to meld. Using a slotted spoon, transfer duck and pineapple to a bowl; cover to keep warm. Strain cooking liquid. If liquid appears greasy, lightly float paper towels on the surface to absorb fat.

Add arrowroot mixture to sauce. Bring to a boil, stirring. Spoon some of this sauce over duck pieces. Serve additional sauce alongside. Garnish with cilantro sprigs and sprinkle with coarsely ground pepper.

Butter chicken

Serves 10 as part of an Indian meal

2 lb (1 kg) chicken thigh fillets

1/4 cup (2 fl oz/60 ml) white vinegar
or lemon juice

1/3 cup coriander seeds

2-inch (5-cm) cinnamon stick, broken
into pieces

5 brown or black cardamom pods

10 green cardamom pods

1 teaspoon whole cloves

3 teaspoons ground turmeric

2 teaspoons chili powder

2 teaspoons paprika

1 teaspoon ground nutmeg

1 teaspoon ground mace

1/4 cup (2 oz/60 g) plain (natural)
yogurt

2 1/2 tablespoons finely chopped garlic

2 1/2 tablespoons grated fresh ginger

2 1/2 tablespoons vegetable oil

salt to taste

FOR SAUCE

1/2 cup (4 fl oz/125 ml) vegetable oil
and melted unsalted butter combined

2 lb (1 kg) yellow (brown) onions, or
about 6 medium, chopped

1 teaspoon salt, plus extra salt to taste

2 1/2 tablespoons grated fresh ginger

2 1/2 tablespoons finely chopped garlic

2 teaspoons chili powder

3 teaspoons ground turmeric

2 teaspoons chopped fresh green chili
peppers

2 lb (1 kg) tomatoes, chopped and
pureed in food processor

2/3 cup (5 fl oz/150 ml) heavy
(double) cream

1/4 cup (2 oz/60 g) unsalted butter

4 teaspoons honey

2 tablespoons dried fenugreek leaves

1/3 cup (1/2 oz/15 g) chopped fresh
cilantro (fresh coriander)

Cut chicken fillets into quarters. In a glass or ceramic bowl, combine chicken with
4 teaspoons vinegar, turning to coat. Set aside.

In a spice grinder, grind coriander seeds, cinnamon, cardamom and cloves to a powder.
Place in a bowl and combine with turmeric, chili powder, paprika, nutmeg, mace,
remaining vinegar, yogurt, garlic, ginger and oil, and mix well. Season with salt and add
to chicken. Mix well, cover and refrigerate to marinate for 30 minutes.

Preheat oven to 475°F (240°C/Gas 9). Oil a shallow roasting pan and arrange chicken
in a single layer. Bake, without turning, for 12 minutes. Remove from oven and set aside.

To make sauce: In a deghchi or large frying pan, heat oil and butter mixture over medium–low heat. Add onions and 1 teaspoon salt, and cook, uncovered, stirring occasionally, until onions are dark golden brown, 15–20 minutes. Add ginger and garlic, and cook, stirring, for 2 minutes. Add chili powder, turmeric and chili, and cook for 1 minute.

Add tomatoes and cook, uncovered, stirring often, until tomatoes are soft, 5–10 minutes. Add cream and butter to pan, and cook, stirring, until butter melts. Stir in chicken, honey and fenugreek, and cook, stirring often, until chicken is cooked through, about 5 minutes. Stir in cilantro. Taste and add salt if necessary. Serve immediately. (Pictured on page 150.)

Chicken and cashew nut curry

Serves 4

FOR SPICE PASTE

1 onion, coarsely chopped

1/3 cup (3 fl oz/90 ml) tomato paste

1/3 cup (2 oz/60 g) roasted cashew nuts

2 teaspoons Garam Masala
  (see page 575)

3 cloves garlic, chopped

1 tablespoon fresh lemon juice

1 teaspoon grated lemon zest

1/4 teaspoon ground turmeric

1 teaspoon sea salt

1 tablespoon plain (natural) yogurt

2 tablespoons vegetable oil

3 oz (90 g) dried apricots

1 lb (500 g) skinless, boneless chicken
  thighs, cut into strips 3/8-inch
  (1-cm) wide

11/4 cups (10 fl oz/300 ml)
  chicken stock (see page 588)

1/4 cup (11/2 oz/45 g) roasted cashew
  nuts, for garnish

1/4 cup (1/4 oz/7 g) fresh cilantro
  (fresh coriander) leaves, for garnish

steamed basmati rice (see page 28),
  for serving

To make spice paste: In a food processor, combine all ingredients and process for 30 seconds, or until smooth. Transfer to a small bowl.

In a wok or large skillet, heat oil over medium heat and fry spice paste until fragrant, about 2 minutes. Add apricots and chicken. Cook for 1 minute. Stir in stock, cover, and simmer over low heat until chicken is tender, 10–12 minutes. Spoon into serving bowls. Garnish with cashews and cilantro leaves. Serve with steamed basmati rice.

Chicken and vegetable hot pot (Mizutaki)

Serves 4

1 lb (500 g) chicken breast fillets, skin removed and cut into bite-sized pieces

6 Chinese (napa) cabbage leaves, coarsely sliced

$^1/_2$ bunch (6 oz/180 g) spinach

$^1/_2$ carrot, finely sliced

4 scallions (shallots/spring onions), cut into 3-inch (7.5-cm) lengths

$^1/_3$ daikon, finely sliced

9 oz (280 g) silken tofu, cut into $^3/_4$-inch (2-cm) cubes

6 oz (180 g) shirataki noodles, cooked in boiling water for 5 minutes, then drained

4 cups (32 fl oz/1 L) boiling water

1 teaspoon instant dashi

Nihaizu (see page 581), for serving

2 oz (60 g) grated daikon mixed with $^1/_2$ red chili, finely chopped

2 scallions (shallots/spring onions), thinly sliced

Arrange chicken, vegetables, tofu and noodles attractively on a large platter. This plate is placed on the table and ingredients are cooked in a large pot on a portable burner or in an electric frying pan.

Fill pot or frying pan two-thirds full with boiling water and add instant dashi. Bring stock to a boil.

When stock is boiling, add firm vegetables and chicken, then gradually add softer vegetables, noodles and tofu. Diners help themselves, retrieving ingredients and stock with chopsticks or serving spoons when cooked to their liking. Keep adding more raw ingredients to stock as more cooked items are removed. Give each diner a small bowl of nihaizu to which daikon–chili mixture and sliced scallions are added to taste. Diners dip vegetables and seafood into sauce bowl.

Note: *Mizutaki is a traditional Japanese dish.*

Chicken chettinad

Serves 8–10 as part of an Indian meal

2 lb (1 kg) chicken thigh fillets, cut into
  1-inch (2.5-cm) pieces
1/2 cup (4 fl oz/125 ml) buttermilk
2/3 cup (5 fl oz/150 ml) vegetable oil
  and melted unsalted butter combined
1-inch (2.5-cm) cinnamon stick
3 green cardamom pods, cracked
3 whole cloves
1 teaspoon powdered asafoetida
5 yellow (brown) onions, chopped
2 1/2 tablespoons grated fresh ginger
2 1/2 tablespoons finely chopped garlic

3–4 teaspoons chili powder
2 1/2 tablespoons ground coriander
4 teaspoons ground turmeric
salt to taste
8 tomatoes, chopped
1 cup (1 1/2 oz/45 g) chopped fresh
  cilantro (fresh coriander)
2 tablespoons crushed black peppercorns
18 fresh curry leaves
steamed basmati rice (see page 28), for
  serving

In a glass or ceramic bowl, combine chicken and buttermilk, and mix well. Place in refrigerator to marinate while preparing sauce.

In a large, heavy saucepan or karhai, heat oil and butter mixture over medium heat. Add cinnamon, cardamom and cloves, and cook until fragrant, about 30 seconds. Immediately stir in asafoetida, then add onions. Cook onions, uncovered, stirring often, until dark golden brown, 10–15 minutes. Add ginger and garlic, and cook, stirring, for 1 minute. Add chili powder, coriander, turmeric and salt to taste, and stir until fragrant, about 1 minute. Add tomatoes and cook, uncovered, stirring occasionally, until tomatoes soften and sauce thickens slightly, 10–15 minutes.

Stir in chicken and buttermilk and cook, stirring often, until chicken is cooked through, 5–10 minutes. Add cilantro, peppercorns and curry leaves, and mix well. Serve with steamed basmati rice.

Chicken donburi-style

Serves 2

1 cup (8 fl oz/250 ml) water

5 tablespoons soy sauce

5 tablespoons mirin

1 teaspoon instant dashi

1/2 teaspoon sugar

8 oz (250 g) chicken thighs, skin removed, cut into bite-sized pieces

1/2 large yellow (brown) onion, sliced

4 tablespoons chopped mitsuba

2 eggs, lightly beaten

2 cups (10 oz/300 g) hot cooked short-grain rice (see page 29)

1 scallion (shallot/spring onion), finely chopped, for garnish

nori, cut into thin strips, for garnish

Place water, soy sauce, mirin, dashi and sugar in a shallow frying pan with a tight-fitting lid. Bring to a boil, then add chicken and onion. Cover, reduce heat to low and simmer until chicken is opaque and onion is soft, 8–10 minutes. Add mitsuba and gradually pour eggs over liquid in pan. Tilt pan so eggs cover bottom. Cover and cook until eggs are almost set, about 1 minute. Remove pan from heat before eggs are completely set. To serve, place rice in individual serving bowls and top with egg, chicken and stock mixture. Garnish with chopped scallion and nori strips.

Chicken teriyaki

Serves 4

4 boneless chicken breasts, skin removed and trimmed of fat

1/2 cup (2 1/2 oz/75 g) all-purpose (plain) flour

2 tablespoons vegetable oil

1/2 cup (4 fl oz/125 ml) Teriyaki Sauce (see page 593)

2 cups (10 oz/500 g) hot cooked short-grain rice (see page 29)

1 teaspoon sesame seeds, toasted

Place each chicken breast on a cutting board and pound gently to flatten. Dredge chicken in flour. Heat oil in a frying pan over high heat, add chicken and brown well on both sides, about 4 minutes. Transfer chicken to a clean pan with teriyaki sauce. Bring to a boil, then reduce heat to low and simmer, covered, for 5 minutes, turning chicken three times, until cooked through. Remove from pan and cut into slices 1/2 inch (12 mm) wide. Serve with rice, topped with teriyaki sauce from pan and garnished with sesame seeds.

Duck and green chili curry

FOR SPICE PASTE

2 fresh green Thai or Anaheim chilies, coarsely chopped

1 onion, coarsely chopped

2 teaspoons ground turmeric

1 tablespoon ground coriander

1 tablespoon raw cashew nuts

2 teaspoons grated fresh ginger

4 cloves garlic, coarsely chopped

2 black peppercorns

2 tablespoons water

3 tablespoons vegetable oil

2 bay leaves

1 stalk lemongrass (white part only), bruised

$1/2$ teaspoon dried shrimp paste

1 lb (500 g) boneless duck or chicken breasts, with skin, cut into 1-inch (2.5-cm) cubes

1 cup (8 fl oz/250 ml) water

1 tablespoon tamarind paste

16 basil leaves

To make spice paste: In a food processor, combine all ingredients and process to a thick paste. Scrape into a small bowl.

In a wok or large skillet, heat 2 tablespoons oil over medium heat and fry spice paste until fragrant, about 1 minute. Add bay leaves, lemongrass and shrimp paste. Stir-fry for 1 minute, then add duck and stir-fry until opaque, 4–5 minutes. Stir in 1 cup (8 fl oz/250 ml) water, reduce heat to a simmer and cook until duck is tender, about 15 minutes. Remove from heat and stir in tamarind paste. Remove lemongrass.

In a small skillet, heat remaining 1 tablespoon oil over medium heat and fry basil leaves in batches. Using a slotted spoon, transfer to paper towels to drain. Spoon curry into serving bowls and garnish each serving with fried basil leaves. Serve with rice.

Duck in crispy fried wontons

Serves 4

10 scallions (shallots/spring onions),
white part only, cut into 2-in (5-cm)
pieces

2 carrots, peeled and julienned

1 Chinese roast duck

6 cups (48 fl oz/1.5 L) vegetable oil, for
deep-frying

16 wonton wrappers

$1/2$ cup (4 fl oz/125 ml) hoisin sauce

Using a sharp knife or scissors, make $1/4$-in (6-mm) cuts into ends of each scallion piece to
make fringe. Place scallions and carrots in a bowl of ice water. Refrigerate until scallions
curl, about 15 minutes. Remove meat and skin from duck and coarsely chop; discard skin
if desired. Heat oil in wok until it reaches 375°F (190°C) on a deep-frying thermometer or
until a small bread cube dropped in oil sizzles and turns golden. Working with one
wonton at a time and using two sets of tongs, hold wonton in taco shape and lower into
oil. Continue to hold wonton until golden and crisp, about 1 minute. Drain on paper
towels. Repeat with remaining wontons. Fill wontons with scallions, carrots and duck.
Drizzle with hoisin sauce and serve immediately.

Duck bread rolls with chili jam

Makes 4 rolls

4 scallions (shallots/spring onions), cut
in 4-inch (10-cm) lengths, discarding
dark green parts

4 dinner rolls or bagels

1 tablespoon hoisin sauce

4 Chinese (napa) cabbage or butter
lettuce leaves

1 carrot, peeled and cut into
matchsticks $2^1/2$ inches (6 cm) long

12 oz (375 g) sliced Chinese roast
duck meat and skin

$1/4$ cup Chili Jam, for serving
(see page 569)

Using a sharp knife, make $1/4$-inch (6-mm) cuts into green end of each scallion. Place in
a bowl of ice water. Refrigerate until scallions curl, about 15 minutes. Drain. Meanwhile,
preheat oven to 325°F (170°C). Wrap rolls in aluminum foil, and bake until heated
through, about 10 minutes. Remove from oven. Using a serrated knife, cut each roll three-
fourths open. Spread cut surface of each roll with hoisin sauce. Divide lettuce, carrot,
scallion, and sliced duck among rolls. Serve chili jam in a small bowl for dipping.

Duck stir-fry with long beans

Serves 4

1 Chinese roast duck

2 teaspoons vegetable oil

4 scallions (shallots/spring onions), chopped

1 tablespoon shredded fresh ginger

8 long beans, cut into 2¹/₂-in (6-cm) lengths

2 tablespoons shredded orange zest

2 tablespoons mirin

1¹/₂ tablespoons light soy sauce

steamed white rice (see page 28), for serving

Cut duck into serving pieces, leaving flesh on bone. Set aside. In a wok, warm vegetable oil over medium–high heat. Add scallions and ginger and stir-fry until softened, about 2 minutes. Add beans, orange zest, duck, mirin and soy sauce and stir-fry until heated through, 3–4 minutes. Serve hot, accompanied by steamed white rice.

Festive duck curry

Serves 4

1 tablespoon grated fresh ginger

4 cloves garlic, finely chopped

2 tablespoons rice vinegar

1 lb (500 g) boneless duck breast fillets, with skin, cut into strips ¹/₄-inch (6-mm) wide

2 tablespoons vegetable oil

1 onion, chopped

2 teaspoons ground cumin

2 teaspoons ground coriander

1 teaspoon chili powder

2 tomatoes, peeled and chopped

1 cup (8 fl oz/250 ml) chicken stock (see page 588)

1 tablespoon fish sauce

1 teaspoon ground pepper

2 tablespoons chopped fresh cilantro (fresh coriander)

steamed rice (see page 28), for serving

In a small bowl, combine ginger, garlic and vinegar. Put duck in a baking dish. Add ginger mixture and toss until well coated. Cover and refrigerate for 1 hour. In a wok or large skillet, heat oil over medium heat and fry onion 1 minute. Add cumin, coriander and chili powder. Fry for 1 minute. Add duck and marinade. Fry until duck is opaque, about 4–5 minutes. Add tomatoes and stir-fry for 3 minutes. Stir in broth, fish sauce and pepper. Reduce heat to low, cover, and simmer until duck is tender, 10–12 minutes. Stir in cilantro. Spoon into serving bowls and serve with steamed rice.

Green curry with chicken

Serves 4–6

2 cups (16 fl oz/500 ml) coconut milk
(see page 24)

1–2 tablespoons vegetable oil (optional)

1/4 cup (2 fl oz/60 ml) Green Curry
Paste (see page 576)

12 oz (375 g) boneless, skinless
chicken breasts, thinly sliced

1/2 cup (2 oz/60 g) chopped eggplant
(aubergine) or 3 round Thai eggplants

1/4 cup (1 oz/30 g) pea eggplants
(optional)

2 tablespoons palm sugar (optional)

2 kaffir lime leaves, stemmed

1/2 cup (1/2 oz/15 g) loosely packed
fresh sweet Thai basil leaves

2 tablespoons fish sauce

1 fresh long green chili, cut into large
pieces

1 fresh long red chili, cut into large
pieces

Let coconut milk stand, allowing the thick coconut milk to rise to the top. Spoon thick coconut milk into a small bowl, and reserve 2 tablespoons of this for garnish.

In a wok or large, heavy frying pan, heat thick coconut milk over medium–high heat for 3–5 minutes, stirring constantly, until it separates. If it does not separate, add optional oil. Add green curry paste and fry, stirring constantly, until fragrant, about 2 minutes.

Add chicken and cook until meat is opaque on all sides, 2–3 minutes. Add remaining thin coconut milk and bring to a boil. Add both the eggplants and simmer until slightly soft, about 4 minutes. If desired, add palm sugar to taste. Tear kaffir lime leaves and basil into pieces. Stir in fish sauce, lime leaves and half of the basil.

Remove from heat and transfer to a serving bowl. Drizzle over reserved 2 tablespoons coconut cream. Garnish with green and red chilies and remaining basil leaves.

Variation: To make green curry with shrimp, substitute an equal amount of shelled and deveined jumbo shrimp (king prawns), with tails attached. If using raw shrimp, add soon after the eggplants and cook briskly for 2 minutes; make sure the liquid is boiling when adding them, lest they turn mushy. Cooked shrimp should be added only during final minute of cooking, to heat through.

Green masala chicken

Serves 8–10 as part of an Indian meal

1 bunch fresh cilantro (fresh coriander), leaves and stems coarsely chopped

$1/4$ cup ($1/2$ oz/15 g) firmly packed fresh mint leaves

5 fresh green chilies, coarsely chopped

4 teaspoons grated fresh ginger

4 teaspoons finely chopped garlic

1 teaspoon coarsely ground black peppercorns

salt to taste

juice of 1 lemon

$1^1/2$ lb (750 g) chicken thigh fillets, halved

4 teaspoons vegetable oil

Preheat oven to 475°F (240°C/Gas 9).

Place cilantro, mint, chili, ginger, garlic, peppercorns and salt in a food processor. Process to form a thick paste, adding enough lemon juice to moisten ingredients. In a glass or ceramic bowl, combine paste with chicken. Mix well to coat chicken and set aside to marinate for 20 minutes.

Brush vegetable oil over a large baking sheet. Place chicken on sheet in a single layer. Bake, without turning, until chicken is cooked through, 20–25 minutes.

Grilled five-spice chicken

Serves 4

2 young chickens (spatchcocks), about
   1 lb (16 oz/500 g) each

1 teaspoon sesame oil

1 tablespoon rice wine

4 tablespoons peanut oil

1 teaspoon five-spice powder

1 teaspoon grated ginger

1 clove garlic, finely chopped

1 tablespoon honey

2 tablespoons soy sauce

1 bunch choy sum, about 16 oz (500 g)

1 red onion, cut into 8 wedges

Clean chickens and pat dry with paper towels. Using poultry shears, cut chickens in half through the backbones and breastbones and place them in a shallow nonmetallic dish. Combine sesame oil, rice wine, 2 tablespoons peanut oil, five-spice powder, ginger, garlic, honey and soy and mix until well combined. Brush mixture over chicken skin, then cover dish with plastic wrap and refrigerate for 3 hours. Drain chicken, reserving marinade.

Preheat a barbecue, then lightly brush grill with the remaining peanut oil. Grill chicken halves on barbecue until golden and tender, about 8 minutes each side, brushing with reserved marinade during cooking. Test chicken by piercing the thickest part with a skewer; chicken is cooked if the juices run clear. Remove from barbecue. Grill onion wedges until lightly browned, 1–2 minutes.

Steam or blanch choy sum in boiling water until tender-crisp, about 2 minutes; drain.

To serve, place some choy sum onto each serving plate, top with a chicken half, and garnish with red onion wedges.

Hint: This recipe is best suited to an outdoor barbecue. However, if only an indoor grill pan is available, grill chicken halves until golden, then bake in a 350°F (180°C/Gas 4) oven for 10–15 minutes to cook through. Otherwise, substitute chicken halves for chicken breast fillets.

Indian braised chicken

Serves 8–10 as part of an Indian meal

2 cups (1 lb/500 g) plain (natural)
  yogurt
1 teaspoon grated fresh ginger
1 teaspoon finely chopped garlic
1/2 teaspoon ground turmeric
1 1/2 tablespoons sesame seeds, ground
8 blanched almonds, ground
salt to taste
2 lb (1 kg) chicken thigh fillets, halved
  or quartered (as desired)

1-inch (2.5-cm) cinnamon stick, broken
  into small pieces
2 green cardamom pods
4 whole cloves
1/2 teaspoon black cumin seeds
1/2 cup (4 fl oz/125 ml) vegetable oil
  and melted unsalted butter combined
3 yellow (brown) onions, thinly sliced
juice of 2 lemons
steamed basmati rice (see page 28), for
  serving

In a glass or ceramic bowl, combine yogurt, ginger, garlic, turmeric, sesame seeds, almonds and salt. Add chicken and mix well. Cover and marinate in refrigerator for 1 1/2 hours.

In a spice grinder, grind cinnamon, cardamom, cloves and cumin to a powder. Set aside.

In a large, heavy saucepan, heat oil and butter mixture over medium heat. Add onions and cook, uncovered, stirring often, until dark golden brown, about 15 minutes. Stir in marinated chicken and mix well. Reduce heat to medium–low and cook, uncovered, turning chicken and stirring sauce occasionally, until chicken is cooked through, 20–25 minutes.

Stir in ground spices and lemon juice, and mix well. Simmer for 2 minutes. Serve with steamed basmati rice.

Japanese marinated crisp-fried chicken

Serves 4

$^1/_2$ cup (4 fl oz/125 ml) sake

$^1/_2$ cup (4 fl oz/125 ml) soy sauce

$^1/_4$ cup (1$^1/_2$ oz/45 g) finely grated fresh ginger

1 teaspoon garlic powder

1 lb (500 g) boneless chicken thighs, skin and fat removed, cut into 1$^1/_2$-inch
 (4-cm) cubes

1 cup (6 oz/180 g) potato flour

vegetable oil, for deep-frying

1 lemon, cut into 6 wedges, for serving

In a large bowl, combine sake, soy sauce, ginger and garlic powder and mix well. Add chicken cubes and stir to coat thoroughly with sauce. Cover with plastic wrap and marinate in refrigerator for at least 30 minutes but no longer than 1 hour. Drain chicken and discard marinade.

Pour oil into a deep, heavy-bottomed frying pan to a depth of 3 inches (7.5 cm). Heat oil until it reaches 375°F (190°C) on a deep-frying thermometer. Place flour on a plate. Working in batches, dredge marinated chicken cubes well in flour. Carefully slip into hot oil and fry until chicken is golden brown, 3–4 minutes. Using a wire skimmer, remove chicken from oil and drain on paper towels.

Place chicken on a warmed serving platter and serve with lemon wedges.

Korean chicken kabobs

3 lb (1.5 kg) chicken breast fillets
salt and freshly ground black pepper
vegetable or sunflower oil, for frying
sesame oil to taste
1 egg, separated
1 daepa or scallion (shallot/spring
onion), cut into 1¹/₂-inch (4-cm) pieces
4 bamboo skewers, 5 inches (12.5 cm)
long, soaked in water for 30 minutes
¹/₂ fresh red chili, seeds removed, cut
into thin strips

FOR SEASONED SOY SAUCE
5 tablespoons light soy sauce
2 tablespoons sugar
1 tablespoon malt liquid (mullyeot)
1 tablespoon ginger juice (obtained by
grating fresh ginger)
1 tablespoon rice wine
¹/₄ cup (2 fl oz/60 ml) water

Wash chicken breast fillets and pat dry with paper towels. Place each fillet between sheets of plastic wrap and pound to about ¹/₄ inch (6 mm) thick with a meat mallet. Cut edges of fillets with a knife tip every 2 inches (5 cm) or so to prevent fillet from curling and shrinking when cooked. Sprinkle with salt and pepper.

Heat 1 tablespoon oil in a frying pan until very hot but not smoking. Add chicken fillets and fry for about 2 minutes on each side. Remove from pan and set aside.

To make seasoned soy sauce: In a saucepan, combine soy sauce, sugar, malt liquid, ginger juice, rice wine and water and boil until thick.

Add chicken to saucepan and simmer for 10–15 minutes. Remove chicken from saucepan, add sesame oil and allow to cool. Slice chicken into strips 1¹/₂ inches (4 cm) long. Fry egg white and yolk to make egg gidan (see page 26). Remove from pan and slice into thin strips. Heat ¹/₂ teaspoon oil in a frying pan and fry daepa for about 30 seconds.

Thread chicken strips and daepa pieces alternately onto skewers. Leave about 1¹/₂ inches (4 cm) free at one end for holding the skewer.

To serve, arrange skewers on an oval plate and garnish with egg gidan and chili strips.

Korean marinated chicken drumsticks

Serves 4

5 chicken drumsticks
1 tablespoon ginger juice (obtained by grating fresh ginger)
1 tablespoon vegetable or sunflower oil
2 tablespoons light soy sauce
1 tablespoon sugar
1 tablespoon malt liquid (mullyeot)
1 tablespoon rice wine
1 tablespoon chopped parsley, for garnish
steamed rice (see page 28), for serving

Score drumsticks all over with tip of a knife to allow ginger flavor to penetrate. Place drumsticks in a medium bowl and drizzle with ginger juice. Marinate for 15 minutes, turning frequently to coat with juice.

Heat 1 tablespoon oil in a frying pan over medium heat. Add drumsticks and fry until golden, about 5 minutes. Remove and keep warm. Keep sauce in pan.

Add soy sauce, sugar, malt liquid and rice wine to pan juices. Boil over high heat until liquid is reduced by half, about 5 minutes.

Using a brush, coat drumsticks with the sauce. Return to frying pan and cook over high heat until sauce caramelizes and chicken is cooked, 5–8 minutes. Test with a skewer; chicken is done when juices run clear.

Transfer drumsticks to a serving plate and wrap the bone ends in foil. Garnish with parsley and serve as finger food with steamed rice.

Korean seasoned whole chicken

4-lb (2-kg) whole chicken, washed, dried and chopped into 2-inch (5-cm) pieces

1 large potato, peeled and cut into 1-inch (2.5-cm) cubes

1 large carrot, peeled and cut into 1-inch (2.5-cm) cubes

3 medium yellow (brown) onions, each cut into 8 wedges

1/2 lengthwise daepa or scallion (shallot/spring onion), cut into 1-inch (2.5-cm) lengths

1 egg, separated

1 tablespoon vegetable or sunflower oil, for frying

FOR SEASONING

3/4 cup (6 fl oz/180 ml) light soy sauce

1/4 cup (2 oz/60 g) sugar

3 tablespoons finely chopped scallions (shallots/spring onions)

3 tablespoons finely chopped garlic

2 tablespoons ginger juice (obtained by grating fresh ginger)

3 tablespoons rice wine

1 teaspoon sesame salt

pinch freshly ground black pepper

sesame oil to taste

To prepare seasoning: In a medium bowl, combine all seasoning ingredients. Set aside to allow flavors to blend.

Meanwhile, place chicken in a large pot and cover with water. Bring to a boil, skimming off any froth from the surface. Pour in half of seasoning mixture and continue boiling for 15 minutes. Add potato, carrot, onions, daepa and remaining seasoning mixture. Continue boiling until vegetables are tender but not mushy, 15–20 minutes. Test chicken by inserting a skewer in a piece of breast meat. Chicken is cooked when juices run clear. Remove from heat. Reserve liquid.

Fry egg white and yolk in oil to make egg gidan (see page 26). Remove from pan and slice into thin strips.

To serve, place segments of chicken in serving bowls, divide reserved liquid among bowls and garnish with egg gidan.

Korean-style fried chicken breast

Serves 4

10 oz (300 g) boneless chicken breast
3 tablespoons light soy sauce
2 tablespoons sugar
2 tablespoons rice wine
1 teaspoon ginger juice (obtained by grating fresh ginger)
1 tablespoon finely chopped garlic
1 daepa or scallion (shallot/spring onion), finely chopped
1 teaspoon sesame salt
pinch freshly ground black pepper
sesame oil to taste
vegetable or sunflower oil, for frying
lettuce leaves, for serving
steamed rice (see page 28), for serving

Wash chicken breast and pat dry on paper towels. Cut into bite-sized pieces, then score with the tip of a knife to allow seasoning to penetrate.

In a glass or ceramic bowl, mix soy sauce, sugar, rice wine, ginger juice, garlic, daepa, sesame salt, pepper and sesame oil. Add chicken and mix well to coat. Cover and refrigerate to marinate for 2–3 hours. The longer chicken marinates, the more intense the flavor and more tender the meat will be.

Heat 2 tablespoons oil in a frying pan until very hot. Add chicken pieces and stir-fry until golden, 3–5 minutes. Remove from pan and drain on paper towels.

Arrange lettuce leaves on a serving plate, top with chicken pieces and serve with steamed rice.

Hint: If you like your chicken spicy, replace the soy sauce with 3 tablespoons red chili paste and salt to taste.

Red curry with roast duck

Serves 4–6

Thai Roast Duck (see page 196), or
about 12 oz (375 g) roasted,
boneless duck meat

2 cups (16 fl oz/500 ml) coconut milk
(see page 24)

2–3 tablespoons vegetable oil (optional)

3 tablespoons Red Curry Paste
(see page 586)

3 kaffir limes leaves, stemmed

1 cup (1 oz/30 g) loosely packed fresh
sweet Thai basil leaves

1/2 cup (2 oz/40 g) fresh green
peppercorns on the stem, or
2–4 tablespoons canned green
peppercorns, drained

1 cup (4 oz/125 g) eggplant
(aubergine) cut into 1/2-inch (12-mm)
pieces, or 4 round Thai eggplants

1/2 cup (2 oz/60 g) pea eggplants
(optional)

1 cup (6 oz/180 g) fresh or canned
pineapple chunks, drained

6 cherry tomatoes

10 grapes

1 fresh long red chili, coarsely chopped

2 tablespoons fish sauce

2 tablespoons soy sauce

1 tablespoon granulated (white) sugar

1 tablespoon palm sugar

Bone and skin duck. Let coconut milk stand, allowing the thick coconut milk to rise to the top. Spoon thick coconut milk into a small bowl, reserving 2 tablespoons for garnish.

In a wok or large, heavy frying pan over medium–high heat, fry the thick coconut milk, stirring constantly, until it begins to separate, 3–5 minutes. If it does not separate, add the optional oil. Add red curry paste and fry, stirring constantly, until fragrant, 1–2 minutes. Add remaining thin coconut milk to wok, increase heat, and bring to a gentle boil. Add duck and simmer until heated through, about 5 minutes. Tear 2 kaffir lime leaves and basil into pieces. Add torn lime leaves, green peppercorns, both varieties of eggplants, pineapple and tomatoes. Reduce heat and simmer for 3 minutes. Add water, if necessary. Add remaining ingredients, reserving a few basil leaves and a kaffir lime leaf for garnish.

Transfer to a serving bowl, garnish with reserved basil and drizzle with reserved thick coconut milk. Roll the remaining kaffir lime leaf into a tight cylinder and cut into fine shreds; sprinkle over curry.

Hint: *You can use roast duck bought from Chinese delicatessens or Asian markets in this recipe.*

Roast duck and long-bean wraps

Makes 4 wraps

1/2 Chinese roast duck

1 tablespoon hoisin sauce, plus 1/4 cup (2 fl oz/60 ml), for serving

1 tablespoon orange juice

1 teaspoon soy sauce

4 scallions (shallots/spring onions), halved lengthwise

1 tablespoon vegetable oil

2 teaspoons grated fresh ginger

8 long beans (snake beans), cut into 3-inch (7.5-cm) lengths

4 pieces lavash or mountain bread

1/2 English (hothouse) cucumber, seeded and cut into 3-inch (7.5-cm) lengths

Remove meat from duck and discard bones. Slice meat and skin into strips about 3 inches (7.5 cm) long. In a small bowl, stir 1 tablespoon hoisin sauce, orange juice and soy sauce together. Set aside. Place scallions in a bowl and add boiling water to cover. Let stand for 1 minute. Drain and rinse under cold running water.

Heat oil in a wok over medium heat and stir-fry ginger and long beans for 2 minutes. Add duck meat and hoisin sauce mixture. Stir-fry for 1–2 minutes, or until duck is heated through. Remove from heat and let stand for 5 minutes.

Place lavash bread on a work surface. Spread duck stir-fry and cucumber evenly over bread. Roll each bread slice into a cylinder and tie at each end with a length of scallion. Cut each roll in half crosswise. Serve immediately.

Roasted chicken with Asian spices

Serves 4

1 chicken, 3 lb (1.5 kg)

3 tablespoons soy sauce

1 tablespoon peanut oil

2 teaspoons Asian sesame oil

2 tablespoons honey

6 star anise

3 cinnamon sticks

6 cardamom pods, bruised

3 cloves garlic, sliced

1 lime

steamed jasmine rice (see page 28), for
serving

Remove neck from chicken cavity and reserve. Rinse chicken inside and out with cold running water and pat thoroughly dry with paper towels. Tuck wing tips under and truss legs with dampened string. Place chicken on shallow platter with neck.

In small bowl, combine soy sauce, oils, honey, star anise, cinnamon, cardamom and garlic to make a marinade. Brush marinade over chicken. Cover and refrigerate for 1 hour.

Preheat oven to 400°F (200°C/Gas 6). Place flat rack in roasting pan. Stack 2 large sheets parchment (baking) paper on rack. Remove chicken from platter, reserving marinade, and place in center of paper. Slip neck alongside. Brush chicken with reserved marinade. Using vegetable peeler, remove lime zest in single long, narrow strip, allowing it to fall onto the breast of chicken. Bring parchment up and over chicken and fold edges over to enclose bird completely. Secure closed with bamboo skewers that have been soaked in water for 30 minutes, or with staples.

Roast chicken until thermometer inserted in thickest part of thigh away from bone registers 175°F (80°C), 50–55 minutes. Alternatively, pierce thigh joint with thin skewer; chicken is ready when juices run clear. Remove chicken to carving board, cover loosely with parchment from pan, and let rest for at least 10 minutes before carving.

Carve chicken, arrange on platter, and serve hot or at room temperature with steamed jasmine rice.

Roasted duck legs with ginger and soba noodles

Serves 4

4 whole duck legs, about $^1/_2$ lb (250 g) each

$^1/_2$ cup ($^1/_4$ lb/125 g) finely grated fresh ginger

7 tablespoons ($3^1/_2$ fl oz/105 ml) mirin

$^1/_4$ cup (2 fl oz/60 ml) rice vinegar

2 teaspoons soy sauce

3 English (hothouse) or Lebanese cucumbers, thinly sliced crosswise

1 teaspoon salt, plus extra for cooking noodles

3 oz (90 g) dried soba noodles

2 tablespoons sliced pink pickled ginger

2 tablespoons finely chopped fresh chives

Preheat oven to 350°F (180°C/Gas 4). Place duck legs in roasting pan just large enough to accommodate them and sprinkle evenly with fresh ginger, mirin, vinegar and soy sauce. Cover with aluminum foil, place in oven, and roast for 45 minutes. Remove foil and continue roasting until skin is crisp and dark brown, about 20 minutes longer.

While duck is roasting, combine cucumbers and 1 teaspoon salt in a bowl. Mix well, cover, and set aside for 30 minutes. Bring large saucepan filled with salted water to boil over high heat, add noodles, and cook until just tender, about 4 minutes. Drain noodles in colander and rinse well under cold running water. Set aside.

Gently squeeze excess water from cucumbers and place in a clean bowl. Add pickled ginger and mix until well combined.

Remove duck legs from oven and divide among warmed dinner plates. Sprinkle chives evenly over duck legs. Place one-fourth of noodles and cucumbers alongside each duck leg and serve immediately.

Soy chicken fresh spring rolls

Makes 4 rolls

1 oz (30 g) cellophane (bean thread) noodles

1 tablespoon dried shrimp, finely chopped or ground in a mortar and pestle

8 cherry tomatoes, quartered

$1/2$ red onion, thinly sliced

1–2 red bird's eye chilies, seeded and chopped to taste

2 tablespoons shredded fresh basil

2 tablespoons roasted peanuts

8 oz (250 g) boneless Chinese soy chicken and skin

8 round rice paper wrappers (8 inches/20 cm in diameter)

4 butter (Boston) lettuce leaves

1 tablespoon crispy fried shallots (French shallots) (see page 24)

Lime, Ginger and Mirin Dipping Sauce (see page 579)

FOR DRESSING

1 tablespoon fresh lime juice

1 tablespoon fish sauce

1 teaspoon tamarind paste

2 teaspoons superfine (caster) sugar

Put noodles in a bowl and add boiling water to cover. Let soak for 10 minutes. Drain. Using scissors, coarsely cut noodles into shorter lengths. In a bowl, combine shrimp, tomatoes, onion, chili, basil, peanuts and noodles. Stir until well combined.

Cut chicken meat and skin into thin strips about $2^{1}/2$ inches (6 cm) long. Combine all dressing ingredients in a screw-top jar and shake to mix. Add chicken and dressing to noodle mixture. Toss to combine. Cover and refrigerate for at least 30 minutes (up to 1 hour).

Remove about 2 inches (5 cm) of center stem from each lettuce leaf. Fill a medium bowl with warm water and place a kitchen towel on your work surface. For each roll, dip 2 rice paper wrappers into water for until soft, about 15 seconds. Stack wrappers on kitchen towel. Arrange a lettuce leaf on one side of rice paper. Spoon over one-fourth of chicken mixture. Sprinkle with fried shallots and spread mixture over lettuce leaf. Starting at lettuce side of wrapper, roll into a cylinder. Cover prepared rolls with a damp kitchen towel to prevent drying out. Repeat with remaining wrappers and filling.

Using a sharp knife, cut each roll into 2–3 slices. Serve with dipping sauce.

Spicy chicken skewers with mint raita

Serves 4

1 lb (500 g) chicken breast fillets

3 teaspoons ground coriander

2 teaspoons ground turmeric

1 small red chili, seeded and finely chopped

4 cloves garlic, finely chopped

2 tablespoons superfine (caster) sugar

1 teaspoon sea salt

12 bamboo skewers

2 tablespoons peanut oil

6$^1\!/_2$ oz (200 g) choy sum or other Asian greens, roughly chopped

Mint Raita (see page 580), for serving

Cut chicken fillets into 1$^1\!/_2$-inch (4-cm) cubes. In a bowl, combine ground coriander, turmeric, chili, garlic, sugar and salt. Toss chicken pieces in spice mixture. Cover bowl with plastic wrap and refrigerate for 2 hours.

Soak bamboo skewers in water for 10 minutes, then drain. Thread chicken pieces onto bamboo skewers.

Preheat a grill pan or barbecue, then brush grill with oil. Grill chicken skewers until golden and tender, 2–3 minutes each side.

Steam or blanch choy sum in boiling water for 3 minutes or until tender-crisp, then drain.

Serve chicken skewers warm with mint raita and choy sum.

Stir-fried chicken with chili and ginger

Serves 4–6

1 cup (2 oz/60 g) cloud or tree ear mushrooms (black or white fungus)

¹/₄ cup (2 fl oz/60 ml) vegetable oil

6 cloves garlic, coarsely chopped

1 small onion, thinly sliced

12 oz (375 g) boneless, skinless chicken breasts, thinly sliced

1 cup (4 oz/125 g) loosely packed, julienned fresh ginger, preferably young ginger

1 tablespoon fish sauce

3 tablespoons oyster sauce

1 tablespoon soy sauce

1 tablespoon soybean paste

2 fresh long red chilies, cut into large pieces

¹/₂ cup (4 fl oz/125 ml) chicken stock (see page 588) or water

8 scallions (shallots/spring onions), white part only, chopped

If using dried mushrooms, soak in water for 10 minutes, then drain. Use scissors to trim hard core, then cut mushrooms into pieces.

Heat oil in a wok or large, heavy frying pan over high heat and fry garlic just until it starts to brown. Immediately add onion and chicken, and stir-fry until meat is opaque on all sides, about 2 minutes.

Add ginger and mushrooms, then fish sauce, oyster sauce, soy sauce and soybean paste. Stir-fry for 1 minute. Add chilies and stock, bring to a boil, and cook for 1 minute. Stir in scallions.

Transfer to a serving dish and serve.

Note: This is a classic Thai-style stir-fry. If cloud or tree ear mushrooms are unavailable, use an equal quantity of straw mushrooms or standard mushrooms.

Sweet chicken wings

Serves 4

6 chicken wings, wing tips removed

pinch sesame salt

1 tablespoon ginger juice (obtained by
grating fresh ginger)

1/4 cup (1 oz/30 g) cornstarch
(cornflour)

1 1/2 cups vegetable or sunflower oil,
for frying

sesame oil to taste

steamed rice (see page 28), for serving

FOR SWEET SAUCE

2 tablespoons light soy sauce

1 tablespoon malt liquid (mullyeot)

1 tablespoon sugar

1 teaspoon ginger juice (obtained by
grating fresh ginger)

1 tablespoon rice wine

3 tablespoons water

5 whole cloves garlic

2 red chilies, halved lengthwise, seeds
removed

2 green chilies, halved lengthwise,
seeds removed

Wash chicken wings and pat dry with paper towels.

Combine sesame salt and ginger juice in a bowl, then add chicken wings. Mix well to
coat in juice. Remove wings and coat with cornstarch.

Heat oil in a wok or deep frying pan until very hot. Fry wings until golden, about
10 minutes. Remove from oil and drain on paper towels.

To make sweet sauce: Combine soy sauce, malt liquid, sugar, ginger juice, rice wine and
water in a medium saucepan and bring to a boil. Add garlic and red and green chilies
and stir in well. Continue boiling the sauce until it is reduced by half.

Add chicken wings to saucepan and mix to coat with sauce. Transfer chicken wings,
garlic and chilies to a serving plate, sprinkle with sesame oil and serve with steamed rice.

Note: This traditional Korean recipe uses chicken wings, but the seasoning goes
well with any type of poultry.

Tandoori-style chicken

4 chicken legs
4 chicken thighs
3/4 cup (6 oz/180 g) plain (natural) yogurt
1 teaspoon Garam Masala (see page 575)
2 teaspoons grated fresh ginger
6 cloves garlic, finely chopped
1/4 teaspoon ground turmeric
1 teaspoon ground coriander
1 tablespoon fresh lemon juice
1/4 teaspoon Chinese powdered red food coloring (see Glossary)
pinch sea salt
1 tablespoon vegetable oil
2 limes, quartered

Using a sharp knife, make 2 slits in skin side of each chicken piece. Place chicken pieces in a baking dish. In a small bowl, combine yogurt, garam masala, ginger, garlic, turmeric, coriander, lemon juice, red coloring, salt and oil. Mix well. Pour over chicken pieces and toss to coat chicken. Cover and refrigerate for 2 hours.

Remove chicken from refrigerator 30 minutes before roasting. Preheat oven to 425°F (220°C/Gas 7). Transfer chicken to a roasting pan. Roast for 25 minutes, or until juices run clear when the chicken is pierced with a sharp knife. Remove from oven. Serve immediately, with lime wedges.

Thai chicken salad (Larb)

Serves 4–6

2 tablespoons sticky (glutinous) rice

2 thin slices fresh galangal

12 oz (375 g) boneless, skinless chicken breasts, ground (minced)

2 tablespoons thinly sliced shallots (French shallots), preferably pink

3 tablespoons fish sauce

2 tablespoons fresh lime juice

2–3 teaspoons chili powder

1 tablespoon coarsely chopped fresh cilantro (fresh coriander) leaves and stems

1 scallion (shallot/spring onion), including green part, coarsely chopped

1 tablespoon coarsely chopped fresh mint

In a wok or small frying pan over low–medium heat, stir rice until golden brown, 3–5 minutes. Transfer to a mortar and pound to a coarse powder with a pestle. Transfer to a bowl and set aside. Pound galangal in the mortar until pulverized.

In a medium bowl, combine ground chicken, galangal, shallots, fish sauce, lime juice, and chili powder to taste; mix thoroughly. Heat a wok or large, heavy frying pan over medium heat and add chicken mixture all at once, stirring vigorously to keep it from sticking into lumps. Cook until opaque throughout, about 5 minutes.

Transfer to a bowl and let cool slightly, then toss with ground rice and all remaining ingredients. If desired, garnish with additional mint leaves, and accompany with vegetable crudités, such as cabbage, carrot, cucumber and long (snake) beans.

Hint: *Ask your butcher to grind the chicken, or do it yourself in a food processor.*

Variation: *To make larb with pork, substitute an equal quantity of ground pork for chicken, and cook as above.*

Thai roast duck (Ped yang)

Serves 4

1 whole duck (about 4 lb/2 kg)

¼ cup (2 fl oz/60 ml) sweet (thick) soy sauce

½ cup (2 1/2 oz/75 g) coarsely sliced fresh ginger

¼ cup (2 fl oz/60 ml) soybean paste (bean sauce)

¼ cup (2 fl oz/60 ml) oyster sauce

6 cloves garlic, crushed

8 fresh cilantro (fresh coriander) roots, or 2 tablespoons coarsely chopped stems

Lightly prick duck skin all over with a fork. Using hands or a pastry brush, coat duck with sweet soy sauce. Let stand to marinate at room temperature for 1 hour, or overnight, covered, in the refrigerator. Preheat oven to 400°F (200°C/Gas 7).

In a small bowl, combine all remaining ingredients, and stir well. Spoon into duck's cavity. Skewer with a toothpick to close cavity. Place duck, breast side up, on a rack in a roasting pan on the lowest shelf of the oven, and roast for 10 minutes. Reduce heat to 350°F (180°C/Gas 4) and roast, turning once, for about 1 hour, or until a leg moves easily in its socket. If duck is over-browning, loosely cover with aluminum foil. Remove from oven and let rest for at least 15 minutes before carving.

When ready to serve, remove and discard stuffing and chop duck into small pieces. This is done easily using a cleaver, cutting through bones, as opposed to carving meat away from the carcass.

Note: In Thailand, duck is eaten well done, though not falling from the bones. When using this meat in another recipe, the duck should be slightly firm, as it will continue cooking in sauce.

Variation: To make Thai roasted duck breasts, prick the skin of 4–6 duck breast halves lightly with a fork. Coat breasts with stuffing (above). Let stand at room temperature for at least 1 hour. Preheat oven to 400°F (200°C/Gas 6). Scrape off stuffing from duck and coat each breast with a spoonful of sweet soy sauce. Place in oven, reduce heat to 350°F (180°C/Gas 4), and roast for 40–50 minutes. Remove from heat and let cool before serving.

Vietnamese chicken salad with herbs

Serves 6

FOR PICKLED ONIONS

1 tablespoon rice vinegar or distilled
   white vinegar

1 teaspoon sugar

2 tablespoons fish sauce

1 lb (500 g) pearl onions or small boiling
   onions (pickling onions) (see Hint)

1 lb (500 g) boneless, skinless chicken
   thighs and/or breasts, or about
   3 cups (18 oz/550 g) coarsely
   shredded cooked chicken, bones and
   skin removed

about 3 cups (24 fl oz/750 ml) water
   or stock for cooking chicken, if
   required

2 cups (4 oz/125 g) bean sprouts,
   rinsed and drained

leaves from 1/2 bunch Vietnamese mint
   (rau ram)

3 fresh long red chilies, seeded and
   coarsely chopped

juice of 3 limes, freshly squeezed

1 teaspoon salt

1/2 teaspoon ground pepper

chilies, for garnish (optional)

To make pickled onions: Plunge pearl onions into boiling water, then drain and slip off the skins. If using pickling onions, peel and quarter. In a medium bowl, combine vinegar, sugar and fish sauce. Add onion and let stand for 10–15 minutes.

If using raw chicken, bring water to a boil in a medium saucepan and add chicken. Immediately reduce heat to a low simmer and cook chicken until opaque throughout, 5–7 minutes. Transfer to a plate and let cool. Shred with your fingers or 2 forks into coarse long shreds. Set aside.

Plunge sprouts in a pot of boiling water, then drain immediately and refresh in cold water. Roll several Vietnamese mint leaves at a time into a tight bundle and cut into thin crosswise slices. Repeat to shred all leaves. At the last moment, in a bowl, toss together onions and their marinade, chicken, bean sprouts, Vietnamese mint and chilies. Season with lime juice, salt and pepper. If desired, garnish with chilies.

Hint: Jars of prepared sweet pickled leeks (cu kieu) are available in Vietnamese markets and some Asian markets. These are time-saving; use in place of pickled onions in this recipe.

Warm tandoori chicken wraps

1/3 cup (3 fl oz/80 ml) plain tandoori paste

2 tablespoons plus 1/2 cup (4 oz/125 g) plain (natural) yogurt

grated zest and juice of 1 lemon

12 chicken tenderloin fillets or 3 skinless, boneless chicken breast fillets

2 carrots

1 English (hothouse) cucumber, halved and seeded

1 clove garlic, finely chopped

2 tablespoons finely chopped fresh mint

6 pieces naan (see page 467), warmed

leaves from 6 fresh mint sprigs

In a small bowl, combine tandoori paste, 2 tablespoons yogurt, lemon zest and juice. Put chicken in a baking dish. Pour tandoori mixture over and stir until chicken is coated. Cover and refrigerate for 2 hours.

Light a fire in a charcoal grill or heat a grill pan. Brush grill or pan lightly with oil. Cook chicken until juices run clear when pierced with a skewer, 4–5 minutes on each side. Transfer to a cutting board and let rest for 5 minutes. Cut each tenderloin into 2 long strips (if using chicken breast fillets, slice each fillet into 4 long strips).

Using a vegetable peeler, cut carrot and cucumber into thin ribbons. In a small bowl, stir 1/2 cup (4 oz/125 g) yogurt, garlic and finely chopped mint together.

Place naan pieces on a work surface. Divide chicken, carrot, cucumber and mint leaves among naan pieces. Drizzle with yogurt mixture. Wrap naan around filling and serve immediately.

Yakitori chicken skewers

Serves 4

1 lb (500 g) boneless chicken thighs
5 thick scallions (shallots/spring onions), cut into 1-inch (2.5-cm) pieces
bamboo skewers
1/4 cup (2 fl oz/60 ml) soy sauce
3 tablespoons brown sugar
1 teaspoon concentrated chicken stock

Remove skin from chicken and cut meat into 1 1/4-inch (3-cm) cubes.

Thread 4 or 5 chicken cubes and 3 or 4 scallion pieces onto each skewer.

In a saucepan over medium heat, combine soy sauce, sugar and stock and bring to a boil. Allow sauce to simmer for 3 minutes, stirring constantly, then remove from heat.

Preheat a broiler (grill). Brush a broiler (grill) pan with oil and lay skewers on pan. Broil (grill), turning several times, until cooked through, 8–10 minutes, depending on thickness and heat level. Make a cut in thickest part of meat to check meat is no longer pink. Brush chicken with sauce. Continue to turn over the chicken skewers and brush with the sauce over a low–medium heat for a few more minutes. Take care not to burn chicken.

Remove chicken skewers from broiler and place on a warmed serving plate. Serve hot.

Hints: Bamboo skewers need to be soaked in water for 10 minutes before using in this recipe. This prevents the skewers from burning while food is cooking. Alternatively, use metal skewers. To make appetizer-sized chicken yakitori, use small skewers and thread 2–3 chicken pieces on each one.

Yellow curry with chicken

Serves 4–6

2 medium potatoes, peeled and cut into $1/2$-inch (12-mm) pieces

2 cups (16 fl oz/500 ml) coconut milk (see page 24)

2–3 tablespoons vegetable oil (optional)

$1/4$ cup (2 fl oz/60 ml) Yellow Curry Paste (see page 595)

1 teaspoon curry powder

12 oz (375 g) boneless, skinless chicken breasts, thinly sliced

2 tablespoons palm sugar

2–3 tablespoons soy sauce

Adjat Sauce (see page 566), for serving

Cook potatoes in a saucepan of salted boiling water until barely tender, 3–5 minutes; drain and set aside. Let coconut milk stand, allowing the thick coconut milk to rise to the top. Spoon thick coconut milk into a small bowl, and reserve 2 tablespoons for garnish.

In a wok or large, heavy frying pan, heat thick coconut milk over medium–high heat for 3–5 minutes, stirring constantly, until it separates. If it does not separate, add optional oil. Add curry paste and curry powder and fry, stirring constantly, until fragrant, 1–2 minutes. Add chicken and potatoes, stirring gently to coat well.

Add remaining thin coconut milk and bring to a boil. Add palm sugar—if using a wok, add it along the edge of the wok so that it melts before being stirred into the curry; if using a standard frying pan, add directly to the curry. Add soy sauce to taste, and simmer for 5 minutes. Transfer to a serving bowl. Accompany with adjat sauce.

Variations: To make yellow curry with chicken drumsticks, add 6 chicken legs to the fried curry paste. Stir in thin coconut milk, bring to a gentle boil and cook, uncovered, until chicken juices run clear when pierced with a knife, 20–30 minutes. Add parboiled potatoes and cook another 5 minutes before serving.

To make vegetarian yellow curry, substitute 1 large carrot, peeled and cubed; 1 sweet potato, peeled and cubed; and $1/3$ cup (2 oz/60 g) peeled and cubed pumpkin for chicken. Cook vegetables in salted boiling water until just tender, about 5 minutes. Drain and proceed as above, adding vegetables with potatoes.

Beef, lamb & pork

meat is the only controversial ingredient in Asian cuisine, and it is in this regard that the nations really stand apart. When it comes to meat, religion often ordains what shall and shall not be consumed. The Indian Hindus cannot eat beef. Muslims, for example in Malaysia and India, cannot eat pork. The Thais generally aren't keen on the strong flavor of beef, and the Chinese aren't overly fond of lamb. Buddhists and other vegetarians, of course, don't eat any meat products at all.

Despite the cultural boundaries, meat is also much prized in Asia as historically it has been scarce and was often exclusive to the rich and royal. Pork is a traditional mainstay in China and Vietnam; lamb and goat in India. Beef, now eaten throughout most of Asia, was primarily a result of Western influence. The Japanese love of beef is fairly recent, only about 150 years old, beginning when Japan opened its doors to the West. Likewise the Vietnamese got their taste for beef (among other foods) from the French, not only in braises and stir-fries, but also in the country's famous pho soup.

Today, meat remains expensive in Asia, with grazing land being in extremely short supply. Rural families still raise their own livestock at home, but meat is more commonly obtained in the cities from the local markets and butchers, where the range on offer is extraordinary, and sometimes too much for Western sensitivities. Almost no part of the animal is wasted, and in some countries the offal is so highly valued that it costs more than a fillet.

Because it is something of a luxury in Asia, both philosophically and cost-wise, meat is treated with appreciation. It is used in small amounts or reserved for main meals, with extravagant dishes, such as whole suckling pig, only appearing on special occasions. As a result, Asian recipes which include meat are quite often ingenious—whether a handful of tender strips tossed in a spicy stir-fry or a big tough cut simmered long and slow until tender—with none more so than the curry.

The word "curry" is believed to originate from the southern-Indian Tamil word "karhi," meaning "sauce." Curries made their way to other parts of Asia via the Indian traders and religious practitioners, thousands of years ago, and now encompass an incredible range of styles, from the furnace-like Indian vindaloo or spicy Malaysian rendang to the delicate Thai green. In the West, curries first became known in meat-based styles, although they are frequently made with vegetables; they are also infamously hot, though traditionally this isn't necessarily so. Curries are, however, renowned for being intensely flavored with spices—these were originally used as preservatives and for their medicinal properties, but today, they are the curry's trademark.

In most Asian recipes, the meat is intrinsically interchangeable—you can make Thai-style red curry with beef, lamb or pork, and you can pretty much grill, braise or stir-fry any type of meat you like. However, contemporary cooks should also try to follow customs where appropriate and avoid, for example, using pork in a Massaman (Muslim) style: not only is this respectful, it results in a more authentic-tasting dish. As well as the great variety of dishes that may be created, cooking with meat in Asian styles is relatively healthy and also conveniently quick and easy.

Buying and preparing meat

Whether you're making beef rendang or stir-fried pork, a good butcher will help to ensure that the result is a success. Each cut of meat comes from a different part of the animal, and will cook in a different way. Your butcher should help you make a sound choice when selecting meat for a particular recipe, but should also advise on what's "good eating" now—organic meat, in particular, can be seasonal. As well as fresh meat, many Asian recipes also used preserved meat products, such as Chinese sausages, which are readily available at Asian markets (see also Glossary). This section includes hints for buying, preparing and cooking meat in Asian styles, as well as tips on grilling.

Choosing cuts of meat

Certain cuts of meat will suit certain recipes and cooking styles, so keep the following points in mind when purchasing meat.

- Cuts that have been worked the most, such as shoulder (blade), chuck (neck), shanks (shins) and round (topside), will be tough and are best cooked long and slow to break down the muscle fibers. In curries and other slow-cooked dishes, this results in melt-in-the-mouth tenderness.

- Prime cuts, such as tenderloin (fillet) or sirloin, are best cooked quickly at high temperatures, such as in stir-fries, preferably just long enough to brown the surface but leave the inside pink (in varying degrees of doneness) and juicy. Because of their lower fat content, prime cuts are very prone to overcooking, which then makes them dry and tough.

Browning and glazing

Many of the Asian recipes start with browning the meat over a high temperature. This seals in the meat juices and also gives it flavor and good color. Browning is often used in slow-cooked dishes such as curries.

Glazing (basting) is another technique favored for meat in Asian cuisine. This usually involves brushing or pouring the pan drippings or a special basting sauce over the meat while it is cooking. A classic example of this style is Chinese barbecued pork.

Grilling meat Asian-style

One of the most authentic ways to cook meat Asian-style is to grill it. Grilling is a way of life throughout Asia, particular as the street food which is so popular in many Southeast Asian countries, from satay skewers to sweet nut-and-sugar sprinkled pancakes.

Asian-style grilling is ideal for everyday meals at home as it generally requires only a small grill or barbecue, such as a brazier or Japanese-style hibachi. However, you can use any cooking implement that is designed to grill: outdoor barbecues are perfect; and although they lack authentic charcoal flavor, electric countertop grills, stove-top grill pans and oven broilers (grillers) make convenient substitutes. Don't forget the general safety rules of grilling, especially if cooking indoors. (See also Equipment, pages 10–19.)

Marinades for meat

Marinating meat is not only an easy way to add flavor, it can help to tenderize the meat. The following marinades are especially suited to Asian-style grilling.

Korean beef marinade (for 1 1/4 lb/625 g beef): In a large glass or ceramic bowl, combine 6 tablespoons Korean soy sauce, 2 scallions (shallots/spring onions) finely chopped, 1 1/2 cups (12 fl oz/375 ml) water (see Hint), 2 tablespoons pan-toasted, ground sesame seeds, 1/4 cup (2 oz/60 g) sugar, 2 tablespoons crushed garlic, 2 tablespoons sesame oil, 1/4 teaspoon freshly ground black pepper and 2 medium yellow (brown) onions, peeled and grated. Add sliced beef and mix well to coat. Cover and refrigerate to marinate for 2–3 hours.

Hint: You can use rice wine or pear juice instead of water; this makes beef more tender.

Asian-style marinade (for 1 lb/500 g beef, lamb or pork): Place 2 tablespoons vegetable oil, 2 tablespoons Thai sweet chili sauce, 3 tablespoons soy sauce, 2 tablespoons lemon or lime juice, 3 chopped cloves garlic, 1 tablespoon chopped cilantro (coriander) leaves and salt and pepper to taste in a screw-top jar, shake to mix, then brush over meat. Cover and refrigerate for 10 minutes or more, then drain and grill.

Dry marinade (for 1 lb/500 g beef, lamb or pork): Combine 1 teaspoon five-spice powder, 1 teaspoon sea salt, 1 teaspoon freshly ground black pepper, 2 tablespoons chopped fresh cilantro (fresh coriander) leaves and 1 small red chili pepper, seeded and chopped. Brush meat lightly with oil then coat with marinade and allow to marinate for several hours before cooking.

Beef and noodle stir-fry

Serves 4–6

6¹/₂ oz (200 g) wheat flour, rice stick or thick egg noodles

2 tablespoons soy sauce

3 tablespoons hoisin sauce

2 cloves garlic, finely chopped

2 teaspoons grated fresh ginger

12 oz (375 g) round (topside) or sirloin (rump) steak, thinly sliced

2 tablespoons vegetable oil

8 fresh shiitake mushrooms, brushed clean and sliced

6 scallions (shallots/green onions), sliced

6 oz (180 g) broccoli, cut into florets

2 tablespoons beef stock

1 tablespoon dry sherry

1 teaspoon Asian sesame oil

Cook noodles as directed on package or on page 442. Drain and set aside.

In glass or ceramic bowl, combine soy and hoisin sauces, garlic and ginger. Add steak slices, turn to coat in marinade, cover and marinate for 30 minutes. Drain and reserve marinade.

In wok or frying pan over medium–high heat, warm vegetable oil. Add steak and stir-fry until meat changes color, 3–4 minutes. Remove from pan. Return pan to medium–high heat, add mushrooms, scallions and broccoli, and stir-fry for 2 minutes. Add noodles, steak, reserved marinade, stock, sherry and sesame oil. Cook until heated through, 1–2 minutes.

Serve immediately, divided among individual plates.

Note: *This is just one adaptation of the dish commonly known as "beef chow mein." Use fresh or dried noodles in this recipe.*

Beef braised in rice wine

Serves 4

1/3 cup (3 fl oz/90 ml) dry rice wine

3 tablespoons fish sauce

1 teaspoon sugar

2 teaspoons ground pepper

2 lb (1 kg) boneless beef shoulder (blade) or chuck, trimmed and cut into 1-inch (2.5-cm) cubes

3 tablespoons vegetable oil

1/2 cup (2 oz/60 g) brown or pink shallots (French shallots), finely chopped

1/2 bulb garlic, finely chopped

2 sticks cinnamon or 1/2 teaspoon ground cinnamon

1/2 teaspoon aniseed

about 1 1/4 cups (10 fl oz/300 ml) water

3 tomatoes, peeled and seeded, with juice strained and reserved

1/4 cup (2 oz/60 g) butter

1/4 cup (1 oz/30 g) all-purpose (plain) flour

crusty bread rolls or baguette, for serving

In a nonmetallic bowl, blend rice wine, fish sauce, sugar and 1 teaspoon pepper. Add beef and let stand at room temperature for 2 hours, or cover and refrigerate for up to 24 hours, stirring several times. Using a slotted spoon, remove beef from marinade and pat dry; reserve marinade.

In a large, heavy pot or Dutch oven, heat oil over medium heat and sauté half of shallots and half of garlic until soft, about 3 minutes. Using a slotted spoon, transfer to a bowl. Add half of beef to pot and cook, stirring frequently, until all sides are lightly seared, about 5 minutes. Using a slotted spoon, transfer to a bowl. Repeat with remaining meat.

In the same pot, combine meat, cinnamon, aniseed and cooked shallots and add remaining garlic. Add 1 cup (8 fl oz/250 ml) water plus any marinade. Cover and simmer over medium–low heat just until beef is tender, about 2 hours. Shake occasionally to prevent scorching. If the braise cooks dry, add a little more water.

In a medium saucepan, combine tomatoes, strained tomato juice and remaining raw shallots, garlic and 1 teaspoon pepper. Add remaining 1/4 cup (2 fl oz/60 ml) water and cook until tomatoes are just starting to break up, about 3 minutes. In a separate saucepan, melt butter over low heat and whisk in flour. Cook, stirring constantly, until it barely begins to brown, about 2–3 minutes. Whisk into tomato mixture and remove from heat. When beef is tender, remove cinnamon sticks, if using, from braise. Stir in tomato mixture. Reduce heat to a simmer, cover and cook until fork tender, 30–60 minutes. Serve with bread rolls or baguette. (Pictured on page 202.)

Beef rendang

Serves 4

FOR SPICE PASTE

1 onion, coarsely chopped

6 cloves garlic

1 tablespoon grated fresh ginger

1 teaspoon chili powder

3 teaspoons ground turmeric

3 teaspoons ground coriander

1 tablespoon coconut milk (see page 24)

1 tablespoon vegetable oil

3 whole cloves

1 cinnamon stick

1^1/$_4$ lb (625 g) lean beef, cut into 1-inch (2.5-cm) cubes

2 cups (16 fl oz/500 ml) coconut milk (see page 24)

2 tablespoons tamarind concentrate

1 teaspoon packed brown sugar

sea salt to taste

steamed basmati rice (see page 28), for serving

To make spice paste: In a food processor, combine all ingredients and process to a smooth paste.

In a wok or large frying pan, heat oil over low heat and stir-fry cloves and cinnamon until fragrant, about 1 minute. Add spice paste and cook for 1 minute. Add beef and cook until beef changes color on all sides, 4–5 minutes.

Stir in coconut milk and bring to a boil. Reduce heat to low and simmer until beef is tender, 15–20 minutes. Add tamarind, sugar and salt.

Spoon beef rendang into serving bowls. Serve with steamed basmati rice.

Beef spare ribs Korean-style

Serves 4

20 oz (600 g) beef spare ribs
4 cups (32 fl oz/1 L) water
1/2 medium daikon or 10 peeled
  chestnuts
1 medium carrot
8 Chinese dried mushrooms, soaked for
  30 minutes in several changes
  of water
1 egg, separated
steamed rice (see page 28), for serving

FOR MARINADE

6 tablespoons light soy sauce
6 tablespoons pear juice or grated pear
3 tablespoons sugar
2 scallions (shallots/spring onions),
  finely chopped
2 cloves garlic, finely chopped
1 tablespoon sesame oil
1 tablespoon pan-toasted, ground
  sesame seeds (see page 30)
2 tablespoons malt liquid (mullyeot)
freshly ground black pepper to taste

Cut beef spare ribs into 2-inch (5-cm) sections. Place in a large bowl of water and soak for 1 hour to clean. Place ribs in a large saucepan, add water and bring to a boil. Boil until liquid reduces by half, 15–20 minutes.

To make marinade: Combine marinade ingredients in a medium glass or ceramic bowl.

Remove ribs from beef stock. Add two-thirds of marinade to beef stock, and cook over medium heat for about 20 minutes.

Peel daikon and carrot and cut into bite-sized cubes. Immerse cubes in rapidly boiling water for about 1 minute, then remove and set aside. Squeeze excess water from the mushrooms. Remove and discard stems. Leave caps whole.

Add remaining marinade, daikon and carrot and beef ribs to stock. Continue cooking until ribs are very tender, about 20 minutes.

Fry egg white and yolk to make egg gidan (see page 26). Remove from pan and cut into diamond shapes 1/2 inch (12 mm) long.

Arrange spare ribs on a serving dish, garnish with egg diamonds and serve with steamed rice.

Beef teriyaki

Serves 4

1 lb (500 g) beef tenderloin (fillet), trimmed of sinew and fat and cut into
  4 uniform steaks
1 cup (8 fl oz/250 ml) soy sauce
1 cup (5 oz/150 g) sugar
1 teaspoon mirin
2 tablespoons chicken stock
1 scallion (shallot/spring onion), thinly sliced
Teriyaki Sauce (see page 593), for serving
sesame seeds, toasted (see page 30), for garnish
steamed rice (see page 28), for serving

In a small saucepan over high heat, combine soy sauce, sugar, mirin and stock. Bring to a boil, stirring to dissolve sugar, and simmer for 1 minute. Remove from heat.

Preheat broiler (grill) and brush broiler pan with oil. Broil (grill) steaks by searing both sides quickly, then cook to your liking. Remove from broiler.

With a sharp knife, cut steaks into $^1/_2$ inch (12 mm) slices. Divide slices among 4 plates. Top with teriyaki sauce and sliced scallions. Sprinkle with sesame seeds. Serve with steamed rice.

Note: This is one of Japan's famous beef dishes; it can also be made with chicken (see page 165).

Hint: The beef may also be cooked on a grill plate or barbecue.

Beef vindaloo

Serves 8–10 as part of an Indian meal

5 dried red chilies, broken into
small pieces

1 teaspoon cumin seeds

1 tablespoon black peppercorns

1 1/2 tablespoons finely grated fresh
ginger

1 1/2 tablespoons finely chopped garlic

1/2 teaspoon ground turmeric

3/4 cup (6 fl oz/180 ml) vegetable oil
and melted unsalted butter combined

1 1/2 lb (750 g) yellow (brown) onions,
(about 4 1/2 medium), finely chopped

1 teaspoon salt, plus extra salt to taste

2 lb (1 kg) beef chuck (neck), excess fat
removed, cut into 1 1/2-inch (4-cm)
pieces

about 4 cups (32 fl oz/1 L) water

4 fresh green chilies, slit lengthwise

1/2 cup (4 fl oz/125 ml) white vinegar

1/2 teaspoon tamarind concentrate

1/2 teaspoon sugar

steamed basmati rice (see page 28),
for serving

In a spice grinder, grind dried chili, cumin seeds and peppercorns to a powder. Place in a bowl and combine with ginger, garlic and turmeric. Set aside.

In a karhai or frying pan, heat oil and butter mixture over medium–low heat. Add onions and 1 teaspoon salt, and cook, uncovered, stirring often, until onions are dark golden brown, 20–25 minutes. Raise heat to medium–high and add beef. Cook, turning beef pieces, for 5 minutes. Add spice mixture and cook, stirring, until fragrant, about 2 minutes.

Pour in enough water to cover beef. Add chilies and bring to a simmer. Cook over low heat, partially covered, stirring occasionally, until liquid is reduced by half, about 1 hour.

Stir in vinegar, tamarind and sugar. Taste and add salt if necessary. Cook, uncovered, until sauce reduces and thickens, about 30 minutes. Serve hot with steamed rice.

Bulgogi (Korean barbecued beef)

Serves 2

7 oz (220 g) beef tenderloin (fillet)

1 pear (preferably nashi), peeled

1^1/$_2$ teaspoons rice wine

4^1/$_2$ teaspoons light soy sauce

1 tablespoon sugar

1 tablespoon finely chopped scallion
  (shallot/spring onion)

1^1/$_2$ teaspoons finely chopped garlic

1 tablespoon pan-toasted, ground
  sesame seeds (see page 30)

1^1/$_2$ teaspoons sesame oil

freshly ground black pepper to taste

1 medium yellow (brown) onion,
  peeled

1 green bell pepper (capsicum), core
  and seeds removed

1 small carrot, peeled

2 lettuce leaves, for serving

Cut beef into ^{1}/$_4$-inch (0.5-cm) thick slices then into thin strips (see Hint below). Score surface with the tip of a knife to allow marinade flavors to penetrate. Grate pear to provide 1 tablespoon of pear juice.

Marinate beef in pear juice and rice wine in a glass or ceramic bowl for 30 minutes. Combine soy sauce, sugar, scallion, garlic, ground sesame seeds, sesame oil and pepper in a large bowl. Mix in beef, cover, and refrigerate to marinate for 2–3 hours.

Cut yellow onion, green pepper and carrot into bite-sized pieces and set aside.

Remove beef slices from marinade and broil (grill) to the preferred tenderness. Arrange beef on lettuce leaves and serve hot, accompanied by pieces of raw vegetable.

Hint: *Traditionally, beef bulgogi is made with wide, thin shavings of beef; however, this recipe uses more commonly available beef cuts for convenience.*

Note: *Bulgogi is one of the most famous dishes of Korea, after kimchi. It is cooked at the table on a specially designed griddle and served wrapped in lettuce leaves, with vegetables and various condiments such as chili paste, green onions and fresh slivers of garlic. Bulgogi is also a popular restaurant dish. The etiquette is to wrap a bit of everything in the lettuce and eat it all in one bite, but this takes some doing if the parcel is large.*

Salt bulgogi

Serves 4

1/2 cup (4 fl oz/125 ml) pear juice or
   1/2 cup (4 oz/125 g) grated pear
   (preferably nashi)
3 tablespoons rice wine
2 lb (1 kg) beef tenderloin (fillet)
1 daepa or scallion (shallot/spring
   onion)
1 fresh red chili
shiso (perilla) leaves or lettuce leaves, for
   serving
steamed rice (see page 28), for serving

FOR MARINADE
2 tablespoons table salt
3 tablespoons sugar
3 tablespoons finely chopped scallions
   (shallots/spring onions)
2 tablespoons finely chopped garlic
1 tablespoon pan-toasted, ground
   sesame seeds (see page 30)
freshly ground black pepper to taste
3 tablespoons sesame oil

Combine pear juice and rice wine in a medium glass or ceramic bowl. Slice beef into strips 1/4 inch (6 mm) thick. Add to bowl and marinate for 30 minutes.

To make marinade: Combine marinade ingredients in a large glass or ceramic bowl.

Drain beef, add to marinade and mix well. Cover, and refrigerate to marinate for 2–3 hours.

Cut daepa into 1 1/2-inch (4-cm) sections, then slice lengthwise into very thin strips. Place in a bowl of cold water for a few seconds, then drain. Slice chili in half lengthwise, remove seeds and membrane and slice into thin strips. Heat broiler (grill). Remove beef strips from marinade and broil (grill) to the desired tenderness.

Arrange shiso leaves on a plate. Place beef on leaves, sprinkle with daepa and chili strips, and serve with steamed rice.

Hint: Drizzle "salt bulgogi" with a little sesame oil to give it a sheen.

Chinese barbecue pork

Makes 8 small servings

2 pork tenderloins (fillets), 12 oz
   (375 g) each
3 tablespoons hoisin sauce
3 tablespoons ground bean sauce
2 cloves garlic, finely chopped

$^1/_4$ teaspoon five-spice powder
3 tablespoons soy sauce
pinch of Chinese red food coloring
   powder (optional)
1 tablespoon brown sugar

Place pork in a shallow dish. Combine hoisin sauce, ground bean sauce, garlic, five-spice powder, soy sauce, red food coloring and brown sugar and mix well. Pour over pork and toss until well coated in marinade. Cover, and refrigerate overnight.

Drain pork and reserve marinade. Place pork on a wire rack over a baking dish. Bake at 350°F (180°C/Gas 4) for 30 minutes, basting with marinade and turning pork during cooking. Remove from oven and allow to stand for 10 minutes before slicing. Serve hot or cold.

Chinese-style grilled pork tenderloin

Serves 4

1 lb (500 g) pork tenderloin (fillet)
3 tablespoons soy sauce
1 tablespoon hot bean paste
2 tablespoons hoisin sauce
4 cloves garlic, finely chopped

$^1/_4$ teaspoon five-spice powder
1 tablespoon shaved palm sugar or
   brown sugar
2 tablespoons vegetable oil
$^1/_4$ Chinese (napa) cabbage, shredded

Place pork in a shallow nonmetallic dish. In a bowl, combine soy, hot bean and hoisin sauces, garlic, five-spice powder and sugar and mix well. Pour mixture over pork, cover dish with plastic wrap and refrigerate for 2–3 hours.

Drain pork, reserving marinade. Preheat a grill pan or barbecue, then brush grill with vegetable oil. Grill pork until tender, 4–5 minutes each side, brushing with reserved marinade during cooking. Remove from grill, wrap in aluminum foil and allow to stand for 5 minutes. Cook cabbage in a saucepan of boiling water until tender, 3–5 minutes. Drain and spoon into serving bowls. Thickly slice pork and serve on top of warm cabbage.

Deep-fried crumbed pork tenderloin (Tonkatsu)

1 teaspoon salt

1 teaspoon garlic powder

$1/2$ teaspoon pepper

1 lb (500 g) pork tenderloin (fillet), trimmed of sinew, cut into slices $1/2$ inch
(12 mm) thick

vegetable oil, for deep-frying

1 cup (4 oz/125 g) all-purpose (plain) flour

2 eggs, beaten

2 cups (8 oz/250 g) panko

4 lemon wedges, for serving

tonkatsu sauce, for dipping

In a small bowl, combine salt, garlic powder and pepper and sprinkle over pork slices.

Pour oil into a deep, heavy-bottomed frying pan to fill it to 3 inches (7.5 cm) deep. Heat oil until it reaches 375°F (190°C) on a deep-frying thermometer. Place flour on a plate. Working in batches, dredge pork slices in flour, shaking off excess. Dip into the beaten egg, letting excess drain away, then coat with panko, pressing crumbs on firmly. Slip pork slices into hot oil and fry until coating is golden brown, 5–6 minutes. To test doneness, make a small cut in thickest part of pork to check it is no longer pink. Using a wire skimmer, remove pork from oil and drain on paper towels.

With a sharp knife, cut each slice into smaller slices 1 inch (2 cm) long; this is a more manageable size to eat with chopsticks. Divide pork among 4 plates. Place a wedge of lemon on each plate. Serve immediately with tonkatsu sauce for dipping.

Note: *This Japanese dish may be accompanied by steamed rice.*

Donburi-style pork (Katsudon)

Serves 2

DONBURI SAUCE

1 cup (8 fl oz/250 ml) water

5 tablespoons soy sauce

5 tablespoons mirin

1 teaspoon instant dashi

$1/2$ teaspoon sugar

$1/2$ teaspoon salt

$1/2$ teaspoon garlic powder

$1/4$ teaspoon pepper

2 pork tenderloins (fillets), 4 oz (125 g)
   each, trimmed of sinew, cut into slices
   $1/2$ inch (12 mm) thick

vegetable oil, for deep-frying

$1/2$ cup ($2^{1/2}$ oz/75 g) all-purpose
   (plain) flour

4 cups (16 oz/500 g) panko

2 eggs, beaten

$1/2$ large yellow (brown) onion, finely
   sliced

2 eggs, lightly beaten

2 cups (10 oz/300 g) steamed rice

2 scallions (shallots/spring onions),
   thinly sliced, for garnish

nori, cut into narrow strips, for garnish

To make donburi sauce: In a small saucepan, bring all ingredients to a boil; immediately remove from heat.

In a small bowl, combine salt, garlic powder and pepper and sprinkle over pork. Pour oil into a deep, heavy-bottomed frying pan to fill it to 3 inches (7.5 cm) deep. Heat oil until it reaches 375°F (190°C) on a deep-frying thermometer. Place flour and panko on separate plates. Working in batches, dredge pork in flour, shaking off excess. Dip into beaten egg, letting excess drain away, then coat with panko, pressing on crumbs to make sure pork is well coated.

Carefully slip pork slices into hot oil and fry until golden brown, 5–6 minutes. Using a wire skimmer, remove from oil and drain on paper towels. Cut into strips $1/2$ inch (12 mm) thick.

Place onions and donburi sauce in a small frying pan over high heat. Bring to a boil, reduce heat to medium and simmer, covered, until the onion softens, about 4 minutes. Add pork, return to a boil, then pour in lightly beaten eggs, tilting pan so eggs cover most of bottom. Cover and cook until eggs are almost set, about 1 minute. Remove pan from heat before eggs are completely set. To serve, place hot rice in a serving bowl, top with pork, egg and sauce, and sprinkle with sliced scallions and nori strips.

Ginger pork

Serves 4

¹/₂ cup (4 oz/125 g) sugar

¹/₂ cup (4 fl oz/125 ml) soy sauce

1 teaspoon mirin

2 tablespoons chicken stock (see page 588) or water

1 lb (500 g) pork tenderloin (fillet), trimmed of sinew, cut into slices ¹/₂ inch
   (12 mm) thick

¹/₂ cup (2¹/₂ oz/75 g) finely grated fresh ginger

2 tablespoons vegetable oil

2 scallions (shallots/spring onions), thinly sliced

1 teaspoon sesame seeds, for garnish

In a small saucepan over medium–high heat, combine sugar, soy sauce, mirin and stock and bring to a boil, stirring to dissolve sugar. Remove sauce from heat and set aside.

Dip both sides of each pork slice into grated ginger. Reserve any leftover ginger. Heat oil in a frying pan over medium–high heat. Add pork and fry, turning once, until pork is no longer pink, 3–4 minutes. Add sauce to pan with any remaining grated ginger and bring to a boil. Reduce heat to low and simmer for 1 minute.

Remove pork from pan and divide among 4 warmed plates. Spoon any remaining sauce from pan over slices. Garnish with sliced scallions and sprinkle with sesame seeds. Serve immediately.

Hint: This Japanese dish may be served with steamed rice.

Green papaya salad with beef

Serves 6

¹/₂ green papaya (about 1 lb/500 g), peeled and seeded

1 carrot, peeled

12 oz (375 g) sirloin (rump) steak, trimmed

1 cup (8 fl oz/250 ml) vegetable oil, for deep-frying

1 cup (6 oz/180 g) peanuts, lightly toasted (see page 30) and chopped

FOR MARINADE

1 tablespoon fish sauce

large pinch sugar

2 cloves garlic, coarsely chopped

1 tablespoon coarsely chopped brown or pink shallots (French shallots)

1 teaspoon chili powder

¹/₄ teaspoon five-spice powder

1 teaspoon ground pepper

¹/₃ cup (¹/₂ oz/15 g) chopped Vietnamese lemon balm

¹/₃ cup (¹/₂ oz/15 g) coarsely torn cilantro (fresh coriander) sprigs

FOR DRESSING

¹/₃ cup (3 fl oz/90 ml) fish sauce

¹/₄ cup (2 fl oz/60 ml) rice vinegar or distilled white vinegar

2 teaspoons sugar

9 cloves garlic

¹/₂ teaspoon ground pepper

¹/₂ teaspoon salt

Grate papaya and carrot into thin long strips. Toss together, cover, and refrigerate until serving. Cut beef into thin, wide pieces. In a medium bowl, stir all marinade ingredients together. Add beef and toss to coat. Refrigerate for 2 hours, stirring occasionally.

To make dressing: Place garlic cloves in a mortar, and using pestle, crush to a paste. In a medium bowl, combine with remaining dressing ingredients.

Prepare a charcoal grill (barbecue) or brazier following directions on page 12, or preheat a broiler (grill). Cook beef, arranged in a single layer, turning once, until lightly browned, about 2 minutes on each side. You may need to cook beef in 2–3 batches. In a wok or deep-fryer, heat 1 cup (8 fl oz/250 ml) oil. Add meat, a few pieces at a time, and fry until slightly crisp, 1–2 minutes. Take care that the oil does not sputter or boil over. Using a slotted spoon, transfer to paper towels to drain. Use kitchen shears or scissors to cut meat into matchsticks, and set aside.

Immediately before serving, add shredded vegetables to dressing and toss to coat. Arrange papaya and carrot on a large, deep platter. Top with meat and sprinkle with peanuts and herbs.

Ground beef stir-fried with basil leaves

Serves 4–6

3 tablespoons vegetable oil

15 cloves garlic, finely chopped

10 fresh red or green chilies, coarsely chopped

1 lb (500 g) ground (minced) beef

1 tablespoon oyster sauce

2 tablespoons fish sauce

1 teaspoon sweet (thick) soy sauce

1 tablespoon granulated (white) sugar, or to taste

2 fresh long red chilies, cut into large pieces

1 cup (8 fl oz/250 ml) chicken stock (see page 594) or water

1¹/₂ cups (1¹/₂ oz/45 g) loosely packed fresh basil leaves, preferably holy basil

Heat oil in a wok or large, heavy frying pan over high heat. Add garlic and chilies and stir-fry until garlic just begins to brown.

Add beef, stirring vigorously to break it up, about 2 minutes, then add oyster sauce, fish sauce, sweet soy sauce and sugar to taste. Stir well to combine, then add chilies.

Add chicken stock and bring to boil. Add basil, cook for 1 minute, then remove from heat.

Transfer to a serving plate and serve.

Note: *Traditionally, this Thai dish is served for lunch.*

Hint: *For a less piquant dish, keep the chilies whole, or seed them.*

Hanglay pork curry

Serves 4–6

2 tablespoons palm sugar

2 tablespoons fish sauce

1 teaspoon curry powder or gaeng hanglay powder (see Note)

3 tablespoons Hanglay Curry Paste (see page 582) or Red Curry Paste (see page 592)

1 lb (500 g) boneless pork loin, butt (leg), or neck, trimmed and cut into ³/₄-inch (2-cm) dice

¹/₄ cup (2 fl oz/60 ml) vegetable oil

2 cups (16 fl oz/500 ml) water

1¹/₂-inch (4-cm) piece fresh ginger, preferably young ginger (see Hint), cut into fine julienne

¹/₄ cup (1 oz/30 g) coarsely chopped roasted peanuts

2–3 tablespoons tamarind puree

In a large bowl, dissolve sugar in fish sauce. Add curry powder and paste. Add pork and toss in marinade. Let stand at room temperature for at least 20 minutes, or cover and refrigerate for at least 1 hour or overnight. If refrigerated, let meat stand at room temperature for 30 minutes before cooking.

Heat oil in a wok or large, heavy frying pan over medium–high heat and add meat and marinade. Stir-fry until pork is opaque on all sides, 2–3 minutes. Add water and bring to a boil. Add ginger, peanuts and tamarind to taste. Reduce heat to a rapid simmer and cook loin for 15 minutes. Pork butt improves with longer cooking; it needs about 45 minutes or until tender. Pork neck will need 1 hour or longer. The sauce should slightly thicken also, for a more flavorsome, richer dish. Add more water to prevent scorching, if necessary.

Note: To make gaeng hanglay curry powder, combine equal amounts of cumin seeds, ground turmeric, ground coriander seeds and mace. In a small, dry pan, lightly toast the spices, stirring constantly, until fragrant. Let cool, grind together in a mortar or spice grinder, then store in an airtight jar in a dark place for up to 6 months.

Hint: If possible, use tender young ginger for the julienne in this recipe; older ginger will be more fibrous. Young ginger, which is available during the summer season, is identifiable by its thin parchmentlike skin.

Japanese sesame beef

Serves 2

1¹/₂ tablespoons sugar

3 tablespoons soy sauce

1 tablespoon sake

1 tablespoon finely chopped garlic

1 tablespoon Asian sesame oil

8 oz (250 g) beef tenderloin (fillet) or sirloin (rump), trimmed of fat and sinew, cut into thin slices

1 tablespoon vegetable oil

¹/₂ large yellow (brown) onion, thinly sliced

2 cups (10 oz/300 g) steamed rice

¹/₂ scallion (shallot/spring onion), thinly sliced

sesame seeds, toasted (see page 30)

In a bowl, combine sugar, soy sauce, sake, garlic and sesame oil. Add beef slices, mix until well combined and allow to marinate for 10 minutes. Heat a wok over high heat, add vegetable oil and stir-fry onions until soft, 2–3 minutes. Add marinated beef and continue to stir-fry until beef is cooked through, 2–3 minutes. Remove from heat. Divide rice among 4 bowls. Spoon beef over rice, scatter sliced scallions over top and sprinkle with sesame seeds.

Japanese wafu steak

Serves 4

¹/₂ cup (4 fl oz/125 ml) soy sauce

¹/₂ cup (4 fl oz/125 ml) mirin

2 tablespoons sake

1 tablespoon rice vinegar

1 teaspoon lemon juice

5 oz (150 g) daikon, finely grated, plus 4 tablespoons for garnish

¹/₄ medium yellow (brown) onion, finely grated

1 lb (500 g) beef tenderloin (fillet), trimmed of sinew, cut into 4 evenly sized steaks

1 scallion (shallot/spring onion), thinly sliced

In a small saucepan over high heat, combine soy sauce, mirin, sake, vinegar, lemon juice, daikon and onion. Stir to mix well and bring to a boil; immediately remove sauce from heat and keep warm. Preheat a broiler (grill) until hot and brush broiler pan with oil. Place steaks on pan and broil (grill) by searing both sides quickly, then cooking steaks to your liking. Remove from grill. With a sharp knife, cut steaks into ¹/₂ inch (12 mm) slices and divide among 4 warmed plates. Pour sauce over slices. Garnish each serving with 1 tablespoon grated daikon and a sprinkling of sliced scallions.

Jungle curry with pork

Serves 4–6

1/4 cup (2 fl oz/60 ml) vegetable oil

1/4 cup (2 fl oz/60 ml) Red Curry Paste (see page 586)

12 oz (375 g) boneless pork butt (leg) or loin, thinly sliced

1/4 cup (1 oz/30 g) chopped eggplant (aubergine)

1/4 cup (1 oz/30 g) pea eggplants (optional)

2 long beans or 8 green beans, cut into 1-inch (2.5-cm) pieces

1/2 cup (2 oz/60 g) julienned krachai (Chinese keys)

1/4 cup fresh green peppercorns on stem, or 1–2 tablespoons canned green peppercorns, drained

6 ears fresh or canned baby corn, rinsed and drained, cut into large pieces

2 cups (16 fl oz/500 ml) chicken stock or water

5 kaffir lime leaves, stemmed

1/2 cup (1/2 oz/15 g) loosely packed fresh basil leaves, preferably holy basil

1/4 teaspoon salt

2 tablespoons fish sauce

1 fresh long red chili, cut into large pieces

Heat oil in a wok or large, heavy frying pan over medium–high heat. Add curry paste and fry, stirring constantly, for 1–2 minutes. Add pork and stir-fry until it changes color on all sides, about 2 minutes.

Add eggplants, beans, krachai, peppercorns, corn and 1 cup (8 fl oz/250 ml) stock. Bring to a boil, stirring often, then simmer, uncovered, for 2 minutes. Add the remaining stock, increase heat and bring to a boil.

Tear kaffir lime leaves and basil into pieces. Stir lime leaves, salt, fish sauce and chili into the curry. Boil for 1 minute. Add basil leaves and immediately remove from heat. Transfer to a serving dish and serve.

Hint: Traditionally, wild boar is used in this Thai recipe. You can replace pork with an equal quantity of thinly sliced beef or chicken.

Korean beef kabobs

Serves 4

7 oz (220 g) beef tenderloin (fillet)

1 oz (30 g) jjokpa or scallions (shallots/spring onions)

1 green bell pepper (capsicum)

4 skewers, 5 inches (12 cm) long, soaked in water for 30 minutes

vegetable or sunflower oil, for frying

lettuce leaves, for serving

FOR MARINADE

2 tablespoons light soy sauce

2 teaspoons sugar

1 scallion (shallot/spring onion), finely chopped

1 teaspoon pan-toasted sesame seeds (see page 30), ground to a powder

1 teaspoon sesame oil

Cut beef into strips about $\frac{3}{4}$ inch x $\frac{1}{4}$ inch x $2\frac{1}{2}$ inches (2 cm x 6 mm x 6 mm). Score surface with the tip of a sharp knife.

To make marinade: Combine all marinade ingredients in a medium glass or ceramic bowl.

Mix beef strips in marinade and marinate for 15–20 minutes.

Cut jjokpa into strips 2 inches (5 cm) long. Remove core and seeds from bell pepper and cut into slices 2 inches (5 cm) long.

Thread pieces of beef, jjokpa and bell pepper alternately onto each skewer, leaving about $1\frac{1}{4}$ inches (3 cm) free for holding skewer.

Heat 1 tablespoon oil in a frying pan over a high heat. Fry kabobs for 2 minutes on each side. Arrange lettuce leaves on a serving plate, place kabobs in center and serve.

Korean marinated beef and bamboo shoots

Serves 4

2 fresh bamboo shoots (about
  10 oz/300 g each)
5 cups (40 fl oz/1.25 L) rice water
  (reserved after washing rice)
1 dried red chili
vegetable or sunflower oil, for frying
2 oz (60 g) Korean watercress stems
  (minari)
3 Chinese dried mushrooms, soaked for
  30 minutes in several changes of
  water
4 oz (125 g) beef tenderloin (fillet),
  thinly sliced into strips about
  1 1/2 inches (4 cm) long
4 oz (125 g) bean sprouts, trimmed
1 egg, separated
1 medium red chili, julienned into
  1 1/2-inch (4-cm) strips
steamed rice (see page 28), for serving

**FOR BEEF AND MUSHROOM
MARINADE**

2 tablespoons light soy sauce
1 tablespoon sugar
4 teaspoons finely chopped scallions
  (shallots/spring onions)
2 teaspoons finely chopped garlic
2 teaspoons sesame oil
2 teaspoons pan-toasted, ground
  sesame seeds (see page 30)
freshly ground black pepper to taste

FOR SEASONING

2 teaspoons light soy sauce
2 teaspoons table salt
2 teaspoons sugar
1 tablespoon white vinegar
2 teaspoons pan-toasted, ground
  sesame seeds (see page 30)

Slice bamboo shoots diagonally into 1 1/2 -inch (4-cm) pieces. Bring rice water to a simmer in a large saucepan. Add bamboo shoots and dried chili, and simmer uncovered for 1 hour. Remove bamboo shoots from water and set aside to cool. Peel and slice in half lengthwise. Heat 2 tablespoons oil in a frying pan and fry bamboo shoot slices over medium heat for 3–5 minutes. Repeat process for watercress stems, removing dried chili.

Squeeze excess water from mushrooms. Remove stems and cut caps into thin slices.

To make beef and mushroom marinade: Combine marinade ingredients in a large glass or ceramic bowl. Add beef and mushrooms and mix well to coat. Heat 1 tablespoon oil in a frying pan and stir-fry beef and mushrooms for 3–5 minutes.

Bring a small saucepan of salted water to a boil. Immerse bean sprouts in boiling water for a few seconds. Remove and drain.

Fry egg white and yolk to make egg gidan (see page 26). Reserve a few slices for garnish.

To make seasoning: Combine all ingredients in a large bowl.

Add everything to seasoning, then mix well to coat. Transfer to a large platter, decorate with the reserved egg gidan and serve with steamed rice.

Korean-style grilled pork

Serves 4

10 oz (300 g) pork tenderloin (fillet)
vegetable or sunflower oil, for grilling

FOR MARINADE

$1/2$ medium yellow (brown) onion, finely chopped

2 tablespoons red chili paste

2 tablespoons light soy sauce

2 tablespoons finely chopped scallions (shallots/spring onions)

1 tablespoon finely chopped garlic

$1^1/2$ teaspoons grated fresh ginger

1 tablespoon sesame oil

1 tablespoon pan-toasted, ground sesame seeds (see page 30)

freshly ground black pepper to taste

steamed rice (see page 28), for serving

Cut pork into strips about $1/4$ inch (6 mm) thick and $1^1/2$ inches (4 cm) long. Score surface with the tip of a knife to allow marinade to penetrate.

To make marinade: Combine all marinade ingredients in a glass or ceramic bowl. Dip pork strips into marinade piece by piece to ensure they are well coated, leave in marinade, cover, and refrigerate to marinate for 2–3 hours.

If you have a portable grill plate, brush it with oil and set in center of serving table. Grill pork strips in front of your guests and serve immediately. Otherwise, broil (grill) pork in a broiler (grill) or in a lightly oiled grill pan or frying pan. Serve with steamed rice.

Lamb biryani

Serves 10–12 as part of an Indian meal

4 yellow (brown) onions, halved and
    thinly sliced

1 teaspoon salt, plus extra salt to taste

1 cup (8 fl oz/250 ml) vegetable oil
    and melted unsalted butter combined

1$^1/_4$ cups (10 oz/300 g) plain (natural)
    whole-milk yogurt

1 cup (1$^1/_2$ oz/45 g) chopped fresh
    cilantro (fresh coriander)

1 cup (1$^1/_2$ oz/45 g) chopped fresh mint

6 fresh green chilies, chopped

1$^1/_2$ tablespoons finely grated fresh
    ginger

1$^1/_2$ tablespoons finely chopped garlic

1$^1/_2$ tablespoons Garam Masala
    (see page 575)

2 tablespoons chili powder

1$^1/_2$ tablespoons ground turmeric

2 lb (1 kg) boneless lamb shoulder,
    diced

pinch saffron threads soaked in
    2 tablespoons hot milk for
    10 minutes

2 lb (1 kg) basmati rice, rinsed and
    soaked in cold water to cover for
    20 minutes

boiling water

juice of 1 lemon

Churri (see page 577), for serving

CRUST

3 cups (15 oz /450 g) whole wheat
    (wholemeal) flour

about 1 cup (8 fl oz/250 ml) water

Preheat oven to 475°F (240°C/Gas 9). In a glass or ceramic bowl, combine onions with
1 teaspoon salt. Set aside for 10 minutes.

In a large deghchi or large, deep ovenproof saucepan, heat oil and butter mixture over
medium–low heat. Add onions and cook, uncovered, stirring often, until onions are dark
golden brown, 20–25 minutes. Strain onions and reserve oil and butter mixture. Let onions
cool slightly.

While onions are cooking, prepare crust. Place flour in a bowl and add enough water
to form a soft dough. Knead gently in bowl until smooth. Cover and set aside.

In a large glass or ceramic bowl, combine yogurt, cilantro, mint, chili, ginger, garlic,
garam masala, chili powder and turmeric. Season with salt. Add cooked onions, lamb,
and saffron mixture, and mix well. Spread lamb mixture in base of deghchi or saucepan.

Drain rice and place in a large saucepan with enough boiling water to cover. Season
with salt. Bring to a boil over high heat and cook, uncovered, for 7 minutes. Drain excess

water from rice. Spread rice evenly over lamb mixture. Pour reserved oil and butter mixture evenly over rice. Cover tightly with lid. Roll crust dough into a thin sausage shape, long enough to extend around top edge of deghchi or saucepan. Place dough around edge, molding it to seal lid.

Place deghchi or saucepan over medium–high heat for 5 minutes, then transfer to oven. Reduce oven temperature to 400°F (200°C/Gas 6) and cook for 40 minutes. Remove from oven and let stand for 15 minutes before breaking away crust and removing lid. Either serve from pan or place a large platter over deghchi or saucepan and then very carefully invert biryani onto platter (you will need two people to do this). Serve immediately, drizzled with lemon juice and accompanied by churri.

Hint: *It is traditional to seal the deghchi with a dough crust; a long piece of aluminum foil can be used, "scrunched" around top edge of the deghchi or saucepan, instead.*

Lamb roganjosh

Serves 8–10 as part of an Indian meal

2 lb (1 kg) lamb shoulder, diced

2 cups (1 lb/500 g) plain (natural) whole-milk yogurt, whisked

1 teaspoon salt, plus extra salt to taste

2/3 cup (5 fl oz/150 ml) vegetable oil and melted unsalted butter combined

1-inch (2.5-cm) cinnamon stick

20 green cardamom pods

5 brown or black cardamom pods

1 teaspoon whole cloves

2 lb (1 kg) yellow (brown) onions, (about 6 medium), chopped

2 tablespoons finely grated fresh ginger

2 tablespoons finely chopped garlic

4 teaspoons chili powder

2 teaspoons ground turmeric

1/3 cup (1/2 oz/15 g) chopped fresh cilantro (fresh coriander)

1 1/2 teaspoons Garam Masala (see page 575)

steamed basmati rice (see page 28) or Paratha (see page 475), for serving

In a large bowl, combine lamb, yogurt and 1/2 teaspoon salt, and mix well. Set aside for 10 minutes.

In a large karhai or frying pan, heat oil and butter mixture over medium heat. Add cinnamon, cardamom and cloves, and cook, stirring, until fragrant, about 30 seconds. Add onions and 1/2 teaspoon salt, and cook over medium–low heat, uncovered, stirring often, until onions are golden brown, 20–25 minutes.

Add ginger and garlic and cook, stirring, for 30 seconds. Drain away any excess oil and butter, leaving onions and spices in pan.

Add lamb and yogurt mixture, chili powder and turmeric to pan, and mix well. Cook over low heat, covered, until lamb is tender, 45–60 minutes. Add cilantro and garam masala, and mix well. Taste and add salt if necessary. Serve hot with steamed rice or paratha.

Note: You can use goat meat in place of lamb.

Massaman lamb curry

Serves 4–6

2 cups (16 fl oz/500 ml) coconut milk (see page 24)

2–3 tablespoons vegetable oil (optional)

1/4 cup (2 fl oz/60 ml) Massaman Curry Paste (see page 580)

12 oz (375 g) boneless lamb leg, thinly sliced

2 potatoes, or 12 oz (375 g) sweet potato, taro, or pumpkin, peeled and cubed

1 teaspoon palm sugar

5 bay leaves

5 cardamom pods, toasted

2–3 tablespoons fish sauce

3–5 tablespoons tamarind puree, to taste

Adjat Sauce (see page 566), for serving

Let coconut milk stand, allowing the thick coconut milk to rise to the top. Spoon the thick coconut milk into a small bowl, and reserve 2 tablespoons for garnish.

In a wok or large, heavy frying pan, heat the thick coconut milk over medium–high heat for 3–5 minutes, stirring constantly, until it separates. If it does not separate, add optional oil. Add curry paste and fry, stirring constantly, until fragrant, 1–2 minutes.

Add meat and potatoes, and cook until lamb is lightly browned on both sides, 2–3 minutes. Add remaining thin coconut milk, increase heat, and bring to a boil. Add palm sugar—if using a wok, add it along the edge of the wok so that it melts before stirring into the curry; if using a standard frying pan, add directly to the curry. Add remaining ingredients and bring just to a boil. Reduce heat and simmer until vegetables are tender, about 20 minutes. Transfer to a serving bowl, and serve with adjat sauce.

Note: Massaman curry is named after Thailand's Muslim minority living in the south, and is consequently never made with pork. It is popular throughout the kingdom.

Variation: To make Massaman curry with beef, substitute an equal amount of cubed stewing beef (chuck steak), round (topside) or blade steak for the lamb. Tougher meat cuts may require thinner slicing and longer simmering.

Mushrooms stuffed with beef

Serves 4

12 dried Chinese mushrooms, soaked
   for 30 minutes in several changes of
   water
3 oz (90 g) beef tenderloin (fillet)
2 oz (60 g) tofu, drained and mashed
   with a fork
2 tablespoons all-purpose (plain) flour
1 egg, beaten
vegetable or sunflower oil, for frying
steamed rice (see page 28), for serving

FOR BEEF SEASONING
1 tablespoon light soy sauce
$4^{1}/_{2}$ teaspoons sugar
2 teaspoons finely chopped scallions
   (shallots/spring onions)
1 teaspoon finely chopped garlic
1 teaspoon sesame oil
1 teaspoon pan-toasted, ground
   sesame seeds (see page 30)
pinch freshly ground black pepper

FOR DIPPING SAUCE
2 tablespoons light soy sauce
1 tablespoon water
1 tablespoon white vinegar
1 tablespoon pan-toasted, ground pine
   nuts (see page 30)

Squeeze excess moisture from mushrooms. Remove and discard stems.

To make beef seasoning: Combine seasoning ingredients in a glass or ceramic bowl.

Add beef and tofu to beef seasoning and mix well. Lightly coat inside of each mushroom
cap with flour, then fill with beef mixture, pressing in firmly.

To make dipping sauce: Mix dipping sauce ingredients together in a small bowl.

Dust filled mushrooms with flour, dip in beaten egg and fry in 1 tablespoon oil over high
heat for about 2 minutes on stuffed side and 1 minute on second side (note: the egg
prevents the stuffing from absorbing too much oil).

Serve mushrooms accompanied by dipping sauce and steamed rice.

Penang pork curry

Serves 4–6

2 cups (16 fl oz/500 ml) coconut cream
plus 2 tablespoons for garnish
see page 24)

2–3 tablespoons vegetable oil (optional)

1/4 cup (2 fl oz/60 ml) Penang Curry
Paste (see page 583) or Red Curry
Paste (see page 586)

12 oz (375 g) pork tenderloin (fillet),
thinly sliced

2 tablespoons palm sugar

2–3 tablespoons fish sauce

7 kaffir lime leaves, stemmed

1/2 cup (1/2 oz/15 g) loosely packed
fresh sweet Thai basil leaves

1 fresh long red chili, cut into thin strips

In a wok or large, heavy frying pan over medium–high heat, cook 1 cup (8 fl oz/250 ml) coconut cream, stirring constantly, until it separates, 3–5 minutes. If it does not separate, add the optional oil. Add the curry paste and fry, stirring constantly, until fragrant, 1–2 minutes.

Add pork, and stir until meat is opaque on both sides, about 2 minutes. Add remaining 1 cup (8 fl oz/250 ml) coconut cream and bring to a boil. Add palm sugar—if using a wok, add it along the edge of the wok so that it melts before stirring into the curry; if using a standard frying pan, add directly to the curry. Stir in fish sauce to taste, and simmer until meat is tender, about 3 minutes.

Roll 4 kaffir lime leaves into a tight cylinder and cut into fine shreds; set aside. Tear remaining 3 kaffir lime leaves and basil into pieces. Add torn kaffir lime leaves and half the basil to curry. Stir to combine. Transfer to a serving dish.

Drizzle with 2 tablespoons coconut cream. Garnish with shredded lime leaves, chili, and remaining basil.

Note: *Tougher cuts of meat require longer cooking: 15–30 minutes. If using, do not add sugar and remaining ingredients until after meat is tender, then proceed as directed.*

Variation: *To make Penang curry with pumpkin, substitute 2 cups thinly sliced and peeled pumpkin or butternut squash for pork. Substitute soy sauce for fish sauce and cook as above, or until tender.*

Pork and lime patties

Serves 4

8 oz (250 g) ground (minced) pork

2 teaspoons fish sauce

1 teaspoon oyster sauce

2 teaspoons sambal oelek

1 egg white, lightly beaten

2 cloves garlic, finely chopped

2 tablespoons cornstarch (cornflour)

2 teaspoon grated lime zest

4 kaffir lime leaves, shredded

1/4 cup (1 oz/30 g) chopped scallions (shallots/spring onions)

1/2 cup (4 fl oz/125 ml) vegetable oil, for frying

Sweet Chili Relish (see page 592), for serving

In bowl, combine pork, fish sauce, oyster sauce, sambal oelek and egg white. Mix well. Add garlic, cornstarch, lime zest, kaffir lime leaves and scallions. Using moistened hands, mix until well combined. Divide mixture into 16 pieces and shape into patties.

In a wok over medium heat, warm vegetable oil. Working in batches, add pork patties and fry, turning once, until tender and golden on both sides, 6–8 minutes. Drain on paper towels.

Serve hot with sweet chili relish.

Hint: *These patties can be simply accompanied by steamed jasmine rice or a salad of Asian greens. They can also be served as an appetizer.*

Pork and nectarine stir-fry

Serves 4–6

2 tablespoons vegetable oil

3 cloves garlic, finely chopped

1 small red chili, seeded and chopped

1 lb (500 g) pork tenderloin (fillet), thinly sliced

1 bunch choy sum or spinach, trimmed and cut into 1¹/₄-in (3-cm) lengths

3 kaffir lime leaves, shredded

2¹/₂ tablespoons light soy sauce

2 teaspoons lime juice

2 firm nectarines, pitted and sliced

steamed rice (see page 28), for serving

In a wok over medium–high heat, warm vegetable oil. Add garlic and chili and stir-fry until aromatic, about 1 minute. Add pork, choy sum or spinach and kaffir lime leaves and stir-fry until pork changes color, 3–4 minutes. Add soy sauce, lime juice and nectarines and stir-fry until heated through, 1–2 minutes. Serve hot, accompanied by steamed rice.

Pork and pumpkin Thai-style

Serves 4–6

¹/₃ cup (3 fl oz/90 ml) vegetable oil

9 cloves garlic, finely chopped

1 lb (500 g) pumpkin or squash, peeled, seeded, and thinly sliced

¹/₂ cup (4 fl oz/125 ml) chicken stock (see page 588) or water

12 oz (375 g) boneless pork loin, cut into thin strips

¹/₄ cup (2 fl oz/60 ml) fish sauce

2 eggs, lightly beaten

fresh sweet Thai basil leaves, for garnish

Heat oil in a wok or large, heavy frying pan over medium–high heat. Add garlic, pumpkin and chicken stock. Bring to a boil.

Add pork, reduce heat, and simmer until meat is opaque throughout and pumpkin is tender, about 5 minutes. Add fish sauce, then stir in eggs to just bind sauce.

Transfer to a serving dish, garnish with basil leaves and serve.

Pork with green onions Korean-style

Serves 4

10 oz (300 g) pork tenderloin (fillet), cut into 1$^1/_2$ x 2-inch (4 x 5-cm) pieces

$^1/_4$ cup (1 oz/30 g) cornstarch (cornflour)

2 cups (16 fl oz/500 ml) vegetable or sunflower oil, for deep-frying

3 cloves garlic, finely sliced

1 fresh red chili, seeds removed, cut into 1$^1/_4$-inch (3-cm) strips

3 daepa or scallions (shallots/spring onions), cut into 2-inch (5-cm) lengths

2 tablespoons light soy sauce

2 tablespoons malt liquid (mullyeot)

freshly ground black pepper

sesame oil to taste

lettuce leaves, for serving

FOR MARINADE

4$^1/_2$ teaspoons table salt

1 tablespoon ginger juice (obtained by grating fresh ginger)

2 tablespoons rice wine

To make marinade: Combine marinade ingredients in a medium-sized glass or ceramic bowl.

Add pork pieces, cover, and refrigerate to marinate for 2–3 hours. Remove pork pieces from marinade and coat with cornstarch. Heat oil in a wok or deep frying pan over high heat. Add pork cubes one at a time so they do not stick together and fry for 1 minute. Remove from oil and drain on paper towels.

Heat 1 tablespoon oil in a wok or frying pan over medium heat and stir-fry garlic and chili for 2 minutes. Add pork and continue stir-frying for 3–5 minutes. Add daepa, soy sauce, malt liquid and pepper and stir-fry for 1 minute. Sprinkle with sesame oil. Arrange lettuce leaves on a large plate, spoon fried pork and daepa into center and serve.

Pork with kimchi and tofu

7 oz (220 g) Chinese (napa) cabbage kimchi

1/2 medium yellow (brown) onion

5 oz (150 g) fresh side pork (pork belly)

vegetable or sunflower oil, for frying

1 tablespoon finely chopped garlic

2 tablespoons finely chopped scallions (shallots/spring onions)

1 tablespoon sesame oil

1 tablespoon pan-toasted, ground sesame seeds (see page 30)

1 block (16 oz/500 g) firm tofu

steamed rice (see page 28), for serving

Slice kimchi into pieces 1–1 1/2 inches (2–4 cm) long. Peel onion and cut vertically into slices. Thinly slice pork. Heat 1 tablespoon oil in a frying pan. Add kimchi, onion, pork, garlic and scallions and stir-fry until pork is well cooked, 3–5 minutes. Turn off heat, add sesame oil and sesame seeds and mix in well.

Bring a medium-sized saucepan of water to a boil. Place tofu in water for a few seconds, then remove and drain. Cut tofu into 1 1/2 x 3/4 x 1/2-inch (4 x 2 x 12-mm) pieces. Place fried kimchi mixture in center of a serving plate, arrange tofu pieces around edge and serve with steamed rice.

Note: This classic Korean stir-fry can be made using the Chinese (napa) cabbage kimchi recipe on page 407.

Shabu–shabu (Japanese beef hot pot)

Serves 4

SHABUTARE (DIPPING SAUCE)

1/2 cup (4 fl oz/125 ml) sesame paste

1/2 cup (4 fl oz/125 ml) white (shiro)
  miso

2 tablespoons rice vinegar

2 tablespoons mirin

2 tablespoons soy sauce

1/2 cup (4 oz/125 g) sugar, dissolved in
  1/4 cup (2 fl oz/60 ml) boiling water

1/2 teaspoon garlic powder

2–3 drops chili oil, or more if desired

1/2 teaspoon Asian sesame oil

1 lb (500 g) lean beef, very thinly sliced

10 oz (300 g) silken tofu

6 1/2 oz (200 g) shirataki noodles,
  cooked in boiling water for 5 minutes,
  then drained and rinsed in cold water

8 fresh shiitake mushrooms

6 Chinese napa cabbage leaves,
  thickly sliced

1/4 bunch (3 oz/90 g) spinach

4 scallions (shallots/spring onions),
  cut into 4-inch (10-cm) lengths

1 small carrot, peeled and finely sliced

5 oz (150 g) daikon, finely sliced

1 teaspoon instant dashi

Nihaizu (see page 581), for serving

steamed rice (see page 28), for serving

To make sauce: In a bowl, combine all ingredients and mix until a smooth paste forms.

Arrange beef slices in a flower shape on a large flat platter. Arrange tofu, noodles and vegetables attractively on another large platter. Bring both platters to the table, where ingredients will be cooked in a large, shallow cast-iron pan over a portable burner, or in an electric frying pan.

Fill pan two-thirds full with water and add instant dashi. Bring stock to boil. Add firm vegetables such as daikon and carrot first. Then gradually add remaining vegetables, noodles and tofu. Dip beef slices into boiling stock separately; each diner holds meat with chopsticks and dips it in stock. Cook for only a few minutes, just long enough for its color to change. Overcooking will toughen meat. Give each diner separate bowls for the two dipping sauces. Serve with steamed rice.

Stir-fried barbecue pork wraps

Makes 24 wraps

1 tablespoon plum sauce

1 tablespoon orange juice

1 teaspoon soy sauce

1 tablespoon vegetable oil

3 cloves garlic, finely chopped

1 Thai red chili, seeded and sliced

5 oz (150 g) choy sum, cut into $2^1/_2$-inch (6-cm) lengths

8 oz (250 g) Chinese barbecued pork, sliced

4 pieces mountain bread or lavash

$^1/_4$ cup fried noodles (flour sticks)

2 tablespoons fried shallots (French shallots)

$^1/_4$ cup (2 fl oz/60 ml) plum sauce, for dipping

In a small bowl, stir 1 tablespoon plum sauce, orange juice and soy sauce together. Set aside.

Heat oil in a wok over medium heat and stir-fry garlic and chili until fragrant, about 1 minute. Add choy sum and stir-fry for 2 minutes. Add pork and plum sauce mixture. Stir-fry until pork changes color, 1–2 minutes. Remove from heat and let stand for 5 minutes.

Place bread on a work surface. Distribute pork stir-fry evenly over bread. Top with fried noodles and shallots. Roll into a cylinder and wrap in a strip of parchment (baking) paper. Cut each roll in half crosswise. Serve immediately, with plum sauce.

Stir-fried beef with Asian greens

Serves 4

10^1/$_2$ oz (315 g) sirloin (rump) or round (topside) steak

3 tablespoons vegetable oil

4 cloves garlic, finely chopped

1 tablespoon grated fresh ginger

2 small red chilies, seeded and chopped

1 bunch Chinese broccoli or 6 celery stalks, trimmed and cut into 1^1/$_4$-in (3-cm) lengths

7 oz (220 g) sugar snap peas or snow peas (mange-tout), trimmed

3^1/$_2$ oz (105 g) fresh bean sprouts, rinsed

1 tablespoon oyster sauce

1 teaspoon sambal oelek

steamed white rice, for serving

Enclose steak in freezer wrap and freeze until slightly firm, about 30 minutes. Remove from freezer and thinly slice. In a bowl, combine beef, 1 tablespoon vegetable oil, garlic and ginger. Cover and refrigerate for 30 minutes.

Drain beef from marinade, discarding marinade. In a wok over medium–high heat, warm remaining 2 tablespoons vegetable oil. Working in batches, add beef and stir-fry until brown, 1–2 minutes. Remove from wok and drain on paper towels. Add chili, broccoli, sugar snap peas and bean sprouts and stir-fry until tender-crisp, 2–3 minutes. Add beef, oyster sauce and sambal oelek. Stir-fry until heated through, about 1 minute.

Serve hot, accompanied by steamed white rice.

Hint: You can substitute other Asian greens in this stir-fry, such as baby bok choy or choy sum.

Stir-fried pork and long beans with red curry paste

Serves 4

1/4 cup (2 fl oz/60 ml) vegetable oil

1 cup (8 fl oz/250 ml) Red Curry Paste (see page 586)

20 oz (625 g) boneless pork butt or loin, thinly sliced

15 kaffir lime leaves, stemmed

1 lb (500 g) long beans or green beans, cut into 1-inch (2.5-cm) pieces

5 fresh long red chilies, seeded and cut into strips

1 tablespoon palm sugar

2 tablespoons granulated (white) sugar

1/4 cup (2 fl oz/60 ml) fish sauce

1 cup (1 oz/30 g) loosely packed fresh sweet Thai basil leaves, coarsely torn

Heat oil in a wok or large, heavy over medium–high heat. Add curry paste and cook, stirring constantly, until fragrant, 1–2 minutes. Add meat and stir until opaque on all sides, 2–3 minutes. Add 10 kaffir lime leaves, beans, and chilies. Cook, stirring frequently, for about 2 minutes, or until meat is barely tender.

Add palm sugar—if using a wok, add it along the edge of the wok so that it melts before stirring into the other ingredients; if using a standard saucepan, add directly to the pan. Add granulated sugar, then fish sauce and basil. Stir well, then remove from heat and transfer to a platter.

Roll remaining kaffir lime leaves into a tight cylinder and cut into fine shreds. Sprinkle over the dish and serve.

Variation: To make with chicken, use an equal quantity of chicken breast fillet, thinly sliced, in place of the pork.

Stir-fried spiced ground lamb with potato

Serves 4

1 tablespoon vegetable oil

4 cardamom pods

1 cinnamon stick

4 whole cloves

1 onion, finely chopped

12 oz (375 g) ground (minced) lamb

2 teaspoons Garam Masala (see page 575)

1 teaspoon chili powder

4 cloves garlic, finely chopped

3 teaspoons grated fresh ginger

1 teaspoon sea salt

6 oz (185 g) potatoes, peeled and cut into 1-inch (2.5-cm) cubes

13 oz (390 g) canned chopped tomatoes

1/2 cup (4 fl oz/125 ml) hot water

2 tablespoons chopped fresh cilantro (fresh coriander)

2 tablespoons chopped fresh mint

Naan (see page 467) or steamed basmati rice (see page 28), for serving

In a wok or large frying pan, heat oil over medium heat and stir-fry cardamom pods, cinnamon stick, and cloves until fragrant, about 1 minute. Add onion and stir-fry until onion is soft, about 2 minutes. Stir in lamb, garam masala, chili powder, garlic, ginger and salt. Stir-fry until lamb changes color, 4–5 minutes. Add potatoes, tomatoes and their juice, and hot water. Reduce heat to low, cover, and simmer until potatoes are tender, about 8 minutes.

Remove from heat and stir in cilantro and mint. Spoon into serving bowls. Serve hot with naan or steamed basmati rice.

Stone-cooked lamb cutlets

Serves 8–10 as part of an Indian meal

1-inch (2.5-cm) cinnamon stick
1 teaspoon black peppercorns
1 teaspoon finely grated fresh ginger
1 clove garlic, crushed to a paste
6 fresh green chilies, crushed to a paste
$1/2$ teaspoon salt
2 lb (1 kg) lamb cutlets
vegetable oil, for brushing
2 red or yellow (brown) onions, thinly sliced into rings, for serving
1 cup (1 oz/30 g) fresh mint leaves, for serving
8–10 lemon wedges, for serving

Prepare a fire in a grill (barbecue), preferably charcoal.

In a spice grinder, grind cinnamon and peppercorns to a powder. Place in a bowl and combine with ginger, garlic, chili and salt.

Rub mixture over both sides of lamb cutlets and set aside to marinate for 30 minutes.

On a grill (barbecue) rack, place a granite slab that is $2^1/2$ inches (7 cm) thick and about 12 inches (30 cm) long and 10 inches (25 cm) wide. When slab is hot, brush oil over surface and place cutlets on top. Cook lamb, brushing with oil when necessary, until cooked to your liking, 3–4 minutes per side.

Serve hot, topped with onion rings and mint leaves and accompanied by lemon wedges.

Hint: If a granite stone is not available, cook lamb on a heavy grill plate or barbecue or on a heated pizza stone.

Thai beef salad

Serves 4–6

$^1/_2$ lb (250 g) beef tenderloin (fillet) or sirloin (rump), trimmed, or roast beef

salt and freshly ground pepper

1 tablespoon vegetable oil

$^1/_3$ cup (3 fl oz/90 ml) fish sauce

$^1/_2$ cup (4 fl oz/125 ml) fresh lime juice

about 25 fresh small green and red chilies, coarsely chopped

1 teaspoon palm sugar

1 cucumber

1 firm tomato

3 tablespoons thinly sliced shallots (French shallots), preferably pink

$^1/_2$ cup (2 oz/60 g) coarsely chopped Chinese or standard celery

5 scallions (shallots/spring onions), cut into 1-inch (2.5-cm) pieces, including
green parts

If using raw beef, cut into 1–2 thick steaks. Season lightly with salt and pepper. In a large frying pan over medium–high heat, heat oil and cook steaks for a total of 7 minutes per inch (2.5 cm) thickness, turning once, for medium rare. Remove from heat and let cool thoroughly.

In a small bowl, combine fish sauce, lime juice, chilies, and sugar. Stir until sugar is dissolved. Cut cucumber in half lengthwise, remove seeds with a spoon if desired, then cut into thin crescents. Core tomato, cut in half vertically, and slice into thin half-moons. Cut meat into thin strips, then toss with fish sauce mixture. Add cucumber, tomato, shallots, celery and scallions, and toss to coat.

Transfer to a serving dish and serve immediately.

Hints: *Tender beef, such as tenderloin or sirloin, is best for this recipe. This is also a good way to use leftover roast beef. For a less spicy salad, leave the chilies whole and lightly bruise them before adding. Although not traditional, this salad is delicious served on a bed of greens, such as green oak leaf lettuce.*

Vietnamese braised pork with young coconut

Serves 6

1¹/₂ lb (750 g) boneless pork shank (shin), leg or shoulder, cut into 1-inch (2.5-cm) cubes

¹/₃ cup (3 oz/90 g) sugar

2 coconuts, preferably young coconuts, or about 4 cups (32 fl oz/1 L) coconut water (see Hint)

2 tablespoons vegetable oil

²/₃ cup (5 fl oz/150 ml) fish sauce

6 hard-boiled eggs, shelled

1 fresh long red or green chili, seeded and thinly sliced

¹/₃ cup (¹/₂ oz/15 g) coarsely chopped Chinese (flat/garlic) chives

6 scallions (shallots/spring onions), including green parts, cut into 1-inch (2.5-cm) pieces

Place pork in a medium casserole dish. Sprinkle with sugar and refrigerate for 1 hour. Traditionally, any rind is retained to enrich the juices, but discard if preferred.

Pierce top of coconuts and drain coconut water; you need about 4 cups (32 fl oz/1 L). If using young coconuts, use a large knife to cut away the top of the coconut (the shell of young coconuts is not as hard as that of older ones). Scoop gelatinous flesh from inside shell and cut into small dice; set aside.

In a medium pot, heat oil over medium heat and cook pork, stirring, until lightly golden on all sides, 3–5 minutes. You may need to do this in 2 batches to prevent crowding. If meat begins to burn because of sugar, add 1–2 tablespoons coconut water. Add fish sauce and remaining coconut water, and, if using, coconut meat. Bring to a low boil, then immediately reduce heat to low, partially cover, and very gently simmer until pork is tender and liquid reduced by half, 2–2¹/₂ hours. Add hard-boiled eggs to the pot for last 30 minutes of cooking time. Serve garnished with chili, chives and scallions.

Notes: This is a southern Vietnamese recipe, popularly sold on the streets of Ho Chi Minh City (Saigon). Cook very slowly to ensure tender results.

Hint: Coconut water is the watery liquid inside a coconut. Try to find young coconuts or packaged coconut water (nuoc dua tuoi). Often, the water is lightly sweetened. If so, omit sugar. Alternatively, the separated clear liquid layer in canned coconut milk can be used.

Vietnamese steamboat with beef

Serves 6

3 lb (1.5 kg) beef tenderloin (fillet),
   trimmed and sliced paper thin
2 teaspoons ground pepper
Table Greens (see page 437), including
   butter (Boston) lettuce and dill sprigs
40 sheets dried rice paper sheets,
   softened (see page 27) (optional)

FOR SOUP STOCK
2 cloves garlic, thinly sliced
1-inch (2.5-cm) knob fresh ginger,
   thinly sliced
1 stalk lemongrass, white part only,
   cut into thin rounds (optional)

1 cup (8 fl oz/250 ml) rice vinegar or
   distilled white vinegar
about 5 cups (40 fl oz/1.25 L) water
1 tablespoon salt
3–4 tablespoons sugar to taste

FOR ACCOMPANIMENTS
about 1 cup (4 oz/125 g) peanuts,
   lightly toasted (see page 30) and
   ground
Nuoc Cham Sauce (see page 582)

Arrange meat attractively on a platter or on individual plates in a single layer, overlapping as little as possible. Sprinkle meat with pepper and cover with plastic wrap and refrigerate until ready to serve, up to several hours in advance. Arrange table greens on a platter. Cover and refrigerate until ready to serve, up to several hours in advance.

To make soup stock: In a large saucepan, combine all stock ingredients and bring just to a boil. Reduce heat to low and simmer until needed. Note that some rice vinegars, especially Japanese brands, are slightly sweet; taste stock before adding extra 1 tablespoon sugar. Strain stock into a fire pot or metal fondue pot on the table. (See page 17 for instructions.) The stock should fill the pot about two-thirds full; if not, add boiling water to the desired depth. At the table, bring to a rapid simmer.

To serve, lay a sheet of rice paper on a plate and top with a lettuce leaf and a few herbs. Take a piece of meat and drop it into simmering liquid for about 10 seconds, or until done as desired. Using a skimmer or chopsticks, retrieve meat and place it on lettuce leaf and herbs. Sprinkle with 1 teaspoon peanuts, then fold to enclose bottom and top. Roll up, as with spring rolls. The finished result should be the size of a thick cigar, about 1 inch (2.5 cm) wide and 4 inches (10 cm) long. Dip in nuoc cham sauce and eat with your fingers.

Seafood

With much of Asia encircled by coastline, it's no surprise that seafood plays such an important role in its cuisine. From China and India to Korea and Vietnam, seafood features in local dishes, at home and in the markets. The island regions, such as Hong Kong and Malaysia, in particular are rich in seafood. In Japan, of course, it is revered in all its wondrous forms as sushi and sashimi.

The choice is abundant, with a dazzling array of fish from the freshwater species beloved by the Koreans to oily mackerel and tuna—the king of sashimi—and a full spectrum of seafood from lobster and other crayfish to abalone, sea urchins and eels (not perhaps seafood by definition, but of watery habitat nonetheless). You can even include snails and frogs, in China and Vietnam.

Seafood is seasonal, so it's always best to buy what nature has on offer. This ensures that you get the best quality but also the best price, because when a particular species is in abundance it will be cheaper than another which is in short supply.

Apart from its appeal to the palate, seafood is renowned for its healthy properties—high in vitamins, minerals and protein, but low in fat, especially saturated fat, and calories. The oily fish such as tuna, salmon, mackerel, sardines and mullet are also rich in omega-3 fatty acids, believed to be highly beneficial.

To ensure that you get the best from your seafood, make sure it is purchased from a reputable supplier. A good fishmonger will do most of the preparation for you, and fish markets stock an amazing range of fresh seafood and seafood-related products. Seafood must be bought as fresh as possible, as it perishes quickly. Temperature plays an important role in maintaining freshness, so when shopping, take an insulated bag or container for carrying your purchase.

Shelf life depends on quality and freshness, but generally seafood should be consumed within two days of purchase. If you are planning to cook seafood on the day of purchase, store it in the original packaging; otherwise transfer it to a plate, rinsing only if it is not completely clean or if there is an ammonia smell from the plastic, then pat dry, and cover with plastic wrap. Keep it in the coldest part of the refrigerator.

Seafood is very adaptable in Asian recipes, allowing you to choose the best of what's in season. You can easily substitute other fish for the fish used in curries, or scallops for shrimp in stir-fries. The recipes in this chapter are especially flexible, and many can be adapted to suit different types of fish or seafood.

Buying and preparing seafood

If you begin by sourcing your seafood from a reputable supplier, either a fish market or a retailer that visits the markets daily, you'll ensure that you're getting the best quality available. Take a good look at the seafood, touch it and have a sniff—fresh fish and seafood always has a pleasant sea smell.

Buying whole fish

- Bright bulging eyes are a sure sign of freshness. Do not reject deep-sea fish if the eyes are bulging but bloodstained, as the blood is due to the fish being rapidly brought to the surface. Bypass fish with dull, sunken or cloudy eyes.

- Overall, the coloring of the fish should be bright or lustrous. Stroke the fish to ensure that the flesh is firm and resilient. Stale fish are less elastic and may feel sticky.

- Scales should be firmly intact and have a glossy sheen. The gills should be bright pink–red and look moist. If the gills are black–red or brown, the fish is not fresh.

- Fish should not have a fishy odor. Some fish develop an ammonia smell when stored in plastic bags—even in the refrigerator; simply run fish under cold water to remove.

Buying fish cuts

- The fish piece should be moist and shiny, with firm, resilient flesh and no dry, brown edges. The flesh should look translucent, not milky.

- Fish pieces should not be sitting in a pool of liquid; this is an indication of poor freezing techniques.

Buying seafood

- Shrimp should have tight shells with no sign of black discoloration along the belly and head. The flesh should be moist and firm with a sweet smell and no hint of ammonia.

- Touch the tentacles of squid and check that the suckers are still active. The skin around the eyes should be clear blue.

- Live shellfish should be tightly closed. If you gently open the shell, it should close by itself. Shells should be uncracked and unbroken.

- Oysters and scallops, sold in the half shell, should have plump, moist, shiny, creamy-colored flesh and clear liquor. Some scallop varieties have roe intact.

Scaling and cleaning fish

When purchasing whole fish from a retailer, it is usually scaled and gutted for you. Whole fish that has not been cleaned should be gutted immediately, as spoilage occurs faster with the insides intact. Rinse the cavity well to remove any blood along the backbone.

If scaling fish at home, use a fish scaler (see Equipment) to avoid damaging the flesh of the fish. Scaling is messy, but this can be reduced if you immerse the fish in a sink of cold water while scaling it. The scales will come away easily and fall directly into the water. When you drain the water, be sure to use a drainer which will collect the scales, so they can be easily discarded

Skinning a fillet of fish

Fish such as mackerel, bonito, sea bream and garfish can be eaten with their skin on. Salmon, tuna, swordfish and cod are usually skinned. To skin a fillet:

1. Place the fillet on a board, skin-side down.

2. Holding the tail end with your left hand, insert the knife blade carefully between the skin and flesh at tail end.

3. Using your left hand to add pressure and to hold onto the fish skin at the tail end, slowly pull skin and flesh, keeping the knife at an angle without moving it and gently let the knife run along the length of the fillet from tail to head, skimming along the skin.

4. Use the side of the knife to push or roll the flesh away as you remove the skin.

Cleaning squid

1. Holding the body part in one hand, use the other hand to pull the tentacles away.

2. Reach inside body cavity and remove remaining parts, including the quill.

3. Insert a finger under the fin to separate, and then pull off the fin and as much skin as possible. Peel off the remaining skin.

4. Use a knife to cut off the tentacles above the eyes and reserve for use in other dishes.

5. Thoroughly wash the body inside and out.

Deveining shrimp

1. Remove shell, then use a small paring knife to lightly score along the back of shrimp, exposing the dark vein.

2. Gently pull vein to remove.

Braised shrimp in ginger-coconut sauce

Serves 4

2 tablespoons peeled and grated fresh ginger

4 cloves garlic, finely chopped

1 tablespoon ground turmeric

1 small red chili, seeded and chopped

2 tablespoons white vinegar

2 tablespoons peanut oil

2 onions, chopped

1 lb (500 g) raw jumbo shrimp (green king prawns), peeled and deveined, tails intact

2 tomatoes, chopped

3/4 cup (6 fl oz/180 ml) coconut milk (see page 24)

2 teaspoons cracked black pepper

2 tablespoons chopped fresh cilantro (fresh coriander)

1/4 cup (1/4 oz/7 g) small whole fresh cilantro (fresh coriander) leaves

Place ginger, garlic, turmeric, chili and vinegar in food processor. Process to form paste.

In a wok over medium–high heat, warm peanut oil. Add onions and spice paste and stir-fry until onions soften, 2–3 minutes. Add shrimp and stir-fry until shrimp change color, 3–4 minutes. Stir in tomatoes and cook until soft, about 2 minutes. Add coconut milk, reduce heat to low, cover, and simmer until sauce thickens slightly and shrimp are tender, 6–8 minutes. Stir in pepper and chopped cilantro.

Serve hot, garnished with cilantro leaves.

Chili crab

2 tablespoons peanut oil
2 red chilies, seeded and finely chopped
2 cloves garlic, chopped
1 tablespoon chopped fresh ginger
¼ cup (2 fl oz/60 ml) oyster sauce
½ cup (4 fl oz/125 ml) fish stock (see page 589)
2 tablespoons Thai sweet chili sauce
2 lb (1 kg) uncooked crab
4 scallions (spring onions/shallots), chopped
steamed jasmine rice (see page 28), for serving

Clean crab by pulling off the apron flap on the bottom of the shell. Pry off top shell, remove gills, intestines and mouth parts. Cut small crabs in half, or large crabs into eight pieces. Twist off claws. Refrigerate until ready to use.

Heat oil in a large frying pan over medium heat. Add chilies, garlic and ginger and sauté until fragrant, about 1 minute. Add oyster sauce, stock and sweet chili sauce and bring to boil. Simmer until slightly thickened, about 4 minutes.

Add crab and scallions and stir to coat with sauce. Simmer, covered, for 15–20 minutes, or until crab is cooked through—to test, crack a shell and see if flesh is tender. Serve with steamed jasmine rice.

Hints: *When serving crabs in the shell, it's important to have the claws cracked to allow your guests easy eating. Claws are easily cracked using a nutcracker or meat mallet.*

Make sure you have lots of finger bowls and hand towels available at the table.

Chili, salt and pepper grilled squid

Serves 2–4

2 small red chilies, seeded and finely chopped

1 tablespoon sea salt

1 teaspoon cracked black pepper

2 tablespoons vegetable oil

16 baby squid (calamari), about 2 lb (1 kg), cleaned and halved

$1^1/_2$ cups ($1^1/_2$ oz/45 g) mizuna

Combine chili, salt and pepper. Brush squid pieces with oil and press chili mix into both sides of squid.

Preheat a grill pan or barbecue. Grill squid pieces for 15–30 seconds each side then remove from grill. Serve squid on a bed of mizuna leaves (pictured).

Chili shrimp stir-fry

Serves 4

1 lb (500 g) raw jumbo shrimp (green king prawns), peeled and deveined, tails intact

pinch chili powder

$^1/_4$ teaspoon ground turmeric

3 tablespoons vegetable oil

3 cloves garlic, finely chopped

1 small red chili, seeded and chopped

1 teaspoon black mustard seeds

1 tablespoon lime juice

lime wedges, for serving

Place shrimp in a bowl. Combine chili powder and turmeric and sprinkle over shrimp. Using hands, rub spices into shrimp.

In a wok over medium–high heat, warm vegetable oil. Add garlic, chili and mustard seeds and stir-fry until seeds begin to pop, 1–2 minutes. Raise heat to high, add shrimp and stir-fry until shrimp change color and are tender, 3–4 minutes.

Remove from heat and stir in lime juice. Serve hot, accompanied by lime wedges.

Crab chettinad

Serves 8 as part of an Indian meal

3 lb (1.5 kg) soft-shell or blue swimmer crabs

1/3 cup coriander seeds

1 cup (8 fl oz/250 ml) vegetable oil and melted unsalted butter combined

1-inch (2.5-cm) cinnamon stick

3 green cardamom pods

3 whole cloves

2 lb (1 kg) yellow (brown) onions, or about 6 medium, chopped

1 teaspoon salt, plus extra salt to taste

2 1/2 tablespoons grated fresh ginger

2 1/2 tablespoons finely chopped garlic

4 teaspoons chili powder

4 teaspoons ground turmeric

2 lb (1 kg) tomatoes (about 7 medium), unpeeled, finely chopped

1 cup (1 1/2 oz/45 g) chopped fresh cilantro (fresh coriander)

18 fresh curry leaves, torn into pieces

4 teaspoons crushed black peppercorns

steamed basmati rice (see page 28), for serving

Remove large top shell from each crab. Remove fibrous matter from inside crab and discard. Rinse crabs well. Use a sharp knife to cut each crab into quarters. Set aside.

In a spice grinder, grind coriander seeds to a powder. Set aside.

In a deghchi or large frying pan, heat oil and butter mixture over low heat. Add cinnamon, cardamom and cloves. Cook until fragrant, about 30 seconds. Add onions and 1 teaspoon salt and cook, uncovered, stirring often, until onions are dark golden brown, 15–20 minutes.

Add ginger and garlic and cook for 1 minute. Add ground coriander, chili powder and turmeric and cook, stirring, for 1 minute. Add tomatoes and cook, uncovered, stirring often, until tomatoes are cooked and soft, about 10 minutes. Add crab and cook, covered, turning pieces occasionally, until crab shells turn red and meat is just cooked, 15–20 minutes.

Use tongs to remove crab pieces to a plate. Add cilantro, curry leaves and peppercorns to sauce in pan, mixing well. Taste and add salt if desired. Return crab pieces to pan and turn to coat with sauce, then serve.

Crab with yellow curry powder

Serves 4–6

1 1/2 lb (750 g) cooked or raw crab in the shell

1 cup (8 fl oz/250 ml) evaporated milk

1 egg, beaten

2 tablespoons soy sauce

1/2 teaspoon granulated (white) sugar

1/2 cup (4 fl oz/125 ml) Chili Oil (see page 569)

1 teaspoon curry powder

1/4 cup (2 fl oz/60 ml) vegetable oil

1 fresh long red chili, cut into strips

4 shallots (scallions/spring onions), coarsely chopped

1/4 cup (1 oz/30 g) coarsely chopped Chinese or regular celery

Clean crab by pulling off the apron flap on the bottom of the shell. Pry off top shell, remove gills, intestines and mouth parts. Cut small crabs in half, or large crabs into eight pieces. Twist off claws. Refrigerate until ready to use.

In a medium bowl, combine milk, egg, soy sauce, sugar, chili oil and curry powder; whisk to blend well.

Heat vegetable oil in a wok or large, heavy frying pan over high heat. Add milk mixture and bring to a boil, stirring constantly. Add crab and cook for 2 minutes, then turn off heat and add chili, scallions and celery. Spoon into a deep serving dish and serve.

Hints: *Make sure you use evaporated milk in this Thai recipe and not sweetened condensed milk.*

For a less piquant dish, replace half the chili oil with vegetable oil and use a mild curry powder.

Fish and tomato curry

Serves 4

FOR SPICE MIXTURE
2 tablespoons vegetable oil
1 onion, finely sliced
3 cloves garlic, finely chopped
1 teaspoon peeled and grated fresh
   ginger
1/2 teaspoon ground turmeric
1 teaspoon ground cumin
2 teaspoons ground coriander
1 teaspoon Garam Masala
   (see page 575)
1/2 teaspoon chili powder

1 lb (500 g) white fish fillets, cut into
   2-inch (5-cm) pieces
13 oz (400 g) canned chopped
   tomatoes
1 teaspoon sea salt
1 teaspoon sugar
2 tablespoons fresh cilantro (fresh
   coriander) leaves
lemon wedges, for serving
steamed basmati rice (see page 28), for
   serving

To make spice mixture: In a wok or large frying pan, heat oil over medium heat and stir-fry remaining ingredients until fragrant, 1–2 minutes.

Add fish, tomatoes with their juice, salt and sugar to the spice mixture in the wok. Reduce heat to low, cover, and simmer, stirring occasionally, until fish is opaque throughout, 8–10 minutes.

Remove from heat and spoon into serving bowls. Sprinkle with cilantro. Serve with lemon wedges and steamed basmati rice.

Fish in coconut sauce

Serves 8 as part of an Indian meal

1 lb (500 g) white-fleshed fish fillets,
such as snapper, barramundi or
ocean perch

3 tablespoons vegetable oil

1 teaspoon brown or black mustard
seeds

1/2 teaspoon fenugreek seeds

3 dried red chilies

1 lb (500 g) yellow (brown) onions
(about 3 medium), halved and thinly
sliced

2 tablespoons grated fresh ginger

2 tablespoons finely chopped garlic

36 fresh curry leaves

3 teaspoons ground turmeric

2–4 tablespoons chili powder

2 tomatoes, unpeeled, coarsely
chopped

1 1/2 cups (12 fl oz/375 ml) coconut
cream

1 teaspoon tamarind concentrate

salt to taste

juice of 1/2 lemon

steamed basmati rice (see page 28),
for serving

Remove skin from fish fillets then cut into 3/4 x 2-inch (2 x 5-cm) pieces. Set aside.

In a karhai or wok, heat oil over low heat. Add mustard seeds and cook until seeds crackle, about 30 seconds. Add fenugreek seeds and chilies and cook, stirring, until seeds turn light golden brown and chilies are deep golden brown, about 30 seconds. Add onions and cook, stirring, until slightly softened, about 1 minute. Add ginger and garlic and cook, stirring, for 1 minute. Add curry leaves, turmeric and chili powder and cook, stirring, for 30 seconds. Add tomatoes and cook until tomatoes are slightly soft, about 3 minutes. Stir in coconut cream and tamarind and season with salt.

Stir in fish pieces and simmer, covered, until fish is just cooked through, about 5 minutes. Stir in lemon juice. Serve immediately with rice.

Fish with green curry paste

Serves 2–4

1/4 cup (2 fl oz/60 ml) vegetable oil

1/4 cup (2 fl oz/60 ml) Green Curry
   Paste (see page 576)

12 oz (375 g) white fish fillets such as
   snapper, sole or cod, thinly sliced

4 kaffir lime leaves, stemmed

1 cup (4 oz/125 g) chopped eggplant
   (aubergine) or 3 round Thai eggplants,
   chopped

1/2 cup (2 oz/60 g) pea eggplants
   (optional)

1/4 cup (2 fl oz/60 ml) fish stock
   (see page 589) or water

1 fresh long red chili, coarsely chopped

1 cup (1 oz/30 g) loosely packed fresh
   sweet Thai basil leaves

1/3 cup (3 fl oz/90 ml) coconut cream
   plus 2 tablespoons, for garnish

1 tablespoon fish sauce

1 tablespoon soy sauce

1 tablespoon granulated (white) sugar

1 tablespoon palm sugar

In a wok or large, heavy frying pan, heat oil over medium–high heat. Add curry paste and fry, stirring constantly, until fragrant, 1–2 minutes. Add fish and gently stir until coated on all sides. Add kaffir lime leaves and eggplants. Cook for 1 minute, then add fish stock.

Bring just to a boil, stirring, then add chili, basil, 1/3 cup (3 fl oz/90 ml) coconut cream, fish sauce, soy sauce and sugars. Cook for 1–2 minutes to heat through. Transfer to a serving bowl, drizzle over the remaining 2 tablespoons coconut cream, and serve.

Note: *This Thai dish is delicious chilled as well as hot; when serving chilled, omit coconut cream garnish.*

Variation: *To make pork with green curry paste, substitute an equal quantity of pork shoulder, loin or tenderloin (fillet) for the fish. Slice thinly and proceed as above. Lamb leg or loin also makes a delicious substitute here, although it is not traditionally Thai.*

Fried fish with Penang curry sauce

Serves 4–6

12 oz (375 g) fish fillets such as
snapper, plaice or halibut, thinly
sliced

1 cup (5 oz/150 g) all-purpose (plain)
flour, for dredging

vegetable oil, for deep-frying

2 cups (16 fl oz/500 ml) coconut cream
plus 3 tablespoons for garnish

2–3 tablespoons vegetable oil (optional)

1/4 cup (2 fl oz/60 ml) Penang Curry
Paste (see page 583) or Red Curry
Paste (see page 586)

2 tablespoons palm sugar

2 tablespoons fish sauce

6 kaffir lime leaves, stemmed

1/2 cup (1/2 oz/15 g) loosely packed
fresh sweet Thai basil leaves

1 fresh long red chili, seeded and
julienned

Pat fish pieces dry with paper towels, then dredge in flour to coat evenly. Shake off any excess flour and set aside.

In a wok or deep-fryer, heat 3 inches (7.5 cm) oil to 350°F (180°C). Fry fish in batches until golden brown, about 3 minutes. Using a skimmer, transfer fish to paper towels to drain briefly. Place in a deep serving dish.

In a wok or large, heavy frying pan over medium–high heat, fry 1 cup (8 fl oz/250 ml) coconut cream, stirring constantly, until it separates, 3–5 minutes. If it does not separate, add the optional oil. Add the curry paste and fry, stirring constantly, until fragrant, 1–2 minutes. Add remaining 1 cup (8 fl oz/250 ml) coconut cream and stir-fry for 1 minute. Add palm sugar—if using a wok, add it along the edge of the wok so that it melts before stirring into the curry; if using a standard frying pan, add directly to the curry. Stir in fish sauce.

Roll kaffir lime leaves into a tight cylinder and cut into fine shreds. Tear basil leaves coarsely into pieces. Add half the kaffir lime leaves, basil and chili to the curry. Stir to combine then pour over fish in serving dish.

Garnish with remaining kaffir lime leaves, basil and chili. Drizzle with reserved coconut cream and serve.

Garlic and chili scallops

Serves 2–3

1 lb (500 g) scallops
3 cloves garlic, finely chopped
$^1/_2$ teaspoon Chinese five-spice powder
1 teaspoon grated fresh ginger
1 small red chili, seeded and finely chopped
2 tablespoons soy sauce
1 tablespoon rice wine
2 tablespoons vegetable oil
3 tablespoons water
1 cup (1 oz/30 g) mizuna

Place scallops in a shallow nonmetallic dish. In a bowl, combine garlic, five-spice powder, ginger, chili, soy sauce and rice wine and pour over scallops. Cover dish with plastic wrap and refrigerate for 30 minutes. Drain scallops, reserving marinade.

Preheat a grill pan or barbecue, then brush grill with oil. Grill scallops until the opaque flesh turns white, 2–3 minutes, turning during cooking. Remove from grill.

Place reserved marinade into a saucepan. Add water, bring to a boil and allow to boil for 1 minute; set aside.

To serve, arrange mizuna on serving plates. Top with scallops and drizzle with warm marinade.

Hint: Scallops in this recipe can also be cooked using a large nonstick frying pan over medium–high heat.

Goan fish

Serves 8–10 as part of an Indian meal

1–1 1/2 cups dried red chilies
  broken into small pieces
1/3 cup coriander seeds
1/4 cup cumin seeds
3/4 cup (6 fl oz/180 ml) white vinegar
1 tablespoon grated fresh ginger
1 tablespoon finely chopped garlic
2 teaspoons ground turmeric
1/2 cup (4 fl oz/125 ml) vegetable oil
  and melted unsalted butter combined
1 lb (500 g) yellow (brown) onions
  (about 3 medium), halved and sliced

2 large tomatoes, unpeeled, quartered
2 fresh green chilies, slit
  lengthwise
2 1/2 cups (20 fl oz/625 ml) coconut
  milk (see page 24)
salt to taste
2 lb (1 kg) white-fleshed fish fillets such
  as snapper, ling, cod or ocean perch
steamed basmati rice (see page 28),
  for serving

In a spice grinder, grind dried chili, coriander seeds and cumin seeds to a powder. Place in a bowl and combine with vinegar, ginger, garlic and turmeric to form a paste. Set aside.

In a large karhai or wok, heat oil and butter mixture over medium–low heat. Add onions and cook, uncovered, stirring often, until soft, about 10 minutes. Add spice paste and cook, stirring, until fragrant, about 3 minutes. Add tomatoes, green chilies and coconut milk and cook, uncovered, stirring often, until tomatoes soften, about 5 minutes. Season with salt.

If fish fillets are large, cut into serving-sized pieces. Add fish to sauce and cook, uncovered, until fish flakes when tested with a fork, about 5 minutes. Serve hot with steamed rice.

Note: Adjust dried chili according to your taste—the full quantity makes a hot dish.

Japanese fried shrimp

Serves 4

12 raw jumbo shrimp (green king prawns), heads and shells removed, tails intact,
   deveined
salt and pepper
1/4 cup (1 1/2 oz/45 g) all-purpose (plain) flour
1 cup (4 oz/125 g) panko
2 eggs, lightly beaten
vegetable oil, for deep-frying
tonkatsu sauce or mayonnaise, for dipping
lemon wedges, for garnish

Make 3 or 4 shallow cuts along underside of each shrimp to prevent it from curling during cooking. Season shrimp lightly with salt and pepper. Place flour and panko on separate plates. Dredge each shrimp in flour, shaking off excess. Dip shrimp into eggs, letting excess drain off, and then coat with panko, pressing crumbs on firmly.

Pour oil into a deep, heavy-bottomed frying pan to a depth of 3 inches (7.5 cm). Heat oil until it reaches 375°F (190°C) on a deep-frying thermometer. Working in batches, carefully slip shrimp into hot oil. Fry until shrimp are golden brown, 2–2 1/2 minutes, using chopsticks to turn shrimp so they cook evenly. Using a wire skimmer, remove shrimp from oil and drain on paper towels.

Divide among 4 plates and serve with tonkatsu sauce and mayonnaise for dipping sauces. Garnish with lemon wedges.

Variation: *To make Japanese fried scallops, use 16 large white scallops, without coral, in place of shrimp and increase all-purpose (plain) flour to 1/2 cup (2 1/2 oz/75 g). Rinse scallops and gently drain, then prepare as for fried shrimp.*

Japanese grilled rainbow trout

Serves 4

4 rainbow trout, about 12 oz (375 g) each, cleaned, heads intact
salt
1/3 cup (3 fl oz/90 ml) Tosa Shoyu (see page 593)
4 tablespoons finely grated daikon
2 teaspoons finely grated fresh ginger

Rinse fish well under running cold water. Sprinkle salt over skin and in cavity of each fish. Coat tail and eye areas well with salt, to prevent burning during cooking. Preheat broiler (grill). Place trout on broiler pan and cook until trout is half cooked, about 8 minutes. Using a spatula, carefully turn trout and continue to broil until cooked through, about 7 minutes. Do not overcook. Cooking time will depend on the size and thickness of fish.

To check if fish is done, make a small cut in thickest part. Transfer fish to plates decorated with a small pyramid of daikon topped with ginger on the side. Serve hot with tosa shoyu for dipping. Diners mix daikon and ginger from each plate into the tosa shoyu to taste.

Japanese grilled sake fish cutlets

Serves 4

4 fish steaks (cutlets), approximately 6 1/2 oz (200 g) each (choose any fish with firm, white flesh, such as sea bass, grouper, halibut, coley or blue-eye cod)
2 teaspoons sea salt
1 teaspoon freshly ground black pepper
2 tablespoons vegetable oil
1 fl oz (30 ml) sake
juice and grated zest of 1 lime
2 cups (2 oz/60 g) baby spinach leaves, for serving
2 tablespoons additional grated lime zest

Sprinkle both sides of fish with salt and pepper. Preheat a grill pan or barbecue, then brush grill with oil. Grill fish until fish changes color and flakes easily with a fork, 2–3 minutes each side. Remove from grill and brush each with combined sake, juice and zest. To serve, arrange spinach leaves on serving plates and top with fish cutlets. Serve with extra lime zest.

Japanese grilled squid

Serves 4

1 whole squid, about 13 oz (400 g), cleaned (see page 263) and
   tentacles trimmed
2 scallions (shallots/spring onions), thinly sliced
1 tablespoon finely grated fresh ginger
soy sauce

Preheat broiler (grill). Place squid on a broiler pan. Broil (grill) squid, turning once, about
4 minutes on each side. Cooking time will depend on thickness of squid. Do not
overcook, as squid will toughen.

Using tongs, transfer squid from broiler to a cutting board. Holding squid with tongs and,
using a sharp knife, cut squid into slices $1/4$ inch (6 mm) thick. Place on a warm serving
plate and sprinkle with grated ginger and scallions. Drizzle with soy sauce to taste.

Japanese grilled tuna with rice noodles

Serves 4

1 egg white
1 tablespoon soy sauce
4 tuna steaks, approximately $6^1/2$ oz
   (200 g) each
$1/3$ cup (1 oz/30 g) sesame seeds

2 tablespoons vegetable oil
4 oz (125 g) rice stick noodles
1 tablespoon sesame oil
lemon wedges, for serving

In a bowl, lightly beat egg white with a fork and add soy sauce. Brush one side of each
tuna steak with egg white mixture, then dip egg white side of tuna into sesame seeds.
Preheat a grill pan or barbecue and brush with vegetable oil. Grill tuna, sesame seed side
down first, for 2–3 minutes each side (tuna should remain pink on the inside). Remove
from grill and allow to stand 5 minutes before slicing in half.

Warm oil in a small saucepan over medium heat for 1 minute. Cook rice stick noodles
according to packet directions, or following instructions on page 442. To serve, place
tuna onto a serving plate and drizzle with warm sesame oil. Serve with noodles and
lemon.

Japanese seafood hot pot (Yosenabe)

Serves 4

2 oz (60 g) harusame

12 oz (375 g) white-fleshed fish fillets
    such as snapper or flathead

8 mussels, scrubbed and debearded

8 pippis or clams, well scrubbed

12 jumbo shrimp (green king prawns),
    heads and shells removed, tails
    intact, deveined

1/2 carrot, thinly sliced

5 oz (150 g) daikon, thinly sliced

6 Chinese (napa) cabbage leaves,
    thickly sliced

8 fresh shiitake mushrooms

1/2 bunch (6 oz/180 g) spinach

2 stems shungiku

4 scallions (shallots/spring onions),
    cut into 3-inch (7.5-cm) lengths

10 oz (300 g) silken tofu

4 cups (32 fl oz/1 L) boiling water

1 teaspoon instant dashi

Nihaizu (see page 581), for serving

8 tablespoons grated daikon, mixed
    with 1/2 red chili, finely chopped, for
    serving

2 scallions (shallots/spring onions),
    thinly sliced, for serving

Soak harusame in hot water for 5 minutes, then drain.

Arrange fish, shellfish, vegetables and tofu attractively on a large platter. This platter is placed on the table and the ingredients are cooked at the table in a large pot on a portable burner or in an electric frying pan.

Fill pot or frying pan two-thirds full with boiling water and add instant dashi. Bring stock to a boil. When stock is boiling add firm vegetables, then gradually add seafood, fish, other vegetables, tofu and harasume in batches.

Diners help themselves, retrieving vegetables, seafood and tofu from stock pot with chopsticks when cooked to their liking. Keep adding raw ingredients to stock as cooked ingredients are removed and eaten. Give each diner a small bowl of nihaizu to which daikon-chili mixture and scallions are added to taste.

Lobster salad Vietnamese-style

Serves 6–8

FOR MARINATED VEGETABLES

1 cucumber

4 carrots

2 stalks celery, julienned finely

6 oz (180 g) pearl onions or small boiling onions (pickling onions)

1 tablespoon rice vinegar or distilled white vinegar

1 teaspoon sugar

1 tablespoon fish sauce

2 teaspoons salt

1 fresh long red chili, seeded and chopped

1 1/2 cups (3 oz/90 g) bean sprouts, rinsed and drained

FOR LOBSTER

1 lb (500 g) shelled meat from lobster tails or langoustines (scampi/ saltwater crayfish), cut into 1/2 inch (12 mm) thick medallions

1 tablespoon fish sauce

1/4 teaspoon ground pepper

1/2 teaspoon chili powder or to taste

2 teaspoons finely chopped brown or pink shallots (French shallots)

1/2-inch (12-mm) knob fresh ginger, finely grated

FOR DRESSING

1 teaspoon Asian sesame oil

2 teaspoons water

1 tablespoon fresh lime juice

1/2 teaspoon grated fresh ginger or ginger juice

1/4 fresh long red chili, seeded and finely chopped

1/2 teaspoon salt

1/4 teaspoon ground pepper

2 tablespoons coarsely chopped fresh cilantro (fresh coriander) sprigs, for garnish

To make marinated vegetables: Cut cucumber lengthwise in half, then use a spoon to scoop out and discard seeds. Cut carrots and cucumber into strips the size of French fries. Plunge pearl onions into boiling water, then drain and slip off the skins. If using pickling onions, peel and quarter. In a medium bowl, combine vinegar, sugar, fish sauce, salt and chili. Add vegetables and sprouts and toss to coat. Let stand for 15–20 minutes.

In a medium bowl, combine fish sauce, pepper, chili powder, shallots and ginger. Add lobster and toss to coat. Let stand for 10 minutes. In a large nonstick frying pan over medium–high heat, sauté lobster until opaque, about 2 minutes. In a small bowl, combine all dressing ingredients. Add to lobster and toss to coat. To serve, drain marinated vegetables and arrange on a serving plate. Layer lobster on top and sprinkle with cilantro.

Lobster tails with rougail sauce

Serves 6

3 rock lobster tails, halved lengthwise,
about 6 oz (180 g) each

FOR ROUGAIL SAUCE
$1/2$-inch (1.2-cm) knob fresh turmeric,
peeled, or 2 teaspoons ground
turmeric
5 garlic cloves, finely chopped
2 tablespoons finely chopped brown or
pink shallots (French shallots)
1 fresh long red chili, seeded and finely
chopped
2 stalks lemongrass, white part only,
peeled and finely chopped
2 tablespoons fish sauce

juice of 1 lime
3 tablespoons vegetable or olive oil
1 teaspoon ground pepper

FOR ACCOMPANIMENTS
Nuoc Cham Sauce (see page 582) or
Vietnamese Chili Fish Sauce (see page
594)
1–2 lemons or limes, quartered or cut
into wedges
1 fresh long red or green chili, seeded
and thinly sliced
fresh cilantro (fresh coriander) sprigs
Marinated Vegetables (see opposite)

To make sauce: If using fresh turmeric, pound in a mortar using a pestle, or use a grater. Soak extracted juice and pulp in 1 tablespoon water, from 3–4 minutes up to a few hours then strain. Wear gloves to prevent turmeric staining your skin. Combine turmeric mixture or ground turmeric and all remaining sauce ingredients. Alternatively, instead of chopping each ingredient separately, combine all sauce ingredients in a food processor and puree.

Rinse lobster halves and pat dry. Place in sauce and let stand for 1 hour, turning occasionally to coat all sides. Prepare a charcoal grill (barbecue) or brazier (see page 12) or preheat an oven broiler (grill). Cook lobster, turning once and spooning additional marinade on top occasionally during cooking, until opaque throughout, about 10 minutes without shell and about 12 minutes with shell. If broiling (grilling), cook lobster, flesh-side up, about 4 inches (10 cm) from heat source, for 10–15 minutes.

Place lobster on serving plate. Serve hot with nuoc cham or chili fish sauce, lemon or lime wedges, chili slices, cilantro sprigs and marinated vegetables.

Note: Rougail is a generic French term applied to any number of spicy sauces, such as this Vietnamese one.

Mussel curry

1 tablespoon vegetable oil
1 onion, finely chopped
6 cloves garlic, finely chopped
2 fresh green Thai or Anaheim chilies, seeded and chopped
1 teaspoon ground turmeric
1/2 cup (4 fl oz/125 ml) white wine vinegar

1 3/4 cups (14 fl oz/440 ml) coconut milk (see page 24)
2 teaspoons sugar
2 lb (1 kg) mussels, scrubbed and debearded
2 tablespoons chopped fresh cilantro (coriander)
sea salt to taste
steamed rice (see page 28), for serving

In a large saucepan, heat oil over medium heat and fry onion, garlic, chilies and turmeric until fragrant, 2–3 minutes. Add vinegar, coconut milk, sugar and mussels. Bring to a boil, reduce heat to low, cover and simmer until mussels have opened, about 6 minutes. Remove from heat and discard any mussels that have not opened. Stir in cilantro and salt.

Transfer mussels to serving bowls. Pour sauce over and serve with steamed rice.

Mussels Japanese-style (Misoyaki)

24 New Zealand green-lipped mussels or other large mussels, scrubbed and debearded

Sumiso Sauce (see page 592)
2 scallions (shallots/spring onions), thinly sliced, for garnish

Preheat broiler (grill). Place mussels on a broiler pan. Broil (grill) until mussels are slightly brown and surface is drying out, about 5 minutes. Do not overcook. Spoon sumiso sauce on mussels and broil for 1 minute. Transfer to 4 plates and garnish with sliced scallions.

Hint: This Japanese method of cooking can be used for most types of shellfish, including oysters and scallops, as well as mussels. Be careful not to overcook the shellfish or they will dry out and toughen.

Pippis steamed with sake

8 oz (250 g) pippis or clams, well scrubbed

2 tablespoons sake

1 teaspoon mirin

1/4 teaspoon instant dashi

1/2 teaspoon salt

2 thin slices of peeled ginger, cut into matchstick strips

1 scallion (shallot/spring onion), thinly sliced

Place pippis in a bowl with 3 cups (24 fl oz/750 ml) water and 1 1/2 tablespoons salt. Let stand overnight to remove any sand. Rinse pippis well.

Place pippis, sake, mirin, dashi, salt and ginger in a heatproof bowl. Place bowl in a steamer set over boiling water and steam for 5–10 minutes. Remove steamer from heat and carefully remove bowl from steamer, placing it on a small heatproof plate. Sprinkle pippis with scallions and serve with a spoon so diners can enjoy the broth.

Note: This recipe uses pippis or clams; however, in Japan, "asari," a small clam-like shellfish that is similar to pippis, is traditionally used.

Hints: Soaking mollusks, such as pippis or clams, in cold water will purge them of sandy residue. The sand will settle at the bottom of the soaking container.

Mollusks that are still in their shells must be alive when cooked. They should be cooked only until the shells open, sometimes for just a few minutes. If overcooked, they will toughen and shrink.

Red curry with fish

Serves 4–6

about 2 cups (16 fl oz/500 ml)
coconut milk (see page 24)

2–3 tablespoons vegetable oil

1/4 cup (2 fl oz/60 ml) Red Curry Paste
(see page 586)

1/2 cup (2 oz/60 g) chopped round Thai
or purple eggplant (aubergine)

1 cup (3 1/2 oz/100 g) coarsely chopped
fresh or canned bamboo shoots,
rinsed and drained

3 kaffir lime leaves, stemmed

1 cup (1 oz/30 g) loosely packed fresh
sweet Thai basil leaves

1–2 tablespoons fish sauce, to taste

12 oz (375 g) fish fillets such as
snapper, bream or perch, thinly sliced

2 fresh long red chilies, cut into large
pieces

Let coconut milk stand until thick coconut milk rises to the top. Spoon thick coconut milk into a bowl, reserving 2 tablespoons for garnish. Heat oil in a wok or large frying pan over medium–high heat and fry curry paste, stirring constantly, until fragrant, 1–2 minutes. Add thick coconut milk, stir to combine and bring to a boil. Add eggplant, bamboo shoots and remaining thin coconut milk. Reduce heat and simmer, uncovered, until vegetables are slightly soft, about 4 minutes.

Tear 2 kaffir lime leaves and basil into pieces. Stir fish sauce and kaffir lime leaves into curry. Add fish and cook for about 2 minutes, or until fish flakes when prodded. Add half the basil leaves and remove from heat.

Transfer curry to a serving dish and garnish with remaining basil. Drizzle with 2 tablespoons of reserved thick coconut milk. Roll the remaining kaffir lime leaf into a tight cylinder and cut into fine strips; sprinkle over curry. (Pictured on page 258.)

Note: Most varieties of fish fillet will suit this authentic Thai recipe, but don't stir too vigorously, or the pieces may break up.

Variation: To make red curry with lobster, remove meat from the shells of 2 rock lobster tails and cut into pieces. Heat 1/4 cup (2 fl oz/60 ml) vegetable oil in a wok or frying pan over high heat and stir-fry lobster meat for 3–4 minutes, or until opaque throughout. Using a slotted spoon, transfer to a bowl. Proceed as above. Just before serving, return lobster meat to the curry to heat through. Garnish and serve.

Roasted whole snapper in salt crust with tamarind-chili sauce

Serves 6

11 cups (6 lb/3 kg) rock salt
2 whole red snappers, each 3 lb
  (1.5 kg), cleaned
3 limes, quartered

TAMARIND-CHILI SAUCE
1/2 cup (5 oz/150 g) tamarind pulp
1/2 cup (4 fl oz/125 ml) boiling water

2 tablespoons sugar
1 teaspoon fish sauce
1 cup (1 oz/30 g) fresh cilantro
  (coriander) leaves
1 cup (1 oz/30 g) fresh mint leaves
1 long, red fresh chili
1/4 cup (1 oz/30 g) crispy fried shallots
  (French shallots) (see page 24)

Preheat oven to 350°F (180°C/Gas 4). Spread half of rock salt in roasting pan; it should be 3–4 inches (7.5–10 cm) deep. Rinse inside and outside of fish with cold running water and pat thoroughly dry with paper towels. Place fish on bed of salt. Divide lime quarters evenly between fish cavities. Cover fish with remaining rock salt.

Place fish in oven and roast until flesh is opaque throughout and flakes when tested with knife tip (scrape away salt near center of fish to test), about 50 minutes.

While fish are roasting, make tamarind-chili sauce: In a small, heatproof bowl, cover tamarind pulp with boiling water and let stand for 4 minutes. Pour through sieve, pressing solids with back of spoon to extract as much flavor as possible. Discard solids. Add sugar and fish sauce to tamarind juice and stir to combine.

Just before fish are done, in a large bowl (to avoid bruising herb leaves), combine cilantro, mint, chili and onions and stir to mix.

Remove fish from oven, scrape away top salt layer and transfer fish to warmed serving platter. Peel away skin from top of each fish. Drizzle half of tamarind-chili sauce over top fillets, sprinkle with half of herb mixture and serve. When top fillets have been removed, remove backbone and lift away bottom fillets from skin. Drizzle bottom fillets with remaining sauce, sprinkle with remaining herb mixture and serve.

Salmon grilled with wasabi butter

Serves 4

1/2 cup (4 oz/125 g) butter, softened
2 teaspoons wasabi paste
grated zest of 1 lime
1 tablespoon lime juice
1/2 teaspoon freshly ground black pepper
2 tablespoons vegetable oil
4 salmon fillets (approximately 6 oz/180 g each), skin and bones removed
fresh cilantro (fresh coriander) leaves, for garnish

FOR CRISPY FRIED POTATOES
3 potatoes, peeled and very thinly sliced
1/2 cup (4 fl oz/125 ml) vegetable oil, for frying

Place butter in a mixing bowl and beat until soft. Add wasabi, rind, juice and pepper and mix until well combined. Refrigerate until firm.

To make crispy fried potatoes: Pat potatoes dry with paper towel. Heat oil over medium heat and, working in batches, fry potato slices until golden and crisp, about 2 minutes. Remove with a slotted spoon and drain on paper towels.

Brush salmon with oil. Preheat a grill pan or barbecue. Grill salmon 2–3 minutes each side (salmon should remain pink in the center), then allow to stand for 5 minutes before cutting in half. Place onto serving plates.

Using a teaspoon or melon baller, scoop wasabi butter onto fish. Serve with crispy fried potatoes and garnish with fresh cilantro.

Hint: Leftover wasabi butter can be stored in a sealed container in the refrigerator for up to 2 weeks.

Semolina-crusted shrimp

Serves 8–10 as part of an Indian meal

¹/₄ cup coriander seeds
1–2 tablespoons vegetable oil
4 teaspoons finely grated fresh ginger
4 teaspoons finely chopped garlic
4 teaspoons tamarind concentrate
2–4 teaspoons chili powder
2 teaspoons fennel seeds
1 teaspoon ground turmeric
18 fresh curry leaves, finely chopped
salt to taste
2 lb (1 kg) medium shrimp (prawns), peeled and deveined
vegetable oil, for deep-frying
1 cup (6 oz/180 g) coarse semolina
juice of 1 lemon

In a spice grinder, grind coriander seeds to a powder. Place in a bowl and combine with oil, ginger, garlic, tamarind concentrate, chili powder, fennel seeds, turmeric, curry leaves and salt to form a paste.

Add shrimp to spice paste and mix well until coated. Set aside to marinate for 5 minutes.

Fill a karhai or wok with vegetable oil to a depth of 2 inches (5 cm) and heat over medium heat to 375°F (190°C) on a deep-frying thermometer. While oil is heating, dip shrimp, one at a time, in semolina to coat. Fry shrimp in batches until light golden, 1–2 minutes. Use a slotted spoon to remove shrimp to paper towels to drain.

Drizzle shrimp with lemon juice and serve hot.

Shrimp, mango and green papaya salad

Serves 4

24 raw jumbo shrimp (green king prawns) peeled and deveined, leaving tails
   intact
2 tablespoons peanut oil
3/4 oz (25 g) cellophane (bean thread) noodles
1/2 green papaya, peeled and cut into matchstick lengths
1 mango, peeled and cut into matchstick lengths
1 cup (1 oz/30 g) loosely packed fresh cilantro (fresh coriander) leaves
1/2 cup (1/2 oz/15 g) loosely packed fresh basil leaves
1/4 cup (3/4 oz/25 g) sliced scallions (shallots/spring onions)

FOR DRESSING

1 small red chili, seeded and finely chopped
3 tablespoons fish sauce
4 tablespoons lime juice
1 teaspoon sesame oil
2 teaspoons grated fresh ginger
1 teaspoon shaved palm sugar or brown sugar

Brush shrimp with oil. Preheat a grill pan or barbecue and grill shrimp until they change
color, 3–4 minutes, turning during cooking. Remove from grill. Place noodles in a
heatproof bowl, pour in boiling water to cover and allow to stand until noodles soften,
about 10 minutes. Drain and, using scissors, roughly cut noodles into shorter lengths.

To make dressing: Place chili, fish sauce, lime juice, sesame oil, ginger and sugar in a
screw-top jar. Shake well to mix.

Combine noodles, shrimp, papaya, mango, cilantro, basil and scallions in a mixing bowl.
Add dressing and toss until well combined. Serve at room temperature or chilled.

Shrimp marinated in spiced yogurt

Serves 8–10 as part of an Indian meal

7 oz (220 g) plain (natural) yogurt

2 red chilies, seeded and chopped

2 cloves garlic, chopped

2 tablespoons chopped fresh cilantro
(fresh coriander) leaves

1 teaspoon Garam Masala (see
page 575)

1 teaspoon turmeric

1 teaspoon grated lemon zest

2 tablespoons lemon juice

2 lb (1 kg) uncooked shrimp (prawns),
peeled and deveined

Combine yogurt, chilies, garlic, cilantro, garam masala, turmeric, zest and juice in a large
bowl. Add shrimp and mix well. Marinate 30 minutes, or overnight in refrigerator if time
allows. Drain excess marinade from shrimp and reserve. Heat a frying pan, broiler (grill)
or barbecue. Cook shrimp for 1–2 minutes per side, basting frequently with marinade.
Serve hot.

Shrimp reiachado masala

Serves 8–10 as part of an Indian meal

1 recipe Reiachado Masala (see page 587)

2 lb (1 kg) medium shrimp (prawns), peeled and deveined

2 tablespoons vegetable oil

juice of 1 lemon

In a glass or ceramic bowl, combine reiachado masala and shrimp and mix well to coat
shrimp. Set aside to marinate for 5 minutes.

In a frying pan, heat oil over medium–low heat until hot. Cook shrimp in batches, turning
once, until browned, about 1–2 minutes. Take care not to scorch marinade. Drizzle
cooked shrimp with lemon juice and serve hot.

Note: *This home-style Indian dish has a strong Portuguese influence.*

Shrimp with wasabi mayonnaise

Serves 4

FOR MAYONNAISE
2 egg yolks, with the thread removed
$1/2$ teaspoon salt
pinch of white pepper
$1/2$ teaspoon sugar
$1/2$ teaspoon instant dashi
$1/2$ teaspoon hot English mustard
$1^1/2$ tablespoons rice vinegar
2 cups (16 fl oz/500 ml) vegetable oil, at room temperature

1 teaspoon wasabi paste
1 teaspoon soy sauce
12 shrimp (prawns), cut in half lengthwise and deveined
1 scallion (shallot/spring onion), thinly sliced, for garnish

In a bowl, beat egg yolks well. Add salt, pepper, sugar, dashi, mustard and a few drops of rice vinegar and beat until yolks are almost white. Very slowly add oil to egg yolks, a few drops at a time, beating constantly, until mixture starts to form an emulsion. Slowly pour in remaining oil, adding remaining vinegar a few drops at a time.

In a bowl, combine mayonnaise, wasabi and soy sauce.

Preheat broiler (grill). Place shrimp on a small baking dish and broil (grill) until almost cooked. Remove and spread liberally with wasabi mayonnaise. Broil again until golden, 1–2 minutes. Transfer to individual plates and garnish with sliced scallions.

Squid bulgogi

3 medium squid tubes (bodies), about
$6^1/_2$ oz (200 g) total, cut open and
cleaned

4 fresh shiitake mushrooms or Chinese
dried mushrooms soaked for
30 minutes in several changes of
water

2 small green bell peppers (capsicums),
cut into bite-sized pieces

2 tablespoons vegetable or sunflower
oil

lettuce leaves, for serving

1 teaspoon pan-toasted sesame seeds
(see page 30)

1 teaspoon freshly ground black
pepper

1 teaspoon thin hot red chili strips

steamed rice (see page 28), for serving

FOR MARINADE

3 tablespoons light soy sauce

2 tablespoons sugar

2 tablespoons finely chopped garlic

2 scallions (shallots/spring onions),
finely chopped

1 teaspoon ginger juice (obtained by
grating fresh ginger)

1 teaspoon sesame oil

Using the tip of a knife, score surface of squid in a crisscross pattern to prevent it
over-curling during cooking. Cut squid into bite-sized pieces.

If using fresh shiitake mushrooms, dip in rapidly boiling water for a few seconds. Remove
and drain on paper towels, then chop roughly. If using dried mushrooms, squeeze out
excess water. Remove and discard stems and roughly chop caps.

To make marinade: Combine marinade ingredients in a small bowl and mix well.

Place squid, mushrooms and bell peppers in a large glass or ceramic bowl with marinade
and marinate for 20–30 minutes.

Heat oil in a frying pan or on a grill until very hot. Drain squid, mushroom and green
pepper pieces and cook over high heat until liquid has evaporated and marinade has
caramelized, about 5 minutes.

Arrange lettuce leaves on individual plates and place squid bulgogi in center. Sprinkle
with sesame seeds, black pepper and chili strips and serve with steamed rice.

Squid sautéed with leeks

Serves 6

1 lb (500 g) cleaned squid (see Hint)

3 tablespoons fish sauce

$^1/_2$ teaspoon ground pepper

2 large leeks or 6 baby leeks, white part only, well rinsed

4 scallions (shallots/spring onions), including green parts, chopped

3 tablespoons vegetable oil

3 small tomatoes, quartered or sectioned

1 onion, coarsely chopped

$^1/_3$-inch (1-cm) knob fresh ginger, peeled and cut into fine julienne

1 tablespoon cornstarch (cornflour) or arrowroot dissolved in 1 tablespoon water

steamed rice (see page 28), for serving

Marinate squid in 2 tablespoons fish sauce and pepper.

Cut leeks and scallions into fine julienne.

In a large frying pan, heat oil over high heat and sauté squid for 1 minute. Add leeks, tomatoes, onion, ginger and scallions. Stir-fry for 2 minutes, then add cornstarch and water mixture. Stir well, then reduce heat to low, cover, and simmer for 3 minutes. Stir in remaining 1 tablespoon fish sauce. Serve hot with steamed rice.

Note: *In Hanoi, Vietnam, young leeks are so tender that they are often eaten raw in salads.*

Hints: *If using uncleaned squid, increase proportion accordingly (see page 275 for directions on cleaning squid). If small, cut squid bodies in half or quarters; larger squid into 1 x 2 inch (2.5 x 5 cm) pieces. To tenderize and beautify larger squid, lightly score inside of flesh with a sharp knife, making a lattice pattern. This works best with larger bodies, as small squid are thin. Do not overcook squid, as it becomes tough and rubbery.*

Squid with sour red chili paste sauce

3 medium squid tubes, about 6¹/₂ oz (200 g) total, cut open and cleaned

2 medium cucumbers

lettuce leaves, for serving

1 tablespoon pan-toasted sesame seeds (see page 30)

steamed rice (see page 28), for serving

FOR SOUR RED CHILI PASTE SAUCE

5 tablespoons red chili paste

3 tablespoons sugar or liquid wheat gluten

3 tablespoons white vinegar

1 teaspoon ginger juice (obtained by grating fresh ginger)

Using the tip of a knife, score the inside surface of squid body in a crisscross pattern to prevent it over-curling during cooking.

Bring a large saucepan of water to a boil. Add squid to the water and boil until it just starts to curl, about 3 minutes. Drain and cut into pieces 1¹/₂ inches (4 cm) long and ³/₈ inch (1 cm) wide.

Cut cucumber in half lengthwise, then slice diagonally into 2-inch (5-cm) lengths. Bring a medium saucepan of water to a boil. Immerse cucumber pieces in boiling water for a few seconds. Remove, rinse in cold water and drain.

To make red chili paste sauce: Combine sauce ingredients in a large bowl.

Add squid and cucumber to chili paste sauce and mix well to coat.

Arrange lettuce leaves on a serving plate and place squid and cucumber in the center. Sprinkle with sesame seeds and serve with steamed rice.

Hint: This is a traditional recipe of Korea. Reduce the amount of red chili paste for a milder sauce.

Steamed ginger fish in nori

Serves 4

FOR MARINADE

1/4 cup (2 fl oz/60 ml) shaoxing wine or dry sherry

1/4 cup (2 fl oz/60 ml) light soy sauce

1 tablespoon fish sauce

1 teaspoon Asian sesame oil

4 fish fillets (snapper, bream, perch, salmon), about 6 oz (180 g) each, and
  5–6 inches (12–15 cm) long

8 scallions (shallots/spring onions)

4 nori sheets

1/2 red bell pepper (capsicum), seeded and thinly sliced

3 tablespoons Japanese pickled ginger

steamed rice (see page 28), for serving

Mix wine, soy sauce, fish sauce and sesame oil in a bowl and pour over fish fillets in a flat dish. Leave for 20–30 minutes, turning once. Drain, discarding marinade.

Cut scallions into same length as fish fillets, leaving some green top on. Lay each fillet diagonally across a sheet of nori. If nori is too big for fillets, trim to smaller square shape. Place 2–3 strips of bell pepper and slices of pickled ginger down center of fish fillet. Add 2 scallions, with one green tip and one white tip at each end. Lightly brush each side flap of nori with water and fold over fish towards center, pressing gently to seal. Fish and vegetable strips will still be visible at either end. Place 2 fish on each level of steamer and cover.

Partially fill a large wok or pot with water (steamer should not touch water) and bring to a rapid simmer. Place steamer over water and steam until fish flakes when tested with a fork and flesh is opaque, 5–8 minutes, depending on thickness of fillets. Switch steamer levels halfway through for even cooking. Remove fish from steamer and serve with remaining pickled ginger and steamed rice.

Stir-fried octopus with long beans and snow peas

Serves 4

1 lb (500 g) baby octopus

1 tablespoon light soy sauce

3 tablespoons vegetable oil

1 tablespoon dry sherry

2 cloves garlic, finely chopped

2 teaspoons grated lime zest

2 tablespoons lime juice

3 small red chilies, seeded and halved

5 oz (150 g) long beans, cut into 4-in (10-cm) lengths

4 kaffir lime leaves, shredded, or 1 teaspoon grated lime zest

5 oz (155 g) snow peas (mange-tout), trimmed and sliced crosswise

Working with one octopus at a time, slit open head and remove intestines. Rinse and place in glass or ceramic bowl. In small bowl, combine soy sauce, 1 tablespoon vegetable oil, sherry, garlic, 2 teaspoons lime zest and lime juice. Pour over octopus, cover and refrigerate for 1 hour. Drain octopus and reserve marinade.

In a wok over medium heat, warm remaining 2 tablespoons vegetable oil. Add chilies and stir-fry until aromatic, 1–2 minutes. Add octopus and stir-fry for 2 minutes. Add beans, kaffir lime leaves, snow peas and reserved marinade. Stir-fry until vegetables are tender-crisp and octopus is cooked through (do not overcook or octopus will toughen), 1–2 minutes. Serve hot.

Variation: To make stir-fried squid with long beans and snow peas, replace octopus with 6 x 1 lb (500 g) baby squid (calamari) bodies, cleaned. Cut squid tubes in half lengthwise. Cut shallow slashes in a criss-cross pattern on outside of squid and cut squid into ³⁄₄-inch (2-cm) strips. Marinate and cook as for octopus.

Tempura seafood

Serves 4

1 egg
1 cup (8 fl oz/250 ml) ice-cold water
1¹/₃ cups (5 oz/150 g) tempura flour
vegetable oil, for deep-frying
¹/₂ cup (2¹/₂ oz/75 g) all-purpose
    (plain) flour
8 scallops, rinsed and cut in half if
    large
12 pieces of white-fleshed fish fillet
    such as snapper, whiting or bream,
    about 1¹/₂ inches x 3 inches
    (4 cm x 7.5 cm) each

2 squid tubes, rinsed and cut
    in half lengthwise, then crosswise
    into slices about 1¹/₂ inches
    x 3 inches (4 cm x 7.5 cm)
4 large or 8 shucked small oysters,
    rinsed well
2 tablespoons finely grated daikon, for
    serving
1 teaspoon finely grated fresh ginger,
    for serving
Tempura Sauce (see page 592), for
    serving

In a bowl, beat egg lightly. Add water, continuing to beat lightly. Stir in tempura flour but do not overmix. The batter will be slightly lumpy.

Pour oil into a deep, heavy-bottomed frying pan so that it is 3 inches (7.5 cm) deep. Heat oil until it reaches 375°F (190°F) on a deep-frying thermometer.

Place all-purpose flour on a plate. Working in batches, dredge seafood in flour, shaking off excess, then dip each piece into tempura batter, allowing excess to drain off. Carefully lower into hot oil. When batter is almost set, use chopsticks to drop a little more batter on each piece of seafood. Cook until batter is light golden brown and seafood is cooked through, 2–2¹/₂ minutes, depending on type of seafood. Using a wire skimmer, remove from oil and drain on paper towels.

Arrange seafood on 4 serving plates, each with a pyramid of grated daikon topped with grated ginger. Each diner mixes daikon and ginger into tempura sauce. Serve immediately.

Tempura shrimp

16 jumbo shrimp (green king prawns), heads and shells removed, tails intact,
  deveined
1 egg
1 cup (8 fl oz/250 ml) ice-cold water
1$^1/_3$ cups (5 oz/150 g) tempura flour
vegetable oil, for deep-frying
$^1/_2$ cup (2$^1/_2$ oz/75 g) all-purpose (plain) flour
2 tablespoons finely grated daikon
1 teaspoon finely grated ginger
Tempura Sauce (see page 592)

Make 3–4 shallow cuts on underside of each shrimp and press gently with hand to flatten slightly. Be careful not to break shrimp. In a bowl, beat egg lightly. Add water continuing to beat lightly. Stir in tempura flour but do not overmix. The batter will be slightly lumpy.

Pour oil into a deep, heavy-bottomed frying pan to fill 3 inches (7.5 cm) deep. Heat oil until it reaches 375°F (190°C) on a deep-frying thermometer.

Place all-purpose flour on a plate. Working in batches, dredge shrimp in flour, shaking off excess, then dip into tempura batter, allowing excess to drain off. Carefully lower into hot oil. When batter is just beginning to set, use chopsticks to drop a little more batter onto shrimp. Continue to cook until batter is light golden brown and shrimp are cooked through, 2–2$^1/_2$ minutes. Using wire skimmers, remove from oil and drain on paper towels.

Arrange shrimp on 4 plates each with a small pyramid of daikon topped with grated ginger. Each diner mixes ginger and daikon into tempura sauce. Serve immediately.

Thai fish cakes

Makes about 25 cakes

1 lb (500 g) fish fillets, such as red fish, cod, monkfish, trout or salmon, skinned
10 kaffir lime leaves, stemmed
1 tablespoon palm sugar
1/3 cup (3 fl oz/90 ml) Red Curry Paste (see page 586)
1 tablespoon fish sauce
1 egg, beaten
1/2 cup (2 oz/60 g) tapioca starch
2 teaspoons baking powder
8 long beans (snake beans), or about 30 green beans, cut into very thin rounds
vegetable oil, for deep-frying
Sweet Chili Relish (see page 592), for serving

In a food processor, pulse fish until finely ground. Roll kaffir lime leaves into a tight cylinder and cut into fine shreds; add to the food processor. Add sugar, red curry paste, fish sauce, egg, tapioca starch and baking powder and process until just blended, no more than 5 seconds. Transfer to a bowl and stir in beans. Cover and keep in the refrigerator for up to 1 day.

To cook, in a wok or deep-fryer, heat 3 inches (7.5 cm) oil to 325°F (170°C/Gas 3). Lightly moisten your fingertips to prevent sticking and form a walnut-sized portion of fish paste into a small patty about 2 inches (5 cm) in diameter and 1/4 inch (6 mm) thick. Carefully add a few fish cakes at a time to the oil and cook until golden brown and well puffed, 2–3 minutes. Using a skimmer, transfer to paper towels to drain. Serve hot, accompanied by sweet chili relish.

Hint: Fish cakes freeze extremely well after cooking. To reheat, first defrost overnight in the refrigerator, then place in a preheated 350°F (180°C/Gas 4) oven until heated through, 15–20 minutes.

Variation: The fish here can be substituted with 1 lb (500 g) boneless, skinless chicken, pork or raw shrimp (prawns).

Thai steamed fish in banana leaves

Serves 8–10

1 tablespoon sticky (glutinous) rice

1/4 cup (2 fl oz/60 ml) vegetable oil

1/4 cup (2 fl oz/60 ml) Red Curry Paste (see page 586)

1/2 cup (2 oz/60 g) chopped eggplant (aubergine) or 2 round Thai eggplants

1/4 cup (1 oz/30 g) pea eggplants (optional)

4 long beans (snake beans) or 12 green beans, cut into 1/2-inch (12-mm) pieces

1/4 cup (2 fl oz/60 ml) chicken stock (see page 588) or water

2 tablespoons fish sauce

8 fresh eryngo (sawtooth coriander) leaves, finely shredded, or 7 sprigs fresh cilantro (fresh coriander), coarsely chopped

12 oz (375 g) firm white fish fillets such as cod, skinned and very thinly sliced

4 kaffir lime leaves, stemmed

1–2 large banana leaves

about 10 fresh piper (betel) leaves, or 2–3 cabbage leaves, each cut into 4 squares

In a wok or small frying pan over low heat, stir rice until golden brown, 3–5 minutes. Transfer to a mortar and pulverize with a pestle; set aside.

Heat oil in a wok or large, heavy frying pan over medium–high heat and fry curry paste, stirring constantly, until fragrant, 1–2 minutes. Add eggplants and beans and stir well to coat. Add chicken stock, fish sauce and eryngo leaves and bring to a boil. Add fish, stirring to coat well, then add ground rice and cook until the mixture is very thick and the fish is just opaque throughout, about 1 minute. Remove from heat.

Roll kaffir lime leaves together into a tight cylinder and cut into fine shreds. Wipe banana leaf with a clean cloth. Spread out each banana leaf and cut each into 8–10 pieces, 8 inches x 6 inches (20 cm x 15 cm) in size, removing the hard center stem. Center a piper leaf on each piece of banana leaf (or alternatively, cut each cabbage leaf into 8–10 small squares and place a piece on each banana leaf) and spoon about 1/4 cup of fish mixture on top. Sprinkle strands of shredded kaffir lime leaf over. Gently roll over sides of banana leaf, overlapping them to make a shape resembling a flat sausage. Fold or pull over 2 opposite ends to the center and secure with a toothpick. Cook parcels in a covered steamer over rapidly simmering water for about 15 minutes. Let cool slightly, then open parcels and serve on the banana leaves.

Thai whole fried fish with chili and basil

Serves 4

1–2 whole fish, about 9¹/₂ inches (24 cm) long, such as snapper, bream, flounder
  or trout, scaled and gutted
vegetable oil for deep-frying, plus 2 tablespoons extra
6 cloves garlic, coarsely chopped
1 onion, finely chopped
5 fresh medium red chilies, thinly sliced
1 fresh long red chili, cut into large pieces
1 fresh long green chili, cut into large pieces
1 tablespoon fish sauce
1 tablespoon soy sauce
¹/₂ cup (2 fl oz/60 ml) chicken stock (see page 588) or water
¹/₂ cup (³/₄ oz/20 g) coarsely chopped sweet Thai basil leaves
¹/₂ cup (³/₄ oz/20 g) chopped cilantro (fresh coriander) leaves

With a very sharp knife, score each side of fish with three deep slashes to the bone.

In a large wok or deep-fryer, heat 4 inches (10 cm) oil to 350°F (180°C). Add fish and cook until crispy and brown on both sides and opaque throughout, 7–10 minutes, depending on thickness. Using a skimmer, transfer fish to paper towels to drain.

Meanwhile, in a wok or heavy frying pan over medium–high heat, heat 2 tablespoons oil and fry garlic, onion and all chilies until garlic just begins to brown. Add fish sauce, soy sauce and chicken stock, stir to combine, then cook for 1 minute. Add basil leaves, stir well and pour over fish. Transfer to a large serving platter, sprinkle with cilantro and serve.

Hints: In Thailand, fish is served whole, with the head intact. If desired, use a cleaver or chef's knife to cut the head of the fish. Discard or retain the head for stock. For a less spicy dish, remove seeds from the chilies.

Variation: This dish can also be garnished with fried basil leaves. In a large frying pan, heat 1 cup (8 fl oz/250 ml) oil. Working in batches, fry about 20 fresh basil leaves. Using a slotted spoon, remove from oil and drain on paper towels.

Vietnamese "cha ca" fish with turmeric

Serves 4

FOR MARINADE

3 tablespoons ground turmeric, or
3-inch (7.5-cm) knob fresh turmeric,
peeled and chopped

1-inch (2.5-cm) knob fresh galangal or
ginger

1–2 fresh long red chilies, seeded

2 tablespoons fish sauce

1/4 cup (2 fl oz/60 ml) water

1 tablespoon rice vinegar

1 tablespoon sugar, or more to taste

1 lb (500 g) skinless catfish, trout or
salmon fillets, cut into bite-sized
pieces

1/4 cup (2 fl oz/60 ml) vegetable oil

1 bunch dill, stemmed and cut into
1 1/2-inch (4-cm) lengths

4 scallions (shallots/spring onions),
including green parts, coarsely
chopped

1/2 cup (2 oz/60 g) thinly sliced brown
or pink shallots (French shallots)

2 cloves garlic, thinly sliced

1/3 cup (2 oz/60 g) chopped peanuts,
toasted (see page 30) and chopped

FOR ACCOMPANIMENTS

Table Greens (see page 437), including
whole butter (Boston) lettuce leaves

5-oz (150-g) packet dried rice
vermicelli, softened (see page 442)
and cut into manageable lengths for
serving

1 cup (8 fl oz/250 ml) Nuoc Cham
Sauce (see page 582)

To make marinade: Pound turmeric, galangal and chili to a paste using a mortar and pestle, or process in a food processor. Add remaining marinade ingredients and stir until dissolved. Pour into a bowl. Add fish, toss to coat and refrigerate for 3 hours. Scrape off marinade from fish and reserve. Pat fish dry with paper towels. Preheat an oven broiler (grill) or barbecue and cook until opaque throughout, 3–4 minutes.

In a medium frying pan, heat oil over medium–high heat until surface shimmers. Add cooked fish, a few pieces at a time, to hot oil, stirring carefully so as not to break up pieces. Fry until flaky to the touch but not crisp, 1–3 minutes. Using a skimmer, transfer to a platter. Reduce heat to medium, add dill and scallions to pan and stir-fry just until wilted, then place on cooked fish. Quickly stir-fry shallots and garlic in same pan, with any reserved marinade, and spoon over fish. Top with chopped peanuts.

To serve, lay out a lettuce leaf, top with greens and rice noodles and add a spoonful of cooked fish. Fold into a parcel, dip into nuoc cham sauce and eat with your hands.

Vietnamese fried shrimp with orange sauce

Serves 4–6

3 lb (1.5 kg) raw jumbo shrimp (green king prawns), shelled and deveined, tails
  left on
about ¹/₂ cup (2 oz/60 g) cornstarch (cornflour)
vegetable oil, for deep-frying
1 orange, for garnish
fresh cilantro (fresh coriander) sprigs, for garnish

FOR ORANGE SAUCE
2 cups (16 fl oz/500 ml) freshly squeezed orange juice (about 5 oranges)
3 tablespoons fish sauce
1 tablespoon arrowroot or cornstarch (cornflour)
1–2 tablespoons sugar (optional)

To butterfly shrimp: Cut them deeply lengthwise along back, but not all the way through;
gently score underside of each shrimp to prevent curling. Cover and refrigerate until ready
to use.

To make orange sauce: Pour orange juice into a non-metallic saucepan and bring to a
boil. Continue boiling until slightly reduced, 5–10 minutes. In a small bowl, stir fish sauce
and arrowroot together until dissolved, then stir this into boiling orange juice. Add sugar to
taste if juice is too acidic. Set aside and keep warm.

Toss shrimp with cornstarch. In a wok or deep-fryer, heat 4 inches (10 cm) oil to 350°F
(180°C) and fry one-third of shrimp at a time until crisp and golden brown, 2–3 minutes.
Using a slotted spoon, transfer to paper towels to drain. Keep warm in a low oven while
cooking successive batches.

To serve, cut orange for garnish in half, then thinly slice each half into half-moon slices.
Arrange slices around sides of a serving plate and spoon some of sauce into center of
plate. Place fried shrimp in center and pour any remaining sauce into a bowl. Sprinkle
with cilantro sprigs.

Hint: *If using frozen shrimp, thaw in the refrigerator prior to using.*

Sushi & sashimi

in the world of cuisine, sushi stands alone. There is nothing quite like it, and its character has barely changed over thousands of years. The signature dish of Japan, sushi represents a national philosophy—food should be prepared with great care, food should be beautifully presented, food should satisfy all the senses.

Sushi (pronounced "zushi" when it follows a vowel) is defined as the combination of vinegared rice with other ingredients, usually fish. It was initially adopted in Japan as a method of preserving fish with rice, and has origins in Southeast Asia as a technique called nare-zushi, a process which involved preserving cleaned raw fish between layers of salt and rice. Edo, the former name for Tokyo, is considered to be the birthplace of sushi as we know it today, beginning with nigiri-zushi (sushi rice topped with fresh raw fish) and evolving into nori rolls and molded sushi.

Over the centuries many more distinctive sushi styles have emerged, both in Japan and, now, worldwide. And although in essence sushi has changed little from the original concept, these new and modern creations utilize an array of ingredients, including shellfish, chicken, beef, pork, vegetables and fruit, as well as herbs and spices. Even the rice, perhaps once considered essential, may be replaced, and the soy or wasabi—sushi's traditional partners—may sit alongside other sauces and accompaniments.

Sashimi essentially consists of fresh seafood fillets cut into bite-sized, oblong strips, and eaten raw with soy sauce and wasabi, but the term can now be used to encompass raw beef, vegetables and even fruit. Sashimi is all in the cutting, and its techniques can be adapted to suit various foods.

Condiments are served with sushi and sashimi not only for their flavor but also to aid digestion. Soy sauce (or shoyu) is an essential accompaniment, served in a small dish, along with daikon, also known as giant white radish, traditionally grated or shredded, its lingering sweetness complementing raw fish, and wasabi, with its intense but refreshing mustard-like flavor. Decorations made from wasabi, vegetables, flowers or leaves add the finishing touch—they are practical, separating the sushi pieces, and also demonstrate the chef's great cutting skills.

Sushi and sashimi can be eaten with chopsticks, a fork and a knife, or the hands. Nigiri-zushi (hand-shaped sushi) is mostly eaten using the fingers, and each diner is provided with a damp hand towel beside their plate to clean their hands. When eating nigiri-zushi, dip the top ingredients rather than the sushi rice into the soy sauce, as the sauce will cause the rice to lose its shape. Nigiri-zushi is designed to be eaten in one bite, without causing a mess, so make sure they are bite-sized.

Cone sushi, or hand rolls, are eaten with the fingers. Rolled sushi and inside-out rolled sushi are eaten with the fingers or chopsticks. Chirashi-zushi (scattered sushi) is eaten with chopsticks, or a spoon or a fork. A fork is often more suitable for molded sushi.

While the training for sushi chefs is traditionally long and hard—an apprentice may spend the first two years learning to cook sushi rice before he even touches any fish—making sushi is easy enough to do at home. The following pages outline the basics of sushi: the specific ingredients and their preparation, and step-by-step instructions for the main sushi and sashimi techniques.

Choosing and preparing fish and seafood

Buy the freshest fish possible for making sashimi and sushi, for reasons of health, taste and beauty. If you can, go to the fish markets, and always buy fish and seafood in season. "Shun wa kusuri ni masaru" is an old saying that means "to eat in season is better than medicine," a belief held dear by many Japanese—this not only ensures the freshness of the ingredients, but also allows you to appreciate foods at their peak of flavor.

Hints for buying

Whenever possible, buy fish whole and fillet them at home so you can ensure that the meat is fresh. (See Buying fish and seafood, pages 262–263.) With bigger fish, it may be inconvenient or uneconomical to buy a whole fish, so buy fillets and smaller cuts. If buying portions for sushi and sashimi:

- Fillets should be moist and have a good color.

- White fish should look almost transparent.

- Cut tuna flesh should have distinct stripes in it around the belly and be clear red without stripes in other parts.

- The head end of fish is more tender than the tail end. With most fish, the back is the most delicious part. Tuna and swordfish are exceptions, with the tender, fatty belly area being the most desired.

Preparing fish and seafood

Most fish types can be consumed soon after catching, but larger fish such as tuna are best after 2–3 days. After purchasing fish, refrigerate as soon as possible. Store in refrigerator no longer than 2 days.

Before cutting the fish, rinse and wipe your cutting board. Either keep a bowl of water beside you to wet your knife and then wipe it, or wipe the knife occasionally with a clean, damp cloth.

Try not to handle the body of the fish too much, as you may cause bruising. Hold the fish by its head or tail whenever possible. If preferred, use a clean kitchen glove on the hand that is holding the fish.

For both sashimi and sushi, fish fillets should be deboned, scaled and, where necessary, skinned (see pages 262–263). The parts of the fish that are not usable for sashimi and sushi may be used in many other ways, such as for rolled sushi, making stock or in other recipes.

You will generally need to cut fish fillets into workable-sized blocks before making sashimi and sushi. The length will depend on the fish being used, but the block should be rectangular in shape, measuring about 3 inches (7.5 cm) across and 1½ inches (4 cm) high. Slices should be ¼–½ inch (6–12 mm) thick. Remember that the slices and resulting sushi should be bite-sized.

To cut fish for sushi and sashimi, always cut with the knife pulling the slice toward you. The flesh should be sliced on the bias along the length of the fish or the fillet to give the best results texturally, visually and for taste.

Preparing tuna block for slicing

Large fish like tuna can be purchased as a block. To trim a tuna block for slicing:

1. Using a sharp sashimi knife or filleting knife, trim tuna block against grain to make it uniform.

2. Cut tuna into rectangular strips about 1 x 2 inches (2.5 cm x 5 cm), ready for slicing. Use leftover pieces for cubic or tataki-style sashimi.

Cleaning and preparing cuttlefish

Cuttlefish have ink sacs and can therefore be messy to clean. As you work, be careful not to break the sac and release the ink. Cuttlefish with a strong smell or an unusually slimy surface should not be used for sashimi. If cuttlefish are unavailable, baby squid (calamari) can be substituted.

1. Holding cuttlefish head with one hand, gently pull out shell with the other hand.

2. Gently pull out tentacles and entrails, being careful not to break the ink sac. Rinse mantle under running cold water. The tentacles can also be used for sashimi; cut them off below the eyes and remove beak. Cut tentacles into bite-sized pieces. Pour boiling water over them to blanch.

3. Slit the edge only halfway on the inside of the mantle. With a firm hold, pull the skin from the edge of the fillet you have cut open. Using a cloth makes skinning easier.

Preparing ingredients for sushi and sashimi

Before you begin making sushi and sashimi, it is best to be prepared. Have all ingredients ready, such as the sushi rice (see page 28), seafood and any other ingredients, such as nori belts and garnishes. Make sure your knives are sharp and equipment is handy, including a bamboo sushi mat, a damp cloth for wiping knives clean and a small bowl of vinegar-water or tezu (a half-half mixture of sushi vinegar and water) for keeping your hands moist. It is best to have a chopping board measuring at least 10 x 15 inches (25 x 38 cm) in size, and even larger for sashimi. (See also Equipment, pages 10–19 and Preparing ingredients, pages 22–33.)

Thin seasoned omelette

Japanese omelettes are used in sushi, for rolling, as filling or as topping. This recipe makes about 8 thin omelettes. To use for nigiri-zushi or as filling for sushi, cut omelette across into $1/2$-inch (12-mm) slices. Omelettes may also be served as a side dish to sushi, with soy sauce and grated daikon, or shredded as garnish.

6 eggs
1 tablespoon mirin
1 tablespoon sugar
$1/4$ teaspoon salt
1–2 teaspoons vegetable oil

Gently beat eggs with mirin, sugar and salt; do not create big air bubbles. Strain mixture to remove any strands of egg. Lightly grease an 8-inch (20-cm) square or 9-inch (23-cm) round frying pan with oil, wiping any excess with paper towel. Heat oiled pan over moderate–low until a drop of water flicked onto surface sizzles. Cover frying pan thinly with egg mixture, tilting pan to spread evenly. Break any air bubbles with chopsticks so omelette lies flat. When almost set and surface begins to look firm and slightly dry, run chopsticks around edges to loosen egg from pan. Flip omelette over and cook other side for only a few seconds; be careful not to overcook. Remove to a plate. Repeat for remaining mixture, lightly greasing pan between omelettes. If a round frying pan is used, trim omelettes to a square shape as required.

Nori belts

Known as "obi-jim," these straps of nori are used to secure toppings that are prone to slide off the rice, such as omelette, scallops, squid (calamari), tofu or snow peas (mange-tout). After forming nigiri-zushi, take a small strip of nori about $1/2$ x 3 inches (12 mm x 7.5 cm) and use this as a belt to wrap around the topping and the rice, holding them together.

Garnishes

Garnishes are an essential component of sushi and sashimi. While decorative, garnishes are also often edible, especially when served with sashimi, the colors and flavors carefully chosen to complement each dish.

Shredded daikon: Using a vegetable-carving knife or paring knife, peel a section of daikon. Alternatively, use a peeler. Placing knife at a right angle to work surface, cut daikon into very thin slices. Separate slices and place in bowl of water, or refrigerate in water for 15 minutes. Drain well before using.

Grated chili and daikon: Especially suited to light-tasting sashimi and white-fleshed fish. Peel daikon (about 7 oz/220 g) and trim ends. Make 2 small holes in ends with chopsticks, large enough for a small chili pepper. Insert 1 small red chili pepper into each hole. Grate daikon with chili in it and mix gently in a bowl.

Red radish flower: Make 3 thin cuts, spacing them evenly around radish. Make 3 more thin cuts about $3/8$ inch (1 cm) behind each of the first cuts, making sure the cuts meet near the bottom of radish. Do not cut all the way through. Holding bottom of radish, gently cut off the top center using tip of knife. Place egg mimosa in middle to create the flower center.

Vegetable flowers: This technique can be used for a variety of vegetables, including daikon, carrot and beet (beetroot). Cut a 2-inch (5-cm) piece of peeled daikon and carrot. Place on end and cut out using a knife or a decorative flower-shaped biscuit cutter. Thinly slice both inside and outside sections of both vegetables to make flower-shaped slices. For a more elaborate garnish, put carrot slices in a daikon surround and daikon slices in a carrot surround.

Decorative leaves: Use whole cleaned leaves such as maple, shiso, citrus or camellia to garnish plates, or arrange condiments on the leaf. Use a sprig of leaves or herbs or a small spray of blossom as a seasonal decoration on the plate, at the place settings, or as a chopstick rest.

Wasabi leaf: Add enough water to wasabi powder to make a soft paste or use fresh wasabi. Roll about 1 teaspoon into a small ball. Gently flatten and shape with fingers into a leaf shape. Using a knife or toothpick, lightly mark a central vein down the middle and side veins at a 45 degree angle.

Sushi and sashimi techniques

There are as many techniques for making sushi and sashimi as there are chefs to create them. A few, however, are considered essential, and once you have mastered these, you'll be ready to invent your own ways of preparing and presenting these exquisite dishes. Following are the main techniques for making sushi and sashimi, as used in the recipes of this chapter. The quick-and-easy techniques, such as hand or cone rolls and nigiri-zushi, are ideal for beginners or family affairs, while the more intricate methods such as decorative rolls or paper-thin slicing will inspire sushi devotees.

Sharpening Japanese knives

When sharpening a Japanese knife, have a whetstone that is used with water rather than with oil. Soak Japanese whetstones in water for about 20 minutes before sharpening.

1. Place whetstone on a wet towel to hold it in place. Wipe clean with a damp towel and hold knife in right hand. Place top half of blade flat on stone at a 40-degree angle to the body. Placing middle and index fingers on blade, apply pressure, and move blade forward and backward. Wipe blade.

2. Once the top is sharpened, proceed to score the base of the blade.

3. As most Japanese knives are single-edged, when blades are honed the shaved pieces cling to the flat side of the blade. To remove, turn knife, place edge of blade on corner of stone at a 45-degree angle. Slide blade down to remove excess metal.

4. Wipe knife clean with a damp towel.

Note: Steps are written for right-edged blade. Check sharpness regularly.

Filleting fish, three-piece technique

Since sashimi-quality fillets are frequently unavailable, the three-piece filleting technique is worth learning. If you buy a whole fish, fillet it and then refrigerate it. The fish will stay fresh longer. A filleting knife with a 5-inch (13-cm) stainless steel blade is ideal. Make sure your knife is sharp.

1. Scale fish if scaling is required. Using a sharp knife, slit belly of fish, remove viscera and rinse briefly. Avoid using too much tap water, as it will affect the taste. Lay fish down on board. Place knife behind gills and cut off head.

2. With one hand holding fish firmly, start cutting into fillet from the head end toward the tail, along backbone of fish, lifting fillet away as you cut. Place first fillet aside. Turn fish over and repeat process.

3. Pluck or trim away any remaining bones in the fillets or around the visceral area.

4. You should now have 3 parts: 2 fillets and 1 part consisting of the skeleton and the tail. Discard skeleton and tail.

Rectangular slicing (Hiki-zukuri)

This is the easiest sashimi technique, ideal for larger fish such as tuna.

Place fillet on board. While holding fillet in the left hand, place sharp edge of knife perpendicular to the fillet and cut into slices $\frac{1}{2}$ inch (12 mm) wide. When cutting leave each piece in its original cut position.

Thinly slicing (Sogi-zukuri)

This sashimi style is mainly used for fish with thinner flesh, such as snapper and mackerel, because these fish types are not thick enough for rectangular slicing. Thinly sliced sashimi is highly suitable for novices at eating raw fish.

1. Place fillet skin down on board and insert knife just below the skin. While supporting fillet with left hand, gently cut parallel to the chopping board to remove skin.

2. Starting from the left of fillet, cut into diagonal slices, inclining the blade to the right at a 45-degree angle. Once fish is cut, raise the blade to a 90-degree angle and slide each slice to the left.

Blanching (Matsukawa-zukuri)

Blanching is a sashimi technique with two functions: to cook the skin and outer layer of fish and to give the fish an attractive appearance. Fish with large scales and firm skin, such as snapper, ocean perch and silver bream, are well suited to this style.

1. Cut fish using the three-piece filleting technique (see page 322).

2. Place 1 fillet on a platter and pour boiling water over it to shrink the skin. Remove to a plate and refrigerate until cool. Repeat with second fillet.

3. Remove fillet from refrigerator and place on a board. Cut fillet in half and slice in the rectangular slicing (hiki-zukuri) style (see above).

Cubic sashimi (Kaki-zukuri)

This modern technique was developed to create sashimi slices of uniform size and thickness, for marinating and dressing. The cubic shape allows the outer layers of the fish to soak up the marinade flavors while the fish maintains its own flavor on the inside of the cube. Fish with soft, thick flesh, such as tuna, salmon, king fish and bonito, are suitable for cubic sashimi.

1. Trim fish to a block approximately 2 x 2 inches (5 x 5 cm) thick and 8 inches (20 cm) in length.

2. Cut block in half lengthwise to make two long pieces. Then cut each piece in half lengthwise to make four long pieces.

3. Using the rectangular slicing (hiki-zukuri) technique (see page 323), cut each piece into 1-inch (2.5-cm) cubes.

Tataki

Originally, tataki meant beating the flesh of fish lightly with a knife to enhance the flavor, but the term has expanded to include other techniques.

Lightly broiled (grilled) tataki: Use for bonito. Before broiling (grilling), cover the fish with salt. This makes the hard skin of the bonito much easier to eat.

Blanched tataki: Blanching seals the flavor of meat and fish. Tuna, swordfish and bonito are suitable.

Lightly ground (minced) tataki: Chopping the fish with the back of the knife helps flavor the fish, as does the addition of other ingredients. Yellowtail, garfish and whiting are suitable.

Ground (minced) tataki: Grinding (mincing) gives fish the texture of pâté. Salmon, ocean trout and king fish are suitable for this style.

Maki-zushi: Thin sushi rolls

These sushi rolls are also known as hosomaki-zushi or tekkamaki, and are easy to make, using a half-sheet of nori, a little sushi rice and a single filling. For the novice sushi maker, it is the best roll to practice on. Although the amount of filling is quite small, the variety that may be used is endless—as well as fresh seafood, you can select fillings from your pantry, refrigerator or freezer.

1. Trim the sides of a halved nori sheet. Place a bamboo sushi mat on a dry work surface and lay nori on mat, glossy side down. Set nori in center of mat, about 1 1/4 inches (3 cm) away from edge of mat closest to you. Wet your hands, and take a small handful of rice. Spread rice evenly over nori, leaving uncovered a 3/4-inch (2-cm) strip

of nori on the side farthest from you. Dab a small amount of wasabi on your finger and spread thinly across center of rice. Top wasabi with fillings of choice, such as cucumber strips.

2. Using your index finger and thumb, pick up edge of sushi mat nearest to you. Place your remaining fingers over fillings to hold them as you roll mat forward tightly.

3. Roll the mat, wrapping rice and nori around fillings. The strip of nori without rice should still be visible.

4. Lift up top edge of mat and continue rolling sushi roll over rice-free portion of nori, encasing roll within the mat. If nori is dry, moisten edge of rice-free strip of nori with your wet fingers.

5. With a gentle press on bamboo mat, form sushi as if molding a rectangular bar with the fingers.

6. Remove mat and transfer sushi roll to a dry cutting board. Wipe knife with a damp towel and slice roll in half. Place 2 pieces side by side and cut them again to make 6 rolls, wiping knife after each cut.

Futomaki-zushi: Thick sushi roll

Futomaki-zushi is thick nori roll made with a full-sized sheet of nori, spread evenly with a layer of rice and enclosing several fillings and sometimes a dab of wasabi. A large variety of fillings may be used, making it a very tasty, versatile type of sushi. The California roll is typical of futomaki. Thick rolls can be made in a variety of ways to create decorative patterns, such as the Inside-out California roll.

It is best to serve futomaki rolls immediately they are made, as the rice inside expands and the nori tends to split. They will keep for up to 30 minutes if they are rolled in paper towel and then plastic wrap.

1. Lay 1 nori sheet on a rolling mat and put $3/4$ cup (4 oz/125 g) sushi rice on it. Spread rice over nori sheet, leaving $3/4$ inch (2 cm) of bare nori at far side and making a small ledge of rice in front of this bare strip.

2. Spoon 2 teaspoons roe or a dab of wasabi along center of rice, using the back of a spoon to spread. Add fillings in layers along center of rice, experimenting in the way you lay out the ingredients to create different patterns.

3. Roll mat over once, away from you, pressing ingredients in to keep roll firm, leaving the $3/4$ -inch (2-cm) strip of nori rice-free. Covering roll (but not rice-free strip of nori), hold rolling mat in position and press all around to make roll firm.

4. Lift up top of rolling mat and turn roll over a little more so that strip of nori on far side joins other edge of nori to seal. Use your fingers to make sure roll is properly closed.

5. Roll entire roll once more, and use finger pressure to shape roll into a circle, an oval or a square. Using a sharp knife, cut each roll in half, then cut each half in half again. Then cut each quarter in half to make a total of 8 equal-sized pieces. Cut gently to maintain shape.

Nigiri-zushi

One of the oldest forms of sushi, this is also the type most often found in today's sushi bars. Nigiri means "squeeze," and these sushi were originally bite-sized pieces of fish or seafood gently pressed together with small balls of sushi rice, usually topped with a dab of wasabi. Now, though, the ingredients used are infinite.

There are three or four commonly used methods for making nigiri-zushi, including the traditional tategaeshi style favored by professional sushi masters. The method following is ideal for making nigiri-zushi at home. And don't forget that sushi is best eaten in a single mouthful: a ball of rice the size of a golf ball and enough topping to cover it is a good guide.

1. Hold topping with left hand. Wet right hand and shape a portion of rice into a finger about $1/4$ inch (6 mm) thick, $3/4$ inch (2 cm) wide, and 2 inches (5 cm) long. With tip of right index finger, dab wasabi on topping.

2. Using your index finger, press rice onto the wasabi-dabbed side of topping.

3. Turn rice and topping over so the nigiri-zushi is right side up. Using your index and middle fingers, mold topping around rice so that there is no rice showing around the edges.

4. With right fingers, turn nigiri-zushi 180 degrees and repeat molding. Serve with soy sauce. To eat, dip the topping, not the rice, into the soy sauce.

Temaki-zushi: Hand or cone rolls

Usually constructed at the table by the person who is going to eat it, these sushi are made from a selection of fillings, along with sushi rice, and each one is rolled into quartered sheets of nori to form a cone that is eaten by hand. It's an easy and fun way for family and guests to make their own sushi (ideal for picnics, too), and allows diners to choose fillings to suit their personal taste. Prepare ingredients beforehand, placing them on a platter or in individual bowls. Give your guests guidance on technique, and then let them make their own. For beginners, start with smaller quantities of rice and ingredients, or use quartered nori sheets to make small cone rolls with more filling and less rice. Hand rolls should be eaten immediately, as they do not hold together well. Prepare a finger bowl with water for each person and provide warmed, dampened towels for guests to wipe their hands on.

1. Cut nori sheet in half. Hold nori flat in your left hand, glossy side down. Wet fingers of your right hand, and take about 1 tablespoon rice and spread it evenly on left side of nori. Add a small amount of wasabi and Japanese mayonnaise to rice.

2. Arrange a selection of fillings in the center of rice.

3. Fold bottom left hand corner of nori over fillings and tuck it under rice, allowing the top to open out somewhat. Roll remainder of nori sheet into a cone-shaped sushi roll.

4. To seal nori, use a little water.

Seasoned tofu pouches (Inari-zushi)

Seasoned pouches can be prepared early and refrigerated until required but should be used within 2–3 days or frozen for up to 3 months. These can also be purchased ready-made at Asian grocery stores.

4 large pieces thin deep-fried tofu (abura-age), 3^1/$_4$ x 5 inches (8 cm x 12.5 cm)
1 cup (8 fl oz/250 ml) Dashi 2 (see page 572)
2 tablespoons sugar
2 teaspoons sake
2 tablespoons shoyu

Put tofu in a saucepan of boiling water and boil to remove excess oil, about 2 minutes. Drain, gently squeezing out excess water.

In a saucepan, combine tofu, dashi, sugar, sake and shoyu.

Poke a few holes in a sheet of foil and shape it to fit it inside saucepan so it rests on top of liquid. This drop-lid allows steam to escape but keeps tofu submerged while cooking. Bring to a boil, reduce heat and simmer for 15 minutes. Remove saucepan from heat and cool tofu in liquid.

Drain, squeezing out excess liquid. Gently roll each piece of tofu with a rolling pin to loosen the center.

Cut each piece in half. Gently ease open cut end of each piece with your fingers, pushing down to each corner to form a pouch. These pouches are now ready to be filled with sushi rice.

Battleship sushi

Makes 8 pieces

1 nori sheet
1 cup (5 oz/155 g) Sushi Rice (see page 28)
wasabi paste
4 oz (125 g) sea urchin, salmon, ocean trout or flying fish roe

Cut the nori into strips about 1 inch (2.5 cm) wide and 6 inches (15 cm) long.

Take a ball of rice, about the size of a golf ball, in your hand and gently squeeze it into a rectangular block with rounded edges. Place on a clean board. Repeat with remaining rice.

With one moist hand holding a rice ball, use the dry fingers of your other hand to pick up a nori sheet.

With rough side of nori facing rice, press end of nori to rice (it will stick) and then wrap nori all around rice. Gently press overlapping edge of nori to form a complete ring (or use a crushed grain of sticky rice to hold the ends together).

Dab a little wasabi on top of rice, then place roe on top of rice inside center of ring of nori.

Hints: *This type of sushi has a wide belt of nori wrapped around the sushi rice, supporting a loose or semi-liquid topping such as caviar, shredded chicken or sea urchin roe. Because of its shape, this sushi is known as gunkan, which means "black ship" or "warrior ship."*

When making battleship sushi, remember that moist hands are good for touching the sushi rice, but it is best to have dry hands when handling nori.

Because nori is like paper, if you are making various kinds of sushi, leave the making of these until last, otherwise the nori will become wet and may break.

Broiled chicken battleships

Makes 8 pieces

2$^1/_4$ nori sheets

1 teaspoon canola oil

1 skinless, boneless chicken breast, about 7 oz (220 g)

2 cups (10 oz/300 g) Sushi Rice (see page 28)

4 tablespoons (2 oz/60 g) Japanese mayonnaise or Wasabi Mayonnaise (see page 595)

8 small curly endive (curly chicory) leaves

2 tablespoons umeboshi (pickled plum) puree

Using cooking scissors, cut $^1/_4$ sheet of nori into very thin strips. Set aside on a plate.

Also using scissors, cut 2 nori sheets into quarters. Set aside on a dry work surface.

Heat a grill pan over medium–high heat and add oil. Add chicken, reduce heat to medium, and cook until cooked through, about 10 minutes. Transfer chicken to a plate and let cool slightly. With your fingers, shred chicken into fine strips. Transfer to a medium bowl, add mayonnaise and stir well.

With wet hands, mold rice into 8 fingers, following the instructions for Battleship Sushi (opposite).

With the dry fingers of one hand, pick up a piece of nori and wrap it around rice (rough side in), sealing one end and leaving other end open like a pouch. Press shredded chicken onto rice through open end. Insert a curly endive leaf and sprinkle with thin nori strips. Repeat with remaining ingredients. Serve with umeboshi puree.

Hint: Umeboshi (pickled plum) puree is sold in tubes or small bottles at Japanese or other Asian markets.

California rolls

Makes 4 rolls (32 pieces)

4 nori sheets
3 cups (15 oz/470 g) Sushi Rice (see page 28)
8 teaspoons ocean trout or flying fish roe
1–2 cucumbers, cut into thin, lengthwise slices
8 jumbo shrimp (king prawns), cooked, shelled, veins and tails removed
1–2 avocados, peeled, pitted and sliced
4–8 lettuce leaves, torn or sliced (optional)

Lay 1 nori sheet on a rolling mat and put ¾ cup (4 oz/125 g) sushi rice on it. Spread rice over nori sheet, leaving ¾ inch (2 cm) of bare nori at far side and making a small ledge of rice in front of this bare strip.

Spoon 2 teaspoons roe along center of rice, using the back of a spoon to spread. Add lettuce if desired. Lay 2 shrimp along center, with one-quarter of cucumber strips. Lay one-quarter of avocado slices along center. Add one-quarter of lettuce.

Roll mat over once, away from you, pressing ingredients in to keep roll firm, leaving the ¾-inch (2-cm) strip of nori rice-free. Covering roll (but not rice-free strip of nori), hold rolling mat in position and press all around to make roll firm. Lift up top of rolling mat and turn roll over a little more so that strip of nori on far side joins other edge of nori to seal roll. Use your fingers to make sure roll is properly closed.

Roll entire roll once more, and use finger pressure to shape roll in a circle, an oval or a square.

Using a sharp knife, cut each roll in half, then cut each half in half again. Then cut each quarter in half to make a total of 8 equal-sized pieces. Cut gently to maintain shape.

Note: *California rolls, as their name suggests, were invented in California, although futomaki (thick sushi) rolls originated in the Osaka area. (See also futomaki rolls on page 325.)*

Chirashi-zushi

Serves 4

1 cucumber

2 cups (10 oz/300 g) Sushi Rice
(see page 28)

2 tablespoons shredded fresh ginger or
gari (see page 585)

2 tablespoons soboro

2 tablespoons shredded nori

1/2 cup (2 oz/60 g) shredded Seasoned
Omelette (see page 320)

4 jumbo shrimp (king prawns), cooked,
shelled, veins and tails removed

5–10 snow peas (mange-tout), blanched

1/2 unagi eel, grilled and cut into
bite-sized pieces

FOR SEASONED KAMPYO

3/4 oz (20 g) kampyo strips

2 cups (16 fl oz/500 ml) Dashi 2 (see
page 573)

1/4 cup (2 fl oz/60 ml) dark soy sauce

1 teaspoon superfine (caster) sugar

**FOR SEASONED SHIITAKE
MUSHROOMS**

4 dried shiitake mushrooms, stemmed

1/2 cup (4 fl oz/125 ml) Dashi 2 (see
page 573)

3 tablespoons light soy sauce

1 tablespoon superfine (caster) sugar

1 tablespoon mirin

To make seasoned kampyo: Soak kampyo in water for at least 2 hours (overnight if possible). Place kampyo and soaking water in a saucepan and boil until translucent and tender, about 10 minutes. Drain. In a saucepan, mix together 1 cup (8 fl oz/250 ml) of dashi, soy sauce and sugar. Add kampyo to mixture and boil for 5 minutes. Drain and set aside to cool.

To make seasoned shiitake mushrooms: Soak mushrooms in lukewarm water for at least 2 hours (or overnight). Drain, reserving liquid. Cut mushrooms into 1/4-inch (6-mm) strips. In a saucepan, mix together remaining 2 cups (16 fl oz/500 ml) dashi, light soy sauce, sugar and mirin. Bring mixture to a boil, add mushrooms and simmer for 10 minutes. Remove from heat and drain mushrooms.

Cut cucumber crosswise into 2-inch (5-cm) pieces, then into thin, lengthwise slices. In a large bowl or 4 individual bowls, spread out sushi rice to make a flat bed, keeping it loosely packed. Add following ingredients one by one, sprinkling them to cover the rice and then each other in layers: shredded ginger, kampyo, shiitake mushrooms, soboro, shredded nori and shredded omelette. Make a decorative display on top with cucumber slices, shrimp, snow peas, and eel. Do not add soy sauce to this dish.

Dragon rolls with barbecued eel and avocado

Makes 4 pieces

1 nori sheet, halved

2 cups (10 oz/300 g) Sushi Rice (see page 28)

$^{1}/_{2}$ English (hothouse) cucumber, halved lengthwise, seeded, then cut into
strips $^{1}/_{4}$ inch (6 mm) thick

$^{1}/_{2}$ fillet barbecued eel, cut into strips

1 avocado, halved, pitted and peeled

4 teaspoons umeboshi (pickled plum) puree

shoyu, for serving

Cover a sushi mat with plastic wrap. Place a half sheet of nori on plastic, glossy side down, and, with wet fingers, spread half sushi rice evenly over nori. Holding surface of rice with one hand, turn over rice and nori so rice is on plastic and nori is on top. Arrange cucumber and eel strips in center of nori. Using sushi mat, roll to enclose fillings, leaving a $^{3}/_{4}$-inch (2-cm) strip of nori visible at end farthest from you. Lift up sushi mat and roll following instructions for maki-zushi on page 324. Press gently to firm shape and seal nori.

Unroll mat, remove plastic and transfer roll to a cutting board. Wipe a sharp knife with a damp towel and cut roll in half. Repeat with remaining ingredients.

With a small sharp knife, slice an avocado half thinly, keeping slices together, and place it over a sushi roll, pushing gently with your fingers to curve avocado slices. Repeat with other avocado half. Arrange rolls on serving plates and top each piece with 3 drops umeboshi puree. Serve with shoyu. Eat with a knife and fork.

Hints: Barbecued eel is sold in airtight bags from Japanese and other Asian markets, and some fish stores. Umeboshi (pickled plum) puree is sold in tubes and bottles in Japanese markets.

Inside-out California rolls

Makes 4 rolls (32 pieces)

4 nori sheets
3 cups (15 oz/470 g) Sushi Rice (see page 28)
8 teaspoons ocean trout or flying fish roe
1–2 cucumbers, cut into thin, lengthwise slices
1–2 avocados, peeled, pitted and sliced
8 jumbo shrimp (king prawns), cooked, shelled, veins and tails removed
4–8 lettuce leaves, torn or sliced (optional)

Cover a rolling mat with a sheet of plastic wrap, folding it over edges and attaching it to back of mat. Turn mat over so plastic-covered side is facing down.

Lay 1 nori sheet on rolling mat. Using about $3/4$ cup (4 oz/125 g) rice to cover nori sheet, cover nori with rice right up to edges, starting with a ball of rice at bottom and then spreading it out. Spread about 2 heaped teaspoons roe over rice, using back of a teaspoon.

Pick up rice-covered nori by corners, quickly turn it over and place upside down on bamboo rolling mat.

Add lettuce, if desired. Place sliced cucumber along center of nori. Add avocado, then shrimp.

With your hands held over base of mat and pressing in on ingredients with your fingers as you go, roll mat over ingredients, leaving $3/4$ inch (2 cm) of nori visible at far end of nori end of roll. Press gently to mold roll together. Lift up mat, roll back a little, then roll forward to join nori edges. Use gentle pressure to firm and mold completed roll into shape, either round, oval or square.

Using a sharp knife, cut each roll in half, then cut two halves in half again. Then cut four quarters in half to make 8 equal-sized pieces. Cut gently to maintain shape.

Korean beef and kimchi rolls

1 teaspoon canola oil
3 oz (90 g) topside steak, thinly sliced
2 tablespoons Korean barbecue sauce
1 cup (5 oz/150 g) Sushi Rice (see page 28)
2 Chinese (napa) cabbage kimchi leaves (see Hint)
2 fresh chives
2 tablespoons white sesame seeds

Heat a heavy frying pan over high heat and add oil. Reduce heat to medium, add steak slices and cook until heated through. Add barbecue sauce and cook for 1 minute. Set aside on a plate until cool.

Cover a sushi mat with plastic wrap. Lay kimchi leaves horizontally on plastic, beginning at end closest to you. With wet fingers, spread the rice over kimchi, leaving uncovered a 3/4-inch (2-cm) strip at end farthest from you. Cover with beef and arrange chives in center. Roll up tightly following instructions for hosomaki-zushi on page 324.

Unroll mat, remove plastic and transfer roll to a cutting board. Wipe a sharp knife with a damp towel and cut each roll in half, then cut each half in half again, wiping knife after each cut. Repeat with remaining ingredients.

Holding each piece with your fingers, dip into sesame seeds on a plate to coat kimchi. Arrange pieces on serving plates and serve.

Hint: Korean barbecue sauce and kimchi are available from Japanese and Korean markets; see also Kimchi with Chinese Cabbage (page 407).

Lobster tempura rolls

1 lobster tail
1 nori sheet
1 cup (5 oz/150 g) Sushi Rice
  (see page 28)
2 tablespoons katakuri starch or
  cornstarch (cornflour)

FOR TEMPURA
canola oil, for deep-frying
a few drops Asian sesame oil
1 cup (8 fl oz/250 ml) cold water
1 cup (5 oz/150 g) tempura flour

2 chives, finely chopped
1 hard-boiled egg yolk, sieved
  (egg mimosa)

FOR DIPPING SAUCE
1/2 cup (4 fl oz/125 ml) rice vinegar
1 tablespoon sugar
1 tablespoon mirin
1 tablespoon shoyu

To make dipping sauce: Combine all ingredients in a bowl and mix well; set aside.

Beginning on the softer underside of lobster, insert tip of a large knife and cut meat from shell, leaving meat in a whole piece. Transfer meat to a board and slice it in half, making sure not to cut all the way through and leaving 3/8 inch (1 cm) uncut, then open it to have 1 large flat slice of lobster. Trim meat to three-quarters size of nori sheet.

Arrange nori sheet, glossy side down, on a sushi mat. Place lobster meat on nori and, with wet fingers, arrange sushi rice over lobster. Roll following instructions for hosomaki-zushi on page 324. If nori is dry, wet edge and press mat to seal. Place katakuri starch in a flat plate and coat lobster roll. Allow roll to rest, seam side down, for 2 minutes. Unroll mat and transfer roll to a cutting board. Wipe a sharp knife with a damp towel and cut roll into 4 even pieces, wiping knife after each cut.

Fill a tempura pan, or deep-fryer one-third full with canola oil and heat over medium–high heat to 365°F (185°C). Add a few drops of sesame oil. Meanwhile, to make tempura batter, put tempura flour in a medium bowl and gradually whisk in cold water until mixture resembles a light pancake batter. Dip 2 rolls in batter and deep-fry, turning as necessary, until golden. Using a wire-mesh skimmer, transfer to a wire rack, or paper towels, to drain. Set aside on paper towels. Repeat with remaining rolls. Transfer rolls to serving plates and top with egg mimosa and chives. Serve with dipping sauce.

Omelette nigiri-zushi

Makes 10 pieces

FOR OMELETTE

8 eggs
1/3 cup (3 fl oz/80 ml) Dashi 1 (see page 572)
1/3 cup (3 oz/90 g) sugar
1 teaspoon mirin
pinch salt
2 tablespoons light soy sauce
vegetable oil, for cooking

1 1/2 cups (8 oz/250 g) Sushi Rice (see page 28)
10 nori belts (see page 321)

In a bowl, beat eggs until just blended. Stir in dashi, sugar, mirin, salt and soy sauce. Heat 1–2 tablespoons oil in a square omelette pan over medium heat. Pour excess oil from pan into a bowl with a piece of greaseproof paper or cloth nearby ready to re-oil pan when needed. Pour a thin layer of omelette mixture into pan. Use chopsticks or a spatula to press out any air bubbles.

When omelette is firm, run chopsticks around it to loosen. Using chopsticks, fold one-third of omelette from far side toward center, then fold this two-thirds over remaining one-third to the side closest to you. Add more mixture, lifting cooked omelette up to let it flow underneath. When firm, fold over as before. Continue adding mixture, cooking until firm and folding. Remove from heat and use a wooden board that fits inside the pan to press down and shape the omelette. Turn omelette onto a board. Allow to cool before using or refrigerating.

Cut omelette into strips 1 inch (2.5 cm) wide and 3 inches (7.5 cm) long. Make sushi following directions for nigiri-zushi on page 326. Use nori belts to strap omelette pieces to sushi.

Hint: *Without the right equipment, it may be difficult to create an omelette of the desired shape. Alternatively, cook omelette, lay it on a bamboo rolling mat and use the mat to flatten and shape it.*

Rainbow rolls

3 arugula (rocket) leaves

3 beet (beetroot) leaves

1 slice cuttlefish or baby squid (calamari)

1 slice salmon

1 slice king fish or yellowtail

1 cooked shrimp (prawn), about $2^3/_4$ inches (7 cm) long without head, shelled, halved and deveined

1 slice mango

1 cup (5 oz/150 g) Sushi Rice (see page 28)

$^1/_2$ teaspoon wasabi paste

shoyu, for serving

Cover a sushi mat with plastic wrap. Begining from one edge of mat, line up arugula and beet leaves one after another, placing them on a slight diagonal, and leaving some space in between for cuttlefish, salmon, king fish, shrimp and mango slices. Place fish and mango slices between arugula and beet leaves.

With wet fingers, form sushi rice into a bar and place on top. Using your index finger, smear rice with a dab of wasabi. Lift up sushi mat and firmly roll sushi, following instructions for hosomaki-zushi on page 324.

Unroll mat and transfer roll to a cutting board. Wipe a sharp knife with a damp towel, and cut roll in half. Cut each half into 3 pieces, wiping knife after each cut. Remove plastic and serve with shoyu.

Hint: In Japan, this sushi is called Tazuna-zushi, which means string-shaped hand rolls. The wrapping reveals the colorful ingredients and makes it more enticing to taste.

Roast pork and scallion rolls

$^1/_2$ nori sheet

1 cup (5 oz/150 g) Sushi Rice (see page 28)

2 strips roast pork, each $^3/_8$ inch (1 cm) wide and 8 inches (20 cm) long

2 scallions (shallots/spring onions), trimmed

Asian chili sauce, for serving

Place nori on a sushi mat, glossy side down. With wet fingers, spread rice evenly over nori. Place pork strips and scallions in center of nori and roll following instructions for hosomaki-zushi on page 324. Unroll mat and transfer roll to a cutting board. Wipe a sharp knife with a damp towel and cut roll in half, then cut each half in half again, wiping knife after each cut. Serve with chili sauce.

Shrimp tempura rolls with basil

1 nori sheet, halved

2 cups (10 oz/300 g) Sushi Rice (see page 28)

4 shrimp tempura (see page 307)

4 fresh Thai basil leaves

1 hard-boiled egg yolk, sieved (egg mimosa)

FOR THAI BASIL SAUCE

1 tablespoon rice vinegar

1 teaspoon fish sauce

leaves from 2 Thai basil sprigs, finely chopped

1 teaspoon packed brown sugar

To make Thai basil sauce: Combine all ingredients in a bowl and mix well. Set aside.

Arrange one half sheet of nori, glossy side down, on a sushi mat. With wet fingers, spread half sushi rice evenly over nori, leaving uncovered a $^3/_4$-inch (2-cm) strip of nori on side farthest from you. Place 2 shrimp tempura over rice, allowing tails to poke out at both ends of nori. Top with 2 Thai basil leaves and roll following instructions for hosomaki-zushi on page 324. If nori is too dry to seal, wet edge and press with mat. Unroll mat and transfer roll to a cutting board. Wipe a sharp knife with a damp towel and cut each roll into 4 pieces, wiping knife after each cut. Repeat with remaining ingredients. Arrange pieces on plates and sprinkle egg mimosa over shrimp tails. Serve with Thai basil sauce.

Spicy barbecued eel in cucumber parcels

Makes 8 pieces

8 kombu (kelp) strips, 3 inches (7.5 cm) long and 1 inch (2.5 cm) wide

1 teaspoon sugar

2 tablespoons rice vinegar

2 small English (hothouse) cucumbers, halved lengthwise

3 cups (15 oz/470 g) Sushi Rice (see page 28)

3 oz (90 g) barbecued eel, heated and cut crosswise into 8 slices

8 kinome (prickly ash) or sansho pepper (Japanese mountain pepper) sprigs

sweet-and-sour chili sauce, for serving (see Hint)

Cut kombu into 8 ribbons, each 1/8 inch (3 mm) wide and 3 inches (7.5 cm) long. Cook kombu strips in boiling water for 1 minute. Combine the sugar and rice vinegar in a bowl. Add kombu strips and let sit for 10 minutes.

Using a vegetable peeler, slice cut side of cucumber lengthwise to make 16 long, thin, wide slices.

Wet your hands and take one-eighth of sushi rice and form it into a ball. Insert a piece of eel in center and form into a ball again. On a dry work surface, place 2 strips of cucumber to make a cross, and place ball on center. Lift the 4 cucumber ends to encase the rice, leaving an opening at the top. Tie a kombu ribbon around the outside to secure. Insert a kinome sprig in the top. Repeat with remaining ingredients to make 7 more pieces. Serve with chili sauce.

Hint: *Barbecued eel is available frozen. After defrosting eel, heat until warm, about 30 seconds in a microwave or 2 minutes in an oven. Sweet-and-sour chili sauce is available from Asian markets.*

Tandoori chicken-daikon ships

1 small boneless, skinless chicken breast, about 5$\frac{1}{2}$ oz (165 g)

$\frac{1}{4}$ cup (2 fl oz/60 ml) tandoori paste

1 large daikon, halved and peeled

1 teaspoon canola oil

2 cups (10 oz/300 g) Sushi Rice (see page 28)

2 tablespoons plain (natural) yogurt

8 caperberries

FOR VINAIGRETTE

2 teaspoons shoyu

1 tablespoon mirin

1 tablespoon rice vinegar

Spread tandoori paste on both sides of chicken and let chicken sit for 20 minutes. Place a daikon half on a cutting board, cut side up, and, holding daikon steady with your hand, use a vegetable peeler to cut 8 long, thin, wide slices. Place slices in a bowl of water and set aside.

Heat a frying pan over medium–high heat and add oil. Add marinated chicken to pan and cook, on both sides, until cooked through. Transfer chicken to a cutting board, let cool slightly, then cut lengthwise into 8 thin slices.

Drain daikon slices and pat dry with paper towels.

With wet hands, mold sushi rice into 8 fingers, following instructions for nigiri-zushi on page 326. Holding rice with one hand, pick up a daikon slice and wrap it around rice, pressing gently to make sure it sticks to rice. Top with a dollop of yogurt and a chicken slice. Repeat with remaining ingredients. Top each sushi with a caperberry.

To make vinaigrette: Combine all ingredients in a bowl and stir to mix. Divide among individual sauce dishes and serve alongside sushi for dipping.

Hint: Tandoori paste is available from supermarkets and Indian or other Asian markets.

Tokyo cone rolls with ao-nori crepes

Makes 4 cones

³/₄ cup (4 oz/125 g) canned tuna,
  drained
2 tablespoons Japanese mayonnaise
2 eggs
1 teaspoon sugar
pinch salt
1 teaspoon mirin
1 tablespoon ao-nori (flaked nori)
1 tablespoon canola oil
1 cup (5 oz/150 g) Sushi Rice
  (see page 28)

wasabi paste to taste
1 English (hothouse) cucumber, cut
  lengthwise into ¹/₄-inch (6-mm) thick
  strips
4 nori strips, each 6 inches x ³/₄ inch
  (15 cm x 2 cm)
8 slices gari (see page 585), drained
shoyu, for serving

In a bowl, combine drained tuna and Japanese mayonnaise and mix well. Set aside.

To make crepes, whisk eggs, sugar, salt and mirin together in a bowl. Add aonori flakes and stir lightly.

In a nonstick frying pan, heat oil over medium heat. Pour one-quarter of egg mixture into pan, swirling to coat the base. Cook until surface of crepe becomes dry. Turn crepe over and cook for 30 seconds. Transfer to a plate and cover. Repeat with remaining mixture to make 4 crepes.

Place 1 crepe on a dry work surface. With a wet hand, pick up about 1 tablespoon sushi rice and spread over center of crepe, in a triangular shape. Smear with wasabi. Spread tuna mixture over rice and place 2–3 cucumber strips on top. Fold edge of crepe over rice and roll up tightly into a cone shape (see temaki-zushi on page 326). Wrap a nori strip in a band around end. To seal nori, apply a little water along edge.

Serve with gari and shoyu.

Hint: Ao-nori (flaked nori) is available from Asian markets, in packets or small bottles.

Beef sashimi

$^1/_2$ lb (250 g) sashimi-quality tenderloin (fillet) trimmed of sinew (see Note)
ice cold water
shredded daikon (see page 321), for garnish
2 lemon slices, for garnish
2 teaspoons finely grated fresh ginger, for serving
daikon-chili mixture (see page 321), for serving
1 scallion (shallot/spring onion), finely chopped, for serving
Ponzu Sauce (see page 585), for serving

Preheat a broiler (grill). Cut beef lengthwise into strips about 2 inches (5 cm) thick. Thread each strip onto a long metal skewer. Quickly sear beef in broiler, turning to brown on all sides. Meat should be still raw in center. Immediately place beef into ice water to halt the cooking process. Refrigerate for at least 30 minutes; this will make beef easier to slice.

Slice beef thinly, into slices about $^1/_8$ inch (3 mm) thick and arrange in a flower shape on a round flat platter. To decorate plate, place a mound of shredded daikon in center of platter along with lemon slices, grated ginger, daikon-chili mixture and chopped scallions. Serve with ponzu sauce. Ginger, daikon-chili mixture and scallions can be added to sauce to taste.

Note: This is a traditional Japanese recipe. Buy fresh, best-quality beef.

Blanched snapper sashimi

Serves 4

3¹/₂ oz (105 g) cucumber
21 oz (625 g) whole snapper
8 lemon slices, halved
pesticide-free flowers, for garnish
wasabi, for serving
shoyu, for serving

Using a vegetable peeler, remove skin from cucumber. Cut into very thin, fine strips using a sharp paring knife. Place in a bowl of cold water until using.

Remove scales from snapper (see page 263). Fillet into 3 pieces (see page 334) and remove any remaining bones with tweezers. Following directions for blanching (matsukawa-zukuri) on page 335, place a snapper fillet on a platter, skin side up. Pour boiling water over fish. When skin shrinks, transfer fish to a plate and refrigerate until cold. Repeat with second fillet.

Before serving, slice fish in rectangular slicing (hiki-zukuri) style (see page 335). You should have 20 pieces.

Place 5 pieces on each plate. Slip lemon slices between pieces. Garnish with cucumber slices and flowers.

Serve with wasabi and shoyu for dipping.

Hints: For blanched snapper sashimi, the texture is best when snapper weighs 2 lb (1 kg) or less. Larger snapper have thicker, tougher skin. Silver bream can also be used in this recipe.

Crabmeat with wasabi mayonnaise

Serves 4

1 tablespoon sake
1 tablespoon salt
8 fresh Alaskan (snow) crab sticks
ice water, for chilling
16 long chives, stemmed
4 strips of daikon 4 inches x $1/2$ inch (10 cm x 12 mm)
$1/4$ punnet mustard cress

FOR WASABI MAYONNAISE
$1^3/4$ oz (50 g) light mayonnaise
$1/3$ oz (10 g) wasabi

Bring a pot of water to a boil and add sake and salt. Wrap the crab sticks with a cotton cloth, and tie so they don't come apart, then boil. When cloth floats to the surface, remove crab and place in ice water. Unwrap the crab sticks once they have cooled.

Mix mayonnaise and wasabi to a smooth consistency. Cut each crab stick in half. Tie 2 crab sticks together with 4 pieces chives. Place a tied crab stick to stand on cut end on each bowl, and top with wasabi mayonnaise, daikon strip and mustard cress.

Hint: Lobster meat can be substituted for crab in this recipe.

Cuttlefish rolls with okra

Serves 4

1 nori sheet
4 cuttlefish or baby squid (calamari)
4 okra
12 shiso (perilla) leaves
4 carrot strips, 4 inches (10 cm) long and 3 inches (7.5 cm) wide
4 daikon strips 4 inches (10 cm) long and 3 inches (7.5 cm) wide
wasabi, for serving
shoyu, for serving

Cut nori sheet into quarters, and set aside. Clean and blanch cuttlefish following the directions on page 319. Place knife blade on edge of fillet and slice in half, without cutting right through (leave about ½ inch/12 mm of joined flesh). Gently open fillet using the knife blade. Cut a piece of nori to the size of one side of the opened cuttlefish fillet. Place nori on one half of the opened fillet. Trim ends of each okra and place 1 okra piece at the edge of the nori, in the center of the cuttlefish fold. Wrap cuttlefish tightly around okra and nori to form a cylindrical roll. Cut into 3 pieces.

Arrange shiso leaves on a plate and top with cuttlefish rolls, cut side up. Holding 1 carrot strip and 1 daikon strip, tie together to form knot in center. Place on plate. Repeat for remaining servings.

Serve with wasabi and shoyu for dipping.

Hint: Buy okra that is young and tender. As a substitute for okra, salmon slices, tuna slices, pickled ginger (gari) and sliced cucumber can be used.

Fine-sliced lemon sole with chives

Serves 4

3^1/$_2$ oz (105 g) shredded carrot
8 taro potato leaves or large basil
   leaves, for serving (optional)
21 oz (625 g) whole lemon sole

1 bunch chives
4 daikon flowers (see page 321)
wasabi, for serving
shoyu, for serving

Divide shredded carrot between 4 plates. If using, place 2 taro potato leaves on each plate, and set aside until ready to use. Fillet lemon sole into 3 pieces (see page 322). Cut lemon sole fillets into thin slices (see sogi-zukuri page 323). Chop chives into 1-inch (2.5-cm) lengths. Lay a lemon sole slice on a board, place 3 lengths of chives in the center and fold lemon sole in half. Place lemon sole on top of taro leaf. Place a daikon flower on each plate. Serve with wasabi and shoyu for dipping.

John Dory, paper-thin style

Serves 4

21 oz (625 g) whole John Dory
^{1}/$_2$ cup (4 fl oz/125 ml) aji-ponzu
   (Japanese citrus vinegar) or rice
   vinegar
juice of 1 lemon or 4 pieces dried or
   frozen yuzu
6 lemon slices, halved, for garnish

16 daikon flowers (see page 321), for
   garnish
4 carrot flowers (see page 321), for
   garnish

Scale fish (see page 263) and cut into 3 pieces (see page 322). Remove any remaining bones with tweezers. Then remove skin. With a sharp knife, trim left side of fillet diagonally. While holding the cut fillet with the left hand, incline the blade at a 45-degree angle to your left. Slice thinly, like paper, from the left to the right of the flesh. Slice each fillet thinly into pieces 2 inches x 1 inch (5 cm x 2.5 cm). Gently place on a plate with chopsticks or a fork.

Mix vinegar and lemon juice in a small bowl. Serve vinegar sauce with sashimi. If using yuzu, put one piece into each dipping sauce bowl. Add 3 lemon slices, 4 daikon flowers and a carrot flower to each serve.

Kaki-oyster cocktail

Serves 4

3 cups (24 fl oz/750 ml) water
1 tablespoon salt
8 oysters
2 nori sheets, quartered
4 tablespoons grated chili and daikon
  (see page 321)
1 tablespoon tobiko (flying fish roe)
8 chive stems, halved
1³/₄ oz (50 g) ugo (salted seaweed)
1³/₄ oz (50 g) shredded daikon

FOR VINAIGRETTE
2 tablespoons rice vinegar
1 teaspoon sugar
¹/₂ teaspoon mirin
2 drops shoyu

Combine all ingredients for vinaigrette in a bowl. Set aside.

Place water in another bowl and stir in salt.

To shuck oysters: Using an oyster opener or a butter knife, hold oyster in palm of one hand and insert knife into the shell where it is joined like a hinge. Push against the hinge and twist knife to open shells.

Dip oysters in salted water to enhance texture. Shape each piece of nori into a cylinder and seal using water. Place oyster in cylinder and cylinder in oyster shell. Place grated chili and daikon in shell. Arrange tobiko between daikon and oyster. Insert 2 chive stems in tobiko. Arrange ugo and shredded daikon in the center of each plate. Top with the oyster cocktail in the center of ugo and daikon bed. Drizzle with vinaigrette mixture.

Hint: Chose plump and lustrous oysters with a fresh smell.

Marinated yellowtail

Serves 4

1 yellow (brown) onion
4 whole yellowtail
1 3/4 oz (50 g) green ginger, grated
1 clove garlic, crushed
1 scallion (shallot/spring onion) stem,
  finely chopped
4 shiso (perilla) leaves, for serving
2 myoga, halved, for serving
3 1/2 oz (105 g) shredded daikon, for
  serving

FOR RED RADISH BASKETS
4 red radishes
2/3 oz (20 g) wasabi

FOR VINEGAR MIXTURE
1/2 cup (4 fl oz/125 ml) rice vinegar
2 tablespoons sugar
1 pinch salt
1 teaspoon mirin

To make red radish baskets: Slice top from each radish and reserve. Scoop out center and fill with wasabi.

In a bowl, add all vinegar ingredients and mix until well combined.

Slice onion. Place slices in a bowl of ice water. Fillet yellowtail (see page 322) and cut into small squares, approximately 3/8 inch (1 cm) wide. Drain sliced onion. Place sliced onion, grated ginger, crushed garlic and chopped scallion in a bowl. Pour in vinegar mixture and mix using chopsticks or a fork. Add yellowtail pieces and mix gently. Remove pieces and place on a board, then lightly grind (mince) with the back of a knife blade to absorb the flavor (see lightly ground tataki, page 324). Lay a shiso leaf on each plate or bowl with crushed ice, then arrange yellowtail pieces on each plate or bowl, and top with condiments from the vinegar mixture. Garnish with a half myoga leaf, shredded daikon and 1 radish basket per plate.

Hint: *Bonito is also suitable for this dish.*

Salmon sashimi

3¹/₂ oz (105 g) ugo (salted seaweed) or shredded daikon

10 oz (300 g) salmon fillet without skin, bones removed

4 daikon flowers, for garnish (see page 321)

wasabi, for serving

shoyu, for serving

Rinse ugo under running water for 10 seconds to extract extra salt, then leave in cold water until needed. Slice salmon in the rectangular slicing (hira-zukuri) technique (see page 335). Place ugo on each plate and arrange 7 slices on top of ugo. Place daikon flower in middle. Serve with wasabi and shoyu.

Salmon tataki

10 oz (300 g) salmon fillet, skin removed

2 chive stems, chopped

1¹/₂ oz (45 g) ginger, grated

1 teaspoon mirin

pinch salt

8 shiso (perilla) leaves

8 quail eggs

red maple leaves, for decoration (optional)

wasabi, for serving

shoyu, for serving

Remove any bones in salmon with tweezers. Julienne fillet, then using a knife, chop finely with the chives and ginger. Mix in mirin and salt. Form into 8 small balls. Cut shiso leaves in half lengthwise along center vein and wrap each salmon ball with 2 leaf halves. If necessary, use a little water to help leaves adhere. Place 2 wrapped salmon balls on each plate. Break a quail egg into a bowl. Carefully spoon out yolk and place on top of salmon. Decorate plate, if desired, with maple leaves. Serve with wasabi and shoyu for dipping.

Salmon with blue cheese and white miso puree

Serves 4

8 oz (250 g) salmon or ocean trout
   fillet, skin removed
1³/₄ oz (50 g) scallions (shallots/spring
   onions), shredded, for serving
1 teaspoon sansho seeds (Japanese
   mountain pepper), for serving

**FOR BLUE CHEESE AND WHITE
MISO PUREE**

1 oz (30 g) blue cheese
1³/₄ oz (50 g) white (shiro) miso paste
2 tablespoons mirin
1 tablespoon light soy sauce

To make blue cheese and white miso puree: Whisk blue cheese and shiromiso in a bowl.
Add mirin and light soy sauce. Slice salmon thinly (see page 323). Arrange shredded
scallion on 4 plates. Place salmon on the scallion on each plate and top with blue cheese
and white miso puree and sansho seeds.

Scallop sashimi

Serves 4

8 scallops in the shell (see Hint)
1 tablespoon salt, dissolved in 3 cups
   (24 fl oz/750 ml) water
4 tablespoons salmon caviar,
   for serving

FOR GREEN TEA MIXTURE

1 tablespoon green tea powder
1 tablespoon white (shiro) miso paste
1 teaspoon mirin

Rinse scallop shells before using. Insert butter knife in shell and open. Cut out scallop meat
and rinse in salted water. Discard veins and roe. Do not discard shells, as they will be
used for presentation.

To make green tea mixture: In a bowl, combine all ingredients. Divide mixture between
4 half-shells. Place 2 scallops in each shell. Top with caviar.

Hint: *Purchase scallops in the shell. If only scallops for cooking are available,
blanch them before making sashimi.*

Trumpeter sashimi

Serves 4

20 oz (600 g) whole trumpeter
3¹/₂ oz (105 g) shredded daikon
8 thin lime slices, halved
4 red radish flowers, for garnish
  (see page 321)

1 hard-boiled egg yolk, sieved
  (egg mimosa)
8 chives, stemmed
wasabi, for serving
shoyu, for serving

Fillet trumpeter into 3 pieces (see page 322) and remove bones. Remove skin from each piece and slice each fillet in rectangular slicing (hira-zukuri) technique (see page 323). You should have 20 slices. Place a small amount of shredded daikon on each plate and top with 5 trumpeter slices. Slip 4 lime slices between trumpeter slices.

Garnish with a radish flower. Place egg mimosa into each flower. Garnish with 2 chives. Serve with wasabi and shoyu for dipping.

Tuna and nori sashimi rolls

Serves 4

10 oz (300 g) tuna block
4 nori sheets, halved
1³/₄ oz (50 g) shredded daikon radish
1³/₄ oz (50 g) shredded beet
  (beetroot)

4 beet (beetroot) flowers (see page
  321)
wasabi, for serving
shoyu, for serving

Cut tuna into cylinders 1 inch (2.5 cm) in diameter and 4 inches (10 cm) long.

Lay a halved nori sheet on board and top with 1 tuna slice. Roll up tightly using both hands. Repeat with remaining tuna slices and nori sheets. Cut each roll into 4 pieces. Divide daikon and shredded beet among 4 bowls. Place 4 rolls in each bowl. Garnish with beet flower. Serve with wasabi and shoyu for dipping.

Hint: Salmon may be used in place of tuna.

Tuna cubes, blanched

Serves 4

10 oz (300 g) tuna block, trimmed of dark flesh and skin
12 small shiso (perilla) leaves or maple leaves, for garnish
pesticide-free flowers, for decoration
shoyu, for serving

Cut tuna block into 2 pieces, approximately 1 inch x 8 inches (2.5 cm x 20 cm) or 1 inch x 6 inches (2.5 cm x 15 cm)—size of pieces will depend on size of block. (See also directions for kaki-zukuri on page 324.)

Bring a saucepan of water to a boil and, using tongs or chopsticks, dip each tuna piece in water for 2 seconds. Remove immediately and place in a bowl of ice water; refrigerate until chilled.

Remove tuna from bowl, and cut into 1-inch (2.5-cm) cubes. Divide leaves among 4 plates. Top with tuna cubes, cut side up. Garnish with flowers. Serve with shoyu for dipping.

Tuna with yam puree

Serves 4

10 oz (300 g) tuna block, trimmed of
dark flesh and skin
2 tablespoons soy sauce

1 3/4 oz (50 g) shredded daikon
3 1/2 oz (105 g) yam puree
1 nori sheet, shredded

Cut the tuna into 1-inch (2.5-cm) cubes following directions for kaki-zukuri on page 324. Place tuna cubes in a bowl, add soy sauce and gently toss. Divide daikon between 4 bowls. Place tuna cubes on daikon in each bowl. Pour the yam puree over tuna and garnish with shredded nori.

Hint: Yam puree is available packaged from Japanese grocery stores.

White fish and chive rolls

3 oz (90 g) white fish such as sea bream (whiting)
8 stalks fresh chives, cut into 1-inch (2.5 cm) lengths
shoyu, for serving
wasabi, for serving

Cut fish into paper-thin slices (see directions for John Dory, Paper-thin Style on page 352). Wrap each slice of fish around 4 or 5 chive lengths. Serve with shoyu and wasabi.

Yellowtail, kelp and daikon rolls

4 sheets of kelp, each trimmed into 4-inch (10-cm) squares, lightly boiled
4 paper-thin daikon slices, each 4 inches (10 cm) long
4 whole yellowtail
2 teaspoons tobiko (flying fish roe), for garnish
nandin leaves, for garnish
wasabi, for serving
shoyu, for serving

To boil kelp: Bring a pot of water to a boil. Add kelp and cook until tender.

To slice daikon: Using a vegetable peeler, peel 4 slices of daikon, starting from top to bottom, ensuring that each slice is about 4 inches (10 cm) long.

Fillet yellowtail into 3 pieces (see page 334). Remove any remaining bones with tweezers. Carefully remove skin from fish with a knife. Place a kelp sheet on a board, then lay fillets on top. Roll tightly. Place a daikon slice on board, top with kelp roll, and roll tightly. Cut roll into 4 pieces. Repeat with remaining kelp, yellowtail and daikon.

Divide rolls among 4 plates and garnish with tobiko and nandin leaves. Serve with wasabi and shoyu for dipping.

Asparagus and sweet red pepper rolls

Makes 6 rolls (36 pieces)

FOR SESAME DRESSING

2 tablespoons white sesame seeds or tahini

2 teaspoons shoyu

2 teaspoons sugar

6 thin asparagus, blanched

1/3 red bell pepper (capsicum), seeded and thinly sliced

3 nori sheets

3 cups (15 oz/450 g) Sushi Rice (see page 28)

2 tablespoons gari (see page 585), for garnish

1/4 cup (2 fl oz/60 ml) shoyu, for serving

To make sesame dressing: Place sesame seeds in a dry frying pan over moderate heat until golden and seeds begin to jump. Grind in a mortar and pestle to a smooth paste. (Alternatively, use tahini.) Combine with shoyu and sugar, stirring until sugar dissolves. If mixture is too thick, add a little water, stock or sake. Prepare rolls following the directions for hosomaki-zushi on page 324, using sesame dressing, asparagus and red pepper strips as fillings. Garnish with gari and serve with shoyu.

Avocado nigiri-zushi

Makes 10 pieces

1–2 avocados, peeled, pitted and sliced

1 cup (5 oz/150 g) Sushi Rice (see page 28)

10 nori belts (see page 321)

White or red miso paste, for garnish

Use 2 slices of avocado for each sushi piece. Make sushi following the directions for nigiri-zushi on page 326. Wrap nori belts around sushi. Top each with a dab of miso.

Variation: To make nigiri-zushi using eggplant (aubergine) instead of avocado, peel 1–2 Japanese eggplants (aubergines), and cut into 1/4 x 1 1/2 x 2 1/2-inch- (6 x 4 x 6-cm) slices. Brush with oil then deep-fry eggplant for about 2 minutes, or until soft. Drain and cool. Make sushi following the directions on page 326. Garnish with white sesame seeds and pour a little sweet soy sauce on top.

Battleships with avocado and cucumber

Makes 10 pieces

1 teaspoon wasabi paste

2 tablespoons mayonnaise

1/2 small avocado, finely diced

1 scallion (shallot/spring onion), green part only, finely sliced

1 cup (5 oz/150 g) Sushi Rice (see page 28)

1 nori sheet, cut into 1 x 5-inch (2.5 x 13-cm) strips

1 teaspoon toasted black sesame seeds

1/4 small English (hothouse) cucumber, seeded and finely sliced, skin on

1/4 cup (2 fl oz/60 ml) shoyu

2 teaspoons beni-shoga

Mix wasabi and mayonnaise until smooth. Carefully fold in avocado and scallion.

Gently shape about 1 tablespoon rice into a small oval or rectangle. Place 1 nori strip against rice, shiny side out. Press gently and continue to wrap strip around rice ball. Use a grain of rice to seal overlapped ends of nori.

Cover top of rice with avocado mixture. Sprinkle with sesame seeds. Tuck 3–4 cucumber slices in at one end. Repeat for remaining sushi. Serve with shoyu and beni-shoga.

Hints: To make mini battleship sushi, use 2 teaspoons of rice and smaller nori strips. (See also Battleship Sushi, page 328.)

Broiled shiitake mushroom nigiri-zushi

Makes 10 pieces

1 tablespoon shoyu
1 tablespoon mirin
10 fresh shiitake mushrooms, stems removed
1 cup (5 oz/150 g) Sushi Rice (see page 28)
$^1/_2$ nori sheet sliced into 10 strips, $^1/_2$ inch x 3 inches (1 cm x 7.5 cm)

Combine shoyu and mirin and brush on shiitake. Grill mushrooms until tender, 2–3 minutes.

With one hand, pick up one tablespoon of rice and gently squeeze and shape it into a rectangle with rounded edges. Pick up a mushroom with the other hand, bending your fingers to form a shallow mold that mushroom can rest in. Place shaped rice ball on mushroom and very gently press down with index and middle fingers, holding your thumb at top end of ball to stop rice being pushed out the end.

Turn over rice ball so mushroom is on top and continue gently pushing topping against rice with your index and middle fingers. Turn sushi 180 degrees and repeat. The topping should look like a roof over rice ball, with very little, if any, rice visible. Place a nori strip on top of mushroom and tuck each end underneath rice ball to keep the mushroom in place.

Hint: See also directions for nigiri-zushi on page 326.

Variations: Combinations of ingredients that suit this recipe include: seasoned omelette slice tied with blanched scallion; sliced avocado with wasabi mayonnaise and toasted sesame seeds; pickled radish (takuan) and shiso leaf, tied with a seasoned kampyo strip (see page 332).

Chirashi-zushi with vegetables

Serves 4

2 large dried shiitake mushrooms

1/2 cup (4 fl oz/120 ml) Dashi 2 (see page 573)

2 teaspoons sugar

2 teaspoons mirin

1 small carrot, peeled and julienned

1/2 cup (1 1/2 oz/45 g) thinly sliced, canned bamboo shoots

2 teaspoons reduced-salt soy sauce

6 thin asparagus spears, blanched

12 snow peas (mange-tout), blanched

1 English (hothouse) cucumber

1 Seasoned Omelette (see page 320)

5 cups (24 oz/750 g) Sushi Rice (see page 28)

2 tablespoons ao-nori (flaked nori)

1/4 cup shredded beni-shoga

2 teaspoons wasabi

1/3 cup (3 fl oz/90 ml) shoyu, for serving

Soak mushrooms in cold water until soft, 20–30 minutes. Discard stems and slice caps thinly.

Put dashi, sugar and mirin in a medium saucepan and bring to a boil over medium heat. Add carrot strips and simmer until cooked but still crisp, about 2 minutes. Using a slotted spoon, remove from liquid and set aside. Add bamboo shoots, mushrooms and soy sauce to liquid and cook about 5 minutes. Remove from heat. Return carrot strips and allow to cool completely. (This preparation can be done ahead.)

Slice asparagus and snow peas diagonally into 1 1/2-inch (4-cm) lengths. Cut cucumber lengthwise into quarters and remove seeds. Thinly slice lengthwise into 2-inch (5-cm) pieces or cut decoratively (see garnishes, page 321). Roll omelette and slice thinly, separating slices with fingertips.

Place rice in lacquered boxes, individual bowls or on one large platter. Arrange a selection of vegetables decoratively on rice and garnish with omelette, aonori and beni-shoga. Serve with wasabi and shoyu.

Hints: *"Scattered" sushi makes a great party or picnic dish or family meal. It features a variety of sushi ingredients arranged on a platter or in a lacquerware bento, a Japanese lunch box which can be transported easily, and eaten with chopsticks. Presentation style and ingredients differ from region to region in Japan.*

You could include scallions (shallots/spring onions), bell peppers (capsicums), lotus root, baby corn or green beans. (See also Chirashi-zushi on page 332.)

Variation: *If you wish, you can season the sushi rice used for chirashi-zushi with chopped vegetables, green peas, chopped fresh ginger, gari, soboro, crumbled nori, toasted sesame seeds, tofu or strips of deep-fried tofu, or various sauces. The dish is then known as "bara-zushi."*

Cucumber and sesame rolls

Makes 6 rolls (36 pieces)

3 nori sheets
3 cups (15 oz/470 g) Sushi Rice (see page 28)
1 teaspoon wasabi paste
2 tablespoons toasted white sesame seeds
1 English (hothouse) or telegraph cucumber, seeded and thinly sliced lengthwise
1 tablespoon gari (see page 585)
1/4 cup (2 fl oz/60 ml) shoyu

Cut each nori sheet in half lengthwise, parallel with the lines marked on the rough side. Place one half nori sheet lengthwise on a bamboo mat about 3 slats from the edge closest to you, shiny side down. Spread one-sixth of rice evenly over nori, leaving a 3/4-inch (2-cm) strip on long side farthest away uncovered. Gently rake fingers across grains to spread rice.

Build a small mound of rice along edge nearest the uncovered nori strip to help keep fillings in place.

Spread a pinch of wasabi across center of rice. Sprinkle with sesame seeds and arrange one-third of cucumber strips, making sure they extend completely to each end. Using your index finger and thumb, pick up edge of mat nearest you. Place remaining fingers over fillings to hold them in as you roll forward, tightly wrapping rice and nori around fillings. The strip of nori without rice should still be visible.

Press gently and continue rolling forward to complete roll. Gently press mat to shape and seal roll. Unroll mat and place roll on chopping board with seam on bottom. Wipe a sharp knife with a damp cloth and cut roll in half. Pick up one half-roll and turn it 180 degrees so cut ends of rolls are on the same side. Cut rolls to make 6 pieces, wiping knife between cuts. Repeat for remaining rolls.

Serve with remaining wasabi, gari and shoyu.

Hints: Many types of fillings can be used in this sushi style, including broiled (grilled) shiitake mushrooms or marinated vegetables. (See also directions for hosomaki-zushi on page 324.)

Futomaki roll with vegetables

Makes 4 rolls (32 pieces)

4 nori sheets

4 cups (20 oz/600 g) Sushi Rice (see page 28)

2 teaspoons wasabi paste

4 strips Seasoned Kampyo (see page 332)

1/2 English (hothouse) cucumber, seeded and thinly sliced

4 strips Seasoned Omelette (see page 320)

4 strips pickled radish (takuan)

2 tablespoons beni-shoga

1/4 cup (2 fl oz/60 ml) shoyu, for serving

Prepare rolls following the directions for futomaki on page 325, layering fillings and making sure that they end extend completely to both ends. Serve with remaining wasabi and shoyu.

Futomaki roll with vegetables, California-style

Makes 4 rolls (32 pieces)

2 teaspoons wasabi

2 tablespoons mayonnaise

4 nori sheets

4 cups (20 oz/600 g) Sushi Rice (see page 28)

1 English (hothouse) cucumber, seeded and thinly sliced

1 avocado, peeled and thinly sliced

1 carrot, coarsely shredded

1 cup (2 oz/60 g) snow pea (mange-tout) sprouts, stems trimmed

4 shiso (perilla) or small lettuce leaves, shredded (optional)

2 tablespoons gari (see page 585)

1/4 cup (2 fl oz/60 ml) shoyu, for serving

In a small bowl, combine wasabi and mayonnaise. Prepare rolls following the directions for futomaki on page 325, spreading wasabi mayonnaise across the rice before adding other ingredients.

Inside-out rolls with vegetables

Makes 4 rolls (32 pieces)

2 nori sheets

3 cups (15 oz/470 g) Sushi Rice (see page 28)

1 tablespoon combined toasted black and white sesame seeds

1–2 tablespoons wasabi paste

1/2 English (hothouse) or telegraph cucumber, seeded and thinly sliced

4 strips Seasoned Kampyo (see page 332)

2 tablespoons beni-shoga

8 snow peas (mange-tout), blanched and thinly sliced

1/2 red bell pepper (capsicum), seeded and thinly sliced

1/4 cup (2 fl oz/60 ml) shoyu

Cut each piece of nori in half lengthwise, parallel with lines marked on rough side. Place one-half nori sheet along long side of a bamboo mat nearest you. Spread one-quarter of rice evenly over nori. Gently rake fingers across grains to spread rice. Sprinkle rice with mixed sesame seeds and cover with a large sheet of plastic wrap.

Pick up mat, carefully turn over so nori is now on top and place back on mat about 3 slats from edge closest to you. Spread a pinch of wasabi and selection of fillings across center of nori. Make sure fillings extend completely to each end. Using your index finger and thumb, pick up edge of bamboo mat and plastic wrap nearest you. Place remaining fingers over fillings to hold them as you roll mat forward tightly, wrapping rice and nori around fillings.

Press gently and continue rolling forward to complete roll. Gently press mat to shape and seal roll. Unroll mat and plastic. Wipe a sharp knife with a damp cloth and cut roll in half. Cut each half in half twice more to make 8 pieces, wiping knife with each cut. Repeat with remaining roll. Serve with remaining wasabi and shoyu.

Variations: Filling combinations which can be used include cucumber, avocado, seasoned tempeh and sesame seeds; or red bell pepper (capsicum), beni-shoga, snow pea (mange-tout) sprouts and cucumber; or shredded carrot, avocado, scallion, snow pea (mange-tout) sprouts and horseradish cream.

Omelette rolls

Makes 2 rolls (16 pieces)

Seasoned Carrot (see page 376),
  julienned
Seasoned Shiitake Mushrooms (see
  page 332), finely chopped
Seasoned Kampyo, thinly sliced (see
  page 332)
2 cups (10 oz/300 g) Sushi Rice (see
  page 28)

2 Seasoned Omelettes (see page 320)
2 nori sheets
1 English (hothouse) cucumber, seeded
  and thinly sliced lengthwise
1/4 cup shoyu, for serving
2 tablespoons gari, for serving

In a bowl, combine seasoned shiitake, seasoned carrot, seasoned tofu and rice, mixing well.

Cover a bamboo mat with a plastic wrap. Lay one omelette on plastic and cover with a sheet of nori. Spread nori with rice mixture, leaving a 1-inch (2.5-cm) strip on long side farthest away uncovered. Lay half cucumber strips across rice, making sure they extend to each end. Pick up mat and plastic with index finger and thumb, holding cucumber in place with remaining fingers and roll and seal nori around cucumber.

Unroll mat and plastic. Place roll on cutting board with seam on bottom. Wipe a sharp knife with a damp cloth and cut roll into 8 pieces, wiping knife before each cut. Repeat for remaining roll. Serve with shoyu and gari.

Variations: To make omelette sushi cones, cut each omelette in half. Place about 1 1/2 tablespoons sushi rice in middle, top with wasabi and fillings. Fold omelette over fillings to form into cone shape.

To make omelette sushi pouches, trim omelettes to 6 inches (15 cm) in diameter. Place sushi rice and filling in middle. Gather up four corners, carefully tying top with a scallion (shallot/spring onion) (trim ends and blanch in boiling water for 30–60 seconds to soften then rinse under cold water). Alternatively, fold omelette over rice like a package, tucking ends underneath, and tie with scallion.

Pickled plum and brown rice rolls

Makes 4 rolls (32 pieces)

1 tablespoon vegetable oil

2 carrots, peeled and cut lengthwise into thin strips

1 clove garlic, finely chopped

1 teaspoon grated fresh ginger

2 eggs, lightly beaten

1 tablespoon shoyu

1 tablespoon umeboshi (pickled plum) paste

1 tablespoon rice vinegar

4 nori sheets

4 cups (20 oz/625 g) Brown Sushi Rice (see page 30)

4 scallions (shallots/spring onions), green parts only

$^1/_4$ cup (2 fl oz/60 ml) shoyu, for serving

Heat oil in a frying pan over medium heat and sauté carrot, garlic and ginger until carrots are just cooked, about 2 minutes. Remove from pan. Combine eggs and tablespoon of shoyu and spread thinly over frying pan. Cook until just set, about 45 seconds. Turn over and cook about 20 seconds longer. Remove from pan and slice into thin strips. Combine plum paste and vinegar and gently fold into rice.

Place a sheet of nori lengthwise on bamboo mat, about 3 slats from edge closest to you, shiny side down. Spread one-quarter of rice evenly over nori, leaving a $^3/_4$-inch (2-cm) strip on long side farthest away from you uncovered. Make an indentation across rice about $^3/_4$ inch (2 cm) from side nearest you and put a quarter of carrots, egg and one scallion evenly from one side of rice to the other. Using your index finger and thumb, pick up edge of bamboo mat nearest you. Place remaining fingers over fillings to hold them as you roll mat forward, tightly wrapping rice and nori around fillings. The strip of nori without rice should still be visible.

Press firmly and continue rolling forward to complete roll. Gently press mat to shape roll. Unroll mat and place roll on cutting board with seam on bottom.

Wipe a knife with a damp cloth and cut roll into 8 pieces, wiping knife with each cut. Repeat with remaining rolls. Serve with shoyu.

Pin wheel rolls

Makes 4 rolls (32 pieces)

4 nori sheets
4 cups (20 oz/600 g) Sushi Rice (see page 28)
2 teaspoons wasabi paste
5–6 fillings per roll (see page 371)
2 tablespoons gari (see page 591), for serving
1/4 cup (2 fl oz/60 ml) shoyu, for serving

Place short side of one nori sheet lengthwise on bamboo mat about 3 slats from edge closest to you, shiny side down. Working from one side to the other, spread one-quarter of rice evenly over nori, leaving a 1-inch (2.5-cm) strip on the long side farthest from you uncovered. Gently rake fingers across grains to spread rice. Spread a pinch of wasabi across center of rice. Place fillings across rice next to each other, beginning about 3/4 inch (2 cm) from edge nearest you and extending to within 1 1/2 inches (4 cm) of opposite edge. Make sure fillings extend completely to each side or there will be no filling in end pieces when cut.

Using your index finger and thumb, pick up edge of bamboo mat nearest you. Roll forward straight down over first filling. Continue rolling forward to complete roll, pulling mat forward as you go so it does not get rolled in with rice. Gently press mat to shape roll. Unroll mat and place roll on cutting board with seam on bottom.

Wipe a sharp knife with a damp cloth and cut roll in half. Pick up one half roll and turn it 180 degrees so cut ends of rolls are on the same side. Cut rolls in half, then in half again to make 8 pieces, wiping knife with each cut. Repeat for remaining rolls. Serve with remaining wasabi, gari and shoyu.

Hints: These sushi rolls are made in the same way as futomaki rolls (see page 325), except the fillings are laid across the rice so when rolled the ingredients and nori form a pin wheel pattern. Alternate different colored ingredients for different effects.

You can also use the same ingredients to make Inside-out Rolls (see page 371) with rice on the outside; sprinkle rice with toasted sesame seeds or fresh herbs.

Seasoned carrot nigiri-zushi

Makes 10 pieces

1 cup (5 oz/150 g) Sushi Rice (see page 28)
10 scallions (shallots/spring onions), green parts only, blanched
1 teaspoon grated fresh ginger
Teriyaki Sauce (see page 593), for dipping (optional)

FOR SEASONED CARROT
1 medium carrot, peeled and cut into thin slices
1/3 cup (3 fl oz/90 ml) Dashi 2 (see page 573) or water
2 teaspoons sugar
1 teaspoon light soy sauce
pinch salt

To make seasoned carrots: In a small saucepan combine carrot, dashi, sugar, light soy sauce and salt. Simmer over low heat until carrot is tender and most of the liquid is absorbed. Remove using a slotted spoon and set aside to cool.

Shape rice into 10 balls following the directions for nigiri-zushi on page 325. Pick up a seasoned carrot slice with one hand, bending your fingers to form a shallow mold that carrot can rest in. Place shaped rice rectangle on carrot and very gently press down with index and middle fingers, holding your thumb at top end of rectangle to stop rice being pushed out the end. Turn rice so carrot is on top and continue pushing topping against rice with your index and middle fingers. Turn sushi 180 degrees and repeat. The topping should look like a roof over rice, with very little, if any, rice visible.

Tie a scallion around each sushi and garnish with grated ginger. Serve with teriyaki sauce for dipping. (Pictured on page 314.)

Seasoned kampyo and radish rolls

Makes 6 rolls (36 pieces)

3 nori sheets

3 cups (15 oz/450 g) Sushi Rice (see page 28)

6 strips pickled radish (takuan), $1/2$ inch x $1/2$ inch x $7^1/4$ inches (1 cm x 1 cm x 18.5 cm)

6 pieces Seasoned Kampyo (see page 332)

1 teaspoon wasabi, for serving

1 tablespoon gari (see page 591), for serving

$1/4$ cup (2 fl oz/60 ml) shoyu, for serving

Prepare rolls following the directions for hosomaki-zushi on page 324, using one strip pickled radish and kampyo per roll.

Serve wasabi, gari and shoyu separately.

Tofu nigiri-zushi

Makes 10 pieces

8 oz (125 g) firm tofu, drained

1 cup (5 oz/155 g) Sushi Rice (see page 28)

10 nori belts (see page 321)

grated fresh ginger, finely chopped scallions (shallots/spring onions),
white or red miso paste or mayonnaise, for garnish

Cut tofu into $1/4$ x 2 x $2^1/2$-inch (6 x 5 x 6-cm) pieces.

Make sushi following the directions for nigiri-zushi on page 326. Wrap nori belts around sushi. Add garnish of your choice.

Vegetables & salads

Vegetables in Asian cuisine are much more than just minor players in a meal. In many cases, it is actually the vegetables which can define the dish. Or, as with Japanese daikon pickles and Korean kimchi, the star vegetable is present at almost every meal.

Throughout the Asian nations—including China, India, Japan, Malaysia, Thailand, Laos, Myanmar, Vietnam, Taiwan and Korea—many people are strictly vegetarian because of their religious beliefs, such as Buddhism which forbids the killing and eating of animals. Some also have a diet based on vegetables due to custom and agricultural circumstances—animal products being so expensive, in comparison with vegetables and grains, they are either reserved for special occasions, eaten in very small quantities, or not eaten at all. As a result, the range of vegetarian food as well as recipes based on vegetables is very broad and enticing in Asia.

There are many compelling reasons for choosing to eat more vegetables—or to be vegetarian—including health and environmental issues, concerns about proper resource management and the treatment of animals, the safety of our food supply and the fact that vegetables are generally less expensive.

Vegetarian Asian food is based on fresh vegetables and fruits combined with grains, seeds and legumes. Soybeans are vegetarian Asia's most important source of non-animal protein.

The amazing array of food products made from soybeans, apart from the beans and sprouts themselves, includes tofu, tempeh, beancurd skins, soy milk, textured vegetable protein (TVP), soy sauce, miso, bean sauces, oil and cheese. In China soybeans are known as the "meat of the earth" and tofu is called "meat without a bone," and over the centuries, generations of Asian cooks have devised ways to make soy products look and taste like any part of fish, meat or poultry.

Many of the recipes in this chapter are vegetarian—vegan (without any animal products at all); lacto-vegetarian (with animal products such as honey, milk, yogurt and cheese, but without any animal meat or meat products); and ovo-lacto vegetarian (with eggs and dairy products). Note that pesco-vegetarians eat seafood; as do some Buddhists in India and Thailand, because seafood is considered to be "fruit of the sea." Some of the recipes, however, also contain seafood, meat or animal products, and while they aren't vegetarian, they could easily be adapted to be so.

Most of the recipes are easy to prepare, with an emphasis on fresh seasonal ingredients and authentic flavor, and have exciting variations. They include vegetable sides, superfast stir-fries, main dishes and hearty one-pot vegetable meals, as well as all the essential elements required for an Asian-style vegetarian banquet.

Buying and preparing vegetables

Vegetables are also popular in Asia because they are so easy to prepare. Some, like herbs and table greens, require nothing more than cleaning. Others, like pickled vegetables, can be made in advance and stored for months, ready for serving at a moment's notice. With vegetables perhaps more than any other food type, it is essential to buy produce that is in season to ensure you get the best quality, price and flavor—if required, simply adapt your chosen recipe to suit the seasonal vegetables available.

Buying and storing vegetables

- When buying roots and tubers (vegetables that grow underground), select firm, unwrinkled specimens that are relatively heavy in proportion to their size. Store roots and tubers, unwashed, with their leaves removed, in a cool, dark place for up to 2 weeks. Store leaves in the vegetable crisper of the refrigerator for up to 1 week. Mature roots and tubers are generally peeled before cooking, but young vegetables, such as baby carrots and new potatoes, can simply be washed and cooked in their skins.

- Store bulb vegetables such as onions and garlic in a cool, dark place for a few weeks. Scallions (shallots/spring onions) and leeks should be stored in a plastic bag in the vegetable crisper of the refrigerator for up to 1 week.

- Squashes are categorized as summer squashes, including zucchini (courgette) and pattypan, which are picked when immature, or winter squashes, such as pumpkin, butternut and acorn, which have tough skin, hard seeds and starchy flesh and are picked when fully grown. Store summer squashes in the vegetable crisper of the refrigerator for 3–4 days, and winter squashes in a cool, dark place for up to 1 month.

- Beans used in Asian cooking include green beans, or snap beans, and long (snake) beans, as well as snow peas (mange-tout), of which both the pods and young growing shoots are eaten. Fresh peas and beans should be stored in the vegetable crisper of the refrigerator, and will keep for several days. Do not shell until ready to use.

- Leaf vegetables, which include all the Asian greens, are best consumed as soon as possible after harvesting. Select unblemished specimens with good color and store, unwashed, in a plastic bag in the vegetable crisper of the refrigerator for up to 4 days.

- Flower vegetables include cabbage and some of its relatives: cauliflower, broccoli and brussels sprouts. These can be stored in the vegetable crisper of the refrigerator for up to 1 week.

- Mushrooms require very little preparation—just wipe the caps clean with a damp paper towel or remove any dirt with a mushroom brush. Store fresh mushrooms in a paper bag in the refrigerator for up to 7 days. Never place mushrooms in a plastic bag; this will cause them to turn soggy.

- Asparagus is best enjoyed when it is in season and plentiful at the market. The most common variety is green, though spears of white asparagus, harvested before they grow aboveground, are sold in some markets. Asparagus is very perishable and should be stored, unwashed, in the vegetable crisper of the refrigerator for no more than 3 days.

Presenting vegetables

Vegetables and fruits in both Asian homes and restaurants are often exquisitely carved and cut—it would be unheard of for many Asian cooks to entertain without considering presentation, from tableware and flower arrangements to carved vegetables. Any dish is transformed with the addition of a chili flower or tomato rose or even some fine chiffonades of herbs (see Preparing ingredients, pages 22–33).

Preserved vegetables and pickles

Fluctuations in food supplies and limited refrigeration across many parts of Asia have resulted in a rich tradition of vegetable preserving techniques, including drying, salting and pickling. Food that has been treated in this way is often pungently flavored and adds a great deal to plainer vegetable and grain dishes. You can add as much or as little of these intensely flavored vegetables as you like, according to availability and taste.

Kimchi is possibly Korea's most famous dish—made by fermenting various kinds of vegetables, but most often Chinese cabbage. It's present at every Korean meal, and so important to national culture that there is a museum dedicated to it in Seoul.

Likewise, Japanese pink pickled ginger (gari) and pickled daikon are well known—no Japanese meal is considered complete without them.

Many of these pickles can be bought ready-made in jars at Asian markets, but as with all good food, it is best to make your own.

Asian greens, peanut and bean thread noodle salad

Serves 4–6

3 oz (90 g) dried cellophane (bean thread) noodles

1 bunch (13 oz/400 g) bok choy, trimmed and washed

1 bunch (16 oz/500 g) choy sum, trimmed and washed

$^1/_4$ Chinese cabbage, washed

1 red (Spanish) onion, peeled and sliced into thin half-moons

$^1/_3$ cup (2 oz/60 g) peanuts, toasted (see page 30) and coarsely chopped

1$^1/_2$ tablespoons white vinegar

3 tablespoons fresh lime juice

1 tablespoon tamarind paste

2$^1/_2$ tablespoons superfine (caster) sugar

3 tablespoons peanut oil

$^1/_4$ cup ($^1/_3$ oz/10 g) chopped fresh Vietnamese or common mint

$^1/_4$ cup ($^1/_3$ oz/10 g) chopped fresh cilantro (fresh coriander)

Soak noodles in cold water until they start to soften, about 15 minutes. Drain and cut into roughly 4-inch (10-cm) lengths. Drop into a pot of boiling water and simmer until just tender, 2–5 minutes depending on the thickness of the noodles. Drain, rinse and drain again. Drain noodles very well or the salad will be watery. Set aside.

Cut bok choy, choy sum and cabbage into roughly 1-inch (2.5-cm) squares, and the coarser stems into fine diagonal slices. Steam until just tender but still crisp, about 2 minutes. Rinse and drain.

In a bowl, combine noodles, steamed vegetables and remaining ingredients. Mix well, cover and chill for 30 minutes before serving.

Asian greens stir-fried with lemon and ginger oil

Serves 4

1/3 cup (3 fl oz/90 ml) sunflower oil

finely grated zest of 2 lemons

1 stalk lemongrass, bottom 3 inches (7.5 cm) only, inner stalks roughly chopped

3 teaspoons grated fresh ginger

1 lb (500 g) mixed Asian greens, such as bok choy, choy sum and Chinese cabbage

pinch sea salt

pinch sugar

juice of 1 lemon

lemon wedges, for serving

Place oil, lemon zest, lemongrass and ginger in a screw-top jar and shake until well combined. Set aside in a warm place for 5 days so flavors infuse oil. After 5 days, strain oil and discard solids. Seal and store lemon and ginger oil in a cool, dark place.

Wash greens well. Pat dry with paper towels. Trim roots from greens and cut into 2-inch (5-cm) lengths. If using bok choy, remove dark outer leaves, separate younger leaves and trim ends.

Warm 2 tablespoons lemon and ginger oil in a wok or frying pan over medium heat. Add greens and stir-fry until tender-crisp, 3–4 minutes. Remove from heat and stir in salt, sugar and lemon juice.

Serve immediately, accompanied by lemon wedges.

Hint: Lemon and ginger oil can be used in stir-fries with other vegetables such as snow peas (mange-tout) or asparagus; it can also be used as a dressing on warm salads.

Asian greens stir-fried with vegetarian oyster sauce

Serves 4

1 bunch (16 oz/500 g) gai larn (Chinese broccoli) or broccolini
pinch salt
2 teaspoons vegetable oil
pinch superfine (caster) sugar
2 tablespoons vegetarian oyster (mushroom) sauce
2 tablespoons hot water
3 tablespoons crispy fried shallots (French shallots), optional (see page 24)

Cut gai larn into 4-inch (10-cm) lengths. To keep the vegetable intact and allow for more even cooking, slice the stalks lengthwise toward the thinner ends without cutting all the way through. Lay gai larn flat in a steamer, sprinkle with salt and steam until tender but still crisp, about 3 minutes.

Heat oil in a medium frying pan or wok over medium–high heat. Add gai larn. Sprinkle with sugar, oyster sauce and water. Bring to a simmer. As soon as sauce simmers, remove from heat. Serve immediately, sprinkled with shallots. Accompany with steamed rice.

Hint: This classic stir-fry recipe suits most forms of Asian greens, such as choy sum or bok choy, as well as other green vegetables such as baby spinach, snow peas (mange-tout), snow pea (mange-tout) shoots or asparagus.

Black-eyed pea and sugar snap stir-fry

Serves 4

1 cup (6¹/₂ oz/200 g) dried black-eyed peas (beans)

2 red onions, sliced

juice of 2 lemons

1 tablespoon vegetable oil

2 teaspoons Asian sesame oil

5 oz (150 g) sugar snap peas or snow peas (mange-tout), trimmed

¹/₂ cup (2 oz/60 g) chopped scallions (shallots/spring onions)

1 cup (1 oz/30 g) mint leaves

¹/₂ cup (³/₄ oz/20 g) snipped chives

1 teaspoon fish sauce

1 teaspoon light soy sauce

Place black-eyed peas in a large bowl, add cold water to cover, cover, and allow to stand overnight. Drain and rinse peas and place in saucepan with plenty of water to cover. Bring to a boil, reduce heat to low and simmer, uncovered, until tender, about 1 hour. Drain and allow to cool completely.

In a bowl, combine onions and lemon juice. Cover and allow to stand for 1 hour.

In a wok over medium–high heat, warm vegetable and sesame oils. Add sugar snap peas and stir-fry until tender-crisp, about 2 minutes. Remove from heat and allow to cool completely. Add black-eyed peas and sugar snap peas to bowl with onions. Add scallions, mint, chives, fish sauce and soy sauce. Mix well, cover and refrigerate for 30 minutes.

Serve chilled.

Braised flowering chives with ginger

Serves 4–6

2 bunches flowering chives

2 tablespoons vegetable oil

2 cloves garlic, finely chopped

2 teaspoons freshly grated ginger

1 small green bell pepper (capsicum),
    seeded and julienned

1 teaspoon sesame oil

2 tablespoons soy sauce

1 teaspoon cornstarch (cornflour),
    dissolved in 3 tablespoons water

steamed rice (see page 28), for serving

Trim about 1 inch (2.5 cm) from the bases and tops of the chives. Warm oil in a medium frying pan or wok over medium–high heat. Add garlic, ginger and bell pepper and stir-fry until they begin to color, about 1 minute. Add chives and toss for 1 minute more. Add remaining ingredients and simmer until the sauce is thick and clear, about 2 minutes. Serve immediately, on its own or with steamed rice.

Hint: *Substitute other green vegetables for chives, such as yard-long (snake) beans, spinach, choy sum or bok choy.*

Chinese chives with oyster sauce

Serves 4 as an accompaniment

2 tablespoons oyster sauce

3 tablespoons chicken stock (see page 588)

2 teaspoons soy sauce

1 teaspoon Asian sesame oil

1 teaspoon cornstarch (cornflour)
    mixed with 1 tablespoon chicken
    stock

1 bunch garlic chives, tied into a
    bundle with string, or choy sum or
    bok choy, trimmed into 4-inch
    (10-cm) lengths and tied with string

In a small saucepan, combine oyster sauce, chicken stock, soy sauce, sesame oil and cornstarch mixture. Bring to a boil over medium heat, stirring until sauce bubbles and thickens. Remove from heat. Blanch garlic chives or Chinese vegetables in a saucepan of boiling water for 1 minute. Remove from pan with a slotted spoon, place on serving plate and remove string. Tie one of the chives around bundle, pour oyster sauce over and serve.

Claypot-cooked vegetables with shiitake mushrooms and five-spice

Serves 4–8

2 tablespoons vegetable oil

12 dried shiitake mushrooms, soaked in hot water for 30 minutes, then drained and finely chopped

2 cloves garlic, finely chopped

1 medium yellow (brown) onion, sliced into half-moons

4 cups (20 oz/600 g) mixed fresh vegetables such as pumpkin, cauliflower, carrot, eggplant (aubergine) or baby corn, cut into 1-inch (2.5-cm) cubes

2 teaspoons Chinese five-spice powder

2 tablespoons brown sugar

1 cup (8 fl oz/250 ml) clear vegetable stock (see page 590)

2 tablespoons vegetarian oyster (mushroom) sauce

1 bunch (15 oz/470 g) choy sum or bok choy, quartered lengthwise

steamed rice, for serving

Soak a Chinese clay pot in water for an hour before using. Alternatively, use a casserole dish. Preheat oven to 400°F (200°C/Gas 6).

Mix all ingredients together and place in cooking pot. Put the pot in a large baking dish filled with enough water to reach halfway up the pot. Bake for 1 hour.

To serve, place the clay pot at the table on a heatproof mat. Accompany with steamed rice.

Creamy lentil and split-pea dal

Serves 6–8 as part of an Indian meal

$^2/_3$ cup (5 oz/150 g) lentils, rinsed and drained

$^2/_3$ cup (5 oz/150 g) yellow split peas, rinsed and drained

1 teaspoon ground turmeric

2 fresh green chilies, halved lengthwise

4 teaspoons vegetable oil

1 teaspoon brown or black mustard seeds

1 teaspoon cumin seeds

2 teaspoons Garam Masala (see page 575)

1 teaspoon ground coriander

$^1/_2$ cup (4 fl oz/125 ml) water

3 tablespoons heavy (double) cream

1 large tomato, unpeeled, chopped

salt to taste

$^1/_4$ cup ($^1/_3$ oz/10 g) chopped fresh cilantro (fresh coriander)

Place lentils and split peas in a bowl and add cold water to cover. Set aside for 30 minutes. Drain.

Fill a large saucepan with water and bring to a boil. Add lentils, split peas, turmeric and chili. Boil, uncovered, until lentils and peas are tender, about 30 minutes. Drain, place in a bowl and mash coarsely. Set aside.

In a saucepan, heat oil over medium–low heat and add mustard seeds. Cook until they crackle, about 30 seconds. Stir in cumin seeds and cook until aromatic, about 30 seconds. Stir in garam masala and coriander. Stir in mashed lentils and peas, water, cream and tomato. Season with salt. Bring to a boil over medium heat, reduce heat to low and simmer, partially covered, stirring often, for 4 minutes. Adjust seasoning. Stir in cilantro and serve hot.

Crispy noodle and bell pepper salad

Serves 4

2 oz (60 g) cellophane (bean thread) noodles or rice vermicelli
vegetable oil, for deep-frying
1 tablespoon sesame seeds
2 tablespoons sunflower seeds
2 tablespoons pumpkin seeds
4 cups (12 oz/375 g) shredded red cabbage
1 red bell pepper (capsicum), seeded and sliced
1 green bell pepper (capsicum), seeded and sliced
3 oz (90 g) button mushrooms (champignons), brushed clean and halved
4 scallions (shallots/spring onions), sliced

Preheat oven to 400°F (200°C/Gas 6). Break or cut noodles into small bundles. Heat oil in a wok or frying pan until it reaches 375°F (190°C) on a deep-frying thermometer or until a small bread cube dropped in oil sizzles and turns golden. Working in batches, fry noodles until golden, 30 seconds. Using slotted spoon, remove from oil and drain on paper towels.

Place sesame seeds, sunflower seeds and pumpkin seeds on a baking sheet and toast until golden, 4–5 minutes. Allow to cool.

In a large bowl, combine cabbage, bell peppers, mushrooms, scallions, toasted seeds and noodles. Gently toss until well combined. Serve immediately. (Noodles will lose crisp texture if left to stand for too long.)

Cumin-flavored potatoes

Serves 8–10 as part of an Indian meal

2 lb (1 kg) uniformly sized desiree or pontiac potatoes, or about 7 medium
salt as needed
2¹/2 tablespoons cold water
1 teaspoon ground turmeric
1/2 teaspoon chili powder
1/4 cup (2 fl oz/60 ml) vegetable oil and melted unsalted butter combined
4 teaspoons cumin seeds
4 teaspoons ground coriander
2 teaspoons finely grated fresh ginger
1/3 cup (1/2 oz/15 g) chopped fresh cilantro (fresh coriander)
juice of 1/2 lemon

Place potatoes and large pinch salt in a saucepan with enough cold water to cover. Bring to a boil over medium–high heat. Reduce heat to medium–low and cook, partially covered, until potatoes are tender, about 20 minutes. Drain potatoes and let cool for 15 minutes. Peel potatoes and cut into 1 1/2-inch (4-cm) cubes. Set aside. In a small bowl, combine cold water, turmeric and chili powder, and set aside.

In a large, heavy saucepan, heat oil and butter mixture over medium–low heat. Add cumin seeds and cook, stirring, until fragrant, about 30 seconds; take care not to burn seeds. Reduce heat to low and add water and turmeric mixture. Cook, stirring, for 30 seconds. Add potatoes and salt to taste, and toss gently until heated through, about 1 minute. Add coriander and toss for 30 seconds. Add ginger and cilantro and toss to combine. Drizzle with lemon juice and serve.

Eggplant broiled Japanese-style

Serves 4

4 small eggplants (aubergines)
1/2 cup (1/8 oz/3.5 g) bonito flakes
1 tablespoon finely grated fresh ginger
Tosa Shoyu (see page 593)

Preheat broiler (grill). Broil (grill) eggplants, turning a few times, until soft, 2–3 minutes. Remove from broiler. Rinse under running cold water and quickly peel away skin. Cut into bite-sized pieces. Divide among 4 plates.

Sprinkle aubergine with bonito flakes and grated ginger. Drizzle with tosa shoyu to taste.

Note: This dish is known as "yaki nasu." Accompany simply with steamed rice.

Eggplant with miso

Serves 2

1 large eggplant (aubergine), cut lengthwise into slices about 3/4 inch (2 cm) thick
vegetable oil, for deep-frying
1/3 cup (3 fl oz/90 ml) Sumiso Sauce (see page 598)
2 scallions (shallots/spring onions), finely chopped
sesame seeds, for garnish

With a small knife, make a shallow cut around outer edge of each eggplant slice and a large shallow X on top surface. Pour oil into a deep, heavy-bottomed frying pan to fill 3 inches (7.5 cm) deep. Heat oil until it reaches 375°F (190°C) on a deep-frying thermometer. Add eggplant and cook until well browned, about 5 minutes. Remove from oil and drain on paper towels. Arrange slices on a serving plate.

Heat sumiso in a small saucepan over low heat and spoon onto eggplant. Garnish with chopped scallions and sprinkle with sesame seeds.

Note: This is a traditional Japanese way of serving eggplant.

Fried tofu Japanese-style

Serves 4

1/4 cup (1 1/2 oz/45 g) potato flour

3/4 cup (1/4 oz/7 g) bonito flakes

vegetable oil, for deep-frying

1 lb (500 g) firm tofu, cut into 12 pieces

2 eggs, beaten

2 cups (16 fl oz/500 ml) Tempura Sauce (see page 593)

4 tablespoons finely grated daikon

1 teaspoon very finely grated fresh ginger

2 scallions (shallots/spring onions), thinly sliced

1 nori sheet, cut into very narrow strips about 3/4 inch (2 cm) long and
   1/8 inch (3 mm) wide

Place potato flour and bonito flakes in a food processor and process to combine. Transfer to a plate. Pour oil into a deep, heavy-bottomed frying pan to fill it to 3 inches (7.5 cm) deep. Heat oil until it reaches 375°F (190°C) on a deep-frying thermometer. Working in batches, coat tofu well with bonito-flour mixture and then dip each piece in beaten egg. Deep-fry until golden brown, about 3 minutes, turning once to ensure that pieces are browned evenly on all sides. Using a wire skimmer, remove tofu from oil and drain on paper towels.

Place 3 pieces of tofu in each serving bowl. Add 1/2 cup (4 fl oz/125 ml) tempura sauce to each bowl. Place 1 tablespoon grated daikon on tofu and top with a little grated ginger. Sprinkle with sliced scallions, then scatter nori strips over top and serve.

Note: This traditional Japanese method of cooking tofu is called "tosa dofu."

Green papaya salad

Serves 4–6

1 lb (500 g) green papaya, peeled and seeded

3 cloves garlic, peeled

10 fresh small green chilies

2 long (snake) beans, or about 8 green beans, cut into 1-inch (2.5-cm) pieces

2 tablespoons dried shrimp

2 tablespoons fish sauce

2 tablespoons fresh lime juice

1 teaspoon palm sugar

1 tablespoon anchovy paste (optional)

1 firm tomato, coarsely chopped, or 5 cherry tomatoes, halved

2 tablespoons coarsely ground roasted peanuts

Using a knife or shredder, shred papaya into long, thin strips. You should have about 3 cups (10–11½ oz/300–350 g); set aside.

In a large mortar or bowl, combine garlic, chilies and beans, and coarsely bruise with a pestle. Add papaya and pound again to just bruise ingredients. Add dried shrimp, fish sauce, lime juice and palm sugar. Stir together until sugar has dissolved. Add anchovy paste, if using, and tomato. Gently pound to combine flavors. Transfer to a serving platter, sprinkle with peanuts and serve.

Notes: *This Thai dish is often served with steamed sticky rice. A complementary fresh herb, kra thin, from the lead tree, is found in many Thai markets, both in Asia and overseas. Faintly resembling acacia in appearance, it tastes similar to arugula (rocket).*

Hint: *If unripe or green papaya is unavailable, use shredded, peeled carrot, cucumber or melon instead.*

Indian mixed vegetables with lentils

Serves 10 as part of an Indian meal

8 cups (64 fl oz/2 L) water

1 1/2 cups (10 oz/300 g) split yellow lentils, rinsed and drained

1 1/2 cups (3 oz/90 g) cauliflower florets

4 oz (125 g) green beans, cut into 1-inch (2.5-cm) pieces

1 carrot, peeled and cut into 1-inch (2.5-cm) sticks

1/3 cup (2 oz/60 g) shelled fresh or frozen green peas

2 teaspoons ground turmeric

salt to taste

1/3 cup (3 fl oz/90 ml) vegetable oil

4 teaspoons brown or black mustard seeds

1 teaspoon powdered asafoetida

1 tablespoon finely grated fresh ginger

1 tablespoon finely chopped garlic

1 teaspoon chili powder

18 fresh curry leaves

juice of 1 lemon

1/2 cup (3/4 oz/20 g) chopped fresh cilantro (fresh coriander)

Place water, lentils, cauliflower, beans, carrot, peas and 1 teaspoon turmeric in a large, heavy saucepan. Bring to a simmer over medium heat, reduce heat to low and cook, partially covered, until lentils are soft and mushy, about 1 hour. Season well with salt and set aside.

In a small, heavy saucepan, heat oil over low heat. Add mustard seeds and cook until they crackle, about 30 seconds. Add asafoetida and stir for 5 seconds. Add ginger and garlic and cook, stirring, for 30 seconds; take care not to burn mixture. Add remaining 1 teaspoon turmeric, chili powder and curry leaves and cook, stirring, for 5 seconds.

Pour mixture over lentils; cover, and set aside for 5 minutes. Stir in lemon juice and sprinkle with cilantro leaves. Serve hot.

Indian-style eggs poached on tomato

Serves 8 as part of an Indian meal

$1/3$ cup (3 fl oz/90 ml) vegetable oil and melted unsalted butter combined

3 yellow (brown) onions, finely chopped

$1/2$ teaspoon salt

$1 1/2$ tablespoons finely chopped fresh ginger

6 cloves garlic, finely chopped

$1/2$ teaspoon ground turmeric

2 lb (1 kg) tomatoes, or about 7 medium, unpeeled, finely chopped

3 fresh green chilies, finely chopped

$2/3$ cup (1 oz/30 g) chopped fresh cilantro (fresh coriander)

8 eggs

In a large, wide, heavy frying pan, heat oil and butter mixture over medium–low heat. Add onions and salt and cook, uncovered, stirring often, until onions are golden brown, 10–15 minutes.

Add ginger and garlic, and cook, stirring, for 1 minute. Add turmeric and cook, stirring, for 30 seconds. Stir in tomatoes and chili, and cook uncovered, stirring often, until tomatoes are soft, about 5 minutes. Add cilantro and mix well.

Spread tomato mixture evenly in pan and use a spoon to make evenly spaced indentations in mixture. Break an egg into each indentation, cover pan and cook over low heat until eggs are just set, about 10 minutes. Serve hot.

Note: This Indian dish is excellent for breakfast or brunch, served with toast or bread rolls.

Indian turmeric beans

Serves 10 as part of an Indian meal

2 lb (1 kg) green beans, trimmed and cut into $^1/_2$-inch (12-mm) pieces
1$^1/_2$ teaspoons ground turmeric
2$^1/_2$ tablespoons vegetable oil
1 teaspoon brown or black mustard seeds
5 dried red chilies
18 fresh curry leaves
1 tablespoon finely grated fresh ginger
2 yellow (brown) onions, chopped
$^1/_2$ teaspoon salt
4 fresh green chilies, chopped
$^1/_2$ cup (2 oz/60 g) finely grated fresh coconut
juice of $^1/_2$ lemon

Fill a saucepan with water and bring to a boil. Add beans and $^1/_2$ teaspoon turmeric and boil for 1–2 minutes. Drain and rinse beans under cold running water. Drain well.

In a karhai or wok, heat oil over medium–low heat. Add mustard seeds and cook until they crackle, about 30 seconds. Add dried chilies, curry leaves and ginger and cook, stirring, for 30 seconds. Add onions, remaining 1 teaspoon turmeric and salt. Cook, uncovered, stirring often, until onions are translucent, about 5 minutes.

Stir in beans and fresh chili, and toss over medium–low heat until well combined and heated through. Sprinkle with coconut and drizzle with lemon juice. Serve hot.

Notes: This Indian dish is known as "beans foogarth." The addition of turmeric when cooking the beans helps to intensify their green color.

Japanese-style okra with bonito

Serves 4

3¹/₂ oz (105 g) small okra, stems removed
¹/₂ teaspoon salt
¹/₂ cup (¹/₈ oz/3.5 g) bonito flakes
Tosa Shoyu (see page 593)

Place okra in a small saucepan with water to cover. Add salt and bring to a boil. Reduce heat to low and simmer about 2 minutes—okra should retain shape and color. Remove from heat and let cool. Cut okra crosswise into slices ¹/₄ inch (6 mm) wide and divide among 4 plates. Top with bonito flakes and drizzle tosa shoyu over to taste.

Variation: Tofu with bonito • *Cut 1 lb (500 g) silken tofu into 4 blocks. Divide among 4 bowls. Top with pickled ginger, bonito flakes, grated ginger and scallions (shallots/spring onions). Add tosa shoyu to taste.*

Japanese-style spinach with bonito

Serves 2

1 bunch spinach
¹/₂ cup (¹/₈ oz/3.5 g) bonito flakes
Japanese soy sauce

Cut roots from spinach and discard. Wash spinach leaves and stems thoroughly, immersing in cold water and draining 3 times to remove all grit.

Half fill a large saucepan with water, add salt and bring to a boil. Add spinach, return to a boil and cook for 2–3 minutes. Drain and let cool.

Squeeze spinach tightly into a cylinder about 4 inches (10 cm) long. Cut in half and place each half, standing on end, in a shallow bowl. Scatter bonito flakes over top and drizzle soy sauce over to taste.

Japanese tofu hot pot

Serves 4

1 teaspoon instant dashi

1 stem shungiku, cut to 4-inch (10-cm) lengths

2 leaves Chinese (napa) cabbage, sliced

3 fresh shiitake mushrooms

1 lb (500 g) tofu, cut into 2$^1/_2$-inch (6-cm) cubes

Nihaizu (see page 581) or shoyu, for serving

3 tablespoons finely grated daikon mixed with $^1/_4$ small red chili, finely chopped

scallions (shallots/spring onions), finely sliced

Fill a large pot three-quarters full with water. Add instant dashi and bring to a boil. Add shungiku, cabbage and mushrooms and cook until softened, 4–5 minutes. Add tofu and heat through.

Serve with a small bowl of nihaizu for dipping. Serve with the daikon mixture and scallions separately, to be added to dipping sauce to taste.

Note: This traditional Japanese dish, "yu dofu," is usually cooked and served in the same pot or in small cast-iron pots or heatproof casseroles.

Kimchi with Chinese cabbage

Makes about 30 cups (240 fl oz/7.5 L)

2 large Chinese (napa) cabbages
4 cups (1 lb/1 kg) coarse sea salt
20 cups (160 fl oz/5 L) water
20 oz (625 g) daikon
2 oz (60 g) jjokpa or scallions
  (shallots/spring onions)
3 oz (90 g) mustard leaves (optional)
4 oz (125 g) Korean watercress stems
  (minari)
2 whole bulbs garlic
2 small knobs (about the size of a
  garlic bulb) fresh ginger

1 small yellow (brown) onion
10 fresh red chilies
1/2 cup (4 oz/125 g) fermented shrimp
1/2 cup (4 oz/125 g) fermented
  anchovies
2 cups (10 oz/300 g) red chili powder
1 oz (30 g) sticky rice powder dissolved
  in 1 1/2 cups (12 fl oz/375 ml) water
1 cup (8 oz/250 g) table salt
1/4 cup (2 oz/60 g) sugar

Remove outer leaves from cabbage. Reserve a few leaves, then cut cabbages in half lengthwise. Combine sea salt and water in a large container. Add cabbage halves and allow to soak until tender, 6–8 hours. Remove cabbage from the salted water, rinse, then squeeze out excess water.

Slice daikon into matchstick-sized pieces. Cut jjokpa, mustard leaves (if using) and watercress stems into 1 1/2-inch (4-cm) lengths and combine with daikon in a large bowl. Peel garlic, ginger and onion. Cut chilies lengthwise and remove cores and seeds. Combine garlic, ginger, onion and chilies with 1/2 cup (4 oz/125 ml) water in a food processor. Blend to a paste, then combine with daikon mixture.

Mix shrimp and anchovies with chili powder. Add sticky rice liquid, table salt and sugar, and mix well. Add to daikon mixture and toss to combine.

Using your fingers, separate leaves of the cabbage halves and spoon some of chili mixture between leaves. Place filled leaves in a kimchi container (clay or glass, with a lid), cover with one reserved large cabbage leaf or plastic wrap, then lid, and store in a cool place for 2–3 days to mature before using. Store any unused kimchi in the refrigerator for up to 1 week.

Kimchi with Korean radish

Makes about 30 cups (240 fl oz/7.5 L)

16 oz (500 g) Korean round radish, cut
 into bite-sized pieces
2 lb (1 kg) Chinese (napa) cabbage, cut
 into bite-sized pieces
1/2 cup (4 oz/125 g) coarse sea salt
1 oz (30 g) jjokpa or scallion (shallot/
 spring onion), white part only
1 clove garlic
1 small knob fresh ginger, about 1/3 oz
 (10 g)

2 hot red chilies
1 oz (30 g) Korean watercress stems
 (minari)
4 oz (125 g) nashi or other firm pear
4 oz (125 g) medium yellow (brown)
 onion
20 cups (160 fl oz/5 L) water
5 tablespoons hot red chili powder

Place radish and Chinese cabbage in a large glass or ceramic bowl. Sprinkle with
1/2 cup (2 oz/60 g) salt and let stand for 15–20 minutes, tossing occasionally so that salt
penetrates vegetables.

Roughly chop jjokpa, garlic, ginger and chilies. Remove and discard leaves from
watercress stems and cut stems into 1 1/2-inch (3-cm) lengths.

Rinse radish and cabbage in cold water to remove salt. Drain, then place in a large
bowl. Add pear, onion, jjokpa, garlic, ginger, chilies and watercress stems. Mix
thoroughly, then transfer to a 20-cup (160-fl oz/5-L) kimchi container (clay or glass, with
a lid).

Pour water into a large bowl and stir in remaining salt. Wrap chili powder in a clean
cloth, tie to make a bundle and immerse in salted water. Stir cloth in the water until chili
powder turns water red. Remove and discard bundle. Pour chili water into kimchi
container. Cover and leave in a cool place for 3–4 days before using. The unused portion
can be stored in the refrigerator for about 5 days.

Hint: If you do not wish to prepare your own, this kimchi is readily available from
Korean markets; it is often known as "watery radish kimchi."

Note: Due to recent changes in the romanization of Korean words, kimchi is also
written as "gimchi."

Korean three-color vegetables

FOR ENOKI MUSHROOMS

4 oz (125 g) fresh enoki mushrooms

1 1/2 teaspoons coarse sea salt

1 1/2 teaspoons finely chopped garlic

1 tablespoon finely chopped scallion
(shallot/spring onion)

1 tablespoon toasted, ground sesame
seeds (see page 30)

1 tablespoon sesame oil

pinch of freshly ground black pepper

vegetable or sunflower oil, for frying

FOR GREEN BELL PEPPER

1 green bell pepper (capsicum)

vegetable or sunflower oil, for frying

1 1/2 teaspoons coarse sea salt

1 1/2 teaspoons finely chopped garlic

1 tablespoon finely chopped scallion
(shallot/spring onion)

1 tablespoon sesame oil

1 tablespoon toasted, ground sesame
seeds (see page 30)

FOR SHIITAKE MUSHROOMS

4 oz (125 g) fresh shiitake mushrooms

1 1/2 teaspoons coarse sea salt

1 1/2 teaspoons finely chopped garlic

1 tablespoon finely chopped scallion
(shallot/spring onion)

1 tablespoon toasted, ground sesame
seeds (see page 30)

1 tablespoon sesame oil

pinch freshly ground black pepper

vegetable or sunflower oil, for frying

Wash enoki mushrooms and discard stems. Bring 3 cups salted water to a boil and immerse mushroom caps in boiling water for a few seconds. Remove and drain, then combine with salt, garlic, scallion, sesame seeds, sesame oil and pepper. Heat 1 teaspoon oil in a frying pan and fry mushroom mixture for 1–2 minutes. Remove from pan and keep warm.

Halve and seed bell pepper, then cut flesh into thin strips. Heat 1 teaspoon oil in a frying pan. Add bell pepper strips and salt, and stir-fry for 1 minute. Add garlic, scallion, sesame oil and sesame seeds. Stir-fry for 1 more minute. Remove from pan and keep warm.

Bring 3 cups salted water to a boil. Immerse shiitake mushrooms in boiling water for a few seconds. Remove, rinse in cold water and drain. Squeeze gently to remove excess water, then slice thinly. In a medium bowl, mix mushroom slices, salt, garlic, scallion, sesame seeds, sesame oil and black pepper. Heat 1 tablespoon vegetable oil in a frying pan and stir-fry mushroom mixture for 2–3 minutes. Remove from pan and keep warm.

Arrange 3 vegetables in separate piles on a white plate or in separate bowls, and serve.

Mushrooms and corn with cilantro

Serves 8–10 as part of an Indian meal

2 ears (cobs) of corn
2 teaspoons unsalted butter
3 tablespoons vegetable oil
1/2-inch (12-mm) cinnamon stick
2 green cardamom pods
2 whole cloves
2 yellow (brown) onions, chopped
1/2 teaspoon salt, plus extra salt
   to taste
1 teaspoon finely grated fresh ginger
1 teaspoon finely chopped garlic
1 teaspoon chili powder

1 tablespoon coriander seeds, crushed
   in a pestle and mortar
1 teaspoon ground turmeric
1 large tomato, unpeeled, finely
   chopped
1 lb (500 g) small button mushrooms,
   wiped clean
juice of 1/2 lemon
1/4 cup (1/3 oz/10 g) chopped fresh
   cilantro (fresh coriander)

Use a sharp knife to remove kernels from ears of corn. In a large saucepan, melt butter over medium–high heat. Add corn and cook, stirring, until softened, 2–3 minutes. Remove to a small bowl and set aside.

In the same pan, heat oil over medium–low heat. Add cinnamon, cardamom and cloves and cook, stirring, until fragrant, about 30 seconds. Add onions and 1/2 teaspoon salt, and cook, uncovered, stirring often, until onions are dark golden brown, 10–15 minutes.

Add ginger and garlic, and cook, stirring, for 30 seconds. Add chili powder, coriander seeds and turmeric and cook, stirring, until fragrant, about 30 seconds. Add tomato and cook, stirring often, until tomato is soft, about 5 minutes. Add mushrooms and corn and cook, tossing occasionally, until mushrooms are slightly soft, 5–10 minutes. Add lemon juice, and salt to taste if necessary. Add cilantro and toss gently. Serve hot.

Paneer (Indian-style cottage cheese)

Serves 8–10 as part of an Indian meal

16 cups (128 fl oz/4 L) whole (full cream) milk
1²/₃ cups (13 fl oz/400 ml) heavy (double) cream
²/₃ cup (5 fl oz/150 ml) white vinegar

Line a large, flat-bottomed sieve with a double layer of cheesecloth (muslin), allowing it to overhang sides of sieve. Place lined sieve inside a large other bowl. Find a large, heavy, non metallic saucepan that fits inside the sieve.

Pour milk into the saucepan and bring slowly to a boil over medium heat. When milk is almost boiling, stir in cream and bring to a boil again. When milk mixture just comes to a boil (it will begin to bubble and froth, and vibrations from boiling mixture can be felt in the handle of a metal spoon held in milk), pour in vinegar and remove from heat. Set aside for 2 minutes; do not stir.

Using a large slotted spoon or spoon-shaped strainer, gently lift curds from whey and place in lined sieve. Once all curds have been placed in sieve, carefully tie loose ends of cheesecloth together to form curds into a thick, round disk about 10 inches (25 cm) in diameter.

Return whey in bowl back to saucepan holding remainder of whey. Place saucepan on top of paneer to weight it. Set aside at room temperature until paneer is firm, about 25 minutes.

Remove saucepan from paneer. Carefully untie cheesecloth and remove paneer. Prepare as directed in individual recipes. If not using paneer immediately, place flat in an airtight container and add enough whey to cover. Store in refrigerator for up to 1 week.

Paneer tikka (Marinated baked cottage cheese)

Serves 8–10 as part of an Indian meal

1 cup (8 oz/250 g) plain (natural) whole-milk yogurt, whisked

1 1/2 tablespoons finely grated fresh ginger

1 1/2 tablespoons finely chopped garlic

2 fresh green chilies, finely chopped

large pinch saffron threads soaked in 1 1/2 tablespoons hot milk for 10 minutes

4 teaspoons vegetable oil, plus extra for brushing

1/2 teaspoon salt

1 recipe Paneer (see opposite), cut into 1 inch x 3 inches (2.5 cm x 7.5 cm) pieces

pinch chat masala

1/3 cup (1 oz/30 g) chopped fresh cilantro (fresh coriander)

juice of 1 lemon

Preheat oven to 475°F (240°C/Gas 9).

In a large bowl, combine yogurt, ginger, garlic, chili, saffron and milk mixture, 4 teaspoons oil and salt. Add paneer pieces and gently turn to coat with marinade. Set aside to marinate for 10 minutes.

Brush a baking sheet with vegetable oil. Place paneer pieces on sheet in a single layer. Bake, without turning, until golden on edges, about 15 minutes.

Place paneer in a serving dish, sprinkle with chat masala and cilantro, and drizzle with lemon juice. Serve hot with a salad of fresh greens.

Paneer with spinach (Cottage cheese with spinach)

Serves 10 as part of an Indian meal

2 bunches spinach, trimmed and rinsed well

1¹/₂ teaspoons ground turmeric

2 tablespoons water

3 tablespoons vegetable oil and melted unsalted butter combined

4 teaspoons cumin seeds

3 yellow (brown) onions, chopped

¹/₂ teaspoon salt

2 tablespoons coriander seeds, crushed in a pestle and mortar

1¹/₂ tablespoons grated fresh ginger

2 fresh green chilies, finely chopped

1 teaspoon chili powder

3 tomatoes, unpeeled, finely chopped

1 recipe Paneer (see page 412), cut into 1-inch (2.5-cm) pieces

1 teaspoon dried fenugreek leaves

Chappati (page 446), for serving

Place spinach in a large saucepan. In a small bowl, combine ¹/₂ teaspoon turmeric with water and add to pan. Cook over medium–high heat, covered, turning spinach occasionally, until spinach is wilted, 3–5 minutes. Remove from heat, drain excess water and let spinach cool. Place spinach in a food processor and puree. Set aside.

In a karhai or wok, heat oil and butter mixture over medium–low heat. Add cumin seeds and cook until fragrant, about 30 seconds. Add onions and salt and cook, uncovered, stirring often, until onions are translucent, about 5 minutes.

Add coriander seeds, ginger, chili, chili powder and remaining 1 teaspoon turmeric and cook, stirring, until fragrant, 2–3 minutes.

Stir in tomatoes and cook, stirring occasionally, until tomatoes are soft, about 5 minutes. Stir in pureed spinach and mix well. Add paneer and stir gently to coat with sauce. Cook over medium–low heat until paneer is warmed through, 2–3 minutes. Sprinkle with fenugreek leaves and serve hot with chappati.

Hint: Adding turmeric to spinach before cooking helps spinach retain a bright green color.

Pumpkin dumplings in malai sauce

Serves 8–10 as part of an Indian meal

1 lb (500 g) pumpkin or butternut
   squash, peeled and grated

2 large desiree or pontiac potatoes,
   10 oz (300g) total, boiled, peeled and
   mashed

1/4 cup (1/3 oz/10 g) chopped fresh
   cilantro (fresh coriander)

1 tablespoon finely grated fresh ginger

3 teaspoons finely chopped fresh green
   chilies

salt to taste

cornstarch (cornflour), for dusting

vegetable oil, for deep-frying

3–4 tablespoons heavy (double) cream

1/2 teaspoon Garam Masala
   (see page 575)

SAUCE

1/4 cup (2 fl oz/60 ml) vegetable oil

1-inch (2.5-cm) cinnamon stick

4 green cardamom pods

4 whole cloves

1 small yellow (brown) onion, halved
   and thinly sliced

1/2 teaspoon salt, plus extra to taste

1 tablespoon finely grated fresh ginger

1 tablespoon finely chopped garlic

3 teaspoons ground turmeric

2 teaspoons chili powder

2 tomatoes, unpeeled, chopped

1 teaspoon honey

1 teaspoon ground mace

Place grated pumpkin or squash in a colander and squeeze well to extract any excess water. Place in a bowl with potatoes, cilantro, ginger and chili. Season with salt and mix well. Set aside.

To make sauce: In a karhai or frying pan, heat oil over medium–low heat. Add cinnamon, cardamom and cloves and cook until fragrant, about 30 seconds. Add onion and 1/2 teaspoon salt and cook, stirring often, until onion is dark golden brown, 10–15 minutes. Stir in ginger and garlic and cook for 30 seconds. Add turmeric and chili powder, and cook, stirring, for 30 seconds. Stir in tomatoes and cook, stirring, until softened, 3–4 minutes. Stir in honey and mace. Cover to keep warm. Meanwhile, shape pumpkin mixture into walnut-sized balls, dust with cornstarch and place on a baking sheet dusted with cornstarch.

Fill a medium saucepan with oil to a depth of 3 inches (7.5 cm). Heat oil over medium–high heat to 375°F (190°C) on a deep-frying thermometer. Carefully add dumplings in batches of five and cook until golden brown, 2–3 minutes. Remove with a slotted spoon and drain on paper towels.

Place dumplings on a serving dish. Stir cream into sauce and pour over dumplings. Sprinkle with garam masala, season with extra salt to taste and serve hot.

Red-cooked tofu and vegetables

Serves 4–8

24 oz (750 g) firm tofu

2 tablespoons peanut oil

1 medium yellow (brown) onion, sliced into half moons

2 cloves garlic, finely chopped

4 cups (20 oz/600 g) mixed fresh vegetables such as pumpkin, baby corn, eggplant (aubergine), mushrooms or carrots

4 teaspoons Chinese five-spice powder

$1/4$ cup (2 oz/60 g) brown sugar

4 teaspoons freshly grated ginger

$1^1/2$ cups (12 fl oz/375 ml) water

$1^1/2$ cups (12 fl oz/375 ml) dark soy sauce

$1/2$ cup (4 fl oz/125 ml) rice wine vinegar or dry sherry

2 teaspoons sesame oil

steamed rice, for serving

4 scallions (shallots/spring onions), finely sliced and curled in ice water (see page 41)

Drain tofu and pat dry with paper towels. Warm oil in a pot just large enough to contain all ingredients. Put single block of tofu in pot and sear on all sides, about 2 minutes total. Add remaining ingredients except sesame oil and scallions. Bring to a boil, cover tightly and simmer for 20 minutes. Turn over tofu, stir, and simmer, covered, for a further 20 minutes. Remove pot from heat and set aside to cool completely and allow tofu and vegetables to absorb all the flavors of the sauce, about 1 hour.

Reheat dish to simmer for 2 minutes. Remove tofu, brush with sesame oil and carve into slices. Divide rice among individual plates. Top with tofu then vegetables, sauce and scattered scallions.

Hint: For a richer flavor, freeze any excess sauce and add to the recipe the next time you make it.

Red lentil and pumpkin salad

Serves 4

DRESSING

1/3 cup (3 fl oz/90 ml) olive oil

2 teaspoons grated lime zest

1/3 cup (3 fl oz/90 ml) lime juice

2 tablespoons chopped fresh cilantro (fresh coriander)

1/2 teaspoon superfine (caster) sugar

ground pepper to taste

SALAD

1 butternut squash or pumpkin, about 1 lb (500 g), peeled and cut into
    1 1/2-in (4-cm) cubes

1/2 cup (3 1/2 oz/105 g) dried red lentils

1 tablespoon vegetable oil

1 small red chili, seeded and chopped

1 teaspoon cumin seeds

2 teaspoons coriander seeds, cracked

To make dressing, place olive oil, lime zest and juice, cilantro, sugar and pepper in a screw-top jar. Shake well to combine.

Line a large steamer with parchment (baking) paper. Half fill wok with water (steamer should not touch water) and bring to boil. Place pumpkin cubes in steamer, cover and place steamer over boiling water. Steam until pumpkin cubes are tender but retain their shape, 10–12 minutes. Add more water to wok when necessary. Remove steamer from wok and allow pumpkin to cool.

Place lentils in saucepan with water to cover. Bring to a boil and cook until tender (do not overcook), about 5 minutes. Drain and allow to cool.

In a wok, over medium–high heat, warm vegetable oil. Add chili and cumin and coriander seeds and cook until aromatic, 1–2 minutes. Add pumpkin and lentils and stir-fry until flavors are blended, about 1 minute. Remove from heat and stir in dressing. Mix well.

Serve warm, or refrigerate for 30 minutes and serve chilled.

Seaweed salad

Serves 4

1 1/2 oz (40 g) hijiki
4 sheets usuage (deep-fried tofu)
boiling water
3 tablespoons vegetable oil
1/2 carrot, peeled and cut into thin matchstick strips
1 teaspoon instant dashi dissolved in 1 cup (8 fl oz/250 ml) water
1/2 cup (4 oz/125 g) sugar
1/2 cup (4 fl oz/125 ml) soy sauce

Wash hijiki well in a large bowl of water. Any dust and sand will settle to bottom of bowl. Scoop hijiki from bowl and then soak in clean water for 20 minutes. Drain well.

Place usuage in a bowl. Add boiling water to cover and soak for 3–4 minutes to remove some of oil. Remove from water, draining well. Cut usuage into strips 1/4 inch (6 mm) wide.

Heat oil in a saucepan over high heat. Add carrot strips and stir-fry until softened, about 2 minutes. Add hijki and stir-fry for 2 minutes. Add usuage and stir-fry for 2 minutes.

Add dashi and sugar, bring to a boil then reduce heat to medium-low and simmer for 4–5 minutes. Add soy sauce and cover pan with a slightly smaller lid. Cook for 20–30 minutes over medium–low heat, stirring occasionally. Liquid should reduce by two-thirds.

Serve warm or cold.

Seaweed salad with wakame

Serves 4

1 cup (1 oz/30 g) dried wakame

2 cups (8 oz/250 g) bean sprouts

1 English (hothouse) cucumber, finely
sliced on an angle

2 tomatoes, cut into wedges

sesame seeds, for garnish

FOR DRESSING

1/2 cup (4 fl oz/125 ml) Nihaizu
(see page 585)

1 1/2 tablespoons Asian sesame oil

Soak wakame in 1 cup (8 fl oz/250 ml) water for 5 minutes to rehydrate (it is not
necessary to drain liquid). In a jar, combine nihaizu and sesame oil and shake until well
combined. Place bean sprouts in a saucepan and add water to cover. Bring to a boil,
turn off heat and strain. Place bean sprouts in a bowl of cold water until cool; strain.

Divide bean sprouts and wakame among 4 bowls. Arrange cucumber slices and tomato
wedges on top. Pour dressing over each salad and sprinkle with sesame seeds.

Snow pea hot and sour salad

Serves 4–6

2 cups (4 oz/120 g) snow peas
(mange-tout), trimmed and steamed
until tender

2 cups (1 oz/30 g) snow pea
(mange-tout) shoots

1 cup (2 oz/60 g) bean sprouts

1 cup (4 oz/125 g) carrots, julienned

1 cup (6 oz/180 g) baby corn, steamed
until tender and halved lengthwise

1 tablespoon umeboshi (pickled plum)
paste

pinch salt

1/4–1/2 teaspoon dried chili flakes

3 tablespoons sesame seeds, toasted
(see page 30)

1 teaspoon soy sauce

2 teaspoons Asian sesame oil

3 tablespoons peanut oil

In a large bowl, combine snow peas, snow pea shoots, bean sprouts, carrots and corn.
Mix the remaining ingredients in a food processor until smooth. Thoroughly mix the
dressing through the vegetables and serve immediately.

Spicy cauliflower

Serves 4 as an accompaniment

3 tablespoons vegetable oil

1 onion, cut into 8 wedges

2 red Thai or Anaheim chilies, seeded and chopped

4 cloves garlic, finely chopped

1 teaspoon ground cumin

1 teaspoon dried shrimp paste

1 lb (500 g) cauliflower, cut into florets

1/3 cup (3 fl oz/90 ml) chicken stock (see page 588)

1 tablespoon sesame seeds, toasted (see page 30)

1 tablespoon fresh cilantro (fresh coriander) leaves

In a wok or large frying pan, heat oil over medium heat and fry onion, chilies and garlic until onion is soft, 1–2 minutes. Add cumin and shrimp paste, mashing with the back of a spoon, and fry for 1 minute. Add cauliflower and toss to coat. Add stock, cover, and cook over low heat until cauliflower is tender, 8–10 minutes. Remove from heat and spoon into a serving dish. Serve immediately, sprinkled with sesame seeds and cilantro leaves.

Spicy mashed potato

Serves 4 as an accompaniment

1 1/2 lb (750 g) potatoes, peeled and chopped

2 tablespoons ghee

1 teaspoon yellow mustard seeds

1 fresh green Thai or Anaheim chili, seeded and sliced

1 fresh red Thai or Anaheim chili, seeded and sliced

1/2 onion, chopped

1/2 teaspoon ground turmeric

1 teaspoon Garam Masala (see page 575)

1 teaspoon sea salt

2 tablespoons fresh lime juice

1 tablespoon chopped fresh mint

1 tablespoon olive oil, for drizzling

In a large saucepan of salted boiling water, cook potatoes until tender, 8–12 minutes. Drain and mash. In a small skillet, melt ghee over medium heat and fry mustard seeds until they pop, about 30 seconds. Add chilies and onion and fry until onion is soft, 1–2 minutes. Remove from heat. Stir in turmeric, garam masala, salt, lime juice and mint. Mix well. Add to mashed potatoes, mixing until well combined. Spoon into a serving dish and drizzle with oil. Serve immediately, with curries.

Spinach with sesame dressing (Gomaae)

Serves 2

SESAME DRESSING
1/2 cup (4 fl oz/125 ml) Japanese soy sauce
1/2 cup (4 oz/125 g) sugar
3/4 cup (3 1/2 oz/105 g) sesame seeds, toasted (see page 30) and ground

1 bunch spinach
1/2 teaspoon salt
sesame seeds, for garnish

In a small saucepan over medium–high heat, bring soy sauce and sugar to a boil, stirring occasionally until sugar is completely dissolved. Remove from heat, let cool slightly, then add in ground sesame seeds, mixing well.

Cut stems from spinach and discard. Wash spinach thoroughly, immersing leaves in cold water and draining 3 times to remove all grit. Half fill a large saucepan with water, add salt and bring to a boil. Add spinach, return to a boil and cook spinach until wilted, 2–3 minutes. Drain and let cool.

Squeeze out as much water as possible from spinach leaves. Place spinach in a bowl and add 1/4 cup (2 fl oz/60 ml) dressing, or more if desired. Divide spinach between 2 bowls and garnish with a sprinkling of sesame seeds. Serve at room temperature or cold.

Hints: This is a traditionally Japanese way of serving spinach. This recipe makes extra dressing, which can be stored in the refrigerator for up to 6 months. It is also good with a salad of blanched asparagus and thinly sliced cucumber.

Variation: To make beans with sesme dressing, omit spinach. Trim ends from 8 oz (250 g) green beans, removing fibrous strings. Cut beans in half, place in a saucepan, add 1/2 teaspoon salt and water to cover. Bring to a boil then reduce heat to low and simmer for 5 minutes; drain. Place beans in a bowl, add 1/2 cup (4 fl oz/125 ml) sesame dressing and toss gently. Divide between 2 plates and garnish with a sprinkling of sesame seeds. Serve hot or cold.

Steamed Asian greens with tempeh and oyster sauce

Serves 2–4

1 bunch bok choy or choy sum, trimmed and cut into 4-inch (10-cm) lengths

3 oz (90 g) tempeh or tofu, cut into $1/2$-inch (12-mm) pieces

3 oz (90 g) enoki mushrooms, trimmed

$3^1/2$ oz (105 g) bottled baby corn, halved

$1/4$ cup (2 fl oz/60 ml) oyster sauce

1 clove garlic, finely chopped

1 teaspoon Asian sesame oil

$1/2$ teaspoon grated fresh ginger

2 scallions (shallots/spring onions), finely chopped

1 tablespoon toasted sesame seeds (see page 30)

Put bok choy, tempeh, enoki and baby corn in a large bamboo steamer or steamer basket. Partially fill a wok or pot with water (steamer should not touch water) and bring to a rapid simmer. Put steamer over water, cover, and steam until vegetables are softened, 3–4 minutes.

Meanwhile, put oyster sauce, garlic, sesame oil and ginger in a small saucepan and mix well. Place saucepan over medium heat to warm sauce, 3–4 minutes.

Remove vegetables from steamer and arrange on serving plates with enoki in the center. Drizzle warm sauce over vegetables. Sprinkle with scallions and sesame seeds. Serve as an accompaniment or light vegetarian dish.

Variations: *To make with shrimp (prawns) or scallops, steam deveined peeled fresh shrimp (prawns) for 3–5 minutes, or scallops for 2–3 minutes, and toss through bok choy just before serving.*

To make with noodles, cook 8 oz (250 g) fresh udon or egg noodles while vegetables are steaming. Serve noodles with vegetables spooned on top.

Tempeh marinated in chili and soy

Serves 4–6

8 oz (250 g) tempeh, cut into $^1/_6$-inch (4-mm) slices

2 tablespoons soy sauce

1 tablespoon ketjap manis (sweet soy sauce)

1 medium yellow (brown) onion, sliced into half moons

$7^1/_2$ oz (235 g) long (snake) or green beans, cut into 2-inch (5-cm) lengths

1 teaspoon freshly grated ginger

2 cloves garlic, finely chopped

1 tablespoon grated palm sugar

1–2 small red chilies, seeded and finely sliced

2 tablespoons vegetable oil, plus extra if required

$^1/_4$ cup ($^1/_4$ oz/7 g) chopped fresh cilantro (fresh coriander)

steamed rice, for serving

In a bowl, combine the tempeh, soy sauce, ketjap manis, onion, beans, ginger, garlic, sugar and chilies. Cover and marinate for 1 hour. Remove only the tempeh strips from the marinade.

Warm oil in a medium frying pan or wok over medium–high heat. Add tempeh strips and fry until golden on both sides, about 4 minutes. Remove from pan and set aside to keep warm. Pour vegetables and marinade into pan or wok. Add 1 teaspoon more oil if required. Stir-fry until golden and cooked, about 5 minutes.

Divide vegetables and tempeh strips among individual plates. Garnish with cilantro. Accompany with steamed rice.

Tempura vegetables

Serves 4

1 egg
1 cup (8 fl oz/250 ml) ice water
1 1/3 cup (5 oz/150 g) tempura flour
vegetable oil, for deep-frying
1/2 cup (2 1/2 oz/75 g) all-purpose
  (plain) flour
1 large zucchini (courgette), cut into
  1/4-inch (6-mm) slices
1 onion, finely sliced
1 carrot, finely sliced
8 oz (250 g) snow peas (mange-tout)
1 eggplant (aubergine), sliced
  crosswise

1 green bell pepper (capsicum), cut
  into strips
8 button mushrooms
1 canned lotus root, thinly sliced
8 green beans
4 asparagus spears
1 sweet potato, sliced and parboiled

2 tablespoons finely grated daikon
1 teaspoon finely grated ginger
Tempura Sauce (see page 593)

In a bowl, beat egg lightly. Add water, continuing to beat lightly. Stir in tempura flour but do not overmix. The batter will be slightly lumpy. Pour oil into a deep, heavy-bottomed frying pan to a depth of 3 inches (7.5 cm). Heat oil until it reaches 375°F (190°F) on a deep-frying thermometer.

Place all-purpose flour on a plate. Set onion and carrot aside. Working in batches, dredge remaining vegetables in flour, shaking off excess, then dip into tempura batter, allowing excess to drain off. Do not completely dip beans, bell peppers, snow peas and asparagus into the batter. Leaving some of these vegetables uncovered with batter is better for presentation. In a bowl, combine onion and carrot. Working in batches, dredge onion and carrot mixture in flour, shaking off excess, then dip into tempura batter, allowing excess to drain off.

Carefully lower vegetables into hot oil. Cook until light golden brown, 30 seconds to 2 minutes, depending on the vegetable. Using a wire skimmer, remove from oil and drain on paper towels.

Arrange vegetables on 4 plates, each with a small pyramid of daikon topped with grated ginger. Each diner mixes ginger and daikon into tempura sauce. Serve immediately.

Three lentil broth (Dal makhani)

Serves 10 as part of an Indian meal

½ cup (3½ oz/105 g) black lentils, rinsed and drained

½ cup (2 oz/60 g) dried red kidney beans, rinsed and drained

¼ cup (2 oz/60 g) split chickpeas (garbanzo beans), rinsed and drained

5 cups (40 fl oz/1.25 L) water

2½-inch (6-cm) cinnamon stick

3 green cardamom pods, cracked

3 whole cloves

1½ tablespoons finely grated fresh ginger

1½ tablespoons finely chopped garlic

2–4 teaspoons chili powder

14 oz (440 g) canned crushed tomatoes

⅔ cup (5 oz/150 g) unsalted butter, chopped

salt to taste

4 teaspoons dried fenugreek leaves, crushed

steamed basmati rice (see page 28) or Paratha (see page 469), for serving

Place lentils, kidney beans, chickpeas and water in a large bowl. Cover and let stand overnight.

The next day, place lentil mixture and liquid in a large, heavy saucepan. Place cinnamon, cardamom and cloves in a square of cheesecloth (muslin), bring up the corners to form a bundle, tie with kitchen twine, and add to pan. Bring to a boil.

Reduce heat to low and cook, uncovered, until lentils, beans and chickpeas are tender, about 1½ hours. Add extra water if necessary to keep lentil mixture covered.

Remove bundle of spices and discard. Add ginger, garlic, chili powder, tomatoes, butter and salt to pan. Raise heat to medium and cook, stirring often, for 10 minutes. The consistency should be like thick soup. If too thick, add a small amount of water.

Taste and adjust seasoning. Stir in fenugreek leaves. Serve hot with rice or paratha.

Tofu and vegetable stir-fry

Serves 4

$1/3$ cup (3 fl oz/90 ml) vegetable oil

$6^1/2$ oz (200 g) firm tofu, cut into 1-in (2.5-cm) cubes

3 cloves garlic, finely chopped

2 teaspoons grated fresh ginger

2 onions, cut into eighths

1 bunch Chinese broccoli, trimmed and cut into $1^1/2$-in (4-cm) lengths

$3^1/2$ oz (105 g) snow peas (mange-tout), trimmed and sliced crosswise

1 red bell pepper (capsicum), seeded and sliced

1 cup (6 oz/180 g) drained canned baby corn

1 bunch bok choy, trimmed and cut into $1^1/2$-in (4-cm) lengths, or 1 bunch spinach, trimmed

2 tablespoons oyster sauce

1 tablespoon light soy sauce

steamed rice (see page 28), for serving

In a wok over medium heat, warm vegetable oil. Working in batches, add tofu and stir-fry until golden on all sides, 2–3 minutes. Using a slotted spoon, remove from wok and drain on paper towels.

Pour off all but 2 tablespoons oil from wok and return to medium heat. Add garlic, ginger and onions and stir-fry until softened, 2–3 minutes.

Add broccoli, snow peas, bell pepper, corn and bok choy or spinach. Stir-fry until vegetables are tender-crisp, 3–4 minutes. Add tofu and oyster and soy sauces and gently stir-fry until heated through, 1–2 minutes.

Serve hot, accompanied by steamed white rice.

Vegetable khurma

Serves 8–10 as part of an Indian meal

1¹/₄ cups (10 fl oz/300 ml) water

4 large fresh green chilies,
   quartered lengthwise

18 fresh curry leaves

¹/₂ teaspoon ground turmeric

1 large desiree potato, cut into 2-inch
   (5-cm) sticks

1 large carrot, cut into 2-inch (5-cm)
   sticks

1 yellow (brown) onion, cut into very
   thin wedges

1 baby eggplant (aubergine), cut into
   2-inch (5-cm) sticks

1 large zucchini (courgette), cut into
   2-inch (5-cm) sticks

4 oz (125 g) green beans, trimmed and
   cut into 2-inch (5-cm) lengths

SPICED YOGURT

¹/₂ cup (4 oz/125 g) plain (natural)
   whole-milk yogurt

¹/₂ teaspoon ground coriander

¹/₂ teaspoon ground cumin

¹/₄ teaspoon ground black pepper

salt to taste

In a large saucepan, combine water, chili, curry leaves and turmeric and bring to a boil over medium–high heat. Add potato, carrot, onion, eggplant, zucchini and beans and mix well.

Cover, reduce heat to medium–low and simmer, stirring occasionally, until vegetables are just tender, about 15 minutes.

While vegetables cook, make spiced yogurt: In a bowl, combine yogurt, coriander, cumin, pepper and salt and mix well.

Drain all but about 1¹/₂ tablespoons liquid from vegetables. Add spiced yogurt and mix gently over very low heat until combined. Do not overheat or yogurt may separate. Serve hot.

Vegetable pulao

Serves 8 as part of an Indian meal

2½ cups (1 lb/500 g) basmati rice

⅓ cup (3 fl oz/90 ml) vegetable oil
and melted unsalted butter combined

¾-inch (2-cm) cinnamon stick

1 brown or black cardamom pod

2 green cardamom pods

2 whole cloves

½ mace blade

2 yellow (brown) onions, halved and
thinly sliced

about 1 teaspoon salt

1 tablespoon finely grated fresh ginger

1 tablespoon finely chopped garlic

2 tomatoes, unpeeled, finely chopped

1 carrot, cut into 1-inch (2.5-cm) sticks

4 oz (125 g) green beans, trimmed and
cut into 1-inch (2.5-cm) sticks

½ cup (2½ oz/75 g) shelled fresh or
frozen green peas

1½ tablespoons chopped fresh green
chilies

3¾ cups (30 fl oz/940 ml) vegetable
stock (see page 590) or water

½ cup (¾ oz/25 g) chopped fresh
cilantro (fresh coriander)

Place rice in a bowl and add cold water to cover. Swirl rice with your hand, let rice settle, then drain off water. Repeat 6 or 7 times. Cover rice with water and set aside to soak for 20 minutes.

Preheat oven to 350°F (180°C/Gas 4). In a large, heavy deghchi or ovenproof saucepan, heat oil and butter mixture over low heat. Add cinnamon, cardamom, cloves and mace, and cook, stirring, until fragrant, about 30 seconds. Add onions and salt, and cook, uncovered, stirring occasionally, until onions are dark golden brown, about 15 minutes. Add ginger and garlic and cook for 30 seconds. Stir in tomatoes and mix well. Stir in carrot, beans, peas and chili and cook, stirring, for 3 minutes.

Drain rice and add to pan, stirring until well combined. Stir in stock and bring to a simmer. Cook, partially covered, until tunnels begin to appear in rice mixture, about 10 minutes.

Cover pan tightly and bake in oven until rice is tender, about 15 minutes. Remove from oven and let stand for 10 minutes. Garnish with cilantro and serve immediately.

Vegetables and spiced coconut steamed in banana leaves

Serves 4–8

2 tablespoons vegetable oil

13 oz (400 g) baby eggplant (aubergine), halved lengthwise then cut into thin strips

1 medium red bell pepper (capsicum), seeded and julienned

1 cup (1 oz/30 g) bean sprouts

2 tablespoons Massaman Curry Paste (see page 580) or other curry paste

1 cup (8 fl oz/250 ml) thin coconut cream (see page 24)

1/2 cup (1/2 oz/15 g) fresh cilantro (fresh coriander) leaves

8 squares banana leaf, each 10 inches (25 cm)

8 strips banana leaf, pandan leaf, string or toothpicks, for tying

2 cups (10 oz/300 g) steamed white rice (see page 28)

2 tablespoons flaked coconut, toasted

Warm oil in a medium frying pan or wok over medium–high heat. Add eggplant and bell pepper and stir-fry until vegetables begin to color, about 3 minutes. Add bean sprouts and curry paste and stir well. Fold in coconut cream and simmer for 2 minutes. Add cilantro leaves.

Soften banana leaf squares and strips in a steamer to prevent splitting, 3–5 minutes. Place banana leaves on a work surface. Divide rice between each leaf and top with vegetable mix. Fold over sides of banana leaf to enclose mixture and secure with strips of banana leaf. Steam parcels for 20 minutes. Open parcels to serve. Garnish with toasted flaked coconut.

Hint: Substitute other green vegetables for chives—long (snake) beans, spinach, choy sum or bok choy, for example.

Vegetarian green curry

Serves 4

5 oz (150 g) firm tofu, drained then cut into 3/4-inch (2-cm) cubes

1 cup (8 fl oz/250 ml) vegetable oil

2 cups (16 fl oz/500 ml) coconut milk (see page 24)

1–2 tablespoons vegetable oil (optional)

1/4 cup (2 fl oz/60 ml) Green Curry Paste (see page 576)

1/2 cup (2 oz/60 g) chopped eggplant (aubergine) or 3 round Thai eggplants, chopped

1/2 cup (2 oz/60 g) pea eggplants (optional)

1 cup (4 oz/125 g) coarsely chopped fresh or canned bamboo shoots, rinsed and drained

6 ears fresh or canned baby corn, rinsed and drained, cut into bite-sized pieces

2 tablespoons palm sugar

2 kaffir lime leaves, stemmed

1 cup (1 oz/30 g) loosely packed fresh sweet Thai basil leaves

2 tablespoons soy sauce

1 fresh long green chili, cut into large pieces

1 fresh long red chili, cut into large pieces

Pat tofu dry with a paper towel. Heat oil in a large frying pan and working in batches, fry tofu cubes until golden. Remove using a slotted spoon and drain on paper towels; set aside. Let coconut milk stand, allowing the thick coconut milk to rise to the top. Spoon thick coconut milk into a small bowl, reserving 2 tablespoons for garnish.

In a wok or large, heavy frying pan, heat thick coconut milk over medium–high heat for 3–5 minutes, stirring constantly, until it separates. If it does not separate, add optional oil. Add green curry paste and fry, stirring constantly, until fragrant, 1–2 minutes. Add vegetables and fried tofu and stir until well coated. Add remaining thin coconut milk and bring to a boil. Reduce heat and simmer until vegetables are slightly soft, about 4 minutes.

Add palm sugar—if using a wok, add it along the edge of the wok so that it melts before stirring into curry; if using a standard frying pan, add directly to the curry. Tear kaffir lime leaves and basil into pieces. Stir in soy sauce, kaffir lime leaves and half the basil.

Remove from heat and transfer to a serving bowl. Drizzle over reserved 2 tablespoons thick coconut milk. Garnish with green and red chilies, and remaining basil leaves and serve.

Vietnamese table greens

Serves 4–6

fresh herbs of choice, such as sprigs of
cilantro (fresh coriander) peppermint
and spearmint, Vietnamese mint (rau
ram), shiso (perilla), Vietnamese
lemon balm, eryngo (sawtooth
coriander), piper (betel) leaf , and
sweet Thai basil

leaves from 1–2 heads butter (Boston)
lettuce
leaves from 1 red or green leaf lettuce
(oak leaf, Lollo Rossa or coral)
2 cups (4 oz/125 g) bean sprouts,
rinsed and drained
1/2 cucumber, seeded and thinly sliced

Trim herb stems and rinse leaves. Keep sprigs whole. Clean lettuce leaves. Rinse sprouts, and remove "tails" if desired. Prepare cucumber. To serve, arrange lettuce leaves and herbs to one side of a large bowl or platter, and place sprouts and cucumber on the other side. (Pictured on page 378.)

Notes: *This is a typical salad to accompany any Vietnamese meal. Vary your use of lettuce and herbs as desired. You can also, to a lesser extent, use pennywort (rau ma), the miniature, cumin-scented rice paddy herb (ngo om) and strong-tasting fish leaf (rau diep ca).*

Unlike a Western salad, where each diner has their own bowl, the greens are picked from a central platter. Lettuce leaves are torn to a suitable size to wrap bite-sized pieces of meat. Softened sheets of rice paper (see page 27) often accompany this salad.

Hints: *Lettuce may be cleaned and refrigerated prior to use; this helps to crisp the leaves. Herbs can be delicate, so they should be kept dry and refrigerated in plastic bags. Only rinse immediately prior to serving.*

Variation: *A smaller selection of fresh herbs, specifically accompanying various soup dishes and some starter courses, includes scallions (shallots/spring onions), eryngo (sawtooth coriander) leaves, cilantro (fresh coriander) sprigs, Vietnamese mint (rau ram), dill and bean sprouts. Accompany with fresh long red chilies cut into small rings, fish sauce or Nuoc Cham Sauce (see page 582), and lemon or lime wedges.*

Rice & noodles

r ice is the definitive food of Asia, along with its relative, the noodle. They are present at every meal, from breakfast through lunch and dinner to dessert, and their variety is nothing short of amazing. Almost every town and city in Asia will have a signature dish, and the mark of every great Asian chef is the perfection of their rice or noodles.

Noodles have been eaten by the Chinese for many hundreds of years, beginning with wheat noodles, which evolved into egg noodles and then became dumplings and wontons. Similarly, rice, the Chinese staple, was made into ground rice flour, and this was mixed with water to form rice stick noodles, rice vermicelli and spring roll wrappers. The ancient Chinese took rice and noodles along with them on their travels, and consequently these are now staples all over Asia and in many other parts of the world.

Thailand is only the sixth-greatest rice-growing nation, yet it is the world's largest rice-exporting country. While sticky (glutinous) rice is favored in parts of the land, particularly in the north and in Isan, and black rice is traditionally used in desserts, long-grain jasmine rice reigns in most Thai kitchens. However, while rice is beloved in the country—the Thai for steamed rice, "khao suey," means beautiful rice—one of Thailand's best known dishes, pad thai, is a noodle.

In Vietnam they also take their rice very seriously. The Vietnamese word for rice, "com," is the same as the word for meal, and some 60 per cent of the land is devoted to rice cultivation. As in Thailand, the preferred steamed rice here is jasmine, and aged rice is the most valued. Besides rice grain, there's a vast array of rice noodles, from the thin rice vermicelli noodles known as "bun," which are eaten unheated, to the wider and more resilient banh pho, used in the country's national soup dish, pho. Thin sheets of rice paper are softened and commonly used to wrap cooked meats at the table, or are filled to make both fresh and fried spring rolls.

The Japanese of course prefer short-grain rice—it's essential in sushi and matches their style of cuisine as well. Short-grain rice is also easier to eat using their elegant pointed chopsticks. The creation of Japanese noodles is renowned as almost an art form, with beautiful bundles of udon, soba or shirataki inspiring a great range of dishes.

India is the exception in Asia because here rice and bread forms the foundation of the nation's diet. The preferred Indian rice is basmati, that low-glycaemic long-grain wonder. Its unique fragrance when cooked, as well as the loose separate nature of the grains, is perfect for spicy dishes and curries. Bread has been part of Indian cuisine since about 1500 BCE, when the Aryans ruled the north of the country and wheat was first introduced. Chappati, naan, poori or paratha—no Indian meal is served without bread.

This chapter contains a wide selection of recipes for rice, noodles and bread, but it is only a small taste of the infinite range of dishes that these staple foods can create. The recipes include traditional methods of cooking rice and noodles, such as Korean bibimbap and Chinese congee, as well as regional dishes and more modern salads and stir-fries. Many of the recipes make substantial meals in themselves, and need only a few accompaniments to complete them.

Preparing rice and noodles

Rice and noodles are intrinsically easy to prepare and cook—they've been that way for thousands of years. When done well, they can be the difference between a good meal and a great one. In this section you'll find hints on buying rice and noodles, and instructions for preparing the commonly used noodles. (See also Preparing ingredients for instructions on steamed rice and sushi rice, and Glossary for descriptions of noodles.)

Buying rice and noodles

In Asia, markets sell many varieties of rice. For example in Thailand and Vietnam, these can range from the freshest new-season's crop, labeled AAA, to "old" rice, which commands a premium price for its special qualities and taste of age.

Most of the basic rice types used in Asian cooking, including jasmine, basmati and short-grain white, are available at good supermarkets; Asian markets will stock a greater variety, including sticky (glutinous) rice, both white and black. Look for clean, dust-free grains that are unbroken.

Noodles were once made only by hand, but are now mass-produced and available in all shapes and sizes. In some noodle bars in Shanghai, Hong Kong and Singapore, you can still see the chef make noodles at your table—an almost acrobatic process that requires great skill and practice and is breathtaking to watch—and needless to say, the resulting noodle is incomparably delicious.

A very good range of noodles is now available from supermarkets, either fresh in the refrigerated section or dried in packets. Of course, Asian markets will stock the freshest and best noodles, as well as a myriad of dried forms. (For descriptions on types of noodles, see Glossary.)

Preparing noodles

There are basically two ways to cook noodles:

1. Place noodles in a heatproof bowl and cover with boiling water. Soak noodles until soft, then drain. This method is suitable only for fine noodles such as cellophane (bean thread) noodles, rice vermicelli and thin egg noodles.

2. Bring a large saucepan of water to a boil, add noodles and cook until tender, then drain. This method is suitable for all noodles.

Always check the package for cooking times and serving ideas. Use the following cooking times as a guide and always check the noodles during cooking by tasting a strand. Noodles for soups should be slightly undercooked, so they don't fall apart. Noodles for most other dishes should be cooked through.

Cellophane (bean thread) noodles: These need only be softened in boiling water for 10 minutes; they do not require boiling. For a crisp texture, deep-fry them in hot oil until golden and crisp, 1 minute or less.

Egg noodles: Cook fresh egg noodles in boiling water for about 3 minutes. Cook dried egg noodles in boiling water for about 5 minutes. Some precooked fresh egg noodles need only be soaked in hot water for 8–10 minutes; check package for directions.

Hokkien noodles: Cook in boiling water for 3–4 minutes or stir-fry in hot oil for 3–4 minutes. Some varieties are precooked; check package for directions.

Ramen noodles: Cook in boiling water for about 5 minutes.

Rice stick noodles: Soften dried noodles in hot water for 15 minutes or cook in boiling water for 2–3 minutes. Stir-fry fresh noodles for 2–3 minutes. Some thin rice stick noodles only require soaking in boiling water before adding to soups or stir-fries. Rice vermicelli can be deep-fried to create a crisp "bird's nest" for serving stir-fry dishes.

Soba noodles: Cook fresh soba noodles in boiling water for about $1\frac{1}{2}$ minutes. Cook dried soba noodles in boiling water for 5–6 minutes.

Somen noodles: Cook in boiling water for about 3 minutes.

Spring roll wrappers: Steam filled wrappers for 5 minutes or deep-fry in hot oil until golden and crisp.

Udon noodles: Cook fresh udon noodles in boiling water for about $2\frac{1}{2}$ minutes. Cook dried udon noodles in boiling water for 10–12 minutes.

Wheat flour noodles: Cook fresh wheat flour noodles in boiling water for 3 minutes. Cook dried wheat flour noodles in boiling water for 4–5 minutes.

Wonton wrappers, white (wheat flour): Cook in boiling water or steam filled wrappers for about 6 minutes; deep-fry until golden and crisp.

Wonton wrappers, yellow (egg dough): Cook in boiling water for about 4 minutes; deep-fry until golden and crisp.

Beijing noodles with snow pea shoots and black vinegar

Serves 4–6

17 oz (500 g) fresh or dried Chinese
  wheat noodles

1 tablespoon dark sesame oil

1/4 cup (2 fl oz/60 ml) peanut oil

4 shallots (French shallots), finely sliced

4 cloves garlic, finely chopped

6 oz (180 g) lotus root, thinly sliced
  pinch salt

3 tablespoons Chinese black vinegar

6 cups (3 oz/90 g) snow pea
  (mange-tout) shoots

1/4 cup (2 fl oz/60 ml) vegetarian
  oyster (mushroom) sauce

5 scallions (shallots/spring onions),
  finely sliced on an angle

**FOR CHILI, BLACK VINEGAR
AND SESAME DRESSING**

1/4 cup (2 fl oz/60 ml) Chinese black
  vinegar

2 small red chilies, seeded and
finely sliced

1 tablespoon finely chopped scallions
  (shallots/spring onions)

1/4 cup (2 fl oz/60 ml) peanut oil

1 teaspoon dark sesame oil

To make dressing: In a bowl, combine vinegar, chili and scallions. Whisk in peanut and sesame oils. Set aside.

Place noodles in a large pot of salted, boiling water and boil for 1 minute. Drain noodles and toss with sesame oil to prevent strands from sticking. Keep warm.

Heat a wok over medium–high heat and add peanut oil. Add shallots and garlic and stir-fry briskly until they begin to color, about 1 minute. Add lotus root and stir-fry until it begins to color, about 3 minutes. Add salt, black vinegar and hot noodles. Reduce heat to medium–low. Add snow pea shoots and stir gently until wilted, about 2 minutes. Stir in oyster sauce.

Divide among individual hot bowls and garnish with scallions. Serve with chili, black vinegar and sesame dressing for dipping. (Pictured on page 438.)

Hint: The recipe for dressing makes 1/2 cup (4 fl oz/125 ml). Store any unused dressing in a glass jar in the refrigerator, for up to 2 weeks. Use to dress salads, tossed through noodle dishes, or as a sauce for steamed mixed vegetables.

Bibimbap with beef and vegetables

Serves 4

2 oz (60 g) red radish, cut into thin strips about 1$\frac{1}{2}$ inches (4 cm) long

2 oz (60 g) Korean round radish, cut into thin strips about 1$\frac{1}{2}$ inches (4 cm) long

2 oz (60 g) carrots, cut into thin strips about 1$\frac{1}{2}$ inches (4 cm) long

2 oz (60 g) cucumber, cut into thin strips about 1$\frac{1}{2}$ inches (4 cm) long

4 shiso (perilla) leaves, cut into thin strips about 1$\frac{1}{2}$ inches (4 cm) long

2 oz (60 g) lettuce leaves, cut into thin strips about 1$\frac{1}{2}$ inches (4 cm) long

4 oz (125 g) beef tenderloin (fillet), cut into thin strips about 1$\frac{1}{2}$ inches (4 cm) long

4 servings hot steamed medium-grain rice (see page 28)

4 fried eggs

FOR BEEF MARINADE

1 tablespoon light soy sauce

1$\frac{1}{2}$ teaspoons sugar

2 teaspoons finely chopped scallions (shallots/spring onions)

1 teaspoon finely chopped garlic

1 teaspoon toasted, ground sesame seeds (see page 30)

1 teaspoon Asian sesame oil

pinch black pepper

FOR HOT CHILI PASTE SAUCE

2 tablespoons hot red chili paste

3 tablespoons beef stock (see page 588)

2 tablespoons sugar

1 tablespoon sesame oil

1 tablespoon toasted, ground sesame seeds (see page 30)

Freshen red radish, radish, carrots, cucumber, shiso leaves and lettuce by dipping them separately in cold water, then draining.

To make beef marinade: Combine marinade ingredients in a glass or ceramic bowl. Add beef to marinade and marinate for 10 minutes. Heat 1 teaspoon vegetable oil in a frying pan and stir-fry beef over medium heat until well done, 3–5 minutes.

To make hot chili paste sauce: Mix chili paste sauce ingredients together and spoon into a serving bowl.

To serve, divide rice among 4 bowls, arrange beef and vegetables over rice, and top with a fried egg. Serve chili paste sauce in separate bowls; each diner mixes sauce into their own bowls of bibimbap.

Chappati (Indian flat bread)

Makes 12 chappati

5 cups (1¹/₂ lb/750 g) whole wheat (wholemeal) flour
1 teaspoon salt
3 tablespoons vegetable oil
about 2 cups (16 fl oz/500 ml) water
vegetable oil and melted unsalted butter combined, for brushing

Sift flour and salt into a large mixing bowl. Make a well in center. Add oil and enough water, adding water in increments, to form a soft dough with your hand. Knead dough lightly in bowl, then cover with a clean damp kitchen towel and set aside for 20 minutes.

Turn out dough onto a lightly floured surface and knead until it almost springs back when touched lightly, about 10 minutes. Cover with a damp towel and set aside for 15 minutes. Knead dough lightly and divide evenly into 12 portions. Shape each portion into a ball, then roll out into a disk 8–10 inches (20–25 cm) in diameter.

Heat a heavy cast-iron griddle over medium heat. When griddle is hot, place a disk of dough on griddle and cook, lightly pressing disk all over with a dry clean kitchen towel, using a dabbing motion, until disk is golden brown in spots, 1–2 minutes. Turn and cook on second side until golden brown in spots and cooked through, about 1 minute. Brush with oil and butter mixture and remove to a serving tray lined with a cloth napkin. Repeat with remaining disks.

Note: *The griddle must not be too hot or chappati will become dry and burnt. You can also make chappati smaller if you prefer. Chappati can be cooked several hours ahead. Before serving, wrap them in a clean kitchen towel, then aluminum foil, and heat in an oven preheated to 225°F (110°C/Gas ¹/₄) for 5–10 minutes.*

Chiang Mai noodles

Serves 6–8

FOR CURRY PASTE

15 dried long red chilies, seeded

³/₄ cup (6 fl oz/180 ml) Hanglay Curry Paste (see page 576)

3 tablespoons grated fresh ginger

1 teaspoon curry powder or gaeng hanglay powder (see page 227)

¹/₃ cup (25 g) chopped cilantro (fresh coriander) roots or stems

1 cup (8 fl oz/ 250 ml) water

FOR SOUP

8 cups (64 fl oz/2 L) coconut milk (see page 24)

6–8 chicken legs

1 cup (8 fl oz/250 ml) chicken stock (see page 588)

2–3 tablespoons palm sugar

2 tablespoons granulated (white) sugar

¹/₂ cup (4 fl oz/125 ml) soy sauce

¹/₂ cup (4 fl oz/125 ml) fish sauce

1 lb (500 g) fresh egg noodles

FOR ACCOMPANIMENTS

about ¹/₂ cup (4 fl oz/125 ml) Chili Oil (see page 569)

about 1 cup (3¹/₂ oz/105 g) pickled cabbage or cucumber, drained

¹/₃ cup (1 oz/30 g) quartered shallots (French shallots), preferably pink

2 limes, cut into small wedges

2 tablespoons ketjap manis

¹/₂ cup (¹/₂ oz/15 g) coarsely chopped cilantro (fresh coriander) leaves and stems

3 scallions (shallots/spring onions), coarsely chopped

To make curry paste: Soak dried chilies in water for 10 minutes to soften, then drain. In a food processor, combine hanglay curry paste, chilies, ginger, curry powder and cilantro. Add water and blend until smooth.

Let coconut milk stand, allowing thick milk to rise to top. Spoon 1 cup (8 fl oz/250 ml) thick coconut milk in a wok and heat for 3–5 minutes, stirring constantly, until it separates. Add curry paste and fry, stirring constantly, until fragrant, 1–2 minutes. Add chicken, stock, remaining thick coconut milk, and half of thin coconut milk. Stir in palm sugar, granulated sugar, soy sauce and fish sauce. Reduce heat to a simmer and cook, uncovered, until chicken is cooked through and tender, about 30 minutes. Add water during cooking if required. Add remaining thin coconut milk and heat through.

In a large pot of boiling water, cook noodles in boiling water for 2 minutes; drain. To serve, divide noodles among individual bowls, top with a chicken leg and ladle in curry sauce. Serve with bowls of accompaniments.

Congee (Chinese rice soup)

Serves 6–8

1 cup (7 oz/220 g) short-grain white rice or premixed congee grains and legumes

6 cups (48 fl oz/1.5 L) water

ACCOMPANIMENTS

1 teaspoon crispy fried shallots (French shallots) (see page 24)

1 tablespoon fried peanuts

1 tablespoon dark sesame oil

2 small red chilies, seeded and finely sliced

1 tablespoon fermented black beans

1 tablespoon light soy sauce

1 tablespoon cilantro (fresh coriander), chopped

1 tablespoon scallions (shallots/spring onions), finely sliced or curled (see page 33)

Put rice or mixed grains and water into a medium-large saucepan over high heat and bring to a boil. Stir rice to make sure it does not stick to base of saucepan. Reduce heat so water is barely simmering and cover tightly so that rice water does not bubble over top. Simmer until rice or mixed grains split and are held in suspension in the water, about 90 minutes.

Transfer congee into individual bowls and offer small quantities of a selection of accompaniments.

Note: The nourishing properties of congee are said to increase with a longer cooking time—of anywhere up to 6 hours. To do this, increase the amount of water up to 10 cups (80 fl oz/2.5 L), cook in a heavy-based saucepan so the rice will not stick, and simmer over very low heat.

Variations: Vary rice congee by adding different single ingredients—such as carrot, celery, fennel, ginger, leek, mustard, sesame seed or spinach—at the beginning of cooking. Instead of white rice, brown or sweet rice may also be used, as can other single grains, such as spelt or millet.

Crisp-fried egg noodles with chicken

Serves 4

6 cups (48 fl oz/1.5 L) vegetable oil for deep-frying, plus 2 tablespoons extra

6^1/$_2$ oz (200 g) fresh thin egg noodles

3 cloves garlic, finely chopped

1 tablespoon grated fresh ginger

1 onion, cut into eighths

1 lb (500 g) skinless chicken thigh fillets, cut into ^{3}/$_4$-in (2-cm) cubes

1 red bell pepper (capsicum), seeded and sliced

1 green bell pepper (capsicum), seeded and sliced

1 bunch choy sum or spinach, trimmed and cut into 2-in (5-cm) lengths

3 tablespoons hoisin sauce

^{1}/$_4$ cup (2 fl oz/60 ml) chicken stock (see page 588) mixed with 1 teaspoon cornstarch (cornflour)

Heat 6 cups (48 fl oz/1.5 L) oil in wok until it reaches 375°F (190°C) on a deep-frying thermometer or until a small bread cube dropped in oil sizzles and turns golden. Working in small batches, add noodles and fry until golden and crisp, 1–2 minutes. Using slotted spoon, remove from oil and drain on paper towels.

In a wok over medium–high heat, warm 2 tablespoons vegetable oil. Add garlic, ginger and onion and stir-fry until onion softens slightly, about 3 minutes. Add chicken and stir-fry until browned, 3–4 minutes. Add bell peppers and choy sum or spinach and stir-fry until tender-crisp, about 2 minutes. Stir in hoisin sauce and stock and cornstarch mixture and cook until sauce boils and thickens slightly, about 2 minutes.

To serve, arrange crisp noodles in a nest on serving plates. Top with chicken and vegetables.

Hint: *You can substitute raw shrimp (prawns) for chicken in this recipe, but cook only until shrimp change color. Or use finely sliced Chinese barbecue pork and add with the vegetables.*

Dosai (Indian rice pancakes)

Makes 10–12 pancakes

3¹/₂ cups (16 oz/500 g) medium to coarse rice flour
1¹/₄ cups (5 oz/150 g) split black lentil flour
salt as needed
cold water as needed
¹/₂ cup vegetable oil and melted unsalted butter combined

In a bowl, combine ¹/₃ cup (2 oz/60 g) rice flour with 2 tablespoons (²/₃ oz/20 g) lentil flour and a pinch of salt. Make a well in center. Stir in enough cold water to form a batter with a dropping consistency. Cover and let stand in a warm place for 12 hours or overnight.

The next day, in a clean bowl, combine ¹/₃ cup (2 oz/60 g) rice flour with 2 tablespoons (²/₃ oz/20 g) lentil flour and a pinch of salt. Make a well in center. Stir in enough cold water to form a batter with a dropping consistency. Stir 1 heaping tablespoon of previous day's batter into new batter. Discard remainder of old batter. Cover new batter and let stand in a warm place for 12 hours or overnight.

The next day, in a large clean bowl, combine remaining rice flour with remaining lentil flour and 1 teaspoon salt. Stir in enough cold water to form a new batter with a soft dropping consistency. Stir 1 heaping tablespoon of previous day's batter into new batter. Discard old batter. Cover new batter and let stand in a warm place for 12 hours or overnight. By this stage, the batter should have increased in volume by about half.

To cook pancakes: Heat a tawa or heavy griddle over high heat and spread a layer of salt over top. Heat for 3–4 minutes and then, using a clean kitchen towel, wipe off salt. This seasons the pan. To test if pan is the right temperature for cooking pancakes, heat pan over medium heat for 2 minutes. Drizzle lightly with oil and butter mixture, and sprinkle with water. If water sizzles immediately on contact, pan is ready. Wipe pan clean.

Use a flat-bottomed metal cup to ladle ¹/₃ cup (2¹/₂ fl oz/80 ml) batter at a time onto pan. Use bottom of cup to spread batter outwards, moving cup in concentric circles. Each pancake should be 7–8 inches (18–20 cm) in diameter. Drizzle pancake with 1 teaspoon oil and butter mixture and cook until crisp and golden underneath, 2–4 minutes. Place filling along center and roll or fold as desired. Place, seam-side down, on a plate. Repeat with remaining batter and oil and butter mixture.

Fresh rice noodles with enoki mushrooms, sesame and soy

Serves 4–6

4 stalks celery, flesh sliced on an angle, and leaves

vegetable oil, for frying

1 lb (500 g) fresh rice sheet noodles

$1/2$ teaspoon plus 2 tablespoons peanut oil

2 cups (4 oz/125 g) bean sprouts

4 oz (125 g) enoki mushrooms

4 oz (125 g) oyster (abalone) or button mushrooms

2 scallions (shallots/spring onions), finely sliced on an angle

1 tablespoon dark sesame oil

1 tablespoon soy sauce plus extra, for serving

2 tablespoons vegetarian oyster (mushroom) sauce

2 teaspoons sesame seeds, toasted (see page 30)

soy sauce, for serving

Heat $3/4$ inch (2 cm) vegetable oil in a wok until hot. Add celery leaves, a few at a time, and cook just until they become transparent, about 15–30 seconds. Remove from oil, and drain. Repeat until all leaves are fried. Leaves will stay crisp for at least 2 hours.

Slice noodles into roughly 1-inch (2.5-cm) strips. Cover with boiling water and carefully separate using a fork or chopsticks. When separate, soak for 5–10 minutes, drain, rinse and drain again thoroughly. Gently stir $1/2$ teaspoon peanut oil through noodles to prevent sticking. Set aside.

Heat 2 tablespoons peanut oil in a medium frying pan or wok over high heat. Add sprouts, mushrooms, scallions and celery slices. Cook until vegetables just begin to collapse, about 4 minutes. Add noodles, sesame oil, soy sauce and oyster sauce and gently stir to combine.

Transfer to individual bowls. Sprinkle with sesame seeds and fried celery leaves. Serve with extra soy sauce.

Ginger-coconut rice

Serves 4–6

2 tablespoons vegetable oil

1 teaspoon Asian chili oil

1 onion, chopped

1 red bell pepper (capsicum), seeded and chopped

3 cloves garlic, finely chopped

3 teaspoons grated fresh ginger

1 1/2 cups (11 oz/330 g) short-grain white rice

1 1/2 cups (12 fl oz/375 ml) chicken stock (see page 588)

1 cup (8 fl oz/250 ml) water

1/2 cup (4 fl oz/125 ml) coconut milk (see page 24)

3 scallions (shallots/spring onions)

3 tablespoons chopped fresh cilantro (fresh coriander)

2 tablespoons unsweetened shredded coconut, toasted

3 tablespoons lemon juice

1/4 cup (1 oz/30 g) unsweetened shredded coconut, for serving

In wok over medium–high heat, warm vegetable and chili oils. Add onion, bell pepper, garlic and ginger and stir-fry until softened, about 3 minutes. Add rice and stir until well coated with oil, about 2 minutes.

Add stock, water and coconut milk and bring to a boil. Reduce heat to low, cover, and simmer until all liquid is absorbed and rice is tender, 15–20 minutes. Remove from heat and stir in scallions, cilantro, toasted coconut and lemon juice.

Serve hot, topped with shredded coconut.

Note: *This ginger-laced rice, which gains a subtle sweetness from both shredded coconut and coconut milk, makes a good accompaniment for Chinese barbecue pork (pictured).*

Hokkien noodles and vegetables with black bean sauce

Serves 4–6

1 1/4 lb (625 g) fresh or vacuum-packed hokkien noodles
3 tablespoons vegetable oil
4 cloves garlic, finely chopped
2 shallots (French shallots), finely chopped
1 cup (6 oz/185 g) baby corn, halved lengthwise
4 oz (125 g) oyster (abalone) mushrooms, coarsely chopped
1/2 bunch (6 oz/180 g) bok choy, halved lengthwise
1/2 bunch (6 oz/180 g) choy sum
1/4 cup (2 fl oz/60 ml) water
1/4 cup (2 fl oz/60 ml) black bean sauce
crispy fried shallots (French shallots) (see page 24), for garnish (optional)
chopped fresh red chili, for garnish (optional)

Cover noodles with boiling water and set aside for 2 minutes. Drain.

Heat oil in a large frying pan or wok over medium–high heat. Add garlic and shallots and stir-fry until they just begin to color, about 30 seconds. Add baby corn, mushrooms, bok choy and choy sum. Sprinkle on water, drizzle on black bean sauce and spread noodles on top. Cover and simmer for 3–5 minutes, depending on how crunchy you like your vegetables. Remove from the heat and stir well.

Divide among individual bowls. Sprinkle with the fried shallots and fresh chili if desired.

Hints: *This classic stir-fry recipe for hokkien noodles can include a variety of ingredients, including strips of chicken, shrimp, fish cakes and tofu. Vegetables can also be varied according to seasonal availability.*

Indian-style pilaf

Serves 4 as an accompaniment

1 1/4 cups (9 oz/280 g) basmati rice
1 tablespoon vegetable oil
1 onion, chopped
2 cloves garlic, finely chopped
1 teaspoon fennel seeds
1 tablespoon sesame seeds
1/2 teaspoon ground turmeric
1 teaspoon ground cumin
1/2 teaspoon sea salt
2 whole cloves
3 cardamom pods, lightly crushed
6 black peppercorns
1 3/4 cups (14 fl oz/440 ml) chicken stock (see page 588)
fresh curry leaves, for garnish

Rinse rice in several changes of cold water until water runs clear. Put rice in a bowl and add cold water to cover. Let stand for 30 minutes. Drain.

In a medium, heavy saucepan, heat oil over medium heat and fry onion and garlic until onion is soft, 1–2 minutes. Stir in fennel, sesame seeds, turmeric, cumin, salt, cloves, cardamom pods and peppercorns. Fry until fragrant, 1–2 minutes. Add drained rice and fry, stirring constantly until rice is opaque, about 2 minutes. Pour in stock and bring to a boil. Cover, reduce heat to low and simmer until rice is tender and all liquid has been absorbed, 15–20 minutes. Remove from heat and let stand, covered, for 5 minutes.

Spoon pilaf into serving bowls and garnish with curry leaves.

Japanese summer noodles

Serves 4

2 eggs
pinch salt
pinch pepper
pinch sugar
1 tablespoon vegetable oil

FOR DRESSING
$1/3$ cup (3 fl oz/90 ml) sugar
$1/3$ cup (3 fl oz/90 ml) water
$1/2$ cup (4 fl oz/125 ml) soy sauce
$1/4$ cup (2 fl oz/60 ml) rice vinegar
1 tablespoon Asian sesame oil

13 oz (400 g) somen or chukasoba noodles, cooked until just tender, then drained
1 English (hothouse) cucumber, cut into matchstick strips
3 oz (90 g) cooked cold fish cake, cut into matchstick strips
5 oz (150 g) cooked pork or chicken breast, cut into matchstick strips
1 tablespoon wakame, soaked in cold water for 5 minutes, drained, then finely sliced
8 slices gari (see page 585), finely sliced
hot English mustard, for serving
sesame seeds, for garnish

In a small bowl, beat together eggs, salt, pepper and sugar. Heat a small frying pan with vegetable oil, add eggs and cook over medium heat, into a thin omelette. Remove from heat, let cool, then cut into thin shreds.

To make dressing: In a small saucepan over high heat, combine sugar and water and bring to a boil, stirring to dissolve sugar. Remove from heat and let cool. Add soy sauce, rice vinegar and sesame oil. Mix together well.

Divide noodles among 4 plates, mounding them in center of each plate. Top with cucumber, fish cake, pork and egg, radiating them around the plate. Place a little wakame and gari in center of noodles. Pour dressing at edge of mound in each plate. Place a little mustard along edge of each plate. Sprinkle with sesame seeds and serve.

Note: *These traditional Japanese noodles are known as "hiyashi chuka."*

Korean mixed noodles (Bibimmyeon)

4 oz (125 g) beef tenderloin (fillet), cut into thin strips about 1¹/₂ inches (4 cm) long

3 dried Chinese mushrooms, soaked for 30 minutes in several changes of water, drained, stems discarded and caps sliced thinly

vegetable or sunflower oil, for frying

1 small cucumber (preferably joseon)

table salt

2 eggs, separated

10 oz (300 g) somyeon (thin, dried wheat noodles)

1 hot red chili, cut into thin strips (optional)

FOR CHILI SAUCE

2 tablespoons chili paste

3 tablespoons Korean soy sauce

2 tablespoons sugar

1 tablespoon sesame oil

1 tablespoon toasted, ground sesame seeds (see page 30)

FOR BEEF MARINADE

1 tablespoon light soy sauce

1¹/₂ teaspoons sugar

2 teaspoons finely chopped scallions (shallots/spring onions)

1 teaspoon finely chopped garlic

1 teaspoon toasted, ground sesame seeds (see page 30)

1 teaspoon sesame oil

freshly ground black pepper to taste

To make chili sauce: In a bowl, combine chili sauce ingredients and mix well, then spoon into a serving bowl. To make beef marinade: In a glass or ceramic bowl, combine marinade ingredients. Add beef and mushrooms and marinate for 20–30 minutes. Heat 1 tablespoon oil to very hot in a frying pan. Stir-fry beef and mushrooms together until browned on all sides, about 3 minutes. Remove from pan and set aside.

Cut cucumber in half lengthwise, then cut diagonally into thin slices. Sprinkle with salt and set aside for 10 minutes to sweat. Squeeze out excess water, then fry in 1 teaspoon oil over high heat for 2–3 minutes. Remove from pan and set aside. Fry egg whites and yolks separately to make egg gidan (see page 26). Set aside.

Bring a pan of water to a boil, then add noodles, stirring to prevent them from sticking together. Cook until soft, about 3 minutes. Remove noodles from water and rinse several times in cold water until water is clear. Drain.

Place noodles and chili sauce in a large bowl and mix well to coat. Add beef, mushrooms and most of the cucumber (reserving a small amount as garnish) and mix well.

Serve noodles in individual bowls, topped with egg gidan, remaining cucumber and strips of hot red chili.

Korean hot noodles (Onmyeon)

Serves 4

10 oz (300 g) piece stewing (gravy) beef

15 cups (120 fl oz/3.75 L) water

1 scallion (shallot/spring onion)

3 cloves garlic

table salt to taste

light soy sauce to taste

vegetable or sunflower oil, for frying

2 eggs, separated

1 medium zucchini (courgette) or cucumber

4 dried Chinese mushrooms, soaked for 30 minutes in several changes of water

10 oz (300 g) somyeon (thin, dried, wheat) noodles

dried hot red chili, chopped, for garnish (optional)

Place beef in a large saucepan with water, scallion and garlic. Bring to a boil, reduce heat to a simmer and cook until beef is tender, about 30 minutes. Remove beef from liquid, reserving liquid, and cut into ½-inch (12-mm) thick slices. Add salt and soy sauce to stock to taste. Fry egg whites and yolks to make egg gidan (see page 26). Remove from pan and cut into thin strips. Set aside to use as garnish.

Cut zucchini in half lengthwise, remove the seeds, then slice into thin strips. Sprinkle strips with salt and leave for 10 minutes to sweat. Squeeze out excess water, then fry for about 1 minute in 1 tablespoon oil. Squeeze excess water from Chinese mushrooms. Remove and discard stems. Slice caps thinly, then fry in 1 teaspoon oil over high heat for 1 minute.

Bring a medium saucepan of water to a boil and add noodles, stirring to prevent the noodles from sticking together. Cook until soft, about 3 minutes. Remove noodles from water and rinse several times in cold water until water is clear. Drain and divide into 4 bowls. Top noodles with beef slices and garnish with egg gidan, zucchini, mushrooms and chili, if desired. Gently pour some stock into each bowl and serve.

Masala dosai (Indian pancakes with potato filling)

Makes 10–12 filled pancakes

1 recipe Dosai (see page 452)
Fresh Coconut Chutney (see page 575),
   for serving

SAMBHAR (LENTIL GRAVY)

1^1/$_2$ cups (10 oz/300 g) split yellow
   lentils, rinsed and drained
8 cups (64 fl oz/2 L) water
1 teaspoon ground turmeric
1 lb (500 g) tomatoes, about
   3–4 medium, unpeeled, chopped
2 yellow (brown) onions, chopped
3 tablespoons Sambhar Masala
   (see page 587)
2 teaspoons tamarind concentrate
18 fresh curry leaves
salt to taste
^{2}/$_3$ cup (1 oz/30 g) chopped fresh
   cilantro (fresh coriander)

POTATO PALLYA (FILLING)

2 tablespoons vegetable oil
1^1/$_2$ teaspoons brown or black mustard
   seeds
1 tablespoon split chickpeas (garbanzo
   beans)
1 tablespoon split black lentils
4 dried red chilies
^{1}/$_4$ teaspoon powdered asafoetida
2^1/$_2$ teaspoons ground turmeric
18 fresh curry leaves
2 yellow (brown) onions, halved and
   thinly sliced
^{1}/$_2$ teaspoon salt, plus extra salt to taste
2 lb (1 kg) cooked desiree or pontiac
   potatoes, about 7 medium, peeled
   and coarsely mashed
^{1}/$_2$ cup (1 oz/30 g) chopped fresh
   cilantro (fresh coriander)

To make sambhar: In a large saucepan, combine lentils, water and turmeric. Bring to a boil. Reduce heat to low and cook, partially covered, until soft and mushy, about 30 minutes. Add tomatoes and onions, and cook, partially covered, stirring occasionally, until soft, about 30 minutes.

Add sambhar masala, tamarind, curry leaves and salt. Bring to a boil. Taste and adjust seasoning. Stir in cilantro. Partially cover and keep warm over low heat until serving.

To make potato pallya: In a heavy saucepan, heat oil over medium–low heat. Add mustard seeds and cook until they crackle, about 30 seconds. Add chickpeas and lentils and stir over low heat until light golden, about 30 seconds; be careful not to burn them. Add chilies and asafoetida and stir for 15 seconds. Add turmeric and curry leaves and stir for 15 seconds.

Add onions and ½ teaspoon salt, and cook, stirring often, until onions are translucent, about 5 minutes. Add potatoes and cilantro, and stir until well combined, 2–3 minutes. Taste and adjust seasoning if necessary. Cover to keep warm and set aside until serving.

Cook dosai following directions on page 452. Spoon one-tenth of potato filling onto each dosai, fold in sides and place on a serving plate, seam-side down. Serve immediately with sambhar and chutney.

Note: *Cook the pancakes just before serving, one at a time unless you have a large, heavy griddle. You can make sambhar 3 days ahead, fresh coconut chutney 1 day ahead, and potato pallya 6 hours ahead.*

Metropole-style fried rice

Serves 6

4 eggs
vegetable oil, for cooking
2 large onions, coarsely chopped
4 oz (125 g) shelled cooked shrimp (prawns), coarsely chopped
1 1/2 cups (9 oz/280 g) diced cooked chicken meat, firmly packed
1/2 cup (4 fl oz/125 ml) fish sauce or to taste
1/4 green bell pepper (capsicum), seeded and finely diced
1/4 red bell pepper (capsicum), seeded and finely diced
4 cups (18 oz/ 550g) steamed rice (see page 28), cooled
2 teaspoons ground pepper
1 tablespoon Asian chili sauce (or to taste)
cilantro (fresh coriander) sprigs, for garnish
shrimp crackers, for serving (optional)

Prepare 4 thin omelettes as described on page 26. Cool omelettes slightly, roll, then cut into strips; set aside.

In a large frying pan or wok, heat 2 tablespoons oil over high heat and stir-fry onions until barely wilted, about 1 minute. Add shrimp and chicken, and stir-fry for 2 minutes. Season with half fish sauce, add bell peppers, and stir-fry for 1 minute. Add rice, pepper, chili sauce and remaining fish sauce to taste. Reduce heat to medium–high and stir-fry for 5 minutes.

Moisten 6 individual rice bowls or small ramekins and pack with fried rice. Alternatively, press all rice into a lightly oiled 6-cup (48-fl oz/1.5-L) bowl. Press firmly, then unmold into the middle of a plate. Sprinkle with omelet strips and cilantro. If desired, accompany with shrimp crackers.

Note: This is a signature dish of the Sofitel Metropole Hotel in Hanoi, Vietnam. Cold steamed rice cooks best in this recipe; if using freshly steamed rice, set the rice aside to cool slightly.

Mi goreng

10 oz (300 g) thin dried egg noodles

¹/₄ cup (2 fl oz/60 ml) peanut oil

2 cloves garlic, minced

1 medium yellow (brown) onion, finely sliced into half moons

2 celery sticks, finely sliced on an angle

3 cups (6 oz/180 g) shredded Chinese cabbage

1 cup (6 oz/185 g) baby corn, halved lengthwise

1 medium red bell pepper (capsicum), seeded and sliced into thin strips

2 tablespoons ketjap manis (sweet soy sauce), plus extra for serving

1 tablespoon soy sauce

2 medium eggs, beaten

2 scallions (shallots/spring onions), finely sliced on an angle

Place noodles into a large pot of boiling, salted water, return to a boil and cook until tender, about 4 minutes. Drain and rinse in cold water. Set aside.

Heat oil in a large frying pan or wok over medium–high heat. Add garlic and onion, and stir-fry until they begin to color, about 2 minutes. Increase heat and add celery, cabbage, corn and bell pepper and continue cooking until vegetables soften, about 4 minutes. Add noodles and both types of soy sauce and stir well to combine. Add beaten eggs and fold gently so eggs just cook, about 1 minute.

Transfer to individual bowls. Sprinkle with scallions. Serve with extra ketjap manis.

Hints: Top each serving with a single fried egg. Alternatively, finely slice 1 thin omelette (see page 26) and sprinkle over each bowl.

Naan

Makes 8 naan

1 oz (30 g) compressed fresh yeast, crumbled

3 teaspoons sugar

1/2 cup (4 fl oz/125 ml) warm water

3 1/2 cups (17 1/2 oz/535 g) all-purpose (plain) flour

1/4 cup (2 oz/60 g) plain (natural) yogurt, plus extra 1/2 cup (4 oz/125 g)

1/2 teaspoon ground cumin

1 egg, beaten

2 oz (60 g) ghee, melted

2 teaspoons sea salt

2 tablespoons black cumin seeds

In a small bowl, combine yeast, 1 teaspoon of sugar, 1/4 cup (2 fl oz/60 ml) warm water and 1/2 cup (2 1/2 oz/75 g) flour. Cover and let stand until foamy, about 10 minutes.

Sift remaining 3 cups (15 oz/470 g) flour and 2 teaspoons sugar into a large bowl. Make a well in center and pour in yeast mixture, yogurt, remaining 1/4 cup warm water, cumin, egg, ghee and salt. Stir until combined. Turn out onto a floured board and knead until smooth and elastic, about 7 minutes. Put dough in a lightly oiled bowl and turn to coat. Cover with a damp tea towel and let rise in a warm place until doubled in bulk, about 45 minutes.

Preheat oven to 400°F (200°C/Gas 6). Line 2 baking sheets with parchment (baking) paper.

Punch down dough, turn out onto a floured board and knead until smooth, 6–8 minutes. Divide into 8 pieces and form into balls. Cover and let rest for 5 minutes. Roll each ball into a 6-inch (15-cm) round. Spread each round with 1 tablespoon yogurt and sprinkle with cumin seeds. Place on prepared baking sheets and bake until golden and crisp, 12–15 minutes. Serve warm.

Hint: This naan bread recipe is a traditional Indian favorite. Serve warm with curries as part of an Indian meal.

Nasi goreng

Serves 4–6

3 teaspoons grated fresh ginger

1 teaspoon ground turmeric

1 teaspoon shrimp paste

2 teaspoons chili sauce

3 tablespoons peanut oil

1 onion, chopped

3 cloves garlic, finely chopped

1/2 red bell pepper (capsicum), seeded and chopped

1 stalk celery, chopped

1 carrot, peeled and chopped

1/2 cup (2 1/2 oz/75 g) thawed frozen peas

4 oz (125 g) Chinese barbecue pork, chopped

1 cup (4 oz/125 g) fresh bean sprouts, rinsed

1 cup (3 oz/90 g) shredded bok choy

4 cups (20 oz/625 g) cold cooked jasmine rice

4 oz (125 g) cooked shrimp (prawns), peeled and deveined, tails intact

1/4 cup (2 fl oz/60 ml) coconut milk (see page 24)

2 tablespoons light soy sauce

Combine ginger, turmeric, shrimp paste and chili sauce in small bowl. Mix to form paste. Set aside.

In a wok over medium–high heat, warm peanut oil. Add onion and garlic and stir-fry until onion softens, about 1 minute. Stir in spice paste, bell pepper, celery, carrot, peas, pork, bean sprouts and bok choy. Raise heat to high and stir-fry until vegetables soften slightly, 3–4 minutes. Add rice and shrimp and stir-fry until rice is heated through, about 3 minutes. Combine coconut milk and soy sauce, add to wok and stir until evenly combined and mixture is hot.

Spoon into individual bowls. Serve hot as main course or as accompaniment to other stir-fried dishes.

Paratha (Indian flaky flat bread)

Makes 24 paratha

5 1/3 cups (26 oz/800 g) all-purpose (plain) flour, plus flour for dusting

1 1/3 cups (6 1/2 oz/200 g) whole wheat (wholemeal) flour

1/4 teaspoon baking soda

a pinch cream of tartar

2 teaspoons sugar

1 1/2 teaspoons salt

1 teaspoon nigella seeds

1 egg

6 tablespoons vegetable oil

1 3/4 cups (14 fl oz/440 ml) buttermilk

about 1/3 cup (3 fl oz/90 ml) water

2 oz (60 g) melted unsalted butter, for brushing

Sift flours, baking soda and cream of tartar into a large mixing bowl. Stir in sugar, salt and nigella seeds. Make a well in center.

In a small bowl, whisk together egg and oil; add to well. Using a wooden spoon or fingers, gradually mix flour into egg mixture, adding buttermilk and enough water to form a soft dough. Knead dough for 10 minutes. Cover with a damp clean kitchen towel and set aside for 15 minutes. Knead for 5 minutes, then cover and set aside for 10 minutes.

Knead dough for 1 minute, then divide evenly into 24 portions. Roll each portion into a ball, dust lightly with flour and cover with a clean kitchen towel.

Roll out each ball on a lightly floured work surface into a disk 7 inches (18 cm) in diameter. Brush lightly with melted butter and dust very lightly with flour. Fold in half. Brush with butter and dust with flour, and fold in half again. Dust lightly with flour, set aside in a single layer and cover with a clean kitchen towel while rolling remaining balls. Roll out each folded portion of dough into a triangle shape about 1/8 -inch (3-mm) thick.

Heat a tawa or heavy griddle over medium heat. Place a triangle of dough on surface and cook, lightly pressing all over with a dry clean kitchen towel, or metal spatula until browned, 2–3 minutes. Turn and cook on second side, and lightly brush cooked side with butter. Turn again and cook on first side for 30 seconds, lightly brushing exposed side with butter. Turn again and cook for 30 seconds on second side.

Note: Paratha can be rolled about 30 minutes before cooking. Keep covered at room temperature.

Phad Thai noodles

Serves 4–6

6 oz (180 g) dried rice noodles

3 tablespoons vegetable oil

3 oz (90 g) firm tofu, rinsed and patted
  dry, cut into small cubes

2 large cloves garlic, finely chopped

1 tablespoon dried shrimp

1/3 cup (3 fl oz/90 ml) chicken stock
  (see page 588) or water

3 tablespoons fish sauce

1 tablespoon soy sauce

1–2 tablespoons tamarind concentrate,
  to taste

2–3 tablespoons granulated (white)
  sugar, to taste

2 eggs, beaten

3 tablespoons chopped roasted peanuts

1 small bunch Chinese (flat/garlic)
  chives, or regular chives, cut into
  1-inch (2.5-cm) pieces

1 cup (2 oz/60 g) bean sprouts

2 limes, cut into wedges

Soak noodles in cold water for about 10 minutes to soften; drain and set aside.

Heat oil in a wok or large, heavy frying pan over high heat. Add tofu, garlic and dried shrimp and stir-fry until garlic begins to brown, about 1 minute. Add noodles and stir-fry carefully, so as not to break them. Add stock and continue cooking for 2–3 minutes, or until noodles are tender. Reduce heat to medium and add fish sauce, soy sauce, tamarind concentrate and sugar. Cook until mixture sputters, then add eggs and stir-fry constantly until eggs are cooked and dry, about 1–2 minutes. Add peanuts, chives and bean sprouts, and stir to mix.

Transfer to a serving dish and serve, garnished with lime wedges.

Hints: Phad Thai is a popular Thai dish found in all parts of the kingdom. The noodles used here are about the thickness of a bean sprout. You can substitute 14 oz (400 g) fresh rice noodles, but do not pre-soak.

For a striking presentation, fry a thin, flat omelette in a nonstick pan, and fold this over the fried noodle mixture. Make a small incision at the top to expose the contents, then serve.

Poori (Indian puffed fried bread)

Makes 50 poori; serves about 10

5 cups (1¹/₂ lb/750 g) whole wheat (wholemeal) flour
1 teaspoon salt
5 tablespoons vegetable oil
2 cups (16 fl oz/500 ml) water
8 cups (64 fl oz/2 L) vegetable oil, for deep-frying

Sift flour and salt into a large bowl. Make a well in center. Add oil and water and mix with your hands to form a firm dough. Knead dough on a lightly floured work surface until it almost springs back when touched lightly, about 10 minutes. Cover with a damp clean kitchen towel and set aside for 20 minutes.

Turn out dough onto a floured work surface and knead lightly. Divide evenly into 50 portions. Roll each portion into a ball, then roll out into a disk 4–6 inches (10–15 cm) in diameter. Lightly dust each disk with flour. Set disks on a baking sheet, partially overlapping them.

In large saucepan, heat oil over medium heat to 375°F (190°C) on a deep-frying thermometer. Carefully slide a disk into oil and keep submerged with a slotted spoon until disk puffs well, rises to surface of oil and is golden brown underneath, 30–60 seconds. Gently turn disk, without piercing surface, and cook second side until golden brown. Remove to paper towels to drain. Repeat with remaining disks.

Note: *Poori are best cooked just before serving but dough can be rolled several hours in advance. Dust with flour and cover with a damp kitchen towel to keep moist.*

Red bean porridge with rice balls

Serves 4–5

1 cup (7 oz/220 g) dried red beans
1 cup (8 oz/250 g) medium-grain rice, soaked for about 30 minutes, then drained
table salt to taste (optional)
sugar to taste (optional)

FOR RICE BALLS
1 cup (7 oz/220 g) sticky rice powder
2 tablespoons hot water
pinch table salt

Wash red beans, then drain. Bring a medium-sized saucepan of water to a boil, add red beans and cook until soft, about 30 minutes. Drain beans, reserving water, and mash with a fork or potato masher. Press through a fine sieve into a medium-sized bowl, diluting mashed bean mixture from time to time with 5 cups (40 fl oz/1.25 L) water to help it through the sieve and separate bean skin from flesh. Discard bean skins from sieve.

Add reserved bean water to bean puree. This creates a two-layered effect, with heavy bean mixture on the bottom and water on top.

Carefully pour bean water into a medium-sized saucepan, add soaked rice and bring to a boil. Reduce to a simmer and cook, covered, until soft, about 20 minutes. Add bean paste and cook uncovered, for 10–15 minutes longer, stirring occasionally with a wooden spoon.

To make rice balls: Combine sticky rice powder, hot water and pinch of salt in a small bowl. Using your hands, form mixture into marble-sized balls. Bring a medium-sized saucepan of water to a boil. Add rice balls and cook until they rise to the surface, 1–2 minutes. Remove from saucepan and wash in cold water.

Add rice balls to the bean and rice mixture and bring to a boil to heat through.

Serve porridge hot in bowls, sprinkled with salt and sugar to taste.

Note: This traditional Korean porridge is known as "patjuk."

Soba noodles with tempura

5 oz (150 g) dried soba noodles
2 cups (16 fl oz/500 ml) water
$^1/_4$ cup (2 fl oz/60 ml) soy sauce
$^1/_4$ cup (2 fl oz/60 ml) mirin
1 teaspoon instant dashi

FOR TEMPURA
1 egg
1 cup (8 fl oz/250 ml) ice water
$1^1/_3$ cup (5 oz/150 g) tempura flour
vegetable oil, for deep-frying
$^1/_2$ cup ($2^1/_2$ oz/75 g) all-purpose (plain) flour
4 raw jumbo shrimp (green king prawns), shells removed, tails left intact, deveined
4 green beans, trimmed
2 slices of bell pepper (capsicum)

2 pinches shredded nori, for garnish

Bring a saucepan of water to a boil. Add soba noodles and stir to keep them from sticking together until water returns to a boil. Reduce heat slightly and gently boil noodles until cooked, about 5 minutes (taste noodles to check if cooked). Drain and rinse in cold water to stop cooking process.

Place water, soy sauce, mirin and dashi in a saucepan and bring to a boil. Remove from heat.

Make tempura following instructions for tempura shrimp (see page 307) and tempura vegetables (see page 428), draining them well on paper towels.

Reheat noodles by dipping in boiling water for 1 minute. Place noodles in 2 bowls and pour hot stock over. Arrange tempura vegetables and shrimp on top of noodles. Garnish with shredded nori.

Spiced garlic rice

3 tablespoons vegetable oil

4 cloves garlic, finely chopped

3 bay leaves

2 teaspoons cumin seeds

1$^1/_2$ cups (11 oz/330 g) basmati rice

2$^1/_2$ cups (20 fl oz/625 ml) water

In a wok or large, heavy saucepan, heat oil over medium heat and fry garlic until fragrant but not browned, about 1 minute. Add bay leaves and cumin seeds and cook for 1 minute. Add rice and stir-fry until rice is opaque, about 2 minutes. Add water, stir, cover, and bring to a boil. Reduce heat to low, and cook, stirring occasionally, until rice is tender, 10–15 minutes. Let stand, covered, for 5 minutes. Remove bay leaves. Serve as an accompaniment to curries.

Steamed savory sticky rice in banana leaves

1 cup (7 oz/220 g) white or black
   glutinous (sticky) rice, soaked
   overnight in water
pinch salt
1 cup (8 fl oz/250 ml) thin coconut
   cream (see page 24), or half thick
   coconut cream and half water

2 kaffir lime leaves, finely sliced
2 tablespoons crispy fried shallots
   (French shallots) (see page 24)
banana leaves, cut into four 6-inch
   (15-cm) squares, rinsed
4 pieces pandan leaves or string,
   for tying

Drain rice after soaking. Mix with salt, coconut cream and kaffir lime leaves. Pour into a heatproof bowl and cover tightly. Steam over boiling water until liquid has evaporated, about 1 hour.

Steam banana leaves to soften and prevent splitting, about 2 minutes. Divide rice into 4 portions and place 1 portion onto each banana leaf square. Top rice with fried shallots and carefully wrap in leaf. Secure with thin strips of pandan leaf or string.

To reheat, steam for 15 minutes. Serve warm with vegetables or curry, or cold as a snack.

Stir-fried egg noodles with bell peppers and mushrooms

Serves 4

5 oz (150 g) fresh egg noodles

6 Chinese dried mushrooms

1 tablespoon vegetable oil

1 teaspoon Asian sesame oil

1 red bell pepper (capsicum), seeded and sliced

1 yellow bell pepper (capsicum), seeded and sliced

1 cup (4 oz/125 g) fresh bean sprouts, rinsed

4 oz (125 g) fresh shiitake mushrooms, sliced

4 oz (125 g) fresh oyster mushrooms, sliced if large

1/4 cup (2 fl oz/60 ml) Thai sweet chili sauce

1 tablespoon light soy sauce

1/4 cup (1/4 oz/7 g) fresh cilantro (fresh coriander) leaves

Bring a saucepan of water to a boil. Add noodles and cook until tender, about 3 minutes. Drain and set aside.

Place dried mushrooms in a small bowl, add boiling water to cover and allow to stand until softened, 10–15 minutes. Drain and squeeze out excess liquid. Thinly slice mushrooms, discarding thick stems.

In a wok, over medium heat, warm vegetable oil and sesame oil. Add bell peppers, bean sprouts and fresh mushrooms and stir-fry until slightly softened, 1–2 minutes. Add noodles, mushrooms and chili and soy sauces and stir-fry until heated through, 2–3 minutes.

Serve hot, garnished with cilantro leaves.

Variation: Add sliced Chinese barbecue pork or cooked chicken or shrimp (prawns), or pieces of fried tofu.

Thai-style fried cellophane noodles

Serves 4–6

6 oz (180 g) cellophane (bean thread) noodles

$1/4$ cup (2 fl oz/60 ml) vegetable oil

3 eggs, beaten

1 onion, cut into wedges

3 firm tomatoes, cut into 4 or 8 wedges

3 cloves pickled garlic, coarsely chopped

2 tablespoons fish sauce

3 tablespoons oyster sauce

1 teaspoon granulated (white) sugar

$1/2$ teaspoon ground white pepper

2 shallots (scallions/spring onions), finely chopped

Soak noodles in cold water for at least 15 minutes, to soften. Drain and cut coarsely with scissors into 6-inch (15-cm) lengths.

Heat half the oil (2 tablespoons) in a wok or large, heavy frying pan over medium–high heat. Add eggs and stir-fry until cooked and dry, 1–2 minutes. Remove with a slotted spoon and reserve. Add remaining 2 tablespoons oil to the wok. Add noodles and stir-fry while adding onion, tomatoes and pickled garlic. Stir-fry for 1 minute to heat through, then add fish sauce, oyster sauce, sugar and white pepper and stir until well combined. Add half of scallions and eggs, stir to combine and remove from heat.

Transfer to a serving dish, sprinkle with remaining half of scallions and serve.

Hint: *This is a traditional Thai recipe for cellophane noodles. If desired, noodles can be soaked several hours in advance, and left in the water until ready to cook.*

Thai cellophane noodle salad

Serves 4–6

4 oz (125 g) cellophane (bean thread) noodles

2 cups (16 fl oz/500 ml) coconut milk (see page 24) or water

4 oz (125 g) ground (minced) pork

12 raw jumbo shrimp (green king prawns), shelled and deveined

2–3 tablespoons fish sauce, to taste

2 tablespoons fresh lime juice

5 cloves pickled garlic

1 tablespoon thinly sliced shallots (French shallots), preferably pink

10–20 fresh small red chilies, thinly sliced, to taste

$^1/_2$ cup (2 oz/60 g) coarsely chopped celery, preferably Chinese celery

1 firm tomato, halved and thinly sliced

1 oz (30 g) fresh or dried cloud or tree ear mushrooms (black or white fungus), trimmed and rinsed, soaked if dried (optional)

$^1/_2$ cup ($^3/_4$ oz/20 g) coarsely chopped cilantro (fresh coriander)

Soak noodles in cold water for 10 minutes to soften. (If required, noodles can be prepared several hours in advance, and left in the water until ready to use.) Drain and coarsely cut with scissors into 6-inch (15-cm) lengths.

In a wok or large saucepan over high heat, bring 1 cup (8 fl oz/250 ml) coconut milk to a boil. Add pork, stirring vigorously to break meat apart, and cook for 2 minutes. Drain, reserving $^1/_4$ cup (2 fl oz/60 ml) of the liquid. Set meat aside. In the same wok or saucepan, bring remaining coconut milk to a boil over high heat. Add shrimp and cook, stirring constantly, until evenly pink, about 1 minute. Drain shrimp and set aside.

In a large pot, bring water to a boil, then pour boiling water into a heatproof bowl. Plunge noodles in and soak for 1 minute; drain, then soak in cold water for 1 minute. (Be precise with timing, as noodles must not become water-logged.)

In a large bowl, combine reserved cooking liquid, fish sauce and lime juice. Add garlic, shallots, chilies to taste, celery, tomato and mushrooms (if using). Toss together, then add noodles. Transfer to a serving plate, sprinkle cooked pork and shrimp over, garnish with fresh cilantro and serve immediately.

Thai fried rice with lemongrass

Serves 4–6

¹/₄ cup (2 fl oz/60 ml) vegetable oil

2 eggs, lightly beaten

¹/₃ cup (2 oz/60 g) shelled, raw or cooked shrimp (king prawns), coarsely diced

1 frankfurter, coarsely chopped

2 Chinese sausages (gun chiang), cut into thin rounds

4 cups (20 oz/625 g) cooked long-grain jasmine rice (see page 28)

4 stalks lemongrass, white part only, peeled and very finely chopped

¹/₄ cup (2 fl oz/60 ml) light soy sauce

1 teaspoon granulated (white) sugar

¹/₂ cup (¹/₂ oz/15 g) loosely packed fresh sweet Thai basil leaves, torn

1 lime, quartered

Heat oil in a wok or large, heavy frying pan over high heat. Add eggs and stir-fry until well cooked and dry, about 30 seconds. Add raw shrimp (if using), and both varieties of sausages, and stir-fry for 1 minute.

Add rice and stir-fry until well mixed and heated through, about 2 minutes. Add lemongrass, soy sauce, sugar and cooked shrimp (if using).

Stir to combine, and remove from heat. Sprinkle with basil and squeeze over fresh lime juice. Transfer to a platter and serve.

Hint: If desired, accompany with shredded green mango, thinly sliced shallot (French shallot) and sliced chilies.

Thai fried rice with pineapple

Serves 4–6

¹/₄ cup (2 fl oz/60 ml) vegetable oil

2 Chinese sausages (gun chiang), cut into small rounds

2 tablespoons butter

¹/₂ teaspoon curry powder

3 cups (15 oz/470 g) cooked long-grain jasmine rice (see page 28)

1 small onion, coarsely chopped

3 shallots (scallions/spring onions), chopped

1 firm tomato, coarsely chopped

¹/₂ cup (3 oz/90 g) raisins (sultanas)

¹/₂ cup (3 oz/90 g) coarsely chopped fresh pineapple pieces, or canned in water,
   and drained

1 teaspoon granulated (white) sugar

2 tablespoons soy sauce

Heat oil in a wok or large, heavy frying pan over medium–high heat and fry the sausages for 1 minute. Using a slotted spoon, transfer to paper towels to drain.

Add butter and curry powder to wok and fry, stirring constantly, until fragrant, about 1 minute. Stir in cooked rice until well coated. Add sausages, onion, shallots, tomato, raisins and pineapple. Stir-fry for about 4 minutes, then add sugar and soy sauce.

Hint: For an impressive presentation, place a pineapple on its side on a cutting board and slice in half or slice off the top third lengthwise. Scoop the flesh from the bottom half or two-thirds to make a cavity. Set aside ¹/₄ cup (3 oz/90 g) pineapple for the recipe, and save the rest for another use. Spoon the fried rice into the hollowed-out pineapple, cover with the "lid," and serve.

Udon noodle hot pot

Serves 2

5 oz (150 g) dried udon noodles
2 cups (16 fl oz/500 ml) water
1/4 cup (2 fl oz/60 ml) soy sauce
1/4 cup (2 fl oz/60 ml) mirin
1 teaspoon instant dashi
6 snow peas (mange-tout)
6 slices cooked chicken breast
4 mitsuba leaves
2 bok choy leaves, cut into 1 inch (2.5 cm) lengths
2 eggs
1 scallion (shallot/spring onion), thinly sliced

Bring a saucepan of water to a boil. Add noodles and stir to keep them from sticking together until water returns to boil. Reduce heat slightly and gently boil noodles until cooked, about 10 minutes. Drain and rinse in cold water to stop cooking process.

Place water, soy sauce, mirin and dashi in a saucepan and bring to a boil. Remove from heat.

Divide noodles between 2 pots, add stock and bring to a boil. Divide snow peas, chicken, mitsuba leaves and bok choy between pots and bring each to a boil. To prevent eggs from breaking when they are added to pot, first break each egg into a bowl, then gently slide into simmering stock. Cover and simmer until egg is cooked, 3–4 minutes. Do not overcook; the yolk should still be soft.

Remove pots from heat, sprinkle with scallion slices and serve.

Vietnamese steamed rice in lotus parcels

25 dried black mushrooms

$^1/_4$ cup (1$^1/_2$ oz/45 g) dried lotus seeds (optional)

3 tablespoons vegetable oil

2 cups (10 oz/300 g) diced cooked chicken meat, firmly packed

2 teaspoons salt

1 teaspoon ground pepper

4 cups (18 oz/550 g) steamed rice (see page 28), cooled

2–3 scallions (shallots/spring onions), including green parts, coarsely chopped

2 tablespoons fish sauce

1–2 large fresh or dried lotus leaves

Soak mushrooms in hot water for 20 minutes, then drain, squeezing to remove all liquid. Use scissors or a small knife to cut tough stems; discard. Cut mushroom caps into small dice and set aside. If using dried lotus seed, soak in warm water for 20 minutes, then use a toothpick inserted from end to end to remove any bitter green sprouts. Cook lotus seed in gently boiling water until tender, about 20 minutes; drain and set aside.

In a wok or large frying pan, heat 2 tablespoons oil over medium–high heat. Add mushroom, chicken and lotus seed, if using, and stir-fry for 5 minutes. Season with salt and pepper and transfer to bowl. In same wok or pan, heat remaining 1 tablespoon oil over medium–high heat and stir-fry rice and scallions for 5 minutes. Season with fish sauce. Add chicken and mushrooms and mix well.

If using a dried lotus leaf, cover it with boiling water to soften, then drain. (Water will become brown and somewhat murky.) Fresh leaves should be wiped clean. Spread out leaf and pile rice mixture in middle. Press lightly to compact into a 10 x 7-inch (25 x 18-cm) mound, 2–3 inches (5–7 cm) high. Leave a 5-inch (13-cm) clearance on all sides. Fold two sides of leaf over each other as if folding an envelope, leaving narrow ends still exposed. Fold one narrow end over, then hold packet upright. Lightly press to compress rice, then fold remaining end over to enclose firmly. Tie packet securely both crosswise and lengthwise with coarse kitchen string. (Recipe can be prepared to this point up to 1 hour ahead, or 3–4 hours if refrigerated.)

Place parcel in a steamer over rapidly boiling water. Cover and steam until heated throughout, about 5 minutes. (Refrigerated parcels will require 15–20 minutes of steaming.) Carefully remove from steamer. To serve, use scissors to cut open parcel, rolling back lotus leaf for a decorative appearance.

Desserts

While desserts as we know them aren't customary in Asia, the people there do love their sweets. In fact, these are enjoyed at any time of day, much like a snack or drink, both at home and at the street stalls and markets. From the most delicate of puddings and icy sorbets to the classic Chinese custard tart and comforting sticky rice or dumplings in syrup, Asian sweets are enormously varied— and also the perfect way to finish an Asian-style meal.

In essence, fruits are the true Asian dessert. Since ancient times when fruit was a rarity, its season celebrated, the Asians have revered their fruit. The coconut reigns in many regions, such as Thailand and the south of India, while in China, Korea and Japan the stonefruits are held in high esteem. Of course, a myriad of fruit abounds in the Southeast tropical climes, where the mango, papaya and pineapple are everyday fare.

Traditionally, fruits in Asia are enjoyed in their natural or near-natural states—simply sliced, served and savored—after meals or as snacks, but in response to modern palates, they are also now frequently found in Asian cakes, ice creams and other desserts.

Rice, not surprisingly, also makes an appearance in desserts—in puddings and slices as well as the ultra-modern sweet sushi. Even the noodle transforms into a treat, such as when wontons are crisp-fried and sugar-dusted. Other Asian staples served sweet include beans (especially favored are azuki, black and mung), tapioca starch, agar (made from seaweed), and tofu in all its guises.

Asian-style desserts are characterized by unique flavors such as palm sugar, with its rich aromatic sweetness, and pandan (screwpine) leaves, for which there is no equivalent. Banana leaves, too, add a distinctive but subtle flavor to any food they enfold. Green tea or matcha gives ice cream both color and fragrance, while rosewater, a Middle Eastern influence, is simply divine when paired with yogurt or coconut cream. Of course spices abound in Asian sweets, particularly ginger, cinnamon, saffron and cardamom.

Despite their often exquisite appearance, Asian sweets can be deceptively simple to create. Some of them contain only a few ingredients—typical of the cultures' love of simplicity—while others are more elaborate but still easy to make at home. In fact many Asian sweets are home-made affairs, and are often associated with special occasions such as births, marriages and religious celebrations; others are intended as snacks, to be made in quantities, stored and then consumed at will.

All of the recipes in this chapter can be served as dessert, but they can also be enjoyed in the Asian manner, as snacks, light meals or with coffee or tea. The range also includes sweets that are ideal to serve with dim sum, and refreshing ice creams to soothe the palate after curry. Some of the recipes feature soy, that archetypal Asian ingredient, in place of dairy products. Others are surprisingly low in fat. As well as spanning the great variety of traditional sweets, the recipes here include many modern Asian-style desserts.

Buying and preparing fruit

Fruit is the favored dessert in Asia, and what a cornucopia there is—from papaya to pear and jackfruit to mango, whatever the season, the local markets are brimming with variety. Likewise in the West, good grocers, providores and even supermarkets will stock a fine selection of suitable Asian fruits; some are even grown locally so you can enjoy these exotics in season. In this section, you'll find some of the basic fruit preparation techniques, used in recipes throughout this book as well as in desserts, and also hints for buying and storing fruit. (See also Preparing Ingredients, and Glossary, for descriptions of individual fruits.)

Buying and storing fruit

For the best taste and nutrition, always select fruit in season, preferably grown locally, and if necessary adapt recipes to suit these. Apart from being more expensive, out-of-season fruits can lack flavor. Whole, uncut fruit should be stored at room temperature in a well-ventilated position, away from direct sunlight. If the fruit is becoming overripe, it may be refrigerated to retard ripening, but should be used as soon as possible. Cut fruit should be wrapped in plastic wrap to prevent drying out, then refrigerated, but should also be used as soon as possible.

Many fruits freeze well for use in recipes, but because the texture of frozen fruit, once thawed is quite soft and mushy, it is unsuitable for recipes requiring fresh fruit with a firm texture and attractive shape. To prepare fruit for freezing, peel, pit and chop as needed. Place in a plastic freezer bag, in convenient portions if preferred, and expel as much air as possible from the bag. Seal securely, label and date. Frozen fruit will keep its flavor well for 2–3 months. Once thawed, it should be used immediately. Fruits suitable for freezing include apricot, banana, berries, cherry, grape, mango, melon, nectarine, papaya, passionfruit, peach, persimmon, pineapple and plum.

Cutting mango

1. Cut the flesh from either side of the pit in one piece, running the knife as close to the pit as possible. (The flat pit runs lengthwise through the fruit, roughly through the center third.)

2. Cut each mango piece in half lengthwise, then run the knife between the peel and the flesh to remove as much flesh as possible. Cut any remaining flesh from the pit.

Removing skin from soft fruit

1. Cut a small X in the bottom of each fruit. Place in a heatproof bowl and cover with boiling water. Let stand for about 1 minute. The skin should start to curl away at the X.

2. Drain and rinse under cold running water. When the fruit is cool enough to handle, slip the skin off with your fingers.

Removing pits from dates

1. Cut through each date lengthwise with a small, sharp knife, working the knife around the pit. Pry out the pit with the knife or your fingers.

Removing pits from fruit

1. Cut around the fruit deep enough just to touch the pit with the knife.

2. Gently twist the halves in opposite directions to release them from the pit. Carefully pull out the pit with your fingers or cut out with a small knife.

Coring and quartering pears

1. Peel the pears, then cut lengthwise into quarters.

2. Using a small sharp knife, cut the core from each quarter.

Preparing pineapple

1. To peel, cut both ends off pineapple with a small, sharp knife. Stand pineapple upright and slice downwards to remove the skin, working your way around the fruit.

2. Cut the pineapple lengthwise into quarters, then cut away the core.

Preparing passion fruit

1. Pierce thick skin with the tip of a knife, then slice passion fruit in half. Do not cut the skin with a sawing motion, as the knife could slip.

2. Scoop the pulp out of the skin with a small spoon.

Juicing pomegranates

1. Cut pomegranate in half crosswise. Use a citrus reamer with a shallow bowl to extract and collect the juice, gently crushing membranes and seeds by pressing pomegranate half against the reamer. Watch out for splashing juice, which will stain fabric.

2. If the juice contains bits of seed or white membrane, pass it through a fine-mesh strainer.

Almond jelly with pandan and lychees

Serves 6

3 cups (24 fl oz/750 ml) water
1 cup (5$^{1}/_{2}$ oz/165 g) whole almonds, blanched
2 pandan (screwpine) leaves
$^{1}/_{2}$ cup (4 oz/125 g) grated palm sugar
2 teaspoons agar-agar powder
$^{1}/_{2}$ teaspoon almond extract (essence)
1 mango, peeled and pureed
12 fresh lychees, peeled
watermelon (optional)

Blend 2 cups (16 fl oz/500 ml) water with almonds and set aside for 3 minutes or until smooth. Press almond mixture through a fine sieve to extract as much of the liquid as possible. This is almond milk.

Bring remaining water to a boil. Add pandan leaves, sugar and agar-agar, stirring constantly until agar-agar dissolves. Add almond milk to sugar mixture and stir. Remove and discard pandan. Pour syrup into individual lightly oiled molds or a single large mold about 4 cups (32 fl oz/1 L) in size. Cover and refrigerate until set, about 1 hour. Serve with mango puree and fruit.

Hints: Asian jellies are usually very firm, unlike their Western counterparts. If you prefer a softer texture, reduce the amount of agar-agar powder.

Variation: Substitute 2 kaffir lime leaves for the pandan leaves and vary the fruit served with the jelly.

Apple-ginger soy puddings

$^3/_4$ cup (6 fl oz/180 ml) soy milk

1$^3/_4$ cups (13 oz/400 g) packed brown sugar

2 eggs, lightly beaten

1$^1/_2$ cups (7$^1/_2$ oz/235 g) all-purpose (plain) flour

$^1/_4$ cup (1 oz/30 g) soy flour

1 teaspoon baking soda

2 teaspoons ground cinnamon

1 teaspoon ground ginger

$^3/_4$ teaspoon salt

$^1/_2$ cup (3 oz/90 g) finely chopped glacé ginger

3 apples, unpeeled, cored and grated

Preheat oven to 350°F (180°C/Gas 4).

In a large bowl, combine soy milk, brown sugar and eggs. Stir until smooth.

Sift flours, baking soda, spices and salt together into a medium bowl. Stir dry ingredients into milk mixture. Stir in ginger and apple. Spoon mixture into 8 large teacups or 1-cup (8-fl oz/250-ml) soufflé dishes. Put cups into a baking dish and add enough water to baking dish to come halfway up sides of cups. Bake for 30 minutes. Remove cups from water and return to oven on a baking sheet for 15–20 minutes, until a skewer inserted in center of pudding comes out clean. Served hot or chilled, with vanilla ice cream if desired.

Hint: *You can also steam these puddings instead of baking them. Cover cups or dishes with plastic wrap and cook in a covered steamer over gently boiling water for 45–50 minutes.*

Bananas in coconut milk Thai-style

Serves 4–6

8 unpeeled, small, slightly green, sugar bananas or 4–6 standard-sized bananas
4 cups (32 fl oz/1 L) coconut milk
2 pandan (screwpine) leaves, bruised and tied into a knot, or 2 drops pandan
extract
2 tablespoons palm sugar
1/4 cup (2 oz/60 g) granulated (white) sugar
pinch salt

Cook bananas in a covered steamer over rapidly simmering water until skin begins to break, about 5 minutes. Or cook bananas in a pot of boiling water for about 2 minutes. Remove bananas from heat, let cool slightly, then carefully peel. Cut each banana into quarters: once lengthwise, then across.

Let coconut milk stand, allowing the thick coconut milk to rise to the top. Spoon about 2 cups (16 fl oz/500 ml) thick milk into a bowl to reserve.

In a large saucepan, over medium–high heat, combine thin coconut milk and pandan leaves. Bring to a boil and add banana pieces, both sugars and salt. Add thick coconut milk, bring to a boil, then reduce heat and simmer gently for about 3 minutes. Remove from heat. Serve either hot or cold in individual bowls.

Hints: *Slightly green bananas work best here, as they are less likely to break up during poaching.*

Hard or loaf palm sugar is preferred in this recipe as it contains tapioca starch, which slightly thickens the sauce.

Variation: *In place of bananas, you can use peeled and cubed pumpkin, squash, sweet potato or taro—steam or boil until just tender, then cook as above, until tender.*

Banana tempura

1 egg
1 cup (8 fl oz/250 ml) ice water
1 1/3 cup (7 oz/220 g) tempura flour
vegetable oil, for deep-frying
4 bananas, sliced in half lengthwise
1/2 cup (2 1/2 oz/75 g) all-purpose (plain) flour
2 tablespoons superfine (caster) sugar
4 scoops vanilla ice cream

In a bowl, beat egg lightly. Add water and continue to beat lightly. Mix in tempura flour; do not overmix. Batter should be slightly lumpy.

Pour oil into a deep, heavy-bottomed frying pan to a depth of 3 inches (7.5 cm). Heat oil until it reaches 375°F (190°C) on a deep-frying thermometer. Working in batches, dredge banana pieces in flour, shaking off excess, then dip in batter, allowing excess to drain away. Carefully slip bananas into hot oil. When batter is beginning to set, use chopsticks to drip a little extra batter on bananas. Cook until bananas are light golden brown, 3–4 minutes. Using a wire skimmer, remove bananas from oil and drain on paper towels.

Arrange 2 pieces banana on each serving plate. Sprinkle lightly with sugar and serve with a scoop of ice cream.

Hint: *This Japanese dessert is a favorite in restaurants worldwide. You can vary the ice cream, but subtle-flavored choices, such as coconut or green tea ice cream, are best.*

Black sticky rice pudding

Serves 4–6

1 cup (7 oz/220 g) black sticky rice
3¹/₂ cups (28 fl oz/850 ml) water
1 cup (8 fl oz/250 ml) coconut cream plus ¹/₄ cup (2 fl oz/60 ml) extra
¹/₄ cup (2 oz/60 g) granulated (white) sugar

In a medium saucepan, over medium–high heat, combine rice and water and bring to a boil. Reduce heat to a simmer and cook until tender, about 30 minutes, stirring occasionally at the beginning and frequently towards the end. Add additional water if necessary.

Once the rice is just tender, and the grains begin to open, add 1 cup (8 fl oz/250 ml) coconut cream and sugar. Stir well, and cook for a few minutes more. Remove from heat.

To serve, spoon pudding into individual bowls and drizzle with extra ¹/₄ cup (2 fl oz/60 ml) coconut cream.

Note: This Thai recipe can be served hot, at room temperature, or chilled, but it is best when eaten on the day it is made.

Hint: This pudding can be served with fresh tropical fruit, peeled and sliced, or sprinkled with fresh grated coconut.

Broiled pineapple with tamarind-chili syrup

Serves 4

TAMARIND-CHILI SYRUP
1/2 cup (2 oz/60 g) grated palm sugar
1/2 cup (4 fl oz/125 ml) water
2 tablespoons unsalted tamarind pulp
1 small red chili, halved

1 whole pineapple, about 2 lb (1 kg), peeled
8 bamboo skewers, soaked in cold water for 30 minutes
4 banana leaves (optional)
1/4 cup (2 fl oz/60 ml) thick coconut cream (see page 24)

To make tamarind-chili syrup: Put palm sugar and water in a small pot and bring to a boil. Reduce heat to simmer and cook, uncovered, for 2 minutes. Add tamarind and chili and simmer for 3 minutes more, breaking up tamarind with the back of a wooden spoon. Press mixture through a sieve and set aside.

Cut pineapple lengthwise into 8 wedges; retain core if the pineapple is young and tender, otherwise remove. Thread each pineapple piece, lengthwise through wedge, onto a prepared skewer. Coat pineapple well with tamarind-chili syrup. Broil (grill) pineapple until golden, about 2 minutes on each side.

Lay banana leaves, if using, on a serving platter or individual plates and place skewers on top. Drizzle coconut cream over pineapple or serve in individiual dipping bowls on the side.

Hints: *Try this recipe with other firm fruit, such as banana or mango. You could also use lemongrass sticks as skewers.*

Add ice and club soda to the tamarind-chili syrup for a refreshing drink.

Carrot and cardamom milk pudding

2 lb (1 kg) carrots, about 9 medium, peeled and grated

8 cups (64 fl oz/2 L) whole (full cream) milk

3 tablespoons green cardamom pods

6–8 saffron threads

1/2 cup (4 fl oz/125 ml) whole (full cream) milk, heated

1/2 cup (2 oz/60 g) sliced (flaked) almonds

1/2 cup (2 oz/60 g) pistachio nuts, sliced

1 cup (8 oz/250 g) sugar

1/3 cup (2 oz/60 g) raisins

2/3 cup (5 oz/150 g) ghee or unsalted butter

Preheat oven to 350°F (180°C/Gas 4). In a large, heavy saucepan over medium–high heat, combine carrots and 8 cups milk and bring to a boil. Reduce heat to medium and cook, uncovered, stirring often, until most of milk is absorbed and carrots are soft, about 1 1/4 hours. While carrots are cooking, grind cardamom to a powder in a spice grinder. Set aside.

In a bowl, combine saffron and hot milk and set aside for 10 minutes.

Spread almonds and pistachios on a baking sheet and toast in oven, stirring nuts occasionally, 6–8 minutes. Remove from oven and let cool.

Add cardamom, saffron mixture, sugar and raisins to carrot mixture and cook, stirring, until sugar dissolves. Simmer, uncovered, stirring often, until all liquid is absorbed, about 45 minutes.

Add ghee or butter, a spoonful at a time, stirring until combined. Cook, stirring often, until pudding begins to pull away from sides of pan, 10–15 minutes. Stir in three-quarters of nuts. Spoon into bowls and sprinkle with remaining nuts. Serve warm.

Hint: *This is a traditional Indian pudding. You can spread the pudding mixture evenly in a shallow 8-inch (20-cm) square baking pan lined with plastic wrap. Refrigerate until cold. Use plastic wrap to lift pudding from pan. Cut pudding into individual portions to serve.*

Chinese custard tarts

FOR PASTRY

3 cups (12 oz/375 g) all-purpose (plain) flour

6 oz (180 g) lard

5 tablespoons hot water

FOR FILLING

3 eggs, beaten

$^1/_3$ cup (2 oz/60 g) superfine (caster) sugar

1$^1/_2$ cups (12 fl oz/375 ml) milk

yellow food coloring (optional)

Preheat oven to 425°F (220°C/Gas 7).

To make pastry: Sift flour into a bowl. Using your fingertips, rub lard into flour, until mixture resembles coarse breadcrumbs. Add hot water and mix to form a firm dough. Turn dough out onto a floured work surface and knead until smooth. Roll out between 2 sheets of parchment (baking) paper to $^1/_8$ inch (3 mm) thick. Using a 3-inch (8-cm) round cutter, cut dough into 24 rounds. Line greased tart (patty) pans with dough.

To make filling: Beat eggs, sugar, milk and a few drops of food coloring, if using, together until smooth. Pour into prepared pastry in tart (patty) pans. Bake for 10 minutes.

Reduce oven temperature to 400°F (200°C/Gas 6) and bake until custard is set, 10–15 minutes. Remove from oven and allow to stand for 10 minutes before transferring to a wire rack to cool. Serve cold or chilled.

Note: These custard tarts are a dim sum favorite.

Coconut milk and rosewater sorbet

Serves 4

6 oz (180 g) dried coconut powder
1/4 cup (2 oz/60 g) superfine (caster) sugar
1/4 cup (2 oz/60 g) grated palm sugar
1 1/2 cups (12 fl oz/375 ml) water
1/4 cup (2 fl oz/60 ml) rosewater
edible rose petals, for garnish
toasted coconut, for serving (optional)

In a saucepan, combine coconut powder and sugars. Whisk in water. Bring to a boil, stirring occasionally. Watch it carefully, because it will quickly boil over. Immediately remove from heat and add rosewater. Refrigerate for 30 minutes, or until chilled.

Churn mixture in an ice cream machine according to the manufacturer's instructions. Alternatively, pour mixture into a plastic container, cover and freeze until solid; periodically whisk the partially frozen sorbet to break up ice crystals and obtain a smoother result.

When completely frozen, serve in chilled glasses or bowls scattered with rose petals and toasted coconut, if using.

Variation: *To make coconut milk and mango sorbet, replace rosewater with 4 tablespoons fresh mango puree and proceed as above. Garnish sorbet with fresh mango slices.*

Coconut rice bars

Makes 16 pieces

2¹/₂ cups (17¹/₂ oz/535 g) glutinous (sticky) rice
2¹/₄ cups (18 fl oz/560 ml) coconut milk
¹/₂ cup (3¹/₂ oz/105 g) superfine (caster) sugar

TOPPING
1¹/₄ cups (5 oz/150 g) unsweetened dried (desiccated) coconut
¹/₄ cup (2 fl oz/60 ml) coconut milk, warmed
3 oz (90 g) grated palm sugar or brown sugar
3 tablespoons water

Place rice in a large bowl, cover with cold water and let stand overnight. Line a large bamboo steamer with parchment (baking) paper and spread drained rice on top. Cover steamer.

Half fill a medium wok with water (steamer should not touch water) and bring to a boil. Place steamer over boiling water and steam rice until tender, about 45 minutes, adding more boiling water to wok when necessary.

Place steamed rice into a medium, heavy-bottomed saucepan. Add coconut milk and sugar. Stir over low heat until the coconut milk has been absorbed, about 10 minutes. Evenly spread rice into a shallow baking pan, about 7¹/₂ x 11 inches (19 x 28 cm) in size, lined with parchment (baking) paper. Refrigerate until firm, about 2 hours.

To make topping: Combine coconut and coconut milk. Place palm sugar and water in a small saucepan and stir over low heat until mixture thickens slightly, 3–4 minutes. Pour into coconut and milk mixture and stir until well combined. Allow to cool to room temperature.

Spread topping over rice and refrigerate for 1 hour. Cut into small squares to serve.

Cream and berry wonton stack

Serves 4

vegetable oil, for deep-frying

8 wonton wrappers

8 oz (250 g) ricotta cheese

1/2 cup (4 fl oz/125 ml) heavy (double) cream

4 tablespoons confectioners' (icing) sugar, sifted

2 teaspoons Grand Marnier

1 teaspoon grated orange zest

5 oz (150 g) fresh raspberries

5 oz (150 g) fresh strawberries, hulled (stemmed) and sliced

3 oz (90 g) fresh blueberries

Heat oil in a wok or frying pan until it reaches 375°F (190°C) on a deep-frying thermometer or until a small bread cube dropped in oil sizzles and turns golden. Working in batches, add wonton wrappers and fry until golden on both sides, about 1 minute. Using slotted spoon, remove from pan and drain on paper towels. Allow to cool.

In a bowl, combine ricotta cheese, cream, 3 tablespoons sugar, Grand Marnier and orange zest. Using an electric mixer beat until light and fluffy, 2–3 minutes. Cover and chill until ready to serve.

In another bowl, combine raspberries, strawberries and blueberries. Cover and chill.

To serve, place one wonton on each plate. Spread with ricotta filling. Spoon berries over filling. Top with second wonton. Dust with some of remaining sugar.

Variation: To make fruit wontons, wrap a slice of a fresh fruit, such as apple, pear or pineapple, in a wonton wrapper. Seal with egg white and deep-fry until golden, about 2 minutes. Serve immediately with cream, ice cream or simply sprinkled with confectioners' (icing) sugar.

Date and walnut wontons

Makes 24 wontons

6¹/₂ oz (200 g) dates, pitted and chopped
¹/₂ cup (2 oz/60 g) walnuts, chopped
6¹/₂ oz (200 g) fresh or canned lychees, pitted and chopped
1 tablespoon grated orange zest
24 wonton wrappers
1 egg, beaten
vegetable oil, for deep-frying
2 tablespoons confectioners' (icing) sugar, sifted

In a bowl, combine dates, walnuts, lychees and orange zest. Mix well. Place wonton wrappers on a work surface and cover with a damp kitchen towel. Working with one wrapper at a time, lay on work surface and place 1 teaspoon of filling in center. Brush edges of wonton with egg, gather edges and twist to seal. Repeat with remaining wonton wrappers.

Heat oil in a wok or frying pan until it reaches 375°F (190°C) on a deep-frying thermometer or until a small bread cube dropped in oil sizzles and turns golden. Working in batches if necessary, add wontons and fry until golden, 1–2 minutes. Using a slotted spoon, remove from pan and drain on paper towels. Allow to cool.

Sprinkled with confectioners' sugar and serve.

Hint: You can use fresh or canned lychees in this recipe. If canned, drain well before using.

Indian cottage cheese dumplings in syrup

SYRUP
4 cups (2 lb/1 kg) sugar
4 cups (32 fl oz/1 L) water
1 green cardamom pod, cracked
small pinch saffron threads

DUMPLINGS
2 cups (6 oz/180 g) whole (full cream) powdered milk
1 cup (5 oz/150 g) all-purpose (plain) flour
$1/4$ teaspoon ground cardamom
about 1 cup (8 fl oz/250 ml) heavy (double) cream
6 cups (48 fl oz/1.5 L) vegetable oil

To make syrup: In a large saucepan, combine sugar, water, cardamom pod and saffron. Stir over low heat until sugar dissolves. Keep warm over low heat.

To make dumplings: In a large bowl, combine powdered milk, flour and ground cardamom. Add cream and, using your hands, gradually incorporate flour mixture into cream to form a soft dough, adding a little more cream if dough is a bit dry. Knead lightly in bowl until smooth.

Shape mixture into 20 walnut-sized balls, making sure surface of each ball is very smooth. If necessary, brush balls very lightly with water and smooth over any cracks.

In a large saucepan, heat oil over medium heat to 350°F (180°C) on a deep-frying thermometer. Fry dumplings in four batches in hot oil, gently stirring them occasionally with a large slotted spoon (do not mar surface), until uniformly golden brown, 3–5 minutes. Remove to paper towels to drain for 2 minutes, then add to warm syrup. Soak in syrup for at least 30 minutes. Serve warm.

Note: In the Indian tradition, you should always serve two or more dumplings per person; it is considered rude to offer only one.

Japanese sweet azuki beans

1 cup (7 oz/220 g) dried azuki beans
1 cup (8 oz/250 g) sugar
pinch of salt

Place azuki beans in a bowl, add water to cover and soak overnight. Drain beans and rinse well. Put beans in a heavy-bottomed saucepan and add water to cover. Bring to a boil, then drain. Return to saucepan and add water to cover beans by $3/8$ inch (1 cm). Bring to a boil and simmer, skimming any scum from surface. Continue to simmer until beans are soft, about 30 minutes. Add more water as necessary; do not let beans go dry.

Add sugar, stirring to dissolve, then bring to a boil. Reduce heat to low and simmer, covered, stirring frequently, until beans thicken, at least another 30 minutes. It is very important to stir beans frequently, as sugar can cause mixture to stick to bottom of the pan. Remove from heat, add pinch of salt and stir well. Let cool.

Serve with vanilla ice cream or Matcha-flavored Ice Cream (see page 519).

Kanten and azuki bean dessert

$1/4$ block kanten
$1^{1}/2$ cups (12 fl oz/375 ml) water
scant 1 cup (6 oz/180 g) azuki beans, cooked (see above)
1–$1^{1}/2$ oz (30–45 g) sugar
pinch salt

Separate strands of kanten, place in a bowl with water to cover and soak for 10 minutes. Drain and squeeze dry. Combine kanten and water in a saucepan over medium heat. Stir continuously until kanten is dissolved. Add sugar, stirring until dissolved, then add sweet azuki beans. Simmer, stirring frequently, for 5 minutes. Remove from heat, add salt, then place saucepan in a bowl of cold water, stirring until mixture cools. Pour into 4 small ramekins that have been rinsed with water and refrigerate until set, about 3 hours. Turn out onto plates and serve.

Lemon sushi rice

Makes 4 rolls (56 pieces)

1¹/₂ cups (10 oz/300 g) short-grain rice
1³/₄ cups (14 fl oz/440 ml) water
¹/₄ cup (2 fl oz/60 ml) lemon juice
2 teaspoons sugar
pinch salt
2 teaspoons finely chopped lemon zest
4 sheets nori
selection of fruit such as strawberries, kiwi fruit and papaya

Rinse rice 3 or 4 times until water runs clear. Drain for 15 minutes. In a medium saucepan, bring rice and water to a boil. Reduce heat and simmer, covered, until most of liquid is absorbed, 12–15 minutes. Remove from heat and let stand, covered, to complete the cooking process, 10 minutes longer. Place hot rice in a large flat bowl or dish.

In a separate bowl, combine lemon juice, sugar, salt and zest, stirring until sugar dissolves. Pour juice over hot rice, cutting through rice with a flat spatula or rice paddle to break up any lumps and distribute flavor evenly. Fan rice to cool to room temperature, about 5 minutes.

Place a nori sheet lengthwise on a bamboo mat, about 3 slats from edge closest to you, shiny side down. Cover nori with rice, except a ³/₄-inch (2-cm) strip on long side opposite you.

Using your index finger and thumb, pick up edge of bamboo mat nearest you and roll mat forward tightly. Press gently and continue rolling forward to complete roll. Gently press mat to shape roll. Unroll mat and place roll on cutting board with seam on bottom. Wipe a sharp knife with a damp cloth and cut roll in half. Pick up one half roll and turn it 180 degrees so both cut ends are at the same side. Cut roll into about ¹/₂-inch (1-cm) pieces, wiping knife with each cut, and arrange fruit decoratively on top. Repeat for remaining rolls.

Hint: *Substitute orange or lime for lemon. Or, slice a nashi (pear) thinly and simply top with lemon or coconut rice and more fruit.*

Lime and coconut puddings with lime-ginger syrup

Serves 6

PUDDING

³/₄ cup (6 oz/180 g) butter

¹/₃ cup (3 oz/90 g) superfine (caster) sugar

1 teaspoon grated lime zest

1 teaspoon vanilla extract (essence)

3 eggs

1 cup (5 oz/150 g) self-rising flour, sifted

1 cup (4 oz/125 g) unsweetened dried (desiccated) coconut

LIME-GINGER SYRUP

¹/₂ cup (4 oz/125 g) decorating (crystal) sugar

3 tablespoons lime juice

1 tablespoon shredded lime zest

1 tablespoon shredded fresh ginger

whipped cream, for serving

Butter six ¹/₂ cup (4 fl oz/125 ml) ramekins and line bottoms with parchment (baking) paper. Set aside. To make pudding, place butter, sugar and lime zest in a bowl. Using an electric mixer, beat until light and creamy, 3–4 minutes. Add vanilla. Add eggs, one at a time, beating well after each addition. If mixture begins to curdle, add 1 tablespoon all-purpose (plain) flour. Fold in flour and coconut and mix well.

Spoon pudding into prepared ramekins. Cover each with a piece of buttered parchment (baking) paper. Half fill wok with water (steamer should not touch water) and bring water to a boil. Arrange ramekins in steamer, cover, and place steamer over boiling water. Steam until puddings are firm to touch, 40–45 minutes. Add more water to wok when necessary.

To make lime-ginger syrup: Place sugar, lime juice and zest and ginger in a small saucepan over low heat. Stir until sugar dissolves. Bring to a boil and allow to boil for 2 minutes. Remove from heat.

Slowly pour warm syrup over warm puddings. Serve garnished with whipped cream.

Little coconut cakes

3/4 cup (6 oz/185 g) butter at room temperature

1 cup (7 oz/220 g) superfine (caster) sugar

2 eggs

1 teaspoon vanilla extract (essence)

1 teaspoon almond extract (essence)

1 1/2 cups (7 1/2 oz/235 g) all-purpose (plain) flour

2 teaspoons baking powder

1/2 cup (4 fl oz/125 ml) buttermilk

2 cups (6 oz/185 g) sweetened dried (desiccated) coconut

Preheat oven to 350°F (180°C/Gas 4). Grease or fit paper liners into 12 muffin cups.

In a large bowl, beat butter and sugar until thick and pale in color. Beat in eggs, one at a time. Beat in vanilla and almond extracts. Sift flour and baking powder together onto a sheet of waxed paper. Alternately, stir flour mixture and buttermilk into egg mixture in thirds. Stir in coconut until blended. Fill prepared cups three-quarters full.

Bake for 25–30 minutes, or until cakes are golden and a skewer inserted in the center of one comes out clean. Let cool in pan for 15 minutes, then unmold onto wire racks to cool completely.

Hints: *These little muffin-like cakes are ideal as a snack or to serve with tea or coffee. For dessert, serve them warm with whipped cream or drizzled with syrup such as Lime-ginger Syrup (see opposite).*

Lychee and ginger granita

Serves 4–6

11 oz (330 g) canned lychees in syrup (see Note)
¹/₄ cup (¹/₂ oz/15 g) candied (crystallized) ginger, chopped
²/₃ cup (5 fl oz/150 ml) water
2 teaspoons freshly squeezed lemon or lime juice
mint sprigs, for garnish

Pour lychees and syrup into a food processor. Add ginger, water and lemon juice, then process until coarsely pureed.

Pour into a shallow pan or ice tray and place in freezer. Stir every 15 minutes until mixture freezes.

To serve, use a heavy spoon to scrape granita crystals into a bowl. Garnish with mint sprigs.

Note: *You can use canned or fresh lychees in this Vietnamese recipe. Most canned lychees are already pitted; if not, cut away and discard seed from each fruit before pureeing. If using fresh lychees, remove both peel and pit, and add ¹/₂ cup (4 fl oz/125 ml) sugar syrup (see page 543) to recipe.*

Hints: *Candied ginger comes both crystallized and in syrup; both varieties suit this recipe. If in season, mild-tasting young ginger, with a pale, parchmentlike skin, can replace the candied form; do not use older ginger, with a darker, thicker skin.*

Granita is a sweetened ice, coarser in texture than sherbet (sorbet) or ice cream. If using an ice cream machine, add ¹/₂ egg white to mixture and process as above. The texture will be lighter in both color and texture.

Mango and tofu puddings

Makes 8 individual puddings

12 oz (375 g) firm silken tofu, drained

2 cups (10 oz/300 g) chopped fresh or drained canned mango

2 teaspoons plain gelatin

3 tablespoons fresh lime juice

1 teaspoon honey

2 egg whites

1 tablespoon grated lime zest, for garnish

In a food processor, puree tofu and mango until smooth. In a small bowl, combine gelatin and lime juice. Place bowl over hot water and stir until gelatin dissolves completely. Gradually stir gelatin and honey into tofu mixture.

In a large bowl, beat egg whites until soft peaks form. Gently fold egg whites through tofu mixture, then spoon mixture into eight 4-fl-oz (125-ml) ramekins or cups and refrigerate until set. Garnish with lime zest to serve.

Mango ice cream

Serves 10

1 ripe mango, about 12 oz (375 g), peeled, pitted and coarsely chopped

1 1/2 tablespoons green cardamom pods

1 2/3 cups (13 fl oz/400 ml) sweetened condensed milk

3 cups (24 fl oz/750 ml) heavy (double) cream

In a food processor, puree mango until smooth. Remove to a large bowl. In a spice grinder, grind cardamom to a powder and add to mango. Add condensed milk and cream to mango mixture and stir until well combined; do not beat or whisk. Divide mixture among 10 ramekins with a 1/2-cup (4-fl oz/125-ml) capacity. Place in freezer until frozen, about 6 hours. Cover ramekins well and keep in freezer until serving.

To serve, briefly dip each ramekin in a bowl of hot water. Invert a serving plate on top and invert plate and ramekin to unmold ice cream. Serve immediately, decorated with thin slices of extra ripe mango or other fresh fruit if desired.

Note: This Indian recipe is known as "mango kulfi."

Mango sushi

2 cups (13 oz/400 g) short-grain rice

2¹/₄ cups (10 fl oz/300 ml) water

¹/₃ cup (3 fl oz/90 ml) coconut milk

1 teaspoon sugar

³/₄ teaspoon lime juice

pinch salt

1 small mango, sliced

10 nori strips, about ¹/₂ inch x 3 inches
  (1 cm x 7.5 cm)

¹/₄ teaspoon lime zest or lemon curls
  (see Garnishes page 33)

FOR PASSION FRUIT YOGURT

1 passion fruit

¹/₃ cup (3 oz/90 ml) yogurt

¹/₂ teaspoon honey, or to taste

To make passion fruit yogurt: Remove passion fruit pulp and combine with yogurt and honey.

Rinse rice 3 or 4 times until water runs clear. Drain for 15 minutes. In a medium saucepan or microwave, bring rice and water to a boil. Reduce heat and simmer, covered, until most liquid is absorbed, 12–15 minutes. Remove from heat and let stand, covered, to complete cooking process, 10 minutes longer.

Place hot rice in a large bowl or dish. In a separate bowl, combine coconut milk, sugar, lime juice and salt, stirring until sugar dissolves. Sprinkle milk mixture over rice, cutting through rice with a flat spatula or rice paddle to break up any lumps and distribute flavor evenly. Fan rice to cool to room temperature, about 5 minutes (this can be done with an electric fan on lowest setting).

Gently shape 1¹/₂–2 tablespoons rice mixture into a rectangular log with rounded edges. Place a slice of mango on top so it looks like a roof over rice log, with very little, if any, rice being visible. Lay a nori strip on top of fruit and tuck each end underneath rice log to keep fruit in place. Top each sushi piece with a small amount of passion fruit yogurt. Garnish with lime zest. Alternatively, serve yogurt and lime zest separately, for guests to add to taste.

Matcha-flavored ice cream

Serves 6

4¹/₂ cups (36 fl oz/1.1 L) high-quality vanilla ice cream
1 teaspoon matcha

Soften ice cream slightly, just enough to be able to work in the matcha. Sprinkle matcha over ice cream. Using a large metal spoon, thoroughly incorporate matcha into ice cream. Return ice cream to freezer for about 2 hours.

Hint: *This is a quick and easy recipe for Japanese-style ice cream; it goes very well with Japanese Sweet Azuki Beans (see page 509).*

Matcha ice cream

Serves 4

6 eggs
6¹/₂ oz (200 g) sugar
²/₃ cup (5 fl oz/150 ml) heavy (double) cream
²/₃ cup (5 fl oz/150 ml) milk
1 teaspoon vanilla extract (essence)
1 teaspoon matcha, or to taste

In a bowl, using an electric mixer, beat eggs and sugar until well combined. Beat in cream, then add milk, vanilla and matcha. Add matcha as desired. Place mixture in an ice-cream maker and freeze according to manufacturer's instructions.

Note: *This Japanese ice cream can be made in advance but you must wrap it well to prevent flavors being absorbed from other foods in freezer.*

Miso-baked pears

4 medium pears, skin on
$1/4$ cup (1 oz/30 g) chopped pecans
1 cup (6 oz/180 g) finely chopped
 dates, loosely packed
4 level teaspoons white (shiro) miso
1 teaspoon firmly packed brown sugar

$1/4$ teaspoon grated lemon zest
pinch Chinese five-spice powder
cooking oil spray

Core pears, reserving tops for use as lids. Preheat oven to 350°F (180°C/Gas 4).

In a small bowl, combine pecans, dates, miso, sugar, lemon zest and five-spice powder. Fill cored pears with mixture and cover with reserved tops. Spray a baking dish with cooking oil spray or line it with parchment (baking) paper. Place pears in dish upright and bake, uncovered, until cooked but still crisp, 20–25 minutes. Serve warm or chilled with coconut cream or vanilla ice cream.

Miso figs with tofu cream

8 fresh figs, chilled
2 teaspoons white miso
4 umeboshi (pickled) plums pitted or
 3 teaspoons umeboshi paste
$1^{1}/_{2}$ tablespoons mirin or sweet white
 wine

FOR TOFU CREAM

$6^{1}/_{2}$ oz (200 g) silken tofu, drained
2 tablespoons maple syrup
1 teaspoon vanilla extract (essence)
1 tablespoon fresh lemon juice
pinch salt

To make tofu cream: In a food processor, combine all ingredients and puree until smooth. Set aside.

In a small bowl, combine miso, umeboshi plums and mirin; stir to blend until smooth. Cut figs in half lengthwise and spread miso mixture on each fig half. Place figs on a small baking sheet and broil (grill) until miso mixture bubbles. Arrange 4 fig halves on each plate with tofu cream and serve immediately.

Orange and chocolate spring rolls

7 tablespoons ($3^1/2$ oz/105 g) unsalted butter, softened

$^1/4$ cup (2 oz/60 g) superfine (caster) sugar

2 teaspoons grated orange zest

1 egg

$^1/2$ teaspoon vanilla extract (essence)

$^3/4$ cup ($3^1/2$ oz/105 g) ground almonds

3 tablespoons (1 oz/30 g) all-purpose (plain) flour

4 oz (125 g) semisweet (plain) chocolate, grated

16 frozen spring roll wrappers, about $8^1/2$ inches (21.5 cm) in size, thawed

1 egg white, lightly beaten

3 cups (24 fl oz/750 ml) vegetable or canola oil, for deep-frying

confectioners' (icing) sugar, for dusting

In a medium bowl, beat butter, sugar and zest together until pale and creamy, about 2 minutes. Add egg and vanilla. Mix until combined. Add ground almonds and flour, mixing until smooth. Fold in chocolate. Cover and refrigerate for 20 minutes, or until firm.

Place 1 spring roll wrapper on a work surface, with one end facing you. Brush edges with egg white. Place 1 heaping tablespoonful of chocolate filling 1 inch (2.5 cm) from end of wrapper. Fold end over filling. Fold in sides and roll into a cylinder. Seal seam with egg white. Repeat with remaining wrappers and filling.

In a wok, heat oil to 375°F (190°C) on a deep frying thermometer, or until a small bread cube dropped in oil sizzles and turns golden. Fry spring rolls in batches until golden, about 2 minutes. Using a wire-mesh skimmer, transfer to paper towels to drain.

Serve warm, dusted with confectioners' sugar.

Peach and coconut sushi roll

Makes 4 rolls (24 pieces)

1 1/2 cups (10 oz/300 g) short-grain rice

3/4 cup (6 fl oz/180 ml) water

1 cup (8 fl oz/250 ml) coconut milk

1 tablespoon sugar

2 teaspoons lime juice

pinch salt

1/3 cup finely chopped glacé ginger

1 peach, cut into slices

1/4 teaspoon Japanese soy sauce

2 sheets nori

Rinse rice 3 or 4 times until water runs clear. Drain for 15 minutes. In a medium saucepan, bring rice, water and coconut cream to a boil. Reduce heat and simmer, covered, until most liquid is absorbed, 12–15 minutes. Remove from heat and let stand, covered, to complete cooking process, 10 minutes longer. Place hot rice in a large bowl or dish. In a separate bowl, combine sugar, lime juice and salt, stirring until sugar dissolves. Sprinkle sugar mixture over rice, cutting through rice with a flat spatula or rice paddle. Stir in glacé ginger. Fan rice to cool to room temperature, about 5 minutes (this can be done with an electric fan on lowest setting). Sprinkle peach slices with soy sauce and set aside.

Cut nori in half, parallel with lines marked on rough side. Place a half nori sheet lengthwise on a bamboo mat, above 3 slats from edge nearest you, shiny side down. Cover nori with rice, leaving a 3/4-inch (2-cm) strip on long side farthest away uncovered. Make a small groove in middle of rice with your finger and lay peach slices evenly from end to end.

Using your index finger and thumb, pick up edge of bamboo mat nearest you. Place other fingers over fillings to hold them in place as you roll mat forward, tightly wrapping rice and nori around fillings. Press gently and continue rolling forward to complete roll. Gently press mat to shape roll. Unroll mat and place roll on cutting board with seam on bottom. Wipe a sharp knife with a damp cloth and cut roll in half. Pick up one half roll and turn it 180 degrees so both cut ends are at the same side. Make 2 cuts through both rolls together to make 6 bite-sized pieces, wiping knife with each cut. Repeat for remaining rolls.

Polenta puddings with mango sauce

Makes 6

POLENTA PUDDING

$^1/_2$ cup (4 oz/125 g) butter

$^2/_3$ cup (5 oz/150 g) sugar

2 teaspoons grated lemon zest

2 eggs

1 cup (5 oz/150 g) self-rising flour

$^1/_2$ teaspoon baking powder

$^1/_4$ teaspoon salt

$^2/_3$ cup ($3^1/_2$ oz/105 g) polenta

$^1/_2$ cup (4 fl oz/125 ml) sour cream

$^1/_3$ cup (3 fl oz/90 ml) milk

MANGO SAUCE

2 mangoes, peeled, pitted and sliced

2 tablespoons confectioners' (icing) sugar

2 tablespoons lime juice

1 teaspoon grated lime zest

Butter six $^1/_2$ cup (4 fl oz/125 ml) ramekins and line bottoms with parchment (baking) paper. Set aside.

To make puddings: Place butter, sugar and lemon zest in a bowl. Using an electric mixer, beat until light and creamy, 3–4 minutes. Add eggs, one at a time, beating well after each addition. If mixture begins to curdle, add 1 tablespoon all-purpose (plain) flour.

Sift flour, baking powder and salt into a bowl. Stir in polenta. Combine sour cream and milk. Fold flour mixture into egg mixture alternately with sour cream mixture. Mix well.

Spoon pudding into prepared ramekins. Cover each with piece of buttered parchment (baking) paper. Half fill wok with water (steamer should not touch water) and bring water to a boil. Arrange ramekins in steamer, cover, and place steamer over boiling water. Steam until puddings are firm to touch, 45–50 minutes. Add more water to wok when necessary.

To make mango sauce: Place mangoes, sugar and lime juice and zest in a food processor. Process until smooth.

Remove steamer from wok and carefully remove ramekins from steamer. Run sharp knife around side of each ramekin. Invert onto plate and unmold pudding. Serve warm with mango sauce.

Rice pudding with grilled pears

Serves 8

1 cup (7 oz/220 g) short-grain rice
40 fl oz (1.25 L) milk
1 vanilla bean
$^1/_2$ cup (3$^1/_2$ oz/105 g) superfine (caster) sugar
$^3/_4$ cup (6 fl oz/180 ml) cream

FOR GRILLED PEARS
4 firm pears, halved
juice of 1 lemon
1 tablespoon honey
2 tablespoons vegetable oil

Preheat oven to 300°F (150°C/Gas 2).

Place rice in a medium-sized heatproof bowl. Cover rice with boiling water, allow to stand 3 for minutes, then drain. Place rice in a medium-sized, heavy-based saucepan. Add milk, vanilla bean and sugar. Stir over a low heat for 35 minutes. Remove vanilla bean and stir in cream. Transfer to a greased medium-sized heatproof dish and bake in preheated oven until rice is tender, about 30 minutes.

To grill pears: Combine lemon juice and honey and brush mixture onto cut side of pears. Preheat a grill pan or barbecue, then brush grill with oil. Grill pear halves, cut side down until golden and slightly softened, about 2–3 minutes. Remove from grill and serve warm with rice pudding.

Variation: To make with pan-fried pineapple, in a large frying pan over medium heat, melt unsalted butter and add fresh pineapple slices. Cook for 1 minute then spinkle with brown sugar and cook, turning occasionally, until sugar is melted and pineapple is translucent, 2–3 minutes.

Rosewater doughnuts

FOR YOGURT SAUCE

6¹/₂ oz (200 g) plain (natural) yogurt

3 teaspoons rosewater

1 tablespoon confectioners' (icing)
sugar, sifted

FOR DOUGHNUTS

2¹/₄ cups (11 oz/330 g) self-rising
flour, sifted

¹/₂ cup (2 oz/60 g) ground almonds

¹/₃ cup (3 oz/90 g) butter or ghee, plus
2 cups (16 fl oz/500 ml) vegetable oil
or ghee, for deep-frying

¹/₃ cup (3 fl oz/90 ml) plain (natural)
yogurt

¹/₄ cup (2 fl oz/60 ml) warm water

2 teaspoons rosewater

grated zest of 1 orange

¹/₃ cup (2¹/₂ oz/75 g) superfine (caster)
sugar

To make yogurt sauce: In a small bowl, combine yogurt, rosewater and sugar. Mix well.
Cover and refrigerate until ready to serve.

To make doughnuts: In a bowl, combine flour and almonds. Using fingertips, rub ¹/₃ cup
(3 oz/90 g) butter or ghee into flour. Stir in yogurt, warm water, rosewater and orange
zest. Mix to form a soft dough. Turn out onto floured work surface. Knead until smooth,
about 2 minutes. Divide dough into 30 pieces. Roll each into a ball.

Heat 2 cups (16 fl oz/500 ml) vegetable oil or ghee in wok until it reaches
375°F (190°C) on deep-frying thermometer, or until small bread cube dropped into liquid
sizzles and turns golden. Working in batches, add doughnuts and deep-fry until golden,
5–6 minutes. Using a slotted spoon, remove doughnuts from wok and drain on paper
towels. Place superfine sugar on plate and roll each doughnut in sugar until well coated.
Serve warm with yogurt sauce.

Saffron and pistachio ice cream

Serves 10

large pinch saffron threads

1/2 cup (4 fl oz/125 ml) milk, heated

1/3 cup (3 1/2 oz/105 g) pistachio nuts

3 tablespoons green cardamom pods

1 2/3 cups (13 fl oz/400 ml) sweetened condensed milk

3 cups (24 fl oz/750 ml) heavy (double) cream

FOR RICH SAUCE

1/2 cup (4 oz/125 g) raw or demarara sugar

1/2 cup (4 fl oz/125 ml) heavy (double) cream

5 star anise

In a bowl, combine saffron and hot milk and set aside for 10 minutes. Place pistachio nuts in a food processor and process until finely chopped. In a spice grinder, grind cardamom to a powder.

Place condensed milk and cream in a bowl. Stir until well combined; do not whisk or beat. Add pistachio nuts, saffron and milk mixture, and ground cardamom. Stir until well combined.

Divide mixture among 10 ramekins with a 1/2-cup (4-fl oz/125-ml) capacity. Place in freezer until ice cream is frozen, about 6 hours. Cover ramekins well and keep in freezer until serving.

To make sauce: In a saucepan, combine sugar, cream and star anise. Stir over low heat until sugar dissolves. Bring to a boil, reduce heat to low and cook, uncovered, stirring often, until slightly thickened, about 10 minutes.

To serve, briefly dip each ramekin in a bowl of hot water. Invert a serving plate on top and invert plate and ramekin to unmold ice cream. Top with sauce and serve immediately.

Note: You can make ice cream up to 2 weeks ahead. Wrap well to prevent flavors being absorbed from other foods in freezer. Make sauce close to serving.

Steamed banana cake

3 cups (12 oz/375 g) grated fresh coconut or unsweetened dried (desiccated)
  coconut
5 ripe bananas, about 1^1/$_2$ lb (750 g), peeled and mashed
1 cup (5 oz/150 g) rice flour or very finely ground rice
^{1}/$_4$ cup (1 oz/30 g) tapioca starch
1^1/$_2$ cups (12 oz/375 g) granulated (white) sugar
^{1}/$_2$ teaspoon salt
^{1}/$_2$ cup (4 fl oz/125 ml) coconut cream

If using unsweetened dried coconut, soak first in cold water for 10 minutes, then squeeze dry. Reserve one-fourth of coconut for garnish.

In a medium bowl, mash bananas then stir in all remaining ingredients except reserved coconut. Lightly oil an 8 x 10-inch (20 x 25-cm) cake pan. Pour in cake mixture and smooth top. Sprinkle with reserved coconut. Cover tightly with plastic wrap, or lay a banana leaf on top. Place cake in a steamer, or on a wire rack in a wok, over gently boiling water. Make sure water does not touch cake pan. Cover steamer, and steam for 30 minutes. Cake will be slightly springy to the touch when done.

Remove pan from heat, and drain away any accumulated water. Let cool completely, then cut into small squares and carefully remove pieces with a spatula. Serve warm or at room temperature.

Note: *Standard servings of this traditional Thai cake, known as "khanom kluay," may prove too large and heavy; smaller servings are better.*

Strawberry tofu ice cream

Serves 4–6

1 cup (8 fl oz/250 ml) water
1 cup (8 oz/250 g) sugar
10 oz (300 g) almond-flavored tofu, drained
2 cups (8 oz/250 g) strawberries, hulled
4–6 chocolate or waffle cups
fresh fruit, for serving
grated dark chocolate, for garnish

In a medium saucepan, combine water and sugar and bring to a boil, stirring until sugar has dissolved. Continue boiling gently for 7 minutes. Remove from heat and let cool to room temperature.

In a food processor, puree tofu until smooth. Add strawberries and puree until smooth. Gradually pour in the cooled syrup and process until combined. Pour mixture into an airtight container and freeze for 2 hours. Remove from freezer and whisk with a fork. Freeze for 2 hours longer. Whisk again and return to freezer until fully frozen.

Use a melon baller or small ice cream scoop to shape balls of ice cream. Serve in chocolate or waffle cups with fresh fruit and grated chocolate.

Hint: Chocolate and waffle cups are available at most supermarkets. You can also cut the ice cream into slices to serve.

Variation: To make mango-coconut tofu ice cream, use coconut-flavored tofu in place of almond-flavored tofu and 1 1/4 cups (8 oz/250 g) diced fresh mango instead of strawberries. Serve in slices or scooped into waffle cups. Sprinkle with toasted shredded coconut and toasted sliced almonds.

Sweet mung bean cake with sesame

2 cups (14 oz/440 g) yellow split mung beans (see Hints)
1 cup (8 oz/250 g) sugar
3 tablespoons sesame seeds, lightly toasted (see page 30)

Place beans in a medium pot or saucepan and add water to cover. Bring to a boil, reduce heat and simmer until tender, about 30 minutes. Drain well, but do not rinse. Let cool slightly, then transfer to a food processor and puree coarsely, or mash in saucepan using a potato masher.

Return puree to pot and stir in sugar. Cook over very low heat, stirring or mashing until puree becomes rather dry and pulls away from pan into a ball, about 5–10 minutes.

Lightly moisten a large bowl or mold with water. Add cooked puree and press compactly into bowl or mold. Turn out and sprinkle with sesame seeds.

Note: This Vietnamese dish, known as "che kho," is popular holiday fare and is especially good as a snack served with hot jasmine tea.

Hints: Dried mung beans—either split yellow or whole green—are available at Asian markets and some natural foods stores; at Indian markets split mung beans are known as moong dal, and whole beans are known as sabat moong.

If using whole green mung beans, soak in water for several hours, then rinse well to remove the outer green shell then proceed as above.

Thai sweet sticky rice with mango

Serves 4–6

4 cups (28 oz/875 g) sticky (glutinous) rice

2 cups (16 fl oz/500 ml) coconut cream

1 cup (8 oz/250 g) granulated (white) sugar plus 2 tablespoons extra

$1/2$ teaspoon salt plus pinch extra

$1/2$ cup (4 fl oz/125 ml) coconut milk

2–3 fresh mangoes, peeled, cut from pit (stone), and thinly sliced

1 tablespoon sesame seeds, lightly toasted (see page 30)

Put sticky rice in a large, deep bowl and add water to cover by 2 inches (5 cm). Soak for at least 3 hours, preferably 8 hours.

Drain, then pour rice into a conical bamboo steamer or steamer basket lined with cheesecloth (muslin). If available, place a small round bamboo mat, about 6 inches (15 cm) in diameter, into the bottom of the basket (this facilitates removal and cleaning later). Set basket over a steamer pot filled with boiling water. The basket should fit snugly deep inside the pot, but not touch the water. Cover rice, then steam until grains are tender, about 20 minutes.

Halfway through the cooking, toss the rice so that it is upended. It should have already formed into a cohesive ball by this point.

In a large bowl, stir together coconut cream, sugar and $1/2$ teaspoon salt. Add hot rice, stirring until grains are well coated. Let cool completely at room temperature. (Do not refrigerate; the rice will harden.) The rice will absorb all the coconut liquid; stir occasionally.

Meanwhile, in a small bowl, combine coconut milk, extra sugar and a pinch of salt.

When ready to serve, divide sticky rice among individual serving bowls. Lay mango slices on top of sticky rice. Pour coconut milk mixture over mangoes and sprinkle with sesame seeds. (Pictured on page 486.)

Note: If fresh mango is unavailable, use canned (tinned) mango, drained, or slices of banana.

Tofu pockets with black sticky rice and lime

Serves 4–6

1 cup (7 oz/220 g) black sticky (glutinous) rice

2¹/₂ cups (20 fl oz/625 ml) water plus ¹/₄ cup (2 fl oz/60 ml) extra

1 cup (8 fl oz/250 ml) coconut milk

1 tablespoon packed palm sugar or dark brown sugar

1 teaspoon soy sauce

6 seasoned tofu pouches (see page 327)

6 unpeeled rambutan, halved and unpeeled, or lychees

1 star fruit, sliced

¹/₄ cup (2 fl oz/60 ml) fresh lime juice

Put rice in a medium bowl and add water to cover. Soak overnight; drain rice.

In a small saucepan, bring 2¹/₂ cups (20 fl oz/625 ml) water to a boil and stir in rice. Return to a boil, reduce heat and simmer, uncovered, for 15 minutes. Drain.

In a medium saucepan, combine rice, coconut milk, palm sugar, soy sauce and ¹/₄ cup (2 fl oz/60 ml) water and cook over medium–low heat, stirring constantly, until rice is thick and most of liquid is absorbed, 20–25 minutes. Let cool slightly.

Open tofu pockets with fingers, pushing down to open each corner. Fill pockets two-thirds full with rice mixture. Fold sides of pouches over filling to form parcels and turn over so folded sides are on the bottom. Cut diagonally across parcels and arrange them on a plate with rambutans and star fruit. Sprinkle with lime juice, or serve lime juice separately to be added according to individual taste.

Hint: *Rambutan and lychees are available from Asian markets. Substitute canned lychees if fresh are not available. Drain canned lychees before using.*

Vietnamese sweet black bean "soup"

1 cup (7 oz/220 g) dried small black beans or black-eyed peas (beans) (see Hints)
8 cups (64 fl oz/2 L) water, for cooking
1 tablespoon arrowroot or tapioca starch
1 cup (8 oz/250 g) sugar
crushed ice

Pre-soaking beans: If using black beans or black-eyed peas (beans), soak beans overnight, or for at least four hours. Alternatively, for a quick soaking method, place the beans in a medium pot with a tight-fitting lid. Cover with water, bring to a boil and cook, uncovered, for 1 minute. Remove from heat, cover tightly and rest for 1 hour. Drain before using.

In a large pot, combine beans and water. Bring to a boil, reduce heat and simmer until beans are barely tender, up to 1½ hours. (Surprisingly, tiny Vietnamese black beans cook much slower than other beans, yet still retain crunchiness.)

Take a spoonful or so of cooking juices and stir into arrowroot, then return mixture to pot. Add sugar and stir to dissolve. Remove from heat and let cool. Refrigerate until chilled, at least 2 hours. Spoon beans and juice into individual glasses or cups, add some crushed ice and serve.

Hints: *In place of beans in this Vietnamese recipe, you can substitute black gram (sabat urad) which is available at Asian markets, some natural foods stores and Indian markets. If using black gram, do not presoak, and cook for about 30 minutes only.*

Sweetened condensed milk can be used to sweeten this recipe.

Vietnamese sweet gingered sticky rice

Serves 4–6

1 cup (6$^1/_2$ oz/200 g) uncooked sticky (glutinous) rice
$^1/_2$ cup (4 oz/125 g) raw sugar or palm sugar, preferably dark
1-inch (2.5-cm) knob fresh ginger, peeled and finely grated
$^1/_2$ cup (2 oz/60 g) fresh or dried (desiccated) coconut (see Note)
2 tablespoons chopped peanuts, lightly toasted (see page 30)

Soak rice in water to cover for at least 3 hours, preferably for 8 hours; drain. Pour into a conical bamboo steamer or steamer basket lined with cheesecloth (muslin). Set over a pot of boiling water, cover, and steam until tender, about 20 minutes. Turn out rice into a medium bowl. Cover and keep warm.

In a small saucepan over high heat, combine sugar and $^3/_4$ cup (6 fl oz/180 ml) water. Stir until dissolved, then boil for 1 minute. Add ginger. Reduce heat and barely simmer for 5 minutes. Pour syrup over cooked rice. Stir lightly until rice is just coated. As it will set while cooling, spoon rice immediately into small individual bowls or molds. Alternatively, flatten into a tray or plate, and cut into 1$^1/_4$-inch (3-cm) cubes. Serve at room temperature, garnished with coconut and peanuts.

Note: *If using fresh coconut, see page 24 for preparation. You will only need a small quantity of coconut for this recipe, so wrap and refrigerate remainder for another use, such as to make coconut milk (see page 24).*

Drinks

no matter where you go in Asia, one thing is for certain —
you'll drink tea. In the ancient towns and temples, in the bustling
cities and markets, in every Asian home, tea is brewing. More than
just a drink, tea is a tradition.

Chinese legend has it that, in 2737 BCE, the Emperor Chen-Nung
discovered tea by accident one day while sipping boiled water in
his garden. A few leaves fell from a tea bush into his cup, the
emperor tasted it and liked it, and the tea-drinking custom began.
Thought to have medicinal and restorative powers, tea was firmly
established in China by the fourth century AD, and soon after in
India and Japan. In the first book ever written about tea, the Cha
King, or Holy Scripture of Tea, the eighth-century poet Lu Yu said
"…tea tempers the spirits, calms and harmonises the mind; it arouses
thought and prevents drowsiness, lightens and refreshes the body,
and clears the perceptive faculties" — qualities which are still
associated with tea today.

The range of tea in Asia is infinite — from the fully fermented black
teas through the greens to the delicate florals — but almost all come
from one plant, *Camellia sinensis*. Native to Southeast Asia, this
evergreen (closely related to the garden camellia) is widely grown
in the mountainous regions of China, India, Indonesia, Sri Lanka
and Japan, its cultivation perfected over thousands of years.

Coffee is a more modern beverage in Asia, having only been
introduced into the mainstream a few hundred years ago. It cannot
compete with tea, though the Malaysians love it (a Middle Eastern
influence) and the Vietnamese inherited a fondness for it from the

French. Reflecting a worldwide trend, however, coffee is increasingly popular with younger generations.

The place of alcohol is somewhat chequered in Asian cuisine. In some countries, alcohol is part of the tradition: Japanese sake, Chinese rice wine and sherry, and Korean soju, made from fermented potatoes. There are also many local brews, like the Thai beers and whiskeys, and folk liquors based on fruits and herbs. However, in many regions, including the Muslim parts of Southeast Asia, alcohol is banned for religious reasons. Alcoholic drinks and wines are popular in restaurants and hotels, though imported products are generally very expensive.

Pure water is the drink most commonly served with meals in Asia, though again a modern preference is for soft drink. Tea is served with dim sum and sweet snacks. There's also a tantalising range of fruit and soy-based drinks on offer, though traditionally most are consumed as snacks or desserts. Asian drinks are governed by the same rules that apply to Asian food—they must be beneficial to the body and taste as good as they look.

This chapter features a varied selection of Asian-style drinks, from authentic teas infused with herbs and spices and fruit punches to modern coolers and crushes. Some are designed to quench a tropical thirst, fast. Others are intended to be slowly sipped, after a long hard day or a memorable meal. The recipes also include drinks that are substantial as well as refreshing, like the yogurt-based lassis and exotic fruit whips. These make ideal snacks, as is the Asian custom.

Preparing tea and other Asian drinks

The preparation of drinks in Asia is given as much care as any other food or dish. Tea, of course, has developed many rituals and customs. However, the making of many other Asian drinks is also regarded as a serious talent, and local vendors can become renowned for their soy milk or lassi. In this section you'll find information on tea and how to make it, and also hints on preparing other Asian drinks.

Making tea

Making tea is regarded as an art form throughout Asia, whether humbly practised at home, in local tea houses or in elaborate tea ceremonies, such as the Japanese Chanoyu, which takes place in a purpose-built tea house and can last for hours.

When making tea, always select good-quality tea leaves and use only freshly boiled water. Good teas can be infused three times—the second time is generally regarded as the best, because by then the tea will release its full fragrance and aroma. About 1 teaspoon of tea is used to make 1 cup. Traditionally, the Chinese use porcelain teapots and tiny porcelain cups without handles. Note that milk or sugar is never added to Chinese teas; the Indians, however, did adopt these additions following British rule.

- Teas from China include: Orange Pekoe, from Shanghai; Oolong, a semi-fermented; Souchong, a whole-leaf black; Jasmine, a green tea infused in the drying process with jasmine flowers; Gunpowder, the most popular green in China; and White, one of the rarest and most expensive teas, harvested for only a few days each year in Fujian province.

- Indian teas include: Darjeeling, considered by many to be the prince of teas; Nilgiri, renowned for its fragrance; and the mighty Assam, from the tea bush *Thea assamica*. The Indians also love their spiced teas, enthusiastically adding spices such as cardamom, cinnamon, cloves and anise to their brews.

- In Sri Lanka the predominant tea is Ceylon and its many varieties, grown extensively for the European and American markets.

- In Japan, only green teas are produced, including: Bancha, a mild, refreshing leaf for everyday consumption; Sencha, a fresh and flowery infusion; and Gyokuro, one of Japan's finest teas used in matcha.

- The Japanese Matcha Uji means "froth of liquid jade," which perfectly describes this brew. Matcha, made from the dried and finely ground leaves of Gyokuro, is the tea of ceremonies, whisked in little bowls and sipped appreciatively. It is also used in other Japanese foods, with none more modern than matcha ice cream.

- Herbal and floral teas also are enjoyed throughout Asia. They can be made from flowers (such as honeysuckle or chrysanthemum), leaves (such as lemongrass or pandan), or roots (such as ginger and Korean ginseng); or infused with fruit, as is lemon tea or the Chinese lychee-flavored tea.

Preparing Asian-style drinks

A good food processor or blender is essential for making drinks such as frappes, crushes and fruit lassis (although you don't need one for a traditional lassi). If possible, choose one that can accommodate ice and keep it away from chilies (which can leave an indelible flavor).

Many of the recipes in this chapter, and Asian drinks in general, contain ice—whether cubed, crushed or blended into the drink. Always ensure that your ice is of the best quality—using bottled or filtered water to make ice for drinks will taste much better than using tap water.

You can easily alter the quantities of these drink recipes to suit the required amount, and also vary the flavors to taste. Asian-style fruit drinks can be quite sweet (in accordance with their customary role as liquid fast food), so adjust added sugar accordingly. Conversely, salty sweet drinks are relished in many parts of Southeast Asia, but the salt can simply be omitted from the recipe.

Sugar syrup

A basic sugar syrup is often used to sweeten Asian-style drinks. The following recipe makes about $1\frac{1}{4}$ cups (10 fl oz/300 ml) of sugar syrup.

In a medium saucepan, combine 1 cup (8 oz/250 g) sugar and 1 cup (8 fl oz/250 ml) water. Cook over low heat, stirring until sugar dissolves. Stop stirring, increase heat to high and bring to a boil. Cook for 3 minutes without stirring. To prevent syrup from crystallizing, brush pan sides with cold water. Remove from heat and let cool completely. Pour into a jar and cover; keep indefinitely in the refrigerator.

To make Vanilla sugar syrup: Add 1 vanilla bean, split lengthwise, to sugar syrup after removing it from heat. Alternatively, stir in $\frac{1}{4}$ teaspoon vanilla extract (essence).

Assam cardamom tea

3$\frac{1}{2}$ cups (28 fl oz/875 ml) water
6 green cardamom pods
1 tablespoon Assam tea leaves

$\frac{1}{2}$ cup (4 fl oz/125 ml) milk
$\frac{1}{4}$ cup (2 oz/60 g) packed brown
  sugar or honey

In a saucepan, bring water to a boil over medium heat. Add cardamom, cover, and boil for 3–5 minutes. Remove from heat and let steep for 5 minutes. Add tea leaves, bring to a boil and boil for 3 minutes. Add milk and sugar or honey. Strain and drink hot.

Note: *Cardamom pods add a special touch to Assam tea. Though it is drunk piping hot, this tea is refreshing and cooling.*

Chamomile and honeysuckle floral tea

2 teaspoons dried honeysuckle flowers
1 teaspoon dried chamomile flowers

1 cup (8 fl oz/250 ml) boiling water

Combine honeysuckle and chamomile in a warmed small ceramic or glass teapot. Add boiling water, cover, and let steep for 10 minutes. Strain, then drink hot.

Note: *Floral teas are highly regarded in China medicinally, but they are also enjoyed for their delightful flavors. This floral blend is ideal after a heavy meal or stressful day.*

Green mango drink

Serves 10

2 lb (1 kg) unripe green mangoes
3 tablespoons green cardamom pods
1/2 cup (4 oz/125 g) sugar
pinch salt
8 cups (64 fl oz/2 L) ice water
crushed ice, for serving

Rinse mangoes and place in a large saucepan. Add enough water to cover and bring to a simmer over medium heat. Cook, partially covered, until mangoes are soft and mushy, 20–30 minutes. Drain, but reserve cooking water. Set mangoes aside to cool.

In a spice grinder, grind cardamom to a powder. Set aside.

Remove mango pulp from skins and pits. Place pulp in a food processor with cardamom, sugar and salt. Puree until smooth, adding some cooking water if necessary to facilitate blending.

Remove mango puree to a bowl and combine with ice water. Taste and adjust sugar and salt if necessary. Pour into tall glasses and add crushed ice. Serve immediately.

Note: This traditional Indian drink is known as "panha."

Variation: To make with fresh mint, omit cardamom from the recipe above and add 1 teaspoon ground, dry-roasted cumin seeds and a handful of fresh mint leaves.

Iced coffee Vietnamese-style (Ca-phe den da)

Serves 1

3–4 heaping teaspoons very finely ground espresso-roast coffee
¹/₃ cup (3 fl oz/90 ml) boiling water
ice cubes, for serving
sugar to taste

Remove top filter or inner screen from a Vietnamese coffee filter by unscrewing it counterclockwise (anticlockwise). (Some versions attach with a clip or a pressure spring. See Note.) Fill fully with coffee, pat to compress and secure filter. Set coffee filter atop a small bistro glass and add boiling water. Cover with top lid to retain heat. The coffee will slowly drip through. Meanwhile, fill a small water glass with crushed ice or ice cubes.

When coffee has fully dripped through, about 3 minutes, remove top lid of filter and invert it as a saucer to catch any remaining drips. Remove coffee filter and place it atop inverted lid. Pour coffee over ice in glass. If desired, sweeten with sugar to taste.

Note: *If a Vietnamese coffee filter is unavailable, a French-press coffeepot is a close equivalent.*

Hint: *If coffee drips too quickly, it is either because the coffee grind is too coarse or because the filter has not been packed tightly with sufficient coffee. Conversely, over-packed coffee may not drip at all.*

Variations: *To make with sweetened milk, carefully pour 2 tablespoons sweetened condensed milk into a small bistro glass. It should form a single layer, and not run down sides. Place coffee filter atop, and proceed as above, allowing coffee to slowly drip into glass. The finished coffee will appear in two layers, similar to a French pousse-café. Serve hot, or pour over ice.*

To make with cinnamon, prepare as for iced coffee, but do not pour over ice. Sweetening with sugar or sweetened condensed milk is optional; use a cinnamon stick to stir. Leave cinnamon in coffee to further flavor it. Alternatively, sprinkle with a pinch ground cinnamon.

Iced lemongrass tea

3 green shoots (leaves) lemongrass (see Hint)
about 1 cup (8 fl oz/250 ml) boiling water
Sugar Syrup (see page 543), to taste

Crush lemongrass shoots and place into a mug or large teacup. Alternatively, wrap leaves attractively into a bunch, tying them together with a leaf. Pour boiling water over, cover, and let steep for 5 minutes. Let cool then pour over ice. Add sugar syrup to taste.

Hint: In Vietnam, this drink is known as "che sa da" or "tra sa da." This recipe uses the green shoot-like leaves at the top of the plant, not the white bulbous base used in cooking. If fresh lemongrass is unavailable, look for dried lemongrass but use this frugally.

Iced lemon tea

5 teaspoons black tea
6 cups (48 fl oz/1.5 L) boiling water
1/4 cup (2 fl oz/60 ml) lemon juice
1/4 cup (13/4 oz/50 g) superfine
  (caster) sugar

1 lemon, sliced
2 sprigs lemon thyme
ice cubes, for serving

Place tea in a large teapot and add boiling water. Let stand for 5 minutes to infuse.

Strain into heatproof container and add lemon juice and sugar, stirring to dissolve sugar. Add lemon slices and thyme and chill, covered, in refrigerator for at least 1 hour.

To serve, place ice cubes in glasses and pour in chilled tea.

Indian masala chai (Indian tea)

4 cups (32 fl oz/1 L) cold water
4 teaspoons finely grated fresh ginger
¹/₃ cup (1 oz/30 g) tea leaves
3 tablespoons milk, plus extra for serving
¹/₂ teaspoon Garam Masala (see page 575)
sugar to taste

In a saucepan, combine water and ginger and bring to a boil over medium heat. Reduce heat and stir in tea leaves. Bring to a boil again and stir in 3 tablespoons milk and garam masala. Remove from heat and cover pan. Set aside for 4 minutes. Strain tea and add sugar to taste. Serve with extra milk.

Note: Indians generally drink their chai strong, with lots of milk and sugar, but you can vary the amounts depending on how strong or diluted you like your chai. As a variation, use ground cardamom instead of garam masala.

Indian sweet lemon drink

1¹/₂ tablespoons green cardamom pods
8 cups (64 fl oz/2 L) ice water
juice of 6 lemons or 10 limes

¹/₃ cup (2 oz/60 g) superfine (caster) sugar or to taste
1 teaspoon black salt (optional)
pinch table salt
crushed ice, for serving

In a spice grinder, grind cardamom to a powder. In a bowl, combine cardamom with ice water, lemon juice, sugar, black salt (if using) and table salt, and whisk well until sugar dissolves. Pour into tall glasses and add crushed ice. Serve immediately.

Hint: This refreshing Indian drink is known as "nimbu pani." Omit black salt if it is unavailable as there is no substitute.

Indonesian sweet potato and coconut drink

Serves 2–4

1 sweet potato (12 oz/375 g), peeled and cubed
3½ cups (28 fl oz/875 ml) water
½ cup (4 oz/125 g) grated palm sugar
1 pandan (screwpine) leaf, folded, or 2 kaffir lime leaves, finely sliced
2 tablespoons sweet potato flour or tapioca balls, cooked until translucent
½ cup (4 fl oz/125 ml) thin coconut cream (see page 24)

Place sweet potato in a pot and cover with water. Add palm sugar and pandan leaf and bring to a boil. Simmer until tender, about 20 minutes. Remove from heat and stir in potato flour balls and coconut cream. Serve in glasses as a drink, either hot or cold.

Hint: Known as "kolak," this Indonesian drink is like many from Asia—more like a dessert or sweet snack than a drink. As a dessert, this recipe can be served hot or cold over shaved ice.

Korean cinnamon and persimmon fruit punch

Serves 4

2 oz (60 g) fresh ginger
6 cups (48 fl oz/1.5 L) water
1 oz (30 g) cinnamon sticks
1½ cups (12 oz/375 g) sugar

4 small dried seedless persimmons or
  2 medium dried seedless
  persimmons, halved
pine nuts, for garnish

Peel ginger and thinly slice. Put sliced ginger, water and cinnamon in a large saucepan. Bring to a boil, then lower heat and simmer for 30–40 minutes. Add sugar and combine well, then strain through a fine-mesh sieve; discard ginger and cinnamon.

Remove stems from persimmon and add persimmons to cinnamon and ginger water 3 hours before serving, to allow them to soften.

Ladle persimmons into glass bowls or wide glasses such as champagne saucers and fill with cinnamon and ginger water. Garnish with 2–3 pine nuts and serve.

Lassi (Chilled yogurt drink)

Serves 10

pinch saffron threads
^{2}/$_3$ cup (5 fl oz/150 ml) milk, heated
3 tablespoons green cardamom pods
8 cups (4 lb/2 kg) plain (natural)
  whole-milk yogurt

^{1}/$_2$ cup (3^1/$_2$ oz/105 g) superfine
  (caster) sugar
crushed ice, for serving

In a bowl, combine saffron and warm milk and set aside for 10 minutes. In a spice grinder, grind cardamom to a powder. In a large bowl, combine saffron mixture, cardamom, yogurt and sugar. Whisk thoroughly until sugar dissolves and mixture begins to froth. Pour into glasses, add crushed ice and serve immediately.

Notes: This traditional Indian drink is a favorite worldwide. Lassis are a refreshing dessert following a curry or other Indian food, but they can also be sipped with the meal, as yogurt provides a soothing counterpoint to dishes containing chili peppers.

Lassi with fruit

Serves 4

1 cup (8 oz/250 g) plain (natural)
  whole-milk yogurt
1 cup (8 fl oz/250 ml) milk
1^1/$_2$ cups (12 oz/375 g) chopped fresh
  fruit (peach, mango or raspberry)

sugar to taste
crushed ice, for serving
fresh fruit, leaves, or flowers, for
  garnish

In a food processor or blender, combine yogurt, milk and 1 cup (8 oz/250 g) chopped fruit. Process until frothy, about 20 seconds. Add sugar. Fill glasses with crushed ice, pour in yogurt mixture and top each with a portion of the remaining ^{1}/$_2$ cup (4 oz/125 g) chopped fruit. Garnish with fruit, flowers or leaves. (Pictured on page 538.)

Lassi with mango and ginger

Serves 2–3

1 large mango, peeled and flesh cut from pit
1 cup (8 oz/250 g) plain (natural) whole-milk yogurt
1/2-inch (12-mm) piece fresh ginger, chopped
1/2 cup (4 fl oz/125 ml) water, chilled
8 ice cubes
2 teaspoons sugar, or to taste

Place all ingredients in a food processor or blender and process until smooth. Taste and add sugar if desired or thin with a little more water.

Lassi with pineapple and mint

Serves 2–3

1/2 pineapple, peeled, cored and chopped
1 cup (8 oz/250 g) plain (natural) whole-milk yogurt
1/2 cup (4 fl oz/125 ml) water, chilled
4 mint leaves
8 ice cubes
2 teaspoons sugar, or to taste

Place all ingredients in a food processor or blender and process until smooth. Taste and add sugar if desired or thin with a little more water.

Hints: Lassis made with fruit are usually processed in a food processor or blender. The sweetness of the resulting drink will depend on the sugar content of the fruit. You can thin lassis by adding milk or water.

Lemongrass drink

2 whole stalks lemongrass, including green top, coarsely chopped
3 cups (24 fl oz/750 ml) water
about 1 tablespoon Sugar Syrup (see page 543), or to taste
ice cubes or crushed ice, for serving

In a food processor or blender, combine lemongrass and water and process for about 2 minutes to puree. Strain liquid through a fine-mesh sieve or cheesecloth (muslin), squeezing, or pressing with a wooden pestle, to extract all liquid.

To serve, pour lemongrass drink into glasses packed with ice and add sugar syrup individually to each glass, to taste.

Note: *This traditional Thai drink is known as "nam takrite."*

Lemongrass tea

3 green shoots (leaves) lemongrass (see Hint)
about 1 cup (8 fl oz/250 ml) boiling water

Crush lemongrass shoots and place into a mug or large teacup. Alternatively, wrap leaves attractively into a bunch, tying them together with a leaf. Pour boiling water over, cover, and let steep for 2–3 minutes. Leave lemongrass in cup while drinking.

Hint: *This recipe for lemongrass tea comes from Vietnam, where it is known as "che sa" or "tra sa." It is made from the green shoot-like leaves at the top of the plant, not the white bulbous base used in cooking. If fresh lemongrass is unavailable, look for dried lemongrass, but use this frugally.*

Lemon soda

Serves 1–2

¹/₃ cup (3 fl oz/90 ml) fresh lemon juice
¹/₃ cup (3 fl oz/90 ml) Sugar Syrup (see page 543), or to taste
pinch salt, or to taste
ice cubes or crushed ice, for serving
about 1 cup (8 fl oz/250 ml) soda water or water

In a small pitcher, combine lemon juice, sugar syrup and salt to taste. Stir to blend. Pour into a glass tumbler packed with ice. Add soda water or water to fill, plus additional sugar syrup if you like.

Lime soda

Serves 1–2

¹/₃ cup (3 fl oz/90 ml) fresh lime juice
¹/₄ cup (2 fl oz/60 ml) Sugar Syrup (see page 543), or to taste
pinch salt, or to taste
ice cubes or crushed ice, for serving
about ¹/₂ cup (4 fl oz/125 ml) soda water or water

In a small pitcher, combine lime juice, sugar syrup to taste and salt to taste. Stir to blend. Pour into a glass packed with ice. Add soda water or water to fill, plus additional sugar syrup if you like.

Note: *These lemon and lime sodas typify the sweet-salty drinks favored in both Thailand and Vietnam. Omit salt if preferred.*

Melon and pineapple crush

Serves 2–3

¹/₂ cup (2 oz/60 g) chopped, seeded watermelon flesh
¹/₃ cup (2 oz/60 g) pineapple chunks
¹/₄ cup (2 fl oz/60 ml) Sugar Syrup (see page 543), or to taste
about 1¹/₂ cups (12 oz/375 g) lightly crushed ice
¹/₂ cup (4 fl oz/125 ml) water

In a food processor or blender, combine all ingredients and process until smooth. Taste and adjust sweetening, if desired. Pour into glasses and serve immediately.

Hint: *You can use other forms of melon for this drink, including honeydew and cantaloupe (rockmelon). Adjust water and sugar syrup to taste.*

Pandan drink

Serves 2–3

5 pandan (screwpine) leaves, cut into 1¹/₂-inch (12-mm) pieces
4 cups (32 fl oz/1 L) water
2–3 tablespoons Sugar Syrup (see page 543), or to taste
ice cubes or crushed ice, for serving

In a large saucepan over high heat, combine pandan leaves and water. Bring to a boil and cook, uncovered, for about 10 minutes. Strain and let cool. To serve, pour pandan drink into glasses packed with ice and add sugar syrup individually to each glass, to taste.

Hint: *Known as "nam bay toey," this classic Thai drink features pandan (screwpine), a signature flavor of Southeast Asia. Pandan leaves are available at Asian markets.*

Papaya, coconut and lime smoothie

Serves 2

1 cup (8 fl oz/250 ml) low-fat coconut milk
1/2 papaya, peeled, seeded and chopped
1/2 lime, peeled and seeded
8 ice cubes

Place all ingredients in a food processor or blender and process until smooth and frothy.

Hint: The tartness of lime offsets the richness of the coconut milk and papaya.

Pineapple, mango and coconut smoothie

Serves 2

1 banana, peeled and chopped
1/4 pineapple, peeled, cored and chopped
1 mango, peeled and flesh cut from pit
1 cup (8 fl oz/250 ml) low-fat coconut milk, chilled
1/2 cup (4 oz/125 g) mango or other tropical-fruit yogurt
4 ice cubes

Place all ingredients in a food processor or blender and process until smooth and frothy.

Hint: This cooling, tangy drink is ideal to prepare on hot days when cooking holds little appeal. Coconut milk is nutritious but is also high in fat; this recipe uses a low-fat product.

Soybean drink

Serves 6

¹/₂ cup (2 oz/60 g) dried yellow soybeans
8 cups (64 fl oz/2 L) warm water
¹/₂ cup (4 fl oz/125 ml) Vanilla Sugar Syrup (see page 543), or to taste
ice cubes or crushed ice, for serving

Rinse and pick over soybeans. Put soybeans in a medium bowl and add warm water. Soak overnight, then drain, reserving soaking water. Rinse beans briskly under cold running water and drain again.

In a blender (a food processor does not work well here), combine beans and about ³/₄ cup (6 fl oz/180 ml) soaking water; puree. Add remaining soaking water, then strain through several layers of cheesecloth (muslin).

In a medium saucepan, bring strained liquid to a boil, reduce heat to low and simmer for 10 minutes. Remove from heat and add vanilla sugar syrup (add more to taste if desired). Let cool, then pour over ice and serve.

Note: Soybean drink is best drunk freshly made. Any leftovers can be kept refrigerated for a day, but stir well before serving.

Hint: Soybean drink is popular throughout many countries in Southeast Asia where it is often called "soy milk." This recipe is from Vietnam, but the method and ingredients vary little from region to region. Unlike Western "soy milk," the Asian soybean drink is not intended as a dairy substitute—it is slightly sweetened, light and refreshing, and always enjoyed icy-cold.

Spiced Himalayan tea

1 bay leaf

1/2 tablespoon fennel seeds or aniseed

3 tablespoons packed brown sugar or honey

3 cardamom pods

6 cloves

1 stick cinnamon

1/4 teaspoon black peppercorns

1 teaspoon grated fresh ginger

3 1/2 cups (28 fl oz/875 ml) water

2 tablespoons tea leaves (preferably Darjeeling)

1/2 cup (4 fl oz/125 ml) milk

Combine all ingredients except tea leaves and milk in a saucepan. Bring to a boil over high heat. Reduce heat to low, cover, and simmer for 20 minutes. Add tea leaves, remove from heat and let steep for 10 minutes. Add milk and bring to a boil over medium heat. Strain, then drink hot.

Note: *This drink is known in India as "garam Himalaya chai."*

Hint: *This hot and spicy tea goes well with sweets after dinner.*

Sauces, stocks & condiments

almost every Asian meal is served with something alongside—a sauce, condiment or pickle. These accompaniments not only enhance the dish, both in flavor and appearance, but also refresh the diner's palate and sometimes even have healthy benefits. This chapter includes a great range of sauces, condiments and pickles, as well as basics such as stocks and dashi, and a myriad of curry pastes—all the essential ingredients to make an Asian-style meal complete.

Soy sauce is one of Asia's definitive foods, along with tea and rice. All soy sauces are made from fermented soybeans. The most basic distinction is whether the sauce is light or dark, with the saltier light types most commonly served as a table condiment and the sweeter, dark version used in cooking. However, from there the range expands and becomes extraordinary—ponzu, a Japanese citrus soy; ketjap manis, an Indonesian sweet soy; shoyu, a Japanese soy aged for 1–2 years; and tamari, a by-product of making miso. There are also reduced-salt versions of soy, along with those which are specific to countries, such as Korean soy. As well as favoring soy sauce in all its forms, Asian cuisine also features soybean sauces, such as yellow soybean, black soybean and hoisin (soybean sauce flavored with garlic, chili and sesame).

Fish sauce is irreplaceable at the Vietnamese table, either in its pure state straight out of the bottle or in one of the many dipping sauces, such as the ubiquitous nuoc cham, or nuoc cham nem, which is served with just about everything in Vietnam, including breakfast. Thailand is another nation built on fish sauce—quite literally, as this pungent liquid provides protein for people living in these countries—and most Thai dishes will contain a liberal splash of it. Even in the

West, fish sauce is no longer considered an acquired taste, but takes its place with soy as a commonly used condiment.

Chili is, of course, one of the predominant flavors of Asian cuisine, though a surprisingly recent introduction. Chilies only arrived in countries like Thailand, Malaysia and Korea in the sixteenth and seventeenth centuries, but these nations have embraced it as their own. In Asia chilies are often served at the table as accompaniments to a meal, in fine slices, perhaps in vinegar, fish sauce or soy, so that diners can add them to taste, but they are also ever-present in the form of chili jam, chili oil, sambal and the many chili sauces.

In some Asian countries, it is the pickles, chutneys and raitas which are de rigueur. These are present at every meal, both to aid digestion and to balance the flavors of the meal; this is the case in traditional Indian dining. A Korean meal without kimchi is unthinkable—incomplete and lacking in grace—while sushi is simply never served without pickles, soy or wasabi.

Many of Asia's favorite sauces and accompaniments can now be purchased ready-made, from supermarkets or specialist Asian markets. And while these ensure that Asian cooking is even easier, it's preferable to make your own, especially when it comes to curry pastes, chutneys and the like. Making your own allows you to vary the ingredients to suit your taste: you can decrease the amount of chilies, for example. In many cases, such as with stocks and curry pastes, you can also make more than you need and store the remainder for future use—as convenient as anything off-the-shelf but much, much better.

Adjat sauce

Makes about ³/₄ cup (6 fl oz/180 ml)

¹/₂ cup (3 oz/90 g) granulated (white) sugar

¹/₂ cup (3 fl oz/90 ml) water

2 tablespoons rice vinegar

¹/₄ cup (2 oz/60 g) peeled, thinly sliced cucumber

1¹/₂ tablespoons ground roasted peanuts

1 tablespoon thinly sliced shallots (French shallots), preferably pink

1 tablespoon coarsely chopped fresh cilantro (fresh coriander) leaves and stems

¹/₄ fresh long red chili, coarsely chopped

In a small saucepan over low heat, combine sugar and water and stir until sugar dissolves. Increase heat, bring syrup to a full boil and cook without stirring for a few minutes. Remove from heat and let cool. Stir remaining ingredients into syrup and serve.

Carrot with yogurt and spices (Carrot pachadi)

Serves 8–10 as an accompaniment

2 cups (1 lb/500 g) plain (natural) whole-milk yogurt

1 lb (500 g) carrots, about 4–5 medium, peeled and grated

salt to taste

1¹/₂ tablespoons vegetable oil

1 teaspoon black mustard seeds

3 dried red chilies

18 fresh curry leaves

¹/₄ teaspoon powdered asafoetida

¹/₄ cup (¹/₃ oz/10 g) chopped fresh cilantro (fresh coriander)

In a bowl, whisk yogurt. Add carrots and mix well. Season with salt. In a small saucepan, heat oil over medium–low heat. Add mustard seeds and cook until they crackle, about 30 seconds. Stir in chilies, curry leaves and asafoetida, and cook, stirring, for 15 seconds. Add to yogurt and carrot mixture and mix well. Sprinkle with cilantro before serving.

Right, clockwise from bottom left: Adjat sauce (above), sweet chili relish (page 592), chili jam (page 569).

Chili dipping sauce

Makes about 1 cup (8 fl oz/250 ml)

15 fresh long green chilies, roasted (see page 23)
1 whole bulb garlic
9 shallots (French shallots), about 3 oz (100 g), preferably pink
1/4 teaspoon dried shrimp paste
1/2 teaspoon salt
1 tablespoon fish sauce

Peel and stem roasted chilies but retain seeds. (For a less piquant sauce, discard some or all of the seeds).

Preheat oven to 400°F (200°C/Gas 6).

Lightly break unpeeled garlic bulb by pressing on a knife handle with the heel of your hand, so that the cloves sit loosely together; do not separate cloves from bulb completely. Separately wrap garlic and shallots in aluminum foil.

Roast on top shelf of oven for about 30 minutes, or until soft to touch. Remove from oven and let cool to touch in foil. Peel shallots and garlic; you should have about 1/3 cup (1 1/2 oz/45 g) shallots.

In a mortar, pound chilies gently with a pestle to break them up. Add garlic and pound briefly, then add shallots. Add shrimp paste and salt and pound again to a coarse paste. Or, pulse ingredients in a food processor. Stir in fish sauce.

Chili jam

Makes about 1³/₄ cups (14 fl oz/440 ml)

2 whole bulbs garlic

4 oz (125 g) shallots (French shallots), preferably pink

15 dried long red chilies

1 cup (8 fl oz/250 ml) vegetable oil

2 tablespoons palm sugar

1 tablespoon granulated (white) sugar

¹/₄ teaspoon salt

Preheat oven to 400°F (200°C/Gas 6). Lightly break unpeeled garlic bulb by pressing down a knife handle with the heel of your hand, so that cloves sit loosely together but are not separated from bulb completely. Wrap garlic and shallots separately in aluminum foil. Roast on top shelf of oven until soft to touch, about 30 minutes. Let cool in foil before peeling.

Roast chilies by tossing them in a wok or large, heavy frying pan over high heat until lightly brown, 2–3 minutes. Remove stems, but retain seeds. In a large mortar, grind chilies to a powder with a pestle. Add roasted peeled garlic and shallots and pound until smooth. (Or, grind chilies in a food processor then add garlic and shallots and process until smooth).

Heat oil in a wok or large, heavy frying pan over medium heat and add chili paste. Reduce heat to low and cook for about 5 minutes, stirring frequently. Add sugars and salt, and stir until dissolved. Remove from heat.

Store in a covered jar in the refrigerator for up to 6 months. Do not drain off any oil from the top, as this helps to preserve the jam. (Pictured on page 567.)

Hint: Chili jam, "nam prik pow," is traditionally served in Thailand as a table condiment; in the West, it is now enjoyed in the same way as ketchup and mustard.

Chili oil

3/4 cup (6 fl oz/180 ml) vegetable oil
1/2 cup dried chili flakes

In a well-ventilated room, heat oil in a wok or small, heavy saucepan over medium to medium–high heat, until surface shimmers.

Add chili flakes. Stir briefly and immediately remove from heat. Let cool. If tightly covered, chili oil will keep indefinitely at room temperature.

Chili sambal

3 small red chilies, seeded and finely sliced
pinch salt
1/4 teaspoon white vinegar
1 teaspoon peanut oil

Mix the chilies, salt and vinegar in a small food processor or crush by hand in a mortar and pestle to form a smooth paste. Do not lean over the mix while blending—the volatile fumes from chili are a potent irritant. Scrape the paste into a small serving dish and cover with peanut oil.

Hint: Serve as a condiment with steamed mixed vegetables and yum cha.

Chili sambal oelek sauce

Makes $1/2$ cup (4 fl oz/125 ml)

2 teaspoons sambal oelek
$1/2$ cup (4 fl oz/125 ml) rice wine
1 teaspoon superfine (caster) sugar

1 tablespoon finely chopped scallions
(shallots/spring onions)

In a bowl, combine all ingredients and mix well. Store in a glass jar in refrigerator.

Cucumber raita (Cucumber and yogurt dip)

Serves 8

$1^1/2$ teaspoons cumin seeds
1 cup (8 oz/250 g) plain (natural)
   whole-milk yogurt
1 English (hothouse) cucumber, finely
   chopped

salt and freshly ground black pepper
   to taste
$1/4$ cup ($1/3$ oz/10 g) chopped fresh
   cilantro (fresh coriander)

In a small saucepan over low heat, dry-roast cumin seeds until fragrant and lightly colored, being careful not to burn them. Let them cool, then grind to a powder in a spice grinder.

In a bowl, whisk yogurt. Add cucumber and ground cumin, and season with salt and pepper. Mix well. Stir in cilantro and mix well.

Hint: Indian raitas are based on yogurt, which is whipped or whisked. You can use either whole-milk (full-fat) or reduced-fat yogurt. This raita can be made up to 6 hours ahead. Store in an airtight container in refrigerator.

Dashi 1

Makes 4$^1/_2$ cups (36 fl oz/ 1.1 L)

4$^1/_2$ cups (36 fl oz/1.1 L) water
1 x 4-inch (10-cm) square kombu

$^1/_2$ oz (15 g) bonito flakes

Use a clean, damp cloth to wipe off white film on surface of kombu. In a saucepan, combine water and kombu. Let soak for up to 2 hours, then place over high heat and bring to a simmer.

When stock begins to bubble slightly, after about 5 minutes, check center of kombu. If it is soft, remove kombu from saucepan and set aside. If it is hard, continue cooking for a few more minutes, then remove. Let mixture come to a boil, then stir. Skim off any bubbles or scum on surface.

Remove from heat and add a small amount of cold water to lower temperature before adding bonito flakes. (Boiling water makes them smell). Add bonito flakes to saucepan. Do not stir. Use chopsticks to press the flakes down gently to bottom of saucepan. Let rest for 3 minutes.

Lay a piece of cheesecloth (muslin) or a clean napkin over a colander and strain mixture into a large bowl to remove bonito flakes. Reserve the drained bonito flakes.

If, after tasting the finished dashi, you wish to strengthen its flavor, return mixture to saucepan and simmer for another 5 minutes.

Note: There are two forms of dashi used in Japanese cooking. Number-one dashi is stronger and is used as the base for clear soup or suimono. It is best prepared on the day it is to be served, but it can be cooled, refrigerated and used the following day.

Hint: You can vary the amounts of kombu and bonito flakes to taste. Choose good-quality kombu with a flat, wide, thick leaf about 10 inches (25 cm) wide. Avoid thin, wrinkled kombu if at all possible. If the kombu expands greatly and develops soft blisters as it simmers, it is of good quality.

Variation: To make vegetarian dashi, omit bonito flakes and double the quantity of kombu.

Dashi 2

Makes 4¹/₂ cups (36 fl oz/1.1 L)

reserved bonito flakes and kombu from Dashi 1 (see opposite)
4¹/₂ cups (36 fl oz/1.1 L) cold water

Put all ingredients in a saucepan. Bring to a boil over high heat and cook for 15 minutes. Remove from heat.

Lay a piece of cheesecloth (muslin) or a clean napkin over a colander and strain mixture into a large bowl. Remove drained bonito flakes. Dashi should be clear.

Note: Number-two dashi uses the leftover ingredients from number-one dashi, combined with water, to make a more diluted stock. This is then mixed with miso paste to make miso soup.

Dashi clear soup (Suimono)

Makes 2¹/₃ cups (19 fl oz/580 ml)

2¹/₃ cups (19 fl oz/580 ml) Dashi 1 (see opposite)
1 teaspoon soy sauce
1 teaspoon salt
¹/₂ teaspoon sake

Place dashi, soy sauce and salt in a saucepan over medium heat. Heat until almost boiling. Remove from heat and add sake.

Hints: Suimono, or Japanese clear soup, is a simple, subtle soup based on dashi. As with miso soup, many ingredients can be added, and the delicate flavors balance well with sushi.

Cook the ingredients you wish to add to the suimono, place them in a bowl then pour the suimono over the top. The ingredients are not cooked in the soup, so the soup remains clear.

Date and tamarind chutney

Makes about 6 cups (48 fl oz/1.5 L)

2 lb (1 kg) pitted, dried dates

3 cups (24 fl oz/750 ml) white vinegar

8 oz (250 g) jaggery or dark brown sugar

$3/4$ cup (6 oz/180 g) salt

1 cup (8 fl oz/250 ml) vegetable oil

$1/3$ cup ($3^1/2$ oz/105 g) tamarind concentrate

$2/3$ cup (3 oz/90 g) chili powder

5 x 3-inch (7.5-cm) sticks cinnamon, broken into 1-inch (2.5-cm) pieces

$2^1/2$ tablespoons green cardamom pods

3 tablespoons whole cloves

4 teaspoons chat masala

In a large, heavy saucepan, combine dates, vinegar, jaggery, salt, oil, tamarind concentrate, chili powder, cinnamon, cardamom and cloves. Cook over medium heat, stirring, until mixture begins to bubble. Reduce heat to low and cook, partially covered, stirring often, until dates are soft, 35–45 minutes.

Remove from heat, add chat masala and mix well. Spoon hot chutney into clean glass jars and immediately seal with lids. Turn jars upside-down and set aside for 5 minutes. Turn upright and set aside to cool. Label with name and date. Store in a cool cupboard for at least 1 week before opening.

Hints: This Indian chutney will keep unopened for up to 1 year in a cool, dark cupboard. After opening, it will keep in the refrigerator for up to 6 months.

The chutney sterilizes the jars and lids because the jars are filled, sealed and inverted while chutney is boiling hot.

Fresh coconut chutney

Serves 8

1 whole fresh coconut

$^1/_2$ cup ($^3/_4$ oz/20 g) coarsely chopped
  fresh cilantro (fresh coriander) leaves
  and stems

2 fresh green chilies, chopped

2$^1/_2$ teaspoons finely grated fresh ginger

salt to taste

3–4 tablespoons cold water

2 teaspoons vegetable oil

1$^1/_2$ teaspoons brown or black mustard
  seeds

$^1/_2$ teaspoon powdered asafoetida

18 fresh curry leaves, chopped

Open coconut, drain water and break into pieces. Use a small, sharp knife to pry coconut meat from shell. Peel tough brown skin from meat. Place meat in a food processor and process until finely chopped. Add cilantro, chili, ginger and salt. Process until all ingredients are finely chopped, adding 3–4 tablespoons water if necessary to facilitate processing. Transfer mixture to a bowl.

In a small saucepan, heat oil over medium heat. Add mustard seeds and cook, stirring, until they begin to crackle, about 30 seconds. Remove from heat and quickly stir in asafoetida and curry leaves, mixing well. Add mustard seed mixture to coconut chutney and mix well. Taste and add salt if necessary.

Garam masala

Makes 1 cup (8 fl oz/250 ml)

1 x 4-inch (10-cm) stick cinnamon,
  broken into small pieces

4 teaspoons whole green cardamom pods

3 brown or black cardamom pods

4 teaspoons whole cloves

4 teaspoons mace pieces

4 teaspoons black peppercorns

4 teaspoons fennel seeds

3 Indian bay leaves, torn into quarters

1 teaspoon freshly grated nutmeg

Heat a small saucepan over low heat. Separately dry-roast cinnamon, cardamom, cloves, mace, peppercorns, fennel seeds and bay leaves until fragrant and only lightly colored. Make sure heat is not too intense, as spices must not overbrown or burn. As each spice is roasted, place in a bowl. Allow roasted spices to cool. Add nutmeg, mix thoroughly and place in an airtight jar. Store in the refrigerator for up to 1 year. Just before using garam masala, grind to a powder in a spice grinder.

Green curry paste

Makes about 1 cup (8 oz/250g)

2 teaspoons coriander seeds

1 teaspoon cumin seeds

1 teaspoon black peppercorns

1 teaspoon salt

6 thin slices fresh galangal, chopped

2 stalks lemongrass, white part only, peeled and chopped

2 teaspoons chopped kaffir lime zest

about 15 cilantro (fresh coriander) roots, or 1/4 cup (1 oz/30 g) coarsely chopped stems

1/4 cup (1 oz/30 g) finely chopped shallots (French shallots), preferably pink

2 large cloves garlic, finely chopped

2 teaspoons dried shrimp paste

2 teaspoons coarsely chopped, peeled fresh turmeric or 1 teaspoon ground turmeric

40 fresh small green chilies

2 cups (2 oz/60 g) loosely packed fresh sweet Thai basil leaves

In a small dry frying pan over medium heat, separately toast each spice, stirring constantly, until fragrant, no more than 90 seconds. Immediately pour into a mortar or spice grinder. Add salt and grind to a fine powder; reserve. Put all remaining ingredients in a large mortar and pound with a pestle until pulverized, 10–20 minutes. Stir in reserved spices. (See also How to make curry pastes, page 25.)

Hanglay curry paste

Makes about 3/4 cup (6 fl oz/180 ml)

6 dried long red chilies

1 teaspoon salt

2-inch (5-cm) piece galangal, coarsely chopped

1 stalk lemongrass, white part only, peeled and chopped

1/4 cup chopped shallots (French shallots), preferably pink

2 large cloves garlic, finely chopped

2 teaspoons dried shrimp paste

2 teaspoons coarsely chopped fresh turmeric or 1 teaspoon ground turmeric

Soak dried chilies in warm water for 10 minutes. Meanwhile, combine all remaining ingredients in a large mortar and pound to a paste with a pestle, 10–20 minutes. Halfway through, drain chilies, coarsely chop, then add them to the mortar and pound until well blended. (See also How to make curry pastes, page 25.)

Herb and ginger yogurt dip (Churri)

Serves 8–10

1 teaspoon cumin seeds

1/2 cup (3/4 oz/20 g) chopped fresh mint

1/2 cup (³/4 oz/20 g) chopped fresh
  cilantro (fresh coriander)

2 teaspoons finely chopped fresh ginger

2 fresh green chilies, coarsely chopped

2¹/2 cups (20 oz/600 g) plain (natural)
  whole-milk yogurt

1 yellow (brown) onion, halved and
  thinly sliced

salt to taste

In a small saucepan over low heat, dry-roast cumin seeds until fragrant and lightly colored, being careful not to burn. Let cool then grind to a powder in a spice grinder. Place mint, cilantro, ginger and chili in a food processor and process until finely chopped. In a bowl, whisk yogurt. Add onion, ground cumin and chopped herb mixture. Mix well and season with salt.

Indian lime pickle

Makes about 4 cups (32 fl oz/1 L)

15 limes, rinsed and thoroughly dried

1 cup (8 oz/250 g) salt

juice of 4 limes

3 tablespoons vegetable oil

1 teaspoon fenugreek seeds

2 teaspoons ground turmeric

1 teaspoon powdered asafoetida

²/3 cup (3 oz/90 g) chili powder

Rinse and thoroughly dry limes. Cut limes into quarters, then cut each quarter evenly into thirds. In a bowl, combine lime pieces, salt and lime juice. Spoon into a 4-cup (32-fl oz/1-L) capacity airtight glass jar that has been thoroughly washed and dried. Seal jar and set aside at room temperature for 1 week.

In a small saucepan or wok, heat oil over medium–low heat. Add fenugreek and cook, stirring, until golden, about 30 seconds. Remove from heat and place seeds in a spice grinder. Add turmeric and asafoetida to oil remaining in pan and cook, stirring, for 30 seconds. Remove from heat. Grind fenugreek to a powder and add to pan.

Pour lime mixture into a large bowl that has been thoroughly washed and dried. Add chili powder and spice mixture, and mix thoroughly. Return lime mixture to jar and seal. Set aside for 2 weeks at room temperature to pickle then store in the refrigerator.

Laksa paste

3/4 cup (4 oz/125 g) dried shrimp
(prawns)

12 dried red chilies

6–8 scallions (shallots/spring onions),
about 6 1/2 oz (200 g), chopped

6 cloves garlic

4-inch (10-cm) piece fresh ginger,
roughly chopped

2 teaspoons dried shrimp paste

2 stalks lemongrass, bottom 3 inches
(7.5 cm) only, chopped

1/2 cup (3 oz/90 g) candlenuts or
blanched almonds

1 tablespoon ground turmeric

1/2 cup (4 fl oz/125 ml) light olive oil

Place shrimp and chilies in a bowl and
add enough boiling water to cover. Allow
to stand for 15 minutes. Drain, then place
shrimp and chili mixture in a food
processor with remaining ingredients.
Process mixture to a fine paste,
2–3 minutes. Transfer paste to a bowl or
sterilized jar, then cover and refrigerate for
up to 10 days.

Lemongrass, chili and soy dipping sauce

1 stalk lemongrass

1/4 cup (2 fl oz/60 ml) light or dark soy
sauce

2 small red chilies, seeded and finely
sliced

Cut off thick base of lemongrass stalk and remove outer leaves. Keep tough stalk and
leaves for use in soups and curries. Bruise the fleshy base then chop it finely. It will be
a little fibrous. Mix lemongrass with soy sauce and chili. Store in a glass jar in the
refrigerator.

Lime and soy dipping sauce

Makes $1/3$ cup (3 fl oz/90 ml)

2 tablespoons rice vinegar
2 tablespoons light soy sauce
1 tablespoon fresh lime juice

1 scallion (shallot/spring onion), thinly
sliced, including light green parts

In a small bowl, combine all ingredients and mix well. Serve with seafood, chicken or vegetables.

Lime cilantro dipping sauce

Makes $1/4$ cup (2 fl oz/60 ml)

2 tablespoons fish sauce
2 tablespoons white vinegar
2 tablespoons fresh lime juice

$1/2$ teaspoon superfine (caster) sugar
2 tablespoons finely chopped fresh
cilantro (fresh coriander)

In a small bowl, combine all ingredients and mix well. Serve with seafood, chicken or vegetables.

Lime, ginger and mirin dipping sauce

Makes $1/2$ cup (4 fl oz/125 ml)

$1/3$ cup (3 fl oz/80 ml) fresh lime juice
1 tablespoon grated fresh ginger
2 tablespoons mirin

In a screw-top jar, combine all ingredients. Shake until well combined. Serve with seafood, chicken or vegetables.

Massaman curry paste

Makes about ³/₄ cup (6 fl oz / 180 ml)

8 dried long red chilies, seeded

¹/₄ cup (²/₃ oz/20 g) coriander seeds

2 tablespoons cumin seeds

4 star anise pods, crushed

2 sticks cinnamon, broken

10 cloves

1 teaspoon salt

²/₃ cup (5 fl oz/150 ml) vegetable oil

6 large cloves garlic, finely chopped

2 tablespoons finely chopped shallots
(French shallots), preferably pink

6 thin slices galangal, chopped

1 stalk lemongrass, white part only,
peeled and chopped

1 teaspoon chopped kaffir lime zest

Soak dried chilies in warm water for 10 minutes. Drain and pat dry. In a small frying pan over medium heat, separately toast each spice, stirring constantly, until fragrant. Immediately remove from heat and pour spices into a large mortar or spice grinder. Add salt and grind to a fine powder. Transfer to a small bowl.

Heat oil in a wok or large, heavy frying pan over medium–high heat. Add garlic, shallots and drained chilies. Fry until slightly golden, 1–2 minutes. Remove with a slotted spoon; reserve solids and discard oil. Place galangal, lemongrass and kaffir lime zest in a large mortar and pound to a paste, 10–20 minutes. Halfway through, add fried garlic, shallots and chilies and pound until smooth. Add ground spices. Alternatively, grind dried spices and coarsely chop fresh ingredients then process in a food processor until finely chopped. If necessary, add a small amount of water, 1 teaspoon at a time. (See also How to make curry pastes, page 25.)

Mint raita (Mint and yogurt dip)

Serves 8

¹/₂ cup (³/₄ oz/20 g) coarsely chopped
fresh mint

¹/₂ cup (³/₄ oz/20 g) coarsely chopped
fresh cilantro (fresh coriander)

4 teaspoons finely grated fresh ginger

2 teaspoons finely chopped fresh green
chilies

1 cup (8 oz/250 g) plain (natural)
whole-milk yogurt

salt to taste

Place mint, cilantro, ginger and chili in a food processor and process until finely chopped. In a bowl, whisk yogurt. Add chopped mint mixture and mix well. Season with salt.

Miso sesame sauce

Makes ³/₄ cup (6 fl oz/180 ml)

¹/₄ cup (2 fl oz/60 ml) rice vinegar

2 tablespoons water or Dashi 1 (see page 572)

1 tablespoon white (shiro) miso paste

1 tablespoon sesame seed paste or tahini

1 tablespoon sugar

1 teaspoon toasted white sesame seeds, for garnish

1 scallion (shallot/spring onion), green part only, thinly sliced, for garnish

In a small bowl, combine rice vinegar, water, miso, sesame seed paste and sugar, stirring well until sugar dissolves. Cover and refrigerate until required. Garnish with sesame seeds and scallion.

Hints: This sesame sauce can be made 2–3 days ahead and refrigerated until needed. Add finely chopped chili or wasabi for extra bite.

Nihaizu (Japanese soy vinegar dipping sauce)

Makes 1 cup (8 fl oz/250 ml)

¹/₂ cup (4 fl oz/125 ml) Tosa Shoyu (see page 593)

¹/₂ cup (4 fl oz/125 ml) rice vinegar

1 teaspoon mirin

In a bowl, combine all ingredients and mix well. Keeps well for up to 2 months in the refrigerator.

Nuoc cham

Makes about 3 1/2 cups (28 fl oz/875 ml)

8 cloves garlic
4 fresh medium red chilies
1/2 cup (4 oz/125 g) sugar

juice of 4 limes
1 cup (8 fl oz/250 ml) fish sauce
2 cups (16 fl oz/500 ml) water

In a mortar, using a pestle, pound garlic and chilies to a paste. Add all remaining ingredients and stir until dissolved. Alternatively, combine all ingredients in a food processor and puree. Store in the refrigerator and use within 2 days.

Nuoc cham nem

Makes about 2 cups (16 fl oz/500 ml)

3 cloves garlic
1 fresh long red chili, seeded
1/2 cup (4 fl oz/125 ml) fish sauce
1/4 cup (2 fl oz/60 ml) rice vinegar or
  distilled white vinegar
2/3 cup (5 fl oz/160 ml) water
3–4 tablespoons sugar, to taste

1 carrot, peeled and finely shredded or
  chopped
1/2 cup (2 oz/60 g) peeled and
  shredded and chopped green
  papaya (see Hint)
1/2 teaspoon ground pepper

In a mortar, using a pestle, pound garlic and chili to a paste. Stir in fish sauce, vinegar, water and sugar, and continue stirring until sugar is dissolved. Alternatively, in a food processor, combine garlic, chili, fish sauce, vinegar, water and sugar; puree. Stir in shredded carrot, papaya and pepper.

Hint: If green papaya is unavailable, substitute shredded, peeled daikon.

Penang curry paste

Makes about ²/₃ cup (5 fl oz/ 150 ml)

25 dried long red chilies

1 tablespoon coriander seeds

1 teaspoon cumin seeds

6 blades mace or 2 teaspoons ground
   mace

4 cardamom pods

2 teaspoons black peppercorns

1 teaspoon salt

1-inch (2.5-cm) piece fresh galangal,
   coarsely chopped

1 stalk lemongrass, white part only,
   peeled and chopped

2 teaspoons chopped kaffir lime zest

8 cilantro (fresh coriander) roots, or
   2 tablespoons chopped stems

1/3 cup (2 oz/60 g) chopped shallots
   (French shallots), preferably pink

4 large cloves garlic, chopped

2 teaspoons dried shrimp paste

Soak dried chilies in warm water for 10 minutes. In a small dry frying pan over medium heat, separately toast each spice, stirring constantly, until fragrant. Immediately pour spices into a large mortar or spice grinder. Add salt and pound or grind to a fine powder. Transfer to a small bowl.

Place all remaining ingredients in a large mortar and pound to a paste, 10–20 minutes. Halfway through, drain chilies, coarsely chop, then add them to the mortar and pound until well blended. Stir in ground spices. Or, coarsely chop all fresh (or wet) ingredients, then put them in a food processor with the ground spices and process to a paste. If necessary, add a small amount of water, 1 teaspoon at a time. (See also How to make curry pastes, page 25.)

Note: This Thai curry is known as "nam prik panaeng" or "phanaeng." Its name does not refer to the Malaysian island Penang.

Hint: In Asia, and some specialist shops, you may be able to get long pepper (phrik haang), a derivative of peppercorns. If available, add 3 long peppers, preferably fresh or green, and decrease the black pepper to ¹/₂ teaspoon.

Pickled cucumber

Serves 4

10 oz (300 g) English (hothouse) cucumber, thinly sliced
3¹/₂ oz (105 g) cabbage, finely shredded
¹/₂-inch (12-mm) piece peeled fresh ginger, cut into fine matchstick strips
1¹/₂ teaspoons salt
sesame seeds, for garnish

In a bowl, gently mix all ingredients except sesame seeds. Cover with plastic wrap, pressing it down on surface of ingredients. Fill a smaller bowl with water and place on covered ingredients to apply weight. Let stand for 1 hour. Remove bowl of water. Drain liquid from cuccumber pickles, garnish with sesame seeds and serve.

Hint: *Japanese pickles accompany main dishes to freshen the palate. These are known as "kyuri no shiomomi."*

Pickled daikon with bonito

Serves 4

1 lb (500 g) daikon
2 teaspoons salt
3 daikon leaves, blanched then finely sliced

1¹/₄-inch (3-cm) piece fresh ginger, finely grated
¹/₆ oz (5 g) bonito flakes
black sesame seeds, for garnish
soy sauce, for serving

Peel daikon and cut lengthwise into quarters. Thinly slice each quarter. Place daikon in a bowl and mix in salt. Set aside until daikon softens, 10–15 minutes. Gently squeeze daikon with your hands, then drain liquid and add sliced leaves. Cover with plastic wrap, pressing it down on surface of ingredients.

Fill a smaller bowl with water and place on ingredients to apply weight. Let stand for 1 hour. Remove bowl of water. Squeeze as much liquid as possible from daikon. Place daikon pickles in 4 bowls. Top with ginger and bonito flakes and sprinkle with sesame seeds. Add a little soy sauce just before serving.

Pickled ginger (Gari)

Serves 4

3–4 pieces fresh ginger, thinly sliced
   along the grain
salt

$^1/_2$ cup (4 fl oz/125 ml) rice vinegar
2 tablespoons sugar, or to taste
$^1/_4$ cup (2 fl oz/60 ml) water

Spread ginger slices in a colander and sprinkle with salt. Let stand until soft, 30 minutes or longer. Drop ginger into boiling water to blanch. Drain and cool.

In a bowl, combine rice vinegar, sugar and water, stirring well until sugar dissolves. Add ginger and refrigerate until well seasoned, about 1 day. The ginger will turn pinkish in the marinade. For more color add a drop of pink food coloring to marinade.

Ponzu sauce

Makes 1 $^1/_2$ cups (12 fl oz/375 ml)

$^1/_2$ cup (4 fl oz/125 ml) daidai or lemon juice
$^1/_2$ cup (4 fl oz/125 ml) soy sauce
$^1/_2$ cup (4 fl oz/125 ml) Dashi 1 (see page 572)

In a bowl, combine all ingredients and mix well. Keeps for up to 2 months in the refrigerator.

Quick sweet-and-sour sauce

Makes 1 $^1/_2$ cups (12 fl oz/375 ml)

1 $^1/_2$ cups (12 fl oz/375 ml) pineapple
   juice
2 tablespoons tomato ketchup

2 teaspoons tomato paste (concentrate)
2 tablespoons superfine (caster) sugar
3 tablespoons white vinegar

In a bowl, combine all ingredients and mix well. Keeps for up to 2 months in the refrigerator.

Red curry paste

Makes about 1 cup (8 oz/250 g)

20 dried long red chilies, seeded

2 tablespoons coriander seeds

4 cardamom pods

1 teaspoon black peppercorns

1 teaspoon salt

1/2-inch (12-mm) piece fresh galangal, coarsely chopped

1/2 stalk lemongrass, white part only, peeled and chopped

2 teaspoons chopped kaffir lime zest

8 cilantro (fresh coriander) roots or 2 tablespoons coarsely chopped stems

1/3 cup (2 oz/60 g) finely chopped shallots (French shallots), preferably pink

6 large cloves garlic, finely chopped

2 teaspoons dried shrimp paste

20 fresh small red chilies

Soak dried chilies in warm water for about 10 minutes. In a small frying pan over medium heat, separately toast coriander seeds, cardamom pods and peppercorns, stirring constantly, until fragrant. Immediately pour into a mortar. Add salt and grind together into a fine powder with a pestle. Transfer to a small bowl.

Place all remaining ingredients in mortar and pound to a paste, 10–20 minutes. Halfway through, drain chilies, coarsely chop, then add to mortar and pound until well blended. Finally, stir in ground spices. Or, coarsely chop all ingredients then process in a food processor until finely chopped. If necessary, add a small amount of water, 1 teaspoon at a time. (See also How to make curry pastes, page 25.)

Note: Although green curry is one of the most popular Thai dishes in the West, red curry or "nam prik gaeng phed" is preferred in Thailand because it is more versatile.

Reiachado masala

Makes about $1/2$ cup (4 fl oz/125 ml)

4 dried red chilies, broken into small pieces
4 teaspoons black peppercorns
1 teaspoon cumin seeds

$1/4$ cup (2 fl oz/60 ml) white vinegar
4 teaspoons finely chopped garlic
$1 1/2$ teaspoons tamarind concentrate
$1/2$ teaspoon ground turmeric

In a spice grinder, grind chilies, peppercorns and cumin seeds (without roasting) to a powder. In a small bowl, combine vinegar, garlic and tamarind. Stir in ground spices and turmeric, and mix well. Set aside to stand for 10–20 minutes before using in recipes.

Sambhar masala

Makes about 2 cups (16 fl oz/500 ml)

$1 1/3$ cups coriander seeds
1 cup dried red chilies broken into small pieces
2 teaspoons fenugreek seeds
$1 1/2$ teaspoons black mustard seeds
1 tablespoon cumin seeds

$1/2$-inch (12-mm) cinnamon stick
$1/3$ cup ($1 3/4$ oz/50 g) unsweetened dried (dessicated) shredded coconut
$1/4$ cup firmly packed fresh curry leaves
$1 1/2$ teaspoons powdered asafoetida

Heat a small saucepan over low heat. Separately dry-roast coriander, chilies, fenugreek, mustard, cumin and cinnamon until fragrant and only lightly colored. Place roasted spices in a bowl.

Toast coconut in pan, stirring constantly, until lightly browned. Add to spices. Dry-roast curry leaves, tossing often, until crisp. Add to spices with asafoetida. Mix well and let cool.

Place mixture in an airtight jar and store in refrigerator for up to 6 months. Just before using sambhar masala, grind to a powder in a spice grinder.

Stocks: Basic chicken stock

Makes 8 cups (64 fl oz/2 L)

1 chicken, whole, about 2 lb (1 kg)
1 large onion, roughly sliced
1 large carrot, peeled and chopped
2 stalks celery, chopped
5 cilantro (fresh coriander) stems, including roots
1 teaspoon sea salt
8 black peppercorns
10 cups (80 fl oz/2.5 L) water

Place chicken, onion, carrot, celery, cilantro, salt and peppercorns in a large saucepan and cover with water. Place over medium–high heat and bring liquid to a boil. Reduce heat to medium–low and simmer for 1–1 $1/2$ hours, skimming surface occasionally to remove scum and fat.

Remove saucepan from heat. Remove chicken and strain liquid. Allow stock to cool completely, then remove remaining fat from surface.

Hints: This stock can be refrigerated for 5 days or frozen for up to 3 months. Chicken meat may be pulled from bones and reserved for another use.

To remove fat, either chill stock until fat hardens, or gently float paper towels on top to extract fat.

Variations: To make basic beef stock, substitute chopped beef bones for chicken. Place beef bones in a large baking pan and brush lightly with oil. Bake in a preheated 400°F (200°C/Gas 6) oven, turning once, until golden brown all over, about 40 minutes. If desired, add vegetables to the baking pan when turning the beef; this results in a rich and flavorsome stock. Follow recipe as above, using baked beef bones and vegetables.

To make with Asian herbs, add 5–6 slices fresh ginger or galangal, or a 2-inch (5-cm) piece of lime zest, or 2 fresh (or 4 dried) kaffir lime leaves with other ingredients.

Basic fish stock

Makes 8 cups (64 fl oz/2 L)

about 2 lb (1 kg) heads and bones of
  2 medium-sized white-fleshed fish
2 tablespoons light olive oil
1 large onion, roughly chopped
1 large carrot, peeled and roughly
  chopped
2 stalks celery, with leaves, roughly
  chopped

3 stems flat-leaf parsley
3 stems cilantro (fresh coriander),
  preferably including roots
3 fresh or 6 dried kaffir lime leaves
  (optional)
8 black peppercorns
1 teaspoon sea salt

Wash fish heads and bones well, removing any gills. Chop bones to fit into a large pot.

Heat oil in a large pot over high heat for 1 minute. Add fish heads and bones and cook, stirring and turning heads and bones, until any remaining flesh starts to cook and is slightly golden, 4–5 minutes.

Add remaining ingredients and stir to combine. Add enough water to cover bones completely (approximately 8 cups/64 fl oz/2 L) and bring liquid to a steady simmer. Reduce heat to medium and simmer for 25 minutes. Skim any scum from surface as stock simmers.

Strain liquid through a very fine sieve. If you don't have a very fine sieve, line your sieve with a double layer of damp cheesecloth (muslin). Discard solids. Let stock cool then cover with plastic wrap and refrigerate if not using immediately.

Hints: Fish stock should be brought only to a low boil, then simmered, or it may turn sour. Fish stock can be refrigerated for 2 days. If stored in tightly covered containers, it can be frozen for 2 months.

Variation: To make quick seafood stock, in a stockpot, combine shells of shrimp (prawns), crab or other crustaceans with weak chicken stock or water. If desired, add 1–2 onions or white portion of 1–2 leeks, some celery leaves, 2 carrots, 1/2 teaspoon whole peppercorns and salt to taste. Alternatively, the cooking liquid from raw crab in its shell makes a delicious and simple seafood stock.

Basic vegetable stock

Makes 8 cups (64 fl oz/2 L)

2 onions, roughly sliced
2 large carrots, peeled and chopped
2 stalks celery, chopped
2 leeks, sliced
4 oz (125 g) mushrooms, sliced

1–2 cloves garlic
handful of fresh parsley, stalks included
1 teaspoon sea salt, or to taste
8 black peppercorns
10 cups (80 fl oz/2.5 L) water

Place onion, carrot, celery, leeks, mushrooms, garlic, parsley, salt and peppercorns in a large saucepan with water. Place over medium–high heat and bring liquid to a boil. Reduce heat to medium–low and simmer for 1–1 1/2 hours, skimming surface occasionally to remove scum.

Remove saucepan from heat. Strain liquid, using the back of a large spoon to press vegetables into the strainer to enhance flavor.

Hints: *This stock can be refrigerated for 2–3 days or frozen for up to 3 months. For maximum flavor, lightly broil (grill) or roast the vegetables before using. You can also retain the vegetable skins to improve flavor and color of the stock.*

Depending on availability and required flavor of stock, you can substitute vegetables including parsnip, tomatoes or butternut squash.

Variations: *To make clear vegetable stock, follow recipe for Basic Vegetable Stock, but do not press vegetables when straining, so that the resulting stock remains clear.*

Variation: *To make Asian-style vegetable stock, use 5 cilantro (fresh coriander) stems, including roots, in place of parsley, and fresh or dried shiitake mushrooms (if dried, soak and rinse before using). Add 5 or 6 slices fresh ginger or galangal, or a 2-inch (5-cm) piece of lime zest or lemongrass stalk, or 2 fresh (or 4 dried) kaffir lime leaves to other ingredients.*

Pho beef stock

Makes 8 cups (64 fl oz/2 L)

10 lb (5 kg) beef bones	6 cloves
1 teaspoon sea salt	1 teaspoon black peppercorns
2-inch (5-cm) piece fresh ginger	1 stick cinnamon
3 medium yellow (brown) onions	5 cardamom pods
2 star anise seeds	2 tablespoons fish sauce

Place beef bones in a large stockpot. Cover with cold water, place over high heat and bring to a boil. Boil for 2 minutes. Strain liquid through a large sieve or colander. Discard liquid and keep bones. Return bones to stockpot. Cover with cold water, add salt and bring to a boil over high heat. Reduce heat to medium–low and simmer for 3–4 hours.

While waiting for water to boil, grill ginger and onions over a gas flame or under a very hot broiler (grill). For ginger, hold with tongs, and turn, cooking until skin can be easily peeled away, about 3 minutes. For onions, hold each with tongs and turn over flame until skin and outer layer are burnt and slightly soft, 3–4 minutes. Remove and discard burnt outer layer.

Heat a frying pan over high heat and lightly roast star anise seeds by swirling them in pan for 2 minutes. Add ginger, onions and remaining ingredients to simmering stock. After stock has simmered 3–4 hours, strain. Discard solids and skim off any residue. Use stock immediately for making a pho, or refrigerate or freeze.

Variation: To make pho chicken stock, substitute 1 large, whole chicken and 2 lb (1 kg) chicken bones for the beef bones. Instead of simmering for 3–4 hours, simmer for 1 1/2 hours.

Sumiso sauce

Makes about 1 cup (8 fl oz/250 ml)

1/4 cup (2 fl oz/60 ml) white (shiro)
  miso paste
2 tablespoons sugar
2 tablespoons sake

2 tablespoons water
1 1/2 tablespoons rice vinegar
2 teaspoons hot English mustard

In a saucepan over high heat, combine all ingredients and bring to a boil, stirring frequently. Remove from heat and let cool before serving. (Pictured on page 562.)

Hint: *Sumiso is a classic Japanese dipping sauce. It keeps well for up to 2 months in the refrigerator. Allow to return to room temperature before serving.*

Sweet chili relish

Makes about 5 cups (36 fl oz/1.25 L)

2 cups (8 oz/250 g) peeled and finely shredded daikon
2 jars pickled garlic, 16 oz (500 g) each, drained and chopped
1 1/2 cups (12 fl oz/375 ml) rice vinegar
3/4 cup (1 oz/30 g) chopped fresh cilantro (fresh coriander) roots and stems
7 fresh long red chilies, finely chopped
3 1/4 cups (28 oz/875 g) granulated (white) sugar
1/4 teaspoon salt

In a large saucepan, combine all ingredients and slowly bring to a boil. Reduce heat, then simmer for 20 minutes. Remove from heat and let cool completely. Store in a tightly covered jar in the refrigerator for up to 1 month. (Pictured on page 567.)

Hint: *This Thai sauce, "nam jim," is fast becoming a standard table condiment in the West. Traditionally, it accompanies fish cakes, grilled or fried dishes, squid rings and spring rolls.*

Tempura sauce

Makes about 1 1/2 cups (12 fl oz/275 ml)

1 cup (8 fl oz/250 ml) Dashi 1
(see page 572)

1/4 cup (2 fl oz/60 ml) soy sauce
1/4 cup (2 fl oz/60 ml) mirin

In a saucepan over high heat, combine all ingredients and bring to a boil. Remove from heat. Let cool before serving. Keeps well for up to 3 days in the refrigerator. (Pictured on page 562.)

Teriyaki sauce

Makes about 2 cups (16 fl oz/500 ml)

1 cup (8 fl oz/250 ml) soy sauce
1 cup (7 oz/220 g) brown sugar

2 tablespoons chicken stock
1 teaspoon mirin

In a saucepan over high heat, combine all ingredients and bring to a boil. Simmer for 5 minutes, being careful not to let sauce boil over. Serve hot. (Pictured on page 562.)

Hint: One of the most famous Japanese sauces, this keeps for up to 2 months in the refrigerator. Reheat gently before serving.

Tosa shoyu

Makes about 2 cups (16 fl oz/500 ml)

1 cup (8 fl oz/250 ml) soy sauce
1 cup (1/6 oz/5 g) bonito flakes

1/4 cup (2 fl oz/60 ml) sake
2 teaspoons mirin

In a saucepan over high heat, combine all ingredients and bring to a boil, stirring constantly. Remove from heat. Strain through a fine-mesh sieve into a bowl. Let cool before serving. Keeps well for up to 2 months in the refrigerator.

Vietnamese bean sauce

Makes about 1¼ cups (10 fl oz/300 ml)

1 tablespoon rice vinegar

2 tablespoons finely chopped brown or
pink shallots (French shallots)

⅓ cup (3 fl oz/90 ml) coconut cream
or coconut milk (see page 24)

⅓ cup (3 fl oz/90 ml) bean sauce
(bean paste) or canned whole salted
soybeans, mashed

½ fresh long red chili, seeded and
finely chopped

2 tablespoons sugar

2 tablespoons peanuts, lightly toasted
(see page 30) and chopped

In a small saucepan, combine vinegar and shallots. Bring to a boil and cook until liquid is almost all reduced. Add coconut cream and bring to a boil. Add bean sauce and cook, stirring, for about 1 minute. Add chili and sugar, and cook, stirring, until sugar dissolves, about 2 minutes. Remove from heat and let cool. Sprinkle with peanuts and serve.

Vietnamese chili fish sauce

Makes 1¼ cups (10 fl oz/310 ml)

1 cup (8 fl oz/250 ml) bottled fish sauce

1–2 fresh small to medium green
and/or red chilies, coarsely chopped

¼ cup (2 fl oz/60 ml) water

pinch sugar

In a small bowl, combine all ingredients and stir to blend.

Variation: To make Thai chili fish sauce, "nam plaa prik," combine 1 cup (8 fl oz/250 ml) fish sauce; 1 cup (5 oz/150 g) thinly sliced, fresh medium red or green chilies; cloves from ½ bulb garlic, finely chopped; and 2–3 tablespoons fresh lime juice, to taste.

Yellow curry paste

Makes about 1 cup (8 fl oz/250 ml)

25 dried long red chilies, seeded

1 teaspoon salt

1-inch (2.5-cm) piece galangal, coarsely chopped

2 teaspoons coarsely chopped fresh turmeric, or 1 teaspoon ground turmeric

2 stalks lemongrass, white part only, peeled and chopped

8 large cloves garlic, finely chopped

2 teaspoons dried shrimp paste

Soak dried chilies in warm water for 10 minutes. In a mortar, combine all remaining ingredients and pound to a paste with a pestle, 10–20 minutes. Halfway through, drain chilies, coarsely chop, and add to mortar. Or, coarsely chop all ingredients and put in a food processor. Process to a smooth paste. If necessary, add a small amount of water, 1 teaspoon at a time. (See also How to make curry pastes, page 25.)

Wasabi mayonnaise

Makes 4 small servings

2 egg yolks, with the thread removed

1/2 teaspoon salt

pinch white pepper

1/2 teaspoon sugar

1/2 teaspoon instant dashi

1/2 teaspoon hot English mustard

1 1/2 tablespoons rice vinegar

2 cups (16 fl oz/500 ml) vegetable oil, at room temperature

1 teaspoon wasabi paste

1 teaspoon soy sauce

In a bowl, beat egg yolks well. Add salt, pepper, sugar, dashi, mustard and a few drops of rice vinegar and beat until yolks are almost white. Very slowly add oil to egg yolks, a few drops at a time, beating constantly, until mixture starts to form an emulsion. Slowly pour in remaining oil, adding remaining vinegar a few drops at a time. Transfer to a clean bowl and mix well with wasabi and soy sauce.

Hint: *You can also make a quick and easy wasabi mayonnaise by combining good quality light mayonnaise (preferably Japanese) with wasabi paste to taste.*

Glossary

Acacia: Pungent-smelling herb with feathery light-green leaves, a spiky stalk and sometimes tiny white flowers. Available in Southeast Asian markets. Pods are also common in Thai markets.

Ajwain seeds: These tiny seeds have the flavor of thyme with peppery overtones and are similar in appearance to celery seeds. Used in Indian breads, fried snacks, and lentil and vegetable dishes.

Anchovies: Dried anchovies are widely used in Asian cuisine, for flavor and nutrition. These salted preserved fish are available in packets from Asian markets. In Thailand, a popular condiment is "pla rah" or "rotten fish;" Western anchovy paste, available in supermarkets and delicatessens, is the closest substitute.

Arrowroot: Because it is cheaper in countries such as Vietnam, arrowroot is more popular than cornstarch (cornflour) for thickening sauces. Unlike cornstarch, arrowroot thins after boiling.

Asafoetida: The dried and ground resinous gum of a giant fennel plant produces this odorous yellow powder. Its unappealing aroma disappears when it is added in small amounts to food; it offers a mild onion or garlic flavor.

Asian sesame oil: This nutty-tasting, fragrant and richly colored oil is made from toasted, crushed sesame seeds. It is available in various grades, at Asian markets and some supermarkets. Only small amounts are required for flavoring. It keeps for up to 1 year at room temperature and almost indefinitely in the refrigerator.

Azuki: This dried red bean is especially popular in Asia. It is often consumed as a sweet snack or in desserts.

Bamboo leaves: Inedible garnish used for sushi and sashimi. Bamboo leaves need sustained moisture and should be kept in water until needed.

Bamboo shoots: These young shoots are boiled to retain their sweet flavor. Most commonly found canned, packed in water.

Banana leaf: Used for wrapping food parcels before, during and after cooking, fresh banana leaves are available from Asian markets and markets. Choose young, flexible leaves if possible. Wipe leaves before using, and tear or cut them to desired size. Laying leaves in the sun for a few hours helps soften them prior to folding; alternatively, run them briefly over a gas flame until the milky (waxy) side becomes shiny.

Basil: The three main basil varieties used in Asian cooking are sweet Thai, holy, and lemon. Sweet Thai basil has smooth green leaves and tastes less of aniseed or licorice than the Western variety. Holy basil, with small notched leaves, often tinged reddish purple, has a very faint aroma of citrus and is slightly hot to the palate. Lemon basil has small leaves that are slightly furry and a distinct lemon essence. Western basils can be substituted, but will taste markedly different.

Bean sauce (bean paste): Also known as soybean paste, these fermented soybeans are ground with water, salt and roasted rice powder or wheat. Used in cooking, not as a table condiment, Thai bean sauce is light brown, sold in jars and bottles. Chinese varieties are darker, sweeter and may contain sesame oil. Korean soybean paste includes chilies. See also Hot bean paste.

Beans, dried (pulses): Dried legumes are one of the Asian staples, especially in India, where they are an essential food. Asian beans are often served sweet, and are generally much smaller than their Western counterparts. Black beans and green mung beans are about the size of standard lentils; black-eyed peas (beans) are only slightly larger. Dried azuki beans or red beans are favored in desserts.

Bean sprouts: Fresh mung bean sprouts are popular for their crisp yet juicy texture when added, at the last minute, to soups, stir-fries and other cooked dishes, or used in salads and fresh spring rolls. Their taste becomes strong with age, so buy them fresh daily and rinse before using. Better still, quickly blanch in boiling water, then soak in ice water until crisp. Purists remove both the bean and hairlike tail, using only the sprout stem.

Beni-shoga: This Japanese pickled red ginger is made with older season ginger and is more savory than the pink variety (gari). Available sliced or shredded in packets or jars.

Black beans, fermented: These salted and fermented soybeans are available in cans or packets from Asian markets. They should be rinsed before use as they can be very salty. Store unused black beans in a covered container in the refrigerator.

Black salt: Known in India as kala namak, black salt, also called rock salt, is mined from quarries in central India. Despite the name, this mineral is not a sodium; it is sulphur based. It turns from black to grayish pink when ground. Used in drinks, snacks and salads, it is also featured in chat masala. Omit if unavailable as there is no substitute.

Bok choy: An Asian variety of cabbage, it has thick white stalks and dark green leaves. Sizes of bunches vary, from longer than celery stalks to baby bok choy about 6 inches (15 cm) long. Bok choy is also known as Chinese cabbage. Substitute Chinese broccoli or choy sum.

Bonito flakes: Known as "katsuobushi" in Japan, dried, smoked, cured bonito fish is commonly available as shaved flakes, in airtight plastic bags. It is also sold in blocks that are shaved with a special utensil. The flakes, rich in minerals, vitamins and proteins, are used to make dashi stocks or as a garnish.

Candlenuts: These hard, oily nuts were once used to make candles, hence their name. Candlenuts are used in curries, especially Malaysian styles, adding a rich texture. They are sold in packets at Asian markets. The closest substitute is the macadamia, though this is sweeter; almonds may also be used.

Carambola (star fruit): Carambola is a star-shaped fruit eaten fully ripened as a sweet snack or unripe as a table green or in salads. The Thais also favor it as a souring agent in soups and stews. Technically, there are two kinds: a yellow variety, and its more sour green cousin.

Cardamom: This key ingredient in garam masala and many other spice mixes is also used in numerous savory and sweet dishes. Whole green cardamom pods are filled with fragrant, tiny black seeds; for best flavor, grind your own just before using. Brown (also called black) cardamom pods yield tiny, smoky-flavored seeds; these are more often used in savory dishes. You can also buy pre-ground cardamom seeds.

Chat masala: This tasty, tart mixture of toasted and ground spices and other flavorings is sprinkled over food just before serving. It may contain any of the following ingredients: black salt, table salt, asafoetida, cumin, coriander, mint, ginger, mace, garam masala, pomegranate seeds, chilies, black pepper and amchur powder (ground dried green mango).

Chickpea (garbanzo bean) flour: Dried chickpeas are ground to a fine yellow flour rich in protein and dietary fiber. Also known as besan and gram flour, it is used in many Indian dishes, both sweet and savory. It has a slightly nutty flavor and is often used in batters, pastries, doughs and vegetarian dishes.

Chickpeas (garbanzo beans): Known as channa dal and gram lentils, the split chickpeas used in Indian cuisine are smaller than the Western sort although the flavor is very similar. Split chickpeas are used in soups, are roasted and ground to flavor snacks and vegetable dishes, and are sometimes used in sweets. Yellow split peas can be substituted, but the flavor will differ and they may take a little longer to cook.

Chilies: There are infinite varieties of fresh chilies used in Asian cuisine. The most common are the long, mild, finger-thick chilies (for example, Anaheim). Medium-length chilies (for example, Serrano) flavor dishes with more heat. The tiny Thai chilies (like Pequin) are the hottest. (See also pages 22–33.) Chilies are also used in their dried forms (whole, flakes, powdered), and in seasonings and sauces.

Chili oil: This is a vegetable oil infused with chilies and often tinged red; available in many varieties. Make sure the base oil is not toasted sesame oil, lest its taste dominates. Chili oil keeps for up to 6 months at room temperature, but retains flavor better if refrigerated. (See recipe on page 570.)

Chili paste: This fiery condiment is made from ground red chilies and sometimes garlic. Use in small quantities.

Glossary

Chili powder: Made from long dried chilies, Asian chili powder is not as piquant as cayenne pepper. Nor is it the same as Mexican chili powder, which includes herbs and spices. If unavailable, use red chili flakes ground to a powder in a mortar or a food processor.

Chili sauce: Asian chili sauces, such as Vietnamese or Thai, are slightly thick, bright orange-red in color, and made with crushed chilies, vinegar, garlic and sugar. Chili sauce is a standard table condiment in Asia, and now worldwide.

Chinese barbecue pork: Also known as char siew, this fatty, boneless pork is marinated and roasted in a traditional Chinese style. It is sold sliced or whole at Asian barbecue stores or markets. It requires no further cooking, and is added to stir-fries and other dishes, or simply enjoyed with steamed rice. Store for up to 2 days in the refrigerator.

Chinese broccoli (gai larn): This Asian type of broccoli has white flowers and a bitter taste. Sometimes confused with choy sum; these can be used in place of each other.

Chinese (napa) cabbage: Although closely related to bok choy, Chinese cabbage or wong bok looks more like an elongated Western cabbage. It has wide, flat, fleshy stems almost white in color and very pale green wrinkly leaves packed closely into a tight head. It has a crisp texture, high water content, and a delicate, almost sweet flavor.

Chinese celery: Straggly and sparse in appearance compared to regular celery, Chinese celery is also a darker green and stronger in flavor. Use both the stems and the leaves. Regular celery can be used instead.

Chinese (flat/garlic) chives: These flat-leaved chives have a distinct garlic odor. The bottom 1 inch (2.5 cm) or so is discarded. Flowering chives, with rounded stems, are usually cooked like a vegetable, although tender shoots can be served raw. Standard chives or scallions (shallots/spring onions) are similar, but not as pronounced in flavor or aroma.

Chinese pork sausages: These sweet and spicy dried pork sausages, with the Chinese name "lop chong," are sold in airtight unrefrigerated packets, or in the refrigerator section of Asian markets, or they may be found hanging from string in Chinese markets. They are added to stir-fries or steamed.

Chinese powdered red food coloring: Traditionally used to color Chinese barbecued pork, this deep red powder is available from Asian markets. Small amounts are added to marinades to color food prior to cooking.

Chinese roast duck: Sold in Chinese markets or barbecue stores, usually displayed hanging in the window, these can be purchased whole or by the half, chopped or not. Store for up to 2 days in the refrigerator.

Chinese roast pork: This roasted pork belly with a crisp crackling crust is sold by weight, chopped or whole, at Asian markets and barbecue stores. Chinese barbecued pork or regular roast pork slices can be substituted.

Chinese soy chicken: This cooked chicken glazed in soy is usually seen hanging in the window of Chinese markets or barbecue stores. Store for up to 2 days in the refrigerator.

Choy sum: A popular and widely available Chinese vegetable, it has yellow flowers, thin stalks and a mild flavor. Every part is used. Also known as flowering cabbage.

Cilantro (fresh coriander): The fresh leaf, stem and root of the coriander plant appears in all forms of Asian cuisine. Stems and leaves are chopped and added to dishes; sprigs are used as garnish or served as an accompaniment or table green; roots add their strong flavor to soups and other cooked recipes. Also known as Chinese parsley.

Cinnamon: Variously called cinnamon quills or sticks, these rolled and layered pieces of bark come from the cinnamon tree. Both the sticks and ground form are readily available.

Cloves: The dried buds of a tree that grows in Southeast Asia and the West Indies, cloves contribute their sharp but sweet flavor to Asian cuisine. Buy good-quality, whole cloves, which have a small stem and the buds still attached.

Coconut: Young coconuts, identifiable by a green husk, or a thick, white fibrous shell that has been hacked clean, are available at Asian markets and some supermarkets. They come laden with a refreshing water and a jellylike flesh. Older coconuts, with hard brown shells, are common at most supermarkets. These have firm flesh which can be grated for many uses.

Coconut milk and cream: Coconut cream is made from the first pressing of freshly grated coconut. Subsequent pressings produce various thick and thin milks (see page 24). Make sure not to buy sweetened coconut milk or "cream of coconut," which is also sweetened. Generally speaking, the less liquid in the can, the richer the coconut cream or milk. Do not shake cans before using. Rather, open carefully, stand and let the thick milk rise to the top before spooning it off to measure.

Coriander seeds: The plant that provides fresh cilantro (fresh coriander) is the source of these seeds, which are usually dry-roasted in a frying pan before being ground. Freshly ground coriander seeds have a fragrance that is both lemony and herbaceous.

Cotton buds: These are the dried flowers from the kapok tree, used in Thai cuisine. Their taste is reminiscent of okra. If unavailable, omit.

Cumin seeds: The seeds of a plant in the parsley family, briefly dry-roasting brings out their flavor, which is earthy, pungent and a little bitter. Used whole or ground. Black cumin seeds have a slightly less bitter flavor.

Curry leaves: From a small tree native to India and Sri Lanka, curry leaves are predominantly used in the south of Asia. The leaves are dark green and shiny, with a strong savory flavor and a hint of citrus. Dried or frozen curry leaves may substitute for fresh, but make sure these have good color and hence flavor.

Daepa/Jjokpa: Sometimes called Korean leeks, these resemble scallions (shallots/spring onions) in flavor but lack the onion aroma. "Daepa," are immature onions with a long, green top section and a shorter, white stem (about 1/2 inch/12 mm in diameter) rising from an undeveloped bulb. "Jjokpa" are thinner, with a milder taste. They can be used interchangeably. Scallions can be substituted.

Daidai: This bitter Japanese orange juice is mixed with soy sauce to make ponzu dipping sauce. Available at Asian and Japanese markets.

Daikon: This Japanese giant white radish, at least 20 inches (50 cm) long, is less pungent than many other radishes. Fresh daikon should be firm and shiny with smooth skin and straight leaves. Peel them just deep enough to remove both the skin and fibers beneath it. Cut into fine slivers or shredded, it is eaten with sushi; paper-thin slices are rolled around sashimi; and grated daikon is added to shoyu and other sauces for texture and flavor. Daikon sprouts are also used as garnish. Daikon contains various enzymes and is good for the digestion.

Dashi, instant: This Japanese stock is best made fresh (see pages 572–573). It is also available as granules, an instant form that can be used in soups and broths.

Eel: Fresh eel is not widely available: much of it worldwide ends up in Japan, where it is made into unagi—the famous Japanese eel. Unagi is steamed and then grilled, after being brushed with soy sauce and mirin. Commonly called barbecued eel, unagi can be bought frozen at Asian and Japanese markets and some fish markets.

Egg mimosa: This Japanese garnish of sieved egg yolk is used to crown sushi or sashimi, as well as in decorations such as carved radish flowers. To make 1 teaspoon egg mimosa: Hard-boil 1 egg. Once cooled, remove white. Place yolk in a sieve and press with a teaspoon to sieve into a small bowl.

Eggplant (aubergine), Asian types: The long green Asian eggplants are softer than standard purple or Italian (globe) eggplants, and grow to 12 inches (30 cm) long. In most cases, you can use standard eggplants, but these should be young and tender. Japanese eggplants are small and thin, usually 6–8 inches (15–20 cm) long and about 2 inches (5 cm) in diameter, with tender, sweet flesh. Pea eggplants are small and firm, with a bitter flavor that transforms cooked dishes; very popular in Thailand, there is no substitute, so omit if unavailable. Round Thai eggplants are about the size of golfballs and can be white to pale green, or yellow when old; although not bitter, their firm texture resembles pea eggplants.

Eryngo (sawtooth coriander): Similar in taste to cilantro (fresh coriander), this herb has long thin leaves with ridged edges. The leaves are used in cooked dishes, as table greens or in salads. Substitute cilantro (fresh coriander).

Fennel seeds: The seeds from the fennel plant, used whole or ground, have an aniseed-like flavor. They are used in savory dishes, desserts, seasonings, pickles and chutneys.

Fenugreek seeds: In Indian cuisine, whole or ground fenugreek seeds, roasted to bring out their bitter, sharp and nutty flavor, are added to spice mixes, breads, chutneys and lentil dishes. Fenugreek leaves have a subtle sweetness. The two forms are not interchangeable.

Fish sauce (nam pla): Fish sauce is made from the fermented extract of salted small fish. Ubiquitous in Thai and Vietnamese cuisines, it is used both as a table condiment and in the kitchen. Fish sauce ranges from the premium first-pressed grade (save this one for the table) to cheaper varieties relegated to cooking; price is a good guide. Avoid those that list "hydrolyzed protein" as an ingredient, as it indicates chemical manufacture. Although labels may boast names suggesting crabs, shrimp and other seafood, these have nothing to do with the bottle's contents. Once opened, it keeps for 1 month at room temperature or refrigerate for up to 6 months; after that, the flavor rapidly deteriorates.

Five-spice powder: Also known as Chinese five-spice powder, this is a combination of ground star anise (the dominant flavor), fennel seeds, cassia or cinnamon, cloves, and black or Szechuan pepper.

Gaeng hanglay powder: This general blend can be used in most Thai dishes. To make, see recipe on page 227.

Galangal: "Greater galangal," a floral-smelling, pink rhizome related to ginger, is the most commonly used form in cooking, and one of the fundamental Southeast Asian flavors. Fresh galangal is thinly sliced and added to soups or in curry pastes; when unavailable, use fresh ginger. Some recipes also call for the ground or powdered forms.

Gari: These delicate pink ginger slices, integral to Japanese cuisine, are pickled in salt and sweet vinegar. Available in bottles and jars from Japanese and Asian markets. (See recipe on page 585.)

Garlic: Fresh garlic ensures better flavor than pastes, dried flakes or the pre-crushed version sold in jars. Generally, the smaller the garlic bulbs, the stronger the flavor. Some recipes specifically use garlic powder, made from dried flakes that have been finely ground.

Ghee: Also called clarified butter, ghee is pure butterfat and very rich. It is used in India for general cooking, in savory and sweet dishes; substitute a mixture of vegetable oil and melted unsalted butter.

Ginger: This thick rootlike rhizome of the ginger plant is a cornerstone of Asian cuisine. Young ginger, available during the summer season, has faintly yellow, thin skin that does not require peeling and tender flesh. Mature ginger has thicker, darker shiny tan skin, which should be peeled, and is more fibrous. Store fresh ginger in the refrigerator for 2–3 days.

Ginseng root: Cultivated in Korea and tasting similar to parsnip, ginseng is used in soups, stews and teas. It is believed to strengthen and rejuvenate the body.

Hijiki: Rich in minerals and proteins, this black seaweed is available dried at Asian markets.

Hoisin sauce: Also known as Chinese barbecue sauce, this sweet, thick sauce is made from soybeans and also contains vinegar, sugar, chili, garlic and other seasonings. Refrigerate after opening.

Hot bean paste: A spicy, thick red-brown sauce made from fermented soybeans, chilies, garlic and spices. Available from Asian markets and some supermarkets, it is sometimes called hot red bean paste or chili bean paste.

Indian bay leaves: Despite their name, Indian bay leaves come from the cassia tree. They are larger and have a slightly sweeter flavor than the European variety.

Jaggery: Made from dehydrated sugarcane juice, this Indian sweetener has a flavor resembling brown sugar and molasses. Dark brown sugar can be substituted, although the flavor will differ.

Japanese mayonnaise: Creamier and less sweet than Western mayonnaise, this is available at Japanese and Asian markets and some supermarkets. For more bite, blend wasabi into the mayonnaise. (See also recipe on page 595.)

Julienne: To cut into long, thin strips, e.g with vegetables.

Kaffir lime: Identifiable by their double-helix shapes, fragrant kaffir lime leaves are fundamental in Southeast Asian cooking. They are added for flavor, not texture, and if they are to be eaten, they should be sliced paper thin, as they are tough. Coarsely torn leaves are commonly added to soups and pounded into curry pastes. Sometimes available frozen, which is preferable to dried; if unavailable, use tender young fresh citrus leaves. The zest of the knobbly fruit of the kaffir lime tree is also used to add a distinctive citrus flavor to dishes; substitute lime or lemon zest.

Kampyo: This Japanese dried bottle gourd or calabash is used in the form of shavings or ribbonlike strips. Before being used in sushi, kampyo is tenderized and seasoned (see page 332 for method).

Kanten (agar): Also called agar-agar, this is a tasteless dried seaweed used as a setting agent. It is much like gelatine, but suitable for vegetarians. Available in blocks, powders or strands, from Asian markets, healthfood stores and some supermarkets.

Karhai pan: Also known as kadai or kadhai, this Indian heavy metal bowl-like saucepan, much like a wok, is used for general cooking and deep-frying.

Katori: This Indian metal measuring cup, about $1/3$–$1/2$ cup (3–4 fl oz/90–125ml) capacity, is used for ladling dosai batter. Its flat base spreads the batter evenly. Substitute a flat-based metal measuring cup or plain metal cup.

Ketjap manis: Also called kecap manis, this thick, dark brown, syrupy soy sauce hails from Indonesia. Sweetened with palm sugar and often seasoned with garlic and star anise, it is used as a marinade, dipping sauce or in stir-fries and other dishes.

Kombu/konbu: Also known generally as dried kelp, this coldwater seaweed grows off the northern coasts of Japan. Kombu is dried for sale and comes in lengths or folded. Do not wash before use; just wipe with a damp cloth.

Korean fermented anchovies/shrimp: These are made by placing alternate layers of anchovies and salt in a ceramic pot which is then sealed and left in a cool place for 2–3 months. Similarly, shrimp are mixed with salt then fermented. Available from Korean markets. Keeps unrefrigerated for 1 year.

Korean round radish: Similar to daikon, but harder to obtain in the West, these are used in kimchi.

Korean watercress: Similar to common watercress, the Korean variety, also known as minari, has a more pungent taste. Only the stems are used in the Korean recipes.

Krachai (Chinese keys): A long, thin rhizome with a subtle, almost medicinal flavor. Krachai is often mistaken for "lesser galangal," which differs in taste and appearance, and confusingly is sometimes also called "lesser ginger." Not commonly found fresh, except in Asia; omit if unavailable.

Lead tree (kra thin): This Thai herb has a flavor similar to arugula (rocket), and resembles acacia in appearance. It is usually eaten raw, as a table green, and in dipping sauces and peanut-based curries or satays.

Lemongrass: This citronella-like herb is very popular in Southeast Asia. The white portion of the stalk is preferred in cooking, but the tough green leaves are also used in drinks and to color tea. To store, stand upright in 1 inch (2.5 cm) of water covered in a plastic bag in the refrigerator for up to 2 weeks.

Lentils, black: Also known in India as urad dal and black gram, these are used whole and unhulled or hulled and split. They are also ground into split black lentil flour (urad flour). Quite small compared with other lentils, they cook more quickly; and the split lentils become mushy when cooked. Used in lentil and vegetable dishes, they are also roasted to add a nutty flavor to savory dishes. The flour is combined with rice flour in dosai.

Lentils, green/brown: Although they are the same lentil, these are sold as brown or green, and are usually whole, not split. A little larger than other lentils, green/brown lentils have a slightly nutty flavor and hold their shape when cooked.

Lentils, yellow split: These small lentils have many names, including toor dal, toovar dal, tour dal, arhar dal and pigeon peas, and are commonly used in Indian vegetarian dishes and soups. Smaller than split chickpeas (garbanzo beans), they have a mild, slightly sweet flavor and tend to become mushy when cooked. Red lentils are also used, and are known as masoor dhal.

Lotus leaves: These are large, voluptuous leaves from the aquatic lotus plant, commonly used to wrap foods, imbuing a slight chestnut flavor to various dishes. Fresh lotus leaves are available from May to September in parts of Southeast Asia, but dried leaves are more common overseas.

Lotus root: This underwater root vegetable has a brown skin and white, starchy flesh with a distinct pattern of holes. When sliced, it takes on the characteristic wheel shape. Lotus root should be peeled before using. It discolors immediately when cut, so place slices in water mixed with 1 teaspoon vinegar. Fresh lotus root can be found at Asian markets but the canned form is more common.

Lotus seeds: Faintly resembling chickpeas, dried lotus seeds are added to soups and stews for a nutty crunch, or served sweetened. Soak briefly, use a toothpick to push out and remove the bitter green shoot from the center; then boil until tender.

Mace: A spice obtained from the outer covering of the nutmeg, but with a stronger flavor. It is available whole (in "blades" or pieces) and ground.

Malt liquid (mullyeot): Used in Korean cooking, malt liquid has a slightly sweet flavor. It is added to dishes for presentation, as it makes them shine.

Matcha: This green-tea powder is a bitter, caffeine-rich form of tea (see page 543), customarily drunk in Japan's tea ceremonies. Price is usually a fair indication of matcha quality.

Mirin: A very sweet, amber-colored Japanese rice wine, used as a flavoring in cooking. Made by mixing steamed sticky (glutinous) rice and malt, it can contain up to 14 percent alcohol, but this usually evaporates during cooking.

Miso: Many varieties of this Japanese fermented soybean paste are available, including red, white, salt-reduced and some mixed with other cereals like rice. The general rule is the darker the color the saltier the taste. Shiromiso, or white miso, is a pale yellow color and has a sweet flavor, with a salt content that varies from 5 to 10 percent. Miso keeps in the refrigerator for 1 year.

Mitsuba: Used in soups and salads, this herb is also known as Japanese wild chervil. It is a form of parsley, which can be substituted but the tastes are not identical; mitsuba is more like celery.

Mizuna: A Japanese herb with bright green, deeply serrated leaves and a mild flavor, mizuna is used fresh as a garnish for sushi, and also as a table or salad green.

Mung beans, dried: Also known as gram, dried mung beans range from green to yellow to black. Substitute the slightly larger azuki, or even dried soybeans, black beans or black-eyed peas (beans).

Mushrooms, dried black: Dried black Chinese or shiitake mushrooms are available in varying grades from Asian markets. Those with dark caps and deep ivory-colored creases are particularly valued. The flavor is more pronounced than for fresh. Store in an airtight container after opening. Soak in hot water for about 20 minutes, then drain, and remove tough stems. Strain soaking water to flavor stock.

Mushrooms, enoki: Easily identified by their pale color and long thin stalks topped by tiny caps, enoki mushrooms have a mild flavor and crunchy texture. Fresh enoki can be purchased in Asian markets and some supermarkets. Trim the root ends of the stalks before using.

Mushrooms, oyster: These creamy white mushrooms have large, soft, fan-shaped caps and a very mild, delicate flavor. They are available fresh in Asian markets and some supermarkets. Substitute button mushrooms if unavailable.

Mushrooms, shiitake: Fresh shiitake are delicious cooked in dishes such as tempura or stir-fries; they are available at Asian markets and some supermarkets.

Mushrooms, straw: Identifiable by their closed-umbrella top, these are sold canned or dried, and occasionally fresh. Rinse and drain canned mushrooms before using; and halve the quantity in recipes if substituting for fresh.

Mushrooms, tree ear or cloud (black or white fungus): Although fairly tasteless in themselves, these add a great deal of texture to dishes and also absorb flavors during cooking. They are most commonly available in dried form: they must be soaked in water to rehydrate, then rinsed thoroughly and drained. Trim tough stems before using. Also known as wood ear mushrooms.

Mustard greens (mustard leaves): Dark green and peppery, these leaves are a prime source of vitamins A and C, thiamin and riboflavin. Available fresh or frozen in Asian markets and some supermarkets.

Mustard seeds: Brown, black and yellow mustard seeds are common in Asian cooking. They are often crackled in hot oil for a few seconds to release their pungent flavor. Mustard seed oil is a popular cooking medium in India.

Myoga: This Japanese ginger has quite a different herbal fragrance from standard ginger. It is sliced thinly as a condiment.

Nigella seeds: Also known as kalonji, these tiny black seeds are used in Indian breads, salads and lentil or vegetable dishes. Sometimes incorrectly called black cumin seeds or onion seeds, they are not related to either. They do have a flavor similar to cumin, but with a slightly bitter, metallic edge.

Noodles, cellophane (bean thread): A thin translucent dried noodle, made from the starch of mung beans and sold in bundles, this noodle has little or no taste. Once softened in hot water, they become gelatinous and slippery; and are added to soups, laksas, stir-fries and fillings. They are also delicious deep-fried or made into crunchy nests for stir-fries. Cellophane noodles are difficult to cut or separate when dried, so it is best to buy them in small bundles if possible. Use thin rice vermicelli if unavailable.

Noodles, egg: Used extensively in all Asian cooking, egg noodles are available in a variety of widths, thin, round or flat, and fresh or dried. They make a satisfying meal, do not stick together when stir-fried, absorb dressings when used in salads, and are also delicious deep-fried.

Noodles, harusame: These transparent Japanese noodles are made from potato or sweet-potato flour which can be served in a hot pot or deep-fried.

Noodles, hokkien: These popular thick, round yellow noodles are readily available fresh in the refrigerated section of most supermarkets. Usually made from wheat flour, egg and water, they are traditionally used in Chinese stir-fries and soups. If unavailable, use fresh or dried egg noodles. Keep in the refrigerator for up to 7 days.

Noodles, ramen: Also known in Japan as chukasoba, ramen noodles are well known for their use in Asian instant soups. These wiggly noodles, made from egg dough, are usually sold dried in brightly colored packages. Substitute thin egg noodles.

Noodles, rice sheet: These solid white sheets of fresh rice noodle are sliced then gently teased apart in boiling water before stir-frying or adding to soups. Buy them as fresh as possible and use at once as they lose their texture quickly.

Noodles, rice stick or vermicelli: Made from ground rice and water, these noodles are widely available dried or fresh in a vast array of sizes and textures. Rice vermicelli, thin rice stick noodles, are used in soups and deep-fried for fillings and garnishes. Medium rice stick noodles are added to soups, stir-fries and salads, and the larger variety is suitable in most Asian cooking. Be careful when purchasing rice vermicelli as it can easily be confused with cellophane noodles, also sold in shiny white bundles.

Noodles, shirataki: These thin Japanese noodles are made from the root of devil's tongue (konnyaku), a plant related to taro.

Noodles, soba: Brown or green in color, and found dried or fresh in Asian markets, soba noodles are made from buckwheat flour and water. Also known as buckwheat noodles, they are one of the most popular noodles eaten in Japan. Their nutty flavor also makes them ideal in summer salads and stir-fries. Soba are more filling than other noodles, so a smaller quantity is usually prepared. If unavailable, use somen noodles.

Glossary

Noodles, somen: A traditional Japanese noodle made from wheat flour and oil, somen are best used in soups, stir-fries and salads. Available fresh or dried in an array of colors. The Korean version is known as somyeon. Substitute udon or rice stick noodles.

Noodles, udon: This soft, creamy white Japanese noodle is made from wheat flour dough, available fresh or dried and sold in bundles in a variety of widths. Udon are ideal for soups and stir-fries. Substitute soba noodles or linguine or fettuccine.

Noodles, wheat flour: Made from wheat flour and available fresh or dried, these traditional creamy white Chinese noodles are heavier in texture than other noodles. They are great for stir-fry dishes that have plenty of sauce. Substitute rice stick noodles or egg noodles.

Nori: This famous dark green seaweed from Japan is mainly used to wrap sushi, but also appears as finely shredded strips used for garnish. It is sold as paper-thin, dried, toasted, square sheets, in packets of ten. The standard size is 8 inches x 7 inches (20 cm x 17 cm); small-sized nori is also available. Ao-nori is the flaked form, usually sprinkled over dishes just before serving so that it doesn't become too moist when eaten.

Nutmeg: Dried nutmeg, a seed, is available whole or ground. It is used in spice mixes and savory dishes, as well as in sweets and desserts. The spice is also thought to help tenderize meat.

Okra: Sometimes known as gumbo, this five-sided pod tapers to a point and has a flowerlike cross-section filled with seeds. Choose crisp, young okra, 2–4 inches (5–10 cm) long; keep for 2–3 days in the refrigerator, loosely wrapped in plastic.

Oyster sauce: This thick, dark brown sauce is used in cooked dishes; it is not served as a table condiment. Its taste is faintly reminiscent of oysters, but it includes soy and many other seasonings. Vegetarian versions are also available. Refrigerate after opening.

Palm sugar: There are two kinds of palm sugar: one from the coconut tree, and the other from the palm, sometimes also known as "date sugar." Although mostly interchangeable, the palm version is more common. Soft palm sugar is bottled in a slightly gooey state, and mainly used in savory dishes. Hard palm sugar is blended with tapioca flour and sold in blocks which must be shaved before using; it is mostly used in desserts, but its tapioca content also helps to thicken sauces. Palm sugar is often blended with cane sugar to lower its cost. Substitute an equal amount of firmly packed light brown sugar.

Pandan (screwpine) leaf: These long, narrow leaves from the screwpine imbue food with a fragrant aroma and taste. Used especially to flavor and color sweets and cakes, pandan is also popular in drinks. It is also used in curry pastes and to infuse rice dishes. Fresh leaves are infinitely better for flavor and are available at some Asian markets; frozen and dried leaves are more easily found.

Panko: These Japanese dried white bread crumbs are available in both fine and coarse types. Used to coat deep-fried foods, they tend to be crunchier than Western varieties.

Papaya, green: Unripe, or green, papaya adds a delicious crunch when tossed into a salad or blended with other ingredients such as in dipping sauces. Because it is very sticky, oil your hands or wear gloves and oil the grater before preparing.

Peppercorns: Before the chili arrived on the scene, the peppercorn was the king of Asian spices. They are used extensively in Asian cooking; whether dried or fresh, black or white, whole, coarsely ground or finely powdered. Green peppercorns are the immature, undried berries or fruit of the pepper vine. Although readily available canned and in jars, fresh berries on the stem taste better and are easier to remove from dishes if their hot taste proves overpowering. When using canned in place of fresh, halve the quantity.

Pickled radish (takuan): Japanese pickled daikon radish is colored yellow and may be flavored with seaweed or chili. Sold whole or sliced in vacuum-sealed packs, it keeps well if refrigerated after opening. Use in sushi rolls or as a side dish.

Pine nuts: These high-fat nuts are mainly used in Korean recipes pan-toasted and ground, then sprinkled on a finished dish as a garnish. If the intense pine flavor of the Chinese variety is too strong, use the Mediterranean type.

Piper leaf (betel leaf): These shiny, dark green leaves are about the size of ivy. Because they look similar to the betel nut leaf, which is the hot and peppery Asian equivalent of chewing tobacco, all sorts of confusion prevails; hence the piper leaf is commonly called "beetle leaf" or "pepper leaf." Mild in taste, fresh piper leaves are eaten raw, used to wrap little portions of food at the table. They can also be used to wrap meat before grilling, or cooked in curries and stir-fries or blanched as a vegetable. Piper leaves can be found fresh in Southeast Asian markets; if unavailable, either omit or substitute a small piece of cabbage leaf or blanched grape leaves.

Plum sauce: This thick, sweet and slightly sour sauce is used as a flavoring, a dipping sauce or added to stir-fries. Available from supermarkets.

Prickly ash: From the tiny dried fruit of a large-canopied tree, this spice smells similar to a blend of Szechuan and white peppercorns, but tastes hotter; it is known as kamchatton in Thailand, where it commonly flavors salads, some sour dishes and curries. If unavailable, omit or use ground white pepper or Szechuan peppercorns. In Japan prickly ash is called "kinome" and the sprigs are used as an edible garnish or herb.

Rambutan: Also known as hairy lychee, this spiky-skinned red fruit has firm, smooth, sweet white flesh that tastes a little like grapes.

Red bean paste: These boiled, mashed and sweetened azuki beans are sold in cans in Asian markets and used in sweet snacks and desserts.

Rice alcohol: A mild Vietnamese version of this is made by fermenting black sticky rice. A more pungent version comes as a neutral spirit, sold in bottles. Substitute vodka.

Rice flour: Made from both sticky (glutinous) and long-grain rice, this is a base for Asian cakes and dough. Medium to coarse rice flour is used in dosai, the Indian pancakes. Finer rice flour is often used in batters and some desserts.

Rice, ground: This is made by toasting raw grains of sticky rice then grinding them coarsely with a stone mortar and pestle. It is added for texture. Do not confuse with rice starch or rice flour.

Rice paper sheets: Originating in Vietnam, these fragile round or square wrappers are made from rice flour and water. Traditionally, batter was poured onto woven mats and then left to dry in the sun. They are used, uncooked, to wrap food, and are also deep-fried. Available fresh or dried at Asian markets.

Rice starch: Various varieties of Asian rice starch (which, confusingly, may be labeled "rice flour") are made from the amylose, or soluble portion, of both sticky (glutinous) and standard white rice. Unlike rice flour, rice starch feels silky to the touch. It is used as a base for a myriad of dumplings, cakes and doughs; do not use to thicken sauces.

Rice vinegar: Both the Chinese and Japanese varieties are fermented from rice and fairly mild in flavor. Use only Japanese rice vinegar for sushi rice.

Rice wine: Also known as shaoxing wine, rice wine is made from sticky (glutinous) rice. It may be either dry or sweet; the sweet form is a delicious chilled aperitif. Substitute dry or sweet sherry. Korean rice wine is a low-alcohol beverage with a slightly golden color, somewhat like that of olive oil.

Rosewater: This fragrant, clear liquid is distilled from rose petals and one of the divine flavors of the Middle East. It makes its way into Asian cuisine via India, where it is relished in desserts and drinks. Available bottled, from good delicatessens as well as Middle Eastern and Indian markets.

Saffron threads: If pepper is king, then saffron is Asia's ruling spice queen. Saffron threads are the dried stigmas from a variety of crocus flower, each of which produces only three stigmas. Harvesting saffron is labor-intensive, making it the most costly spice in the world. Saffron threads are soaked in a warm liquid to release their intense gold-yellow color and pungent, earthy aroma and flavor.

Sake: Essential in Japanese cuisine, sake is available in a wide range of prices and flavors (from extra dry to quite sweet). It is customarily drunk warm and, with an alcohol content of around 16 percent, is quite potent. High-quality sake is preferred at ambient temperature or chilled. Buy cooking sake or inexpensive drinking sake for making sushi. After opening, cap the bottle and refrigerate; sake keeps for a few months.

Sambal oelek: This spicy Indonesian paste consists of ground chilies, salt and sometimes vinegar. Refrigerate after opening.

Sansho pepper: Also called Japanese mountain pepper, sansho pepper is usually bought ground, since it keeps its aroma well. Sansho seeds are more commonly available cooked with soy, sugar, kelp stock and other ingredients.

Seaweed, Vietnamese: Dried Vietnamese seaweed or moss can be gray to tan in color, and is extremely thin, like angel hair. Do not confuse with Japanese seaweed, such as wakame, which is much thicker. Soak before using, and rinse very well to remove grit.

Semolina: Ground from the endosperm of durum wheat, semolina has little flavor but a pleasantly coarse texture. Coarse semolina makes a crunchy coating on fried food; finer semolina can be used instead. Both forms are used in Indian sweets and some breads.

Sesame salt: A combination of white sesame seeds and table salt, this Korean seasoning can be made in large quantities and stored. To make, toast seeds until light brown, mix in salt, then remove from pan. When cool, grind to a powder. Store in an airtight container until required.

Sesame seeds: The seeds of a plant that grows in India and other parts of Asia, sesame seeds come in three colors: black, white and golden, with the golden having the strongest aroma. Whole or ground white sesame seeds are used in many Asian savory dishes and sweets. The seeds can be toasted to enhance their flavor.

Shallots (French shallots): Resembling clustered tiny onions, shallots may be brown, gold, pink or purple. (There is also an elephantine variety, confusingly called "golden shallot.") The white parts of scallions (shallots/spring onions) can be substituted.

Shiso (perilla): Also known as Japanese basil, this aromatic herb is related to basil and mint. Buy fresh green leaves from Asian supermarkets. A red variety is preferred in Vietnam, and is also used in Japanese pickles. Shiso is also available in a powdered form.

Shoyu: Although there several varieties of Japanese soy sauce, only two are commonly used: heavy soy sauce (koikuchi shoyu) and light soy sauce (usukuchi shoyu). Both are used in cooking, and heavy soy is also served at the table. Chinese soy sauces are quite sweet and should not be substituted.

Shrimp, dried: Available unrefrigerated at Asian markets, these strong-tasting shrimp are added straight into recipes, or soaked briefly in warm water, drained, then used. They also make a quick base for soup. Either omit, or substitute chopped fresh or canned shrimp.

Shrimp paste, dried: Made from fermented shrimp, this is a pungent, darkly colored hard paste. Available unrefrigerated at Asian markets, often under its Malaysian name "balachan," the paste is usually in a paper-wrapped block but also in cans and jars. It keeps indefinitely, but once open, it should be sealed tightly. Only a small amount is needed to flavor curry pastes and dipping sauces. In Asia, shrimp paste is usually roasted prior to flavoring dishes, but this is optional. To roast, wrap shrimp paste in aluminum foil and broil (grill) for 2 minutes on each side or until fragrant. Or, bake foil-wrapped packets in a preheated hot oven for 20–30 minutes. When unavailable, omit.

Shungiku: These are chrysanthemum leaves used as a vegetable. They have a strong flavor, not unlike spinach.

Soboro: Made from white fish, this is a Japanese ingredient used in chirashi-zushi. Available ready-made, in jars.

Soybeans: Dried soybeans are readily available in supermarkets, natural foods stores and Asian markets. There are many varieties, the most common being the yellow (actually beige in color) and the black. Soaking and cooking times may vary depending on the age of the beans, but lengthy cooking is almost always necessary. Keep dried soybeans in an airtight container. Cooked whole yellow soybeans are sold in cans of various sizes; drain and rinse all types before use. (See also Black beans, fermented.)

Soy sauce: Made from soybeans and used in cooking and as a table condiment, there are a myriad of soy sauces. Dark soy sauce, usually used in cooking, is thicker and often less salty than light soy sauce, which is served at the table and added to dipping sauces. Thai soy sauces are made in a range of strengths, from 1 to 6. (See also Ketjap manis and Shoyu.) In all types, the flavor of naturally brewed soy sauce is best. Use soy sauce within 1 month of opening, or keep refrigerated for up to 6 months.

Split peas: These dried regular peas are readily available from health food stores and supermarkets. Called matar dal in India, split yellow peas are used in dal and in vegetarian soups. You can use split green peas instead, although the color and flavor differs a little.

Spring roll wrappers: Sometimes called "spring roll skins," these thin lacy wrappers made from rice flour are available at Asian markets and many supermarkets. They are sold frozen in packages of 10 or 25, usually 8½ inches (21.5 cm) square or round. Thaw in the refrigerator before opening the package then separate before using (trim the edges for easier separation). While working with the wrappers, keep them covered with a damp kitchen towel to prevent drying out. Seal unused wrappers and store in the refrigerator for up to 7 days, or refreeze for up to 1 month.

Star anise: This spice is the dried fruit from a variety of evergreen magnolia tree. Commonly used in Chinese cooking, and the dominant flavor in five-spice powder, star anise is also used in Indian cuisine. Identifiable by its eight-arched pods, forming a star, its flavor is similar to aniseed, but has more depth and sweetness.

Starch balls: Many drinks or desserts in Asian countries include clear balls or beads of starch. These are tasteless, but they provide a much loved gelatinous texture. Sago, tapioca and potato flour balls are just some of the possibilities available at Asian markets and markets.

Sticky (glutinous rice): Available in black or purple and white, which is the most common, this short-grain rice becomes sticky after cooking because of its high starch content. Many Asian rice desserts use this variety, and it is also wrapped in lotus or banana leaves and steamed. It can take longer than other rice varieties to cook, as it must be steamed not boiled, so soaking in water overnight is often recommended.

Sticky rice powder: Made from ground sticky (glutinous) rice, the powder is used as a spongy dough for sweet dumplings, cakes, pastries and wrappers.

Stone-cooking: In Indian cuisine, a large flat stone is sometimes used for cooking. Granite is the best stone to use (don't use limestone). The stone needs to be seasoned before using—place in the oven and bring the temperature to 225°F (110°C/Gas ¼) then use good oven mitts to transfer it to the sink to cool. Return it to the oven and bring slowly to 400°F (200°C). Transfer it to the sink once again, place a drop of water on the edge: if it sizzles immediately (and the stone doesn't crack), it's ready to use. Cool, then place over a gas flame to heat. Stone-cooking is healthy because there is no need for oil to be used. You can use a pizza stone instead.

Sugarcane: The stalk of the sugarcane plant is rich in sweet nectar, which is the basis of white sugar, as well as a refreshing liquid beverage. Fresh sugarcane must be hacked into usable pieces. Canned sugarcane pieces are more convenient; they are available at Asian markets.

Szechuan pepper: Not related to black pepper, the Szechuan has a tingly citrus rather than hot taste. It is an essential ingredient in many Chinese dishes. Use it roasted and ground with salt as seasoning or in place of black pepper and salt over cooked foods.

Tahini: A thick paste made of ground sesame seeds, tahini is available from delicatessens and some supermarkets. Substitute for sesame paste.

Tamarind: The tart and sour pulp of one variety of tamarind pod, fresh tamarind pulp is soaked in boiling water, then strained before using. Tamarind paste is sold in blocks and must be diluted in hot water then strained. More convenient are ready-made tamarind pulp, puree, concentrate or water; all are sold in jars at supermarkets and Asian markets. Because there can be a difference in sourness, quantities required are variable.

Tapioca starch: Made from the cassava or manioc root, this is used like flour to thicken sauces or to coat meat or bind ground meat prior to cooking. It is also blended with sticky (glutinous) rice starch in some cakes and drinks. It adds a chewy texture and glossy sheen. Substitute arrowroot or cornstarch (cornflour).

Taro stem: Known in Japan as zuiki, and sometimes called "elephant ear," or "Vietnamese rhubarb" (though not related to European rhubarb), taro must be purchased only from reputable Asian markets, as some varieties are toxic. Peel before using. Its taste is rather innocuous, like yam, but its crunch is delicious.

Tawa: An Indian flat iron hotplate, either square or round, used for cooking roti and dosai. See Dosai (page 463) for instructions on seasoning the tawa.

Tempeh: Originally from Indonesia, tempeh is still that country's most popular form of soy food. Tempeh is a cake of fermented, cooked soybeans, sometimes in combination with grains, that is held together by a white mold (mycelium). It has a mild nutty, yeastlike flavor and a texture similar to meat. Fermentation also makes it more digestible than other soy foods. Readily available in refrigerated vacuum-sealed packets, tempeh, like tofu, is versatile and absorbs flavors well. It can be cooked in almost any way, or eaten on its own. Premarinated tempehs are also available.

Tempura flour: This rice-based flour is used specifically to make tempura batter. It is widely available from Asian markets and some supermarkets.

Thai sweet chili sauce: This is a mild, sweet sauce usually used as a dipping sauce. Refrigerate after opening.

Tofu: Fresh tofu is made from soybean milk and is also known as bean curd or soybean curd. The two most popular types of tofu are the Chinese style, which is coarser, more grainy and has a higher protein content, and the Japanese style, which is softer and more delicate. (For tofu preparation, see page 39.) Refrigerated packets of dessert-style or flavored tofu and tofu ice cream are also readily available from supermarkets.

Tofu, deep-fried: These come in a variety of shapes and sizes suitable for different cooking uses. Refrigerated and frozen packets can be found in Asian markets, natural foods stores and some supermarkets. Pouring boiling water over deep-fried tofu, or lightly boiling it for 1 minute before use, will remove excess oil. Squeeze gently to remove the water and pat dry with paper towels.

Tofu, firm: Fresh firm tofu is more commonly available as a Chinese-style, firm-textured tofu, packed in water in refrigerated containers. It is sold as "fresh tofu" in Asian markets. Japanese brands tend to be smoother and have a slightly different flavor. Extra-firm tofu is even more solid and holds its shape during cooking or can be shredded or crumbled like feta cheese; available in refrigerated vacuum-sealed packs and shelf-stable cartons.

Tofu, silken: Made like yogurt, silken tofu is not pressed, and available in soft, firm and extra-firm varieties. It is similar to "soft tofu" but, as its name suggests, has a silky texture. Available in refrigerated vacuum-sealed containers and shelf-stable cartons.

Tofu, soft: With its smooth, creamy texture and delicate taste, soft tofu is used in simple dishes that require little handling of the tofu, as it breaks easily. Available in refrigerated vacuum-sealed packs and shelf-stable cartons.

Tofu, usuage or aburaage: This Japanese fried thin tofu is often used as a pouch for fillings but may also be thinly sliced and added to cooked dishes. Atsuage is similar, but thickly sliced, with a crispy surface and soft, silken interior.

Tonkatsu sauce: Known as "usuta sosu," this is a less pungent Japanese version of Worcestershire sauce.

Turmeric: This spice brings a sharp flavor as well as golden color to Asian dishes. Fresh turmeric, a rhizome, is grated, then soaked, and both the soaking water and pulp are used. Peeling before using is optional, but do wear gloves when preparing fresh turmeric, as it can stain. Ground dried turmeric is also widely used, especially in India; the darker Alleppey variety is preferred, as its flavor is closer to the fresh rhizome.

Ugo: Ugo is salted green seaweed, sold in packet in Asian markets. Before using, rinse well.

Umeboshi plums: These are actually pickled apricots, not plums, used whole or as a puree or paste in Japanese food and as an aid to digestion. Umeboshi, usually red, has a deliciously salty, sour and fruity flavor. The pickling liquid is also available as a vinegar. Keep opened packets in the refrigerator.

Vietnamese lemon balm: Stronger in flavor than Western lemon balm, the Vietnamese type tastes of both mint and citrus. Substitute perilla or peppermint.

Vietnamese mint: The slightly fiery polygonum has green to purple leaves and often, but not always, a smudge-like blotch in the leaf's center. With an astringent tang, it is also called hot mint, laksa leaf or Vietnamese basil.

Vietnamese pickles: A large variety of vegetables are pickled as Vietnamese table accompaniments and are also used in some dishes. The "sweet pickled leeks" (cu kieu) are made with ingredients such as miniature leeks or scallions. All are available at Asian markets.

Vinegar: Asian vinegars are made from wine, beer hops, fruits, grains, sap or honey. They are used in Asian food as a preservative and for flavoring. White, black, red, rice and sweet vinegars are the most common, but are vastly different from one another. Try to use the specific vinegar called for in the recipes, as this affects the resulting dish.

Wakame: This Japanese seaweed is sold in dried form and is reconstituted in water, becoming bright green. Highly nutritious, wakame is available dried or salted and is used in soups, salads and simmered dishes, as well as finely chopped with cooked rice.

Wasabi: This Japanese horseradish has roots that are olive green with bumpy skin. Fresh wasabi is expensive and largely unavailable outside Japan, so powdered or paste forms are commonly used. The powder, which is mixed with a small amount of tepid water to make a paste, is the more economical of the two. You can sometimes buy frozen grated wasabi, or you can mix Western horseradish with wasabi powder. Served as an accompaniment to sushi, wasabi is sometimes made into a decorative shape, such as a leaf.

Water chestnuts: The tubers of a plant grown in Asia, they are round in shape with light-colored flesh that is crunchy and subtly sweet. Water chestnuts are widely available canned; after opening, store in the refrigerator for up to 3 weeks.

Water spinach: In Asia, this fresh vegetable comes in two sorts: the Chinese style, which has long green leaves on a green stalk; and the Thai variety, which has broader ivy-like leaves and thicker stems. Their flavors are similar, but the Chinese style is more commonly available outside of Thailand.

Wonton wrappers: Widely available fresh or frozen in a variety of colors and shapes. The white dumpling wrappers, also called potsticker or gow gee wrappers, are made from wheat-based dough, and are generally used for steamed or boiled dumplings. Yellow wonton skins are made from an egg-based dough, and are used for boiled or fried wontons. Wrappers are usually 3½ inches (9 cm) square, though they also may be round. Fresh wrappers will keep for up to 7 days in the refrigerator, or they can be frozen.

Wrappers, gyoza: These thin circles of dough, made with eggs, are used for Japanese dumplings. They are similar to Chinese gow gee or wonton wrappers.

Yuzu (Japanese citron): Used mostly for its zesty aroma, yuzu is available dried, powdered or frozen from Japanese grocery stores.

Guide to weights and measures

The conversions given in the recipes in this book are approximate. Whichever system you use, remember to follow it consistently throughout a recipe, to ensure proportions are correct.

Weights

Imperial	Metric
1/3 oz	10 g
1/2 oz	15 g
3/4 oz	20 g
1 oz	30 g
2 oz	60 g
3 oz	90 g
4 oz (1/4 lb)	125 g
5 oz (1/3 lb)	150 g
6 oz	180 g
7 oz	220 g
8 oz (1/2 lb)	250 g
9 oz	280 g
10 oz	300 g
11 oz	330 g
12 oz (3/4 lb)	375 g
16 oz (1 lb)	500 g
2 lb	1 kg
3 lb	1.5 kg
4 lb	2 kg

Volume

Imperial	Metric	Cup
1 fl oz	30 ml	
2 fl oz	60 ml	1/4
3 fl oz	90 ml	1/3
4 fl oz	125 ml	1/2
5 fl oz	150 ml	2/3
6 fl oz	180 ml	3/4
8 fl oz	250 ml	1
10 fl oz	300 ml	1 1/4
12 fl oz	375 ml	1 1/2
13 fl oz	400 ml	1 2/3
14 fl oz	440 ml	1 3/4
16 fl oz	500 ml	2
24 fl oz	750 ml	3
32 fl oz	1 L	4

Oven temperature guide

The Celsius (°C) and Fahrenheit (°F) temperatures in this chart apply to most electric ovens. Decrease by 25°F or 10°C for a gas oven or refer to the manufacturer's temperature guide. For temperatures below 325°F (160°C), do not decrease the given temperature.

Oven description	°C	°F	Gas Mark
Cool	110	225	1/4
	130	250	1/2
Very slow	140	275	1
	150	300	2
Slow	170	325	3
Moderate	180	350	4
	190	375	5
Moderately hot	200	400	6
Fairly hot	220	425	7
Hot	230	450	8
Very hot	240	475	9
Extremely hot	250	500	10

Useful conversions

1/4 teaspoon	1.25 ml
1/2 teaspoon	2.5 ml
1 teaspoon	5 ml
1 Australian tablespoon	20 ml (4 teaspoons)
1 UK/US tablespoon	15 ml (3 teaspoons)

Butter/Shortening

1 tablespoon	1/2 oz	15 g
1 1/2 tablespoons	3/4 oz	20 g
2 tablespoons	1 oz	30 g
3 tablespoons	1 1/2 oz	45 g

Recipe list

Appetizers & entrees

Soups

Chicken & duck

Beef, lamb & pork

Seafood

Recipe list

Sushi & sashimi

Sushi

Sashimi

Vegetable sushi

Vegetables & salads

Rice & noodles

Desserts

Drinks

Sauces, stocks & condiments

Index

Index

Index

Index

Index

Index

Index